CW00766662

MONASTIC WANDERERS

Nāth Yogī Ascetics in Modern South Asia

VÉRONIQUE BOUILLIER

MANOHAR
2017

First published 2017

© Véronique Bouillier, 2017

All rights reserved. No part of this publication may be
reproduced or transmitted, in any form or by any means,
without prior permission of the author and the publisher

ISBN 978-93-5098-154-2

Published by
Ajay Kumar Jain *for*
Manohar Publishers & Distributors
4753/23 Ansari Road, Daryaganj,
New Delhi 110 002

Typeset by
Ravi Shanker
Delhi 110 095

Printed at
Salasar Imaging Systems
Delhi 110 035

MONASTIC WANDERERS

In memoriam

DOMINIQUE-SILA KHAN

1949-2016

Contents

Illustrations

Acknowledgements

This book is dedicated to the many Yogīs whom I met in various places in Nepal and India. I am immensely grateful for the warm welcome they accorded to me and my persistent questioning, also for their patience, for their lack of prejudice regarding the strangeness of my position. I hope that they will recognize themselves in this book in which I intend to provide a picture as fair as possible of the present condition of the Nāth *sampradāya* and of the richness of its tradition.

I am very grateful to the Nepalese Yogīs of Gorkha, Kathmandu and Dang Valley monasteries, who were the first to introduce me to their universe, and especially to the late Giribarnath, my first guru in Gorkha. I am also especially thankful to the head of the Fatehpur monastery, Mahant Narharinathji, and to Daya Fatehpuria who generously helped me in many ways. In Mangalore, I am particularly indebted to the late Anandanathji and Keshavnathji who patiently guided me and made possible my understanding of the long ceremony of the enthronement of the head of Kadri Math. I also thank the authorities of the Yogi Mahasabha, and particularly Mahant Candnathji of Asthal Bohar, for their help, as well as the dozen of Yogīs met on the road or in their monasteries, in Caughera, Mṛgasthali, Gorakhpur, Varanasi, Asthal Bohar, Jaipur, Jodhpur, Pushkar, Udaipur, Gwalior, Mangalore, Vittal, and in several places of Shekhavati.

My most sincere thanks to the many collegues and friends who shared my interests and generously gave me the occasion of fruitful exchanges, particularly France Bhattacharya, Catherine Clémentin-Ojha, Nalini Delvoye, Marc Gaborieau, Phyllis Granoff, Monika Horstmann, Dominique-Sila Khan, James Mallinson,

Françoise Mallison, André Padoux, Heidi Pauwels, Catherine Servan-Schreiber, and last but certainly not least David White.

My gratitude also goes to the Centre d'Etudes de l'Inde et de l'Asie du Sud and to the CNRS, which made possible these many years of research.

And finally I wish to heartily thank my family, involved by force in the Nāth universe, but nevertheless always encouraging and supportive.

VÉRONIQUE BOUILLIER

A Note on the Transliteration

Words transcribed from Hindi, Nepali, Sanskrit are transliterated according to standard diacritical conventions. I have added English plural mark (s) on vernacular terms, as it is currently practiced in English texts. For Sanskrit/Hindi words I have preferred Hindi transliteration to the Sanskrit one, i.e. without short a, however, I kept the Sanskrit form for some words, more familiar to us under this spelling, such as liṅga and not liṅg, or Śiva and not Śiv. I have not used diacritical marks for well-known geographical places and surnames.

Introduction

The figure of the Hindu ascetic has captured the attention and the imagination of the outside observers since Alexander's first encounter with the naked gymnosophists. These religious virtuosi have most often been given the name of 'yogī' and their mysterious powers and wondrous deeds have been widely celebrated in many popular narratives all over South Asia.

The term yogī has thus been widely used both inside and outside India to designate various categories of ascetics, who appear with very different characteristics according to time and place. Such a general appellation may subsume both an ultra-mundane spiritual quest and mysterious supranatural powers, as the yogī seeking the highest goal, liberation from bondage, appears also as the one who has gained control over the constituents of the cosmos, and who has then developed these powers so that he can fly through the air or enter another's body. Thus, as an encompassing category, the yogī was interpreted differently in different contexts, ranging in conceptualization from a religious virtuoso to a 'sinister' performer (White 2009), from a serious practicioner of Yoga as defined by the Patañjali's *Yogasūtra*, to a malevolent magician.

However, if the term yogī can be employed in a generic sense, it can also designate more precisely the members of a sectarian movement, who are the subject of this book. The Nāth Yogīs[1] are the only ones to have referred to themselves as yogīs

[1] I use the upper case Yogī to refer to the members of the sect and yogī for the general designation.

throughout their history and to claim the appellation as their identity marker.

As we shall see, it is difficult to place a specific date on their emergence as an organized order. As far as we can reconstruct their history, it seems that, from the diverse ascetic lineages belonging to the loose category of yogīs, a specific group slowly emerged and formed an entity united by a common identity grounded on some shared particularities. Then, beginning with the sixteenth century, we can distinguish details in the Indian or foreign descriptions and narratives about yogīs that refer precisely to the Nāth Yogīs as a specific order in contrast to the generic yogī. References are made to wandering troups of yogīs clad in ochre or in patched rags, with matted locks or strange headdresses, wearing conspicuous earrings (hence the name of Kānphaṭā, or 'splitted ears' often given to them) and carrying small horns that they blow before begging, their bodies smeared with ashes, shouting *Alakh, Alakh*; allusion is made to their supposed powers, particularly the power of controlling the breath and thus being able to stay buried in a grave-like cave for days. The combination of these visible characteristics helped characterize the Nāth Yogīs as a *sampradāya*, or specific order grounded on the transmission of a shared tradition. Are these features still identity markers? Who are the Nāth Yogīs? What has been the trajectory of the sect and how has it succeeded in maintaining its specific tradition? What is its present situation in the Indian religious landscape? Such are the questions that this book seeks to answer.

The Nāth Yogīs are not particularly well known in the modern Indian religious landscape. They have not been much studied. Except for a few mentions in some late colonial censuses and gazetteers that mostly concerned householder Yogīs, and the translations of the legends related to the Nāth heroes Gopīcand by George Grierson (1885) and Gūgā by Richard Temple (1885), the first study entirely devoted to the Nāth Yogīs was the 1938 seminal work of George Weston Briggs. Briggs associates factual, detailed observations with historical data, textual and oral traditions. However, the accumulation of contradictory details and the various levels of analysis fail to give an encompassing survey of the *sampradāya*.

After Briggs, various authors tried to find a global overview of the sect by focusing on their philosophy and soteriological tradition, relying upon the treatises attributed to Gorakhnāth. We may cite as examples of this approach the following scholars: Kalyani Mallik (1954); Hariprasad Dvivedi (1981), who translated many of Briggs' passages into Hindi; Akshaya Kumar Banerjea (1983); Christian Bouy (1994), who demonstrated the Nāths' influence on the *Yoga Upaniṣads*; Shashibhusan Dasgupta (1976), who relocated the Nāth tradition in the Bengali context of 'obscure religious cults'; Mariola Offredi (1999), who edited three manuscripts of works attributed to Gorakhnāth; David White (1996, 2002), who saw the roots of the Nāth movement in the ancient alchemical tradition of the Nāth Siddhas; and James Mallinson (2011a, b), who reflected on the early history and literature attributed to the Nāths and questioned the alleged Gorakhnāthi connection with Haṭha Yoga.

Anthropological studies of the *sampradāya* are recent and not very numerous. Let us cite first the many studies of Daniel Gold and Ann Grodzins Gold concerning the Nāth Yogīs in Rajasthan. A few articles by Daniel Gold dealt with the relationships between ascetic and householder Nāths and Nāth local tradition, which Ann Grodzins Gold has documented in her book transcribing the local versions of the songs of Gopīcand and Bhartṛhari (1992). Simon Digby (2000) focused on traditional legends while David White (2001) provided a modern version in the form of a foundational narrative of a monastery, which appears as a palimpsest. Gunther Unbescheid (1980) gave the first historical and ethnographical account of the Nāth Yogīs in Nepal. The study of the Jakhbar monastery in Panjab by B.N. Goswami and J.N. Grewal (1967) was based on archives recording the donations of Mughal emperors. A recent volume edited by David N. Lorenzen and Adrian Muñoz combined textualist and anthropological approaches and presented new data on 'the vernacular folklore and poetry' (2011: VII, see also Muñoz 2010), as did another study by Gordan Djurdjevic.[2] Last, I must also here mention the invaluable work done by Yogī Vilāsnāth (2004, 2005) in collecting Nāth ritual traditions and giving the corresponding mantras.

My own work is anthropological and for twenty years I have published articles and books, mainly in French, focused on different aspects and places belonging to the Nāth Yogīs' tradition. This book aims to present the English speaking reader with a new synthesis, based on my previous works, which focuses on the organization of the sect, the working of its institutions, and the numerous rituals they perform.[3]

My first encounter with the Nāth Yogīs was in 1992 in Nepal. I was then studying what I called 'the ascetic castes', meaning the social groups born from renouncers who went back to a householder life. After studying householder Dasnāmī Sannyāsīs from the Giri subgroup, followed by other communities like the Jangams of the Kathmandu Valley, I met the Nāth Yogīs first as a village community; their duty was to officiate for the palace temple in the town of Gorkha, the place of origin of the last royal dynasty. Having noted the link between the Nāth Yogīs, the disciples of the famous guru Gorakhnāth, and the Nepalese kingship blessed by the same Gorakhnāth, I wrote a few articles centred on the close relationship that developed in various places between wonder-worker Nāth Yogīs and conqueror kings and on their mutual process of legitimation. The same relationship was exemplified in the legendary accounts and in the history of the Caughera monastery, situated in a valley of Inner Terai in Nepal. This monastery was the subject of my 1997 book, *Ascètes et rois. Un monastère de Kanphata Yogis au Népal*. This first insight into the Nāth monastic tradition was a lucky one, since Caughera was representative of the traditional organization of

[2] For a detailed study of the bibliography on the Nāth Yogīs, see Bouillier 2013.

[3] Given a more global perspective and the need for abbreviation, I will, if needed, refer the reader to the detailed versions already published.

the sect and included many emblematic elements, a fact that I discovered later by comparison. After its legendary foundation by a renouncer-king, Caughera benefited from successive royal patronages and expanded its protection upon successive dynasties. Villages had been granted to the monastery together with various economic and judiciary rights. Documents kept in the Nepalese State Archives allowed the reconstruction of the conflicting relationships between the monastery, its dependent peasants and the king's authority. Alongside this political importance, the monastery was also the seat of spectacular ceremonies that were at the heart of the tradition, such as the installation of its head or the annual pilgrimage to a Devī temple. Furthermore, the place was grounded on complex legends that held great popular appeal and were kept alive in small locally-printed booklets and in paintings on the walls of the sanctuaries.

The inscription of the local legends in a wide network of narratives, as well as my encounters with the many Indian Yogīs gathered in Caughera for various festivals, made me aware of the necessity to cross national boundaries and to compare my observations to the overall Indian context. Was Caughera unique? Or was it representative of a broader trend? Only further inquiries could provide an answer.

A first survey in Rajasthan showed numerous but decayed vestiges of ancient temples or monasteries, where only a solitary ascetic guarded a few tombs. However, other places soon modified this first impression of decay. The first was the Pushkar monastery, an impressive building on the lakeshore, which was granted by the Mahārājā of Jodhpur, Man Singh, famous for his unconditional patronage of the Nāth sect. Every year, hundreds of Yogīs gather here for a worship ceremony, which appeared to me quite similar to the Caughera rituals. Yet the difference between this and another Rajasthani monastery situated in the Shekhavati town of Fatehpur was striking. Here the monastery, which is new and undergoing constant transformation, was busier with lay devotees than with ascetics. Since the beginning of the twentieth century, the disciples of the founder of the lineage have scattered across the surrounding area and built a network of successful branches that attest to the vitality of the Nāth *sampradāya*. Together with another example of successful adaptation to modernity – the monastery of Asthal Bohar in Haryana – the Fatehpur monastic establishment was the subject of the second half of my 2008 book: *Itinérance et vie monastique. Les ascètes Nāth Yogīs en Inde contemporaine*.

A few random conversations that I had with various people during the Fatehpur festival led me to discover the part played in the sect by the main monastic settlement in south India, the Kadri Math in Mangalore (Karnataka), which neither Briggs nor Dvivedi had mentioned. I then had the opportunity to attend the widely frequented festival of the renewal of the head of the monastery, which happens every twelve years, and to participate in the last part of the pilgrimage that precedes it and which had started six months previously during the Nasik Kumbh Melā. This spectacular and meaningful experience was the topic of the first part of my book *Itinérance et vie monastique* and will also constitute one of the main parts of the present book.

Thanks to other fieldwork that I conducted in Haryana (Asthal Bohar), Punjab (Bhatinda), Uttar Pradesh (Gorakhpur) Uttarakhand (Haridwar) and Rajasthan (Jodhpur, Jaipur, Gogamedhi) I was able to confirm my views on the structure of the *sampradāya* and delve deeper into some precise points like the relationship between the Nāth Yogīs and Islam (Bouillier 2004, 2015) or the link between the sect and the parallel organization of the Har Śrī Nāth (Bouillier 2009).

* * *

The present volume attempts to give a broad overview of the organization of the Nāth Yogī sect, anchoring the analysis on emblematic examples that will be examined in detail.

The first part gives a general introduction to the Nāths by focusing on their identity markers. Chapter 1 starts with the main characteristics that define the Yogīs: how they present themselves, their appellation, their affiliation with the guru they claim as their founder, Gorakhnāth, and their spiritual worldview. Chapter 2 refers to the way the Yogīs belong to the *sampradāya*, how they enter the sect through different initiations, how their funerals confirm and achieve their affiliation and then how they are part of the general organization of the sect, which found a modern development in the Yogī Association. Chapter 3 focuses on the ideal self-image that the sect presents in the person of the wandering ascetic. The valorization of wandering is an ideal that legitimizes the existence of the sect and found its incarnation in a group of itinerant Yogīs called *jamāt*, whose characteristics will be described in depth.

Parts II and III are devoted to the monastic organization of the Nāth Yogīs. Monasteries are the backbone and the collective anchorage that give the sect its permanent structure. They belong to two different categories with different functions: the collective monasteries and the personal monasteries. Part II deals with the collective or *pañcāyatī* monasteries, the common property of the sect, in which the large-scale rituals that gather together the dispersed sect members are performed. Chapters 4 and 5 present the monastery of Kadri (Mangalore, Karnataka), its long history and legendary roots and then the very complex procedures for the nomination and enthronement of its head, which occurs once every twelve years, starting with the Kumbh Melā of Nasik and an eight-month-long pilgrimage to the monastery. Chapters 6 and 7 focus on the monastery of Caughera in South Nepal and the special relationship with kingship demonstrated by local history and foundational legend, with a focus on the enigmatic figure of the legendary founder Ratannāth. Archival documents allow for an insight into the complex network of economic and political relationships that the proprietary status of the monastery supposes.

Part III presents three personal monasteries, or *nījī maṭhs* as they are called, and explores the way in which these institutions ensure their success and permanency in a modern environment characterized by religious competition for followers and legitimacy. Chapters 8 and 9 are devoted to the Amrit Ashram of Fatehpur (Shekhavati, Rajasthan) and to the role played by the hagiography of the historical founder (d. 1916) in the expansion and consolidation of the institution, grounded on the worship of the tomb and the throne. Chapter 10 emphasizes the role played by lay followers in these monasteries and thus by the involvement of their heads (*mahants*) in forming new relationships with the surrounding society. This kind of involvement with the surrounding world finds its most extreme expression in the political engagement of the last three *mahants* of the Gorakhpur monastery in the Hindutva movement. The monastery of Asthal Bohar, which is the subject of Chapter 11, offers a successful synthesis between traditional rootedness in sectarian identity and modern preoccupations with welfare and social development.

Part IV examines briefly those many people who claim the label of 'yogī' and form a vast community of yogīs by caste, characterized by their householder or *grihastha* status. They may share with the ascetic Nāth Yogīs such characteristics as a common reference to Gorakhnāth, some peculiar rituals of initiation, or burial practices; however, the extreme diversity of their various conditions and our ignorance of the history of their development leave open many questions regarding their relationship with the *sampradāya.*

In addition, beyond presenting a study of a particular sect in the form of the Nāth Yogīs, this book also aims to question more generally the nature of the Hindu ascetic orders and to reflect on the type of organization that has secured their continuity. I stress the importance of monastic institutions in this context and propose that we consider the dialectic between itinerant and settled monastic life a key structural feature of the ascetic sectarian movement. Monastic institutions do not 'tame' the ascetics, as is sometimes said, but rather provide a lasting and solid framework that allows for both the cohesion of the group and the solitary individual spiritual journey.

PART I

NĀTH YOGĪS' IDENTITY

The purpose of this first part is to give a general overview of the Nāth Yogīs before focusing in the subsequent chapters on their institutions, especially their monasteries. This exploration will be devoted to the way the Nāth Yogīs of today see themselves, their self-definition and what they consider to be the most important parts of their identity. My perspective is grounded on the Nāths' practices and beliefs as they are expressed in their daily way of life. I will first describe the community of the Nāth Yogīs by summarizing its main characteristics: its name, founder historical background and references, deities and cults. Then I will follow the path of an individual Yogī from the different initiations he could receive to the last rites performed after his death. I will also look at the institutional integration of the individual ascetic by studying the internal organization of the sect, its various branches, its administration and the part played by the Yogī Association. The last chapter will be devoted to those who embody the sect's ideals, the wandering ascetics.

The Nāth Yogīs of today present themselves as belonging to a *sampradāya*, a term which A. Malinar explains as 'a community following and transmitting a religious teaching' (2011: 157).[1]

[1] See A. Malinar (2011: III, 156-64): 'The term is derived from the verbal compound *sam+pra+dā-*, "to hand over", "to pass on", and refers in particular to the handing down of knowledge; it is a transmission that constitutes a knowledge tradition. The word *sampradāya* comprises the process as well as the result. It is "tradition as transmitted" [...] It still needs to be studied in detail when *sampradāya* starts to denote a community in which a particular tradition of religious knowledge *cum* practice is handed down.' (156).

The transmission of knowledge inside religious communities supposes the sharing of a number of characteristic elements that help the *sampradāya* to define and delimit itself, including the name of the founder with which the community has chosen to identify. The main role that transmission plays in the constitution of a *sampradāya* is also manifested in the use of the term *paramparā* (from the Skt *para*, 'next', thus *param-para*, 'following each other') to mean 'succession,' equally employed by the Yogīs to stress the transmission from guru to disciple. The community grounded on this transmission can also be designated as *panth* (meaning 'path', 'way', or 'religious pathway') but generally the Yogīs prefer to use the word *panth* for their internal subdivision into twelve branches (see passim). Their English publications often use the term 'sect'.

CHAPTER 1

References

The Nāth Yogīs, as they prefer to be called now, are known under different appellations that refer to different characteristics and histories.

NINE NĀTHS AND EIGHTY-FOUR SIDDHAS

In calling themselves Nāth Yogīs, members of this group qualify their tradition as 'the one of the Nine Nāths and Eighty-four Siddhas', therefore inscribing it in the vast Tantric current that developed in medieval India around esoteric practices which included bodily techniques (like breath control), complex rituals, and alchemical manipulations. As David White (1996: 2) explains,

> as a common noun, *siddha* means 'realized, perfected one', a term generally applied to a practitioner who has through his practice realized his dual goal of superhuman powers (*siddhis*, 'realizations', 'perfections') and bodily immortality. As a proper noun, *Siddha* becomes a broad sectarian appellation, applying to devotees of Śiva in the Deccan, alchemists in Tamil Nadu, a group of early Buddhist tāntrikas from Bengal, the alchemists of Medieval India and, most especially, a mainly north Indian group known as the Nāth Siddhas.

The cult of the Siddhas developed later in Tibetan Buddhism with a rich iconography and legendary narratives about those heroic figures who were known as the Eighty-four Mahāsidhas (Dowman 1985, Linrothe 2006). The lists of Siddhas kept varying according to time, place, and sectarian traditions, retaining, however, the number eighty-four as a symbol of completeness.

The Nāth Yogīs share this common heritage but they add the distinction, which to my knowledge is specific to them, between Nāths and Siddhas, even though the distinction is rather unclear. The Nāth Yogīs call the founding ancestors of the sect Nāths or 'Lords' and they consider them to be superior to the Siddhas. However, different variants of this classification are known, and in some cases Siddhas in one list are considered Nāths in another. Today the authorities of the Nāth *sampradāya* have decided on a list that they reproduce in their publications.[1] It starts with Ādināth, the foundational guru who is the only common member of all the lists: Ādināth is no other than Śiva himself. Then his six disciples: Udaynāth, Santoṣnāth, Gajbalī Gajkanthaṛnāth, Acal Acambhenāth, Satyanāth, and Matsyendranāth, plus Matsyendranāth's disciple Gorakṣanāth and Gorakṣanāth's disciple Cauraṅgināth. Some names are associated with a god's name: Udaynāth with Pārvatī, Satyanāth with Brahmā, and Santoṣnāth with Viṣṇu. This list is almost identical to the list given by Briggs (1973: 136)[2] and includes names rarely mentioned elsewhere while excluding more famous figures like Jalendranāth and Kanipā (depicted in the legends as rivals of Gorakhnāth). Besides the list of the nine Nāths, the same Nāth publication gives a list of the Eighty-four Siddhas.[3]

Almost all the lists of the Nine Nāths include Matsyendra, who, according to a very popular legend, which justifies his name of 'Fish-Lord' or 'Lord of the Fishes', overheard the secret teaching of Śiva to Pārvatī while he was in the belly of a fish. His importance in the Nāth Yogī tradition points to a link with

[1] Yogī Vilāsnāth 2010, Śrī Nāth Siddh Pāṭh: 48-9.

[2] See the various lists given by Dvivedi (1981: 23-4), Dasgupta (1976: 202-7), White (2006: 92-3).

[3] Yogi Vilāsnāth 2010. The website of the Nāth *sampradāya* organization provides vivid images of the 84 Siddhas as represented by statues in the former seat of recently deceased guru Anandanāth in Galna (Maharashtra). They are listed by alphabetical order in English. (http://www.yogīgorakshnāth.org/index.php/gallery.html, consulted 16/1/2014).

the medieval Tantric school known as the Yoginī Kaula, of which Matsyendra was reputed to be the founder (see Muñoz 2011). Matsyendra was the author of the *Kaula-jñāna-nirṇaya* and the *Matsyendra-saṃhitā* and a proponent of clearly transgressive sexual-yogīc practices involving effective sexual union. Yoginī Kaula was divided into four lines of transmission (*āmnāya*); from a study of the *Matsyendra Saṃhitā*, Csaba Kiss deducts that 'of the four āmnāyas of the Kaula tradition (cf. Sanderson 1988: 680 ff.), the Paścimāmnāya [i.e. Western Transmission] (the cult of the goddess Kubjikā) and the Dakṣināmnāya [Southern Transmission] (the cult of Tripurā or Tripurasundarī [...]) prominently feature in the text' (Kiss 2011: 144-5). Both traditions intermingled in the Śāmbhava system, an important south Indian variant of the Kubjikā's cult ('a South Indian manifestation of a masculinized version of the worship of Kubjikā and her partner', id.: 145), and had a major influence on the formation of the Nāth Yogīs' soteriology.[4]

GORAKHNĀTH

Matsyendranāth's disciple Gorakṣanāth, or Gorakhnāth, is claimed by the Nāth Yogīs as their supreme Guru and the founder of their *sampradāya* (religious tradition) from whom they trace their *paramparā* (line of succession). They call themselves Gorakhnāthīs, the followers of Gorakhnāth. The common tendency of the various sects and denominations is to trace their genealogy from a prestigious ancestor in order to stress the antiquity of their tradition. But who, then, is Gorakhnāth? We have seen that he was listed as one of the Nine Nāths, but was not

[4] One example of this is the *Gorakṣasaṃhitā* (or one of the three works known under this name, White 1996: 140), which is attributed to Gorakhnāth even though it 'contains no references to Gorakṣa other than in its colophons'; it 'is an expansion of the *Kubjikāmatatantra*, an important Paścimāmnaya Kaula work' (Mallinson 2011a: 424). Dated from the thirteenth century, it is mostly devoted to the Tantric worship of the Goddess, with some discussion on Haṭha Yoga.

first in the succession line, as he was a disciple of Matsyendra. However, many legends told by the Yogīs play on a complex relationship between Matsyendra and Gorakh in which guru and disciple invert their roles or act reciprocally. And as some of the legends tell it, even though Gorakhnāth is Matsyendra's disciple, he was created by Śiva himself. He is no other than the pure form of Śiva, his ascetic self. Thus the Nāth Yogīs claim no other ancestry than the Supreme God himself and they worship Gorakhnāth as *śivrūp*, the quintessential form of Śiva.

This is clearly the message given by one version of the creation myth of Gorakhnāth as explained in one of the booklets published by the Yogī Press, *Siddha Ratnanāth Caritāmṛt*, which I summarize from the Nepali text (Bijayanāth 2043 vs: 17-21):[5]

Matsyendranāth, who in the belly of the giant fish heard Śiva's teaching to Pārvatī about the 'tale on immortality' (*amarkathā*), practised austerities until he was blessed by Śiva and granted the privilege that God himself would become incarnate as his companion to help him on the yogic path.

Later, as Śiva and Pārvatī quarrelled, Pārvatī, with a vain mind, told Śiva: 'Ādideva, everywhere you are, I am. You do not exist without me. You do not exist apart from me!' Mulnāth answered: 'Maheśvarī, everywhere you are, I am. This is true. But to say that everywhere I am, you are – this is not true. It is like when there is a jar, there is always earth, but when there is earth, there is not always a jar.' In order to give a lesson to Pārvatī, Śiva divided himself in two parts, one as himself and the other as Gorakhnāth.

Gorakhnāth, the true form of Śiva immaculate, went to a remote place and entered into deep meditation. Śiva and Pārvatī later approached the place and Śiva told the goddess that there was a great Yogī who had been meditating there for a long time. Upon seeing a Yogī as radiant as a thousand suns, Pārvatī understood that he was a form of Śiva and wondered if he was not a creation of Mahādev intended as a response to her previous assertions. She thus decided to test the Yogī. 'If the acts of Māyā are irresistible, moreover Māyā herself must be irresistible,'

[5] See a similar version in Muñoz 2010: 82-4, quoting Śambhuśarmā 1964.

she said. 'My name is Māyā. My power is superior.' Using the power of her *māyā*, she filled the universe with her presence. But Gorakhnāth remained unprovoked and did not turn from his meditation. Pārvatī then went back to Śiva and said, 'Lord, you were right. You can be without me. I have seen it. Who is this Yogī who did not consider my power and stayed in *samādhi*?' Maheśvar answered, 'This Yogī you saw is Gorakhnāth. He is superior to all gods and men. He is free from *māyā*, he is the death of death. I am Gorakhnāth. Gorakhnāth is my essential form – we have no difference between us. Light is not different from light. I took the form of Gorakhnāth in order for Veda, Cow and Earth to be safe. Whosoever has the knowledge of yoga can vanquish death.' Gorakhnāth then went to look for Matsyendranāth.

The divine guru Śiva was incarnated in Gorakhnāth and became the disciple of his own disciple Matsyendranāth, helping him in his efforts to propagate the doctrine of yoga.

An echo of this legend is found in Dasgupta, who comments: 'Bengali literary traditions make him the purest and strongest of all the yogīs. The erotic charm even of the goddess Durgā herself was repeatedly put to shame by the purity and strength of his character' (1976: 388).[6]

Many other stories playing with etymology tell of the miraculous apparition of Gorakhnāth. According to Rose (1919: II, 390), the name was explained as originating from *ghor*, meaning 'filth', 'because the formless creator from the sweat of his own breast created Gorakhnāth'. Most often the name is explained as 'Lord of cattle', alluding to his miraculous birth in a cowshed or on cowdung from ashes given by Śiva to a barren woman who, incredulously, threw them on a heap of cowdung or into a cowshed. Twelve years later, Mahādev – or in some versions, Matsyendranāth – discovered there a twelve-year-old boy whom

[6] The Bengali *Gorakṣa Vijaya* by Sekh Phayajulla is quite explicit: Gorakh is the only one among the yogīs to resist the charms of Devī. She comes to him naked when he is seated in deep meditation under a tree. He takes a leaf and uses it to close the entrance to her vagina (*yoni dvār*), and then disappears. Devī is ashamed (with many thanks to France Bhattacharya who translated this passage for me from Bengali).

he named Gorakhnāth. Matsyendranāth became his guru (Levi 1905: I, 351; Rose 1919: II 390; Briggs 1973: 182).

Two groups of legends link Matsyendranāth and Gorakhnāth. The first group is specific to the Nepalese tradition, in which Matsyendra is an important syncretic deity; the Tantric Siddha incorporates an ancient Newar god Bungadyaḥ and the boddhisattva Avalokiteśvara.[7] Matsyendra's arrival in Nepal is explained in all the recent Nepalese chronicles (the *vaṃśāvalis* of the nineteenth century) as the consequence of Gorakhnāth's action. After Gorakhnāth was poorly received by the inhabitants of Kathmandu valley, he wanted to punish them by causing a terrible drought; he sat, meditating, on the Nāgas, the serpent-gods and givers of rain, thus preventing them from moving. The Newar king and his counsellors found that the only way to oblige Gorakhnāth to rise from his seat and release the Nāgas was to force him to greet his guru Matsyendra. They persuaded Matsyendra to come from Kamrup (Assam), where he was staying in the form of a young prince. When he arrived in the valley, Gorakhnāth went to greet him, thereby releasing the Nāgas who were then able to resume their task. The rain began to fall profusely. The king and the valley inhabitants worshipped the two yogīs as everything returned to order.

The second group of legends has a pan-Indian diffusion (we shall see in Chapter 4 a version specific to the Mangalore Nāth tradition) and appeared as an echo of the promise made by Śiva to Matsyendra that he would be incarnated as his companion to come to his help. This is exactly the role ascribed to Gorakhnāth, who became the saviour of his guru.

According to the summary of the legend made by Adrian Muñoz from the *Gorakh carit* and *Gorakhnāth Caritra*,

> It is said that once Matsyendra arrived in the Kingdom of Women, in the Kadali Forest. There, he joined Queen Mainākinī and became her lover.

[7] On the cult and legends of Matsyendranāth in Nepal, see the seminal work of J. Locke (1980), as well as S. Lienhard (1978), G. Toffin (1993, Chap. VI), A. Vergati (1985).

> For a long period of time, Matsyendra enjoyed sensual pleasures [...] Meanwhile, Gorakh got to know about his guru's situation and decided to act to save him (from becoming controlled by physical pleasures).

He succeeded in entering the kingdom, disguised as a female musician. During the performance in front of the royal couple,

> Gorakh made the drum emit words that only his guru could understand: 'Wake up Matsyendra. You are a great knower of yoga, Guru-ji; it isn't proper for you to give in to sexual pleasures and be embraced by the net of Māyā. [...] Abandon all Kaula practices. If you continue to cherish the tigress Māyā, you'll dry up the *amṛt* (nectar of immortality) [...] I'm here to remind you of the Nāth sādhanā. [...] Matsyendra finally recalled his former condition. (2011: 115-17]

After other episodes in which Gorakhnāth brutally killed the son (or sons) of Matsyendra and the queen, and restored him (or them) to life, both he and Matsyendra left the women's kingdom and went on pilgrimage.

This widespread story allows for a more philosophical and eventually historical interpretation, Gorakhnāths' teachings superseding those of Matsyendra, and the Nāth *sādhanā* replacing that of Kaula. Thus we can see in the legend a metaphor for a change from the overtly sexual tantric practices of the Kaula, involving exchanges of seminal fluids, to more internalized, and more Haṭha yogīc bodily techniques. As White explains,

> the mythic perils of Matsyendranāth are very likely a reflection of a cleavage within the tantric tradition. While a number of sects, including the Matsyendra's Yogīnī Kaula, incorporated sexual intercourse into their practices, others, including the Nāth Siddhas, whose main doctrinal exponent was Gorakh, were overtly misogynous, treating sexuality as a trap into which the yogīn could fall and thereby lose all the benefits of his prior effort. (White 1996: 235)

Compared to the many legends about Gorakhnāth's birth, his encounters with many disciples and wondrous deeds, historical data about his life are very poor. To talk about a historical Gorakhnāth is more of a hypothetical discussion than a certainty (see White 1996: 90-2). Scholars disagree about the date and the place of his birth (Punjab for Mallik 1960, Dasgupta 1976 and White 1996; eastern Bengal for Briggs 1938; Deccan for Mallinson 2011a). It is generally accepted that he lived in the twelfth century, since his name is mentioned from the thirteenth century onwards in spiritual lineages related to the many Tantric Śaiva schools flourishing at that time. The first inscription to mention Gorakhnāth is dated to 1279 CE and was found in Karnataka, near the Kallesvara temple in Mysore State. It gives a series of Nāths, beginning with Ādināth and including Gorakhnāth, listing them as the spiritual gurus of a yogī beneficiary of a royal grant (Saletore 1937: 18-19). Other stone inscriptions from late fourteenth century come from the Kathmandu Valley: the Itum Bahal rock inscription dated 1382 CE and the Pharping inscription dated 1391 CE, which records how Yogī Acintanāth established stone footprints of Gorakhnāth in a nearby cave sanctuary. Many other inscriptions mentioning Gorakhnāth are found all over Nepal, mostly dated to the sixteenth century onwards (Unbescheid 1980, Locke 1980).

Textual references to Gorakhnāth start from the early thirteenth century. Noteworthy are 'the various mentions in Harihara's Kannada *Ragales*, in particular the *Revaṇasiddheśvara Ragale*, in which Revaṇa defeats Gorakha in a magic contest' (Mallinson 2011a: 413) and the mentions in the *Jñāneśvarī*, the 1290 CE Marathi commentary of the *Bhagavadgītā* by Jñāndev, who quotes Gorakhnāth as the guru of Gahīṇīnāth, himself the guru of Nivṛittināth, who is in turn the guru of Jñāndev. Other references are found in the early works on Haṭha Yoga that are attributed to Gorakhnāth or in which his name is mentioned.

GORAKHNĀTH'S TEXTUAL CORPUS

If the person of Gorakhnāth is rather enigmatic, he is nevertheless credited with the authorship of many Sanskrit and vernacular treatises and poems about Haṭha Yoga.[8] All these texts are now

[8] See the lists of Briggs (1973: 251-7), Dvivedi (1981: 98-101), Banerjea (1962: 26-8).

part of what can be called the Nāth tradition, even though, as we shall see, the connection between the practice of Haṭha Yoga and the present Nāth Yogīs is rather dubious, which may explain the observations of Adrian Muñoz:

> The Nāth yogīs have made no real attempt at organizing their various texts so as to form a canonical corpus. Their prodigality apart, all of these texts respond to different needs, and the approaches and concepts in them vary greatly. This fact makes it all the more difficult to try to 'unify' the Nāth traditions. ... For the most part, the allegedly early works in Sanskrit are attributed to Gorakh, whereas the later Sanskrit texts on Haṭha yoga are not. (2011: 109-10)

The history of these texts is particularly complex, as many are overlapping and appear to be the same work under different titles. Two of the earliest works on Haṭha Yoga, the *Vivekamārtaṇḍa* and the *Gorakṣaśataka*, are dated to the thirteenth century and attributed to Gorakhnāth (Mallinson 2012); they are followed by many other texts ascribed to his authorship and edited as such by the sectarian authorities (see the list in Briggs 1973: chap. 12). However, this claim is now contested by scholars: matters such as dates, exact edition, and even real authorship are quite difficult to ascertain because we find many interpolations, as well as identical passages mentioned under different names (Bouy 1994, Mallinson 2012).

For a clearer view of this issue, let us take the example of the *Gorakṣaśataka*, 'the Hundred Verses of Gorakṣa'. According to James Mallinson, many manuscripts appear under this title; however, what was later called *Gorakṣaśataka* 'was originally known as the *Vivekamārtaṇḍa*.'[9] The first *Gorakṣaśataka* was probably composed around the fourteenth century and the author seems to distinguish himself from Gorakh, as 'he says

[9] These are the versions edited and translated into German by Nowotny, a shorter version translated into English by Briggs (1973, Chap. 14), and a critical edition in French by Tara Michaël 2007. According to her, the *Gorakṣaśataka* is known in an expanded version as the *Gorakṣa-paddhati* (2007: 33).

that he is describing Gorakṣa's method of yoga, which he has experienced thanks to his guru's teaching' (2012: 264). The text 'contains some of the earliest teachings on *haṭha yoga* to be found in Sanskrit texts.[10] It is the first text to describe complex methods of *prāṇāyāma*, breath control, and the first to teach [a...] technique for arousing Kuṇḍalinī, the coiled serpent goddess' (id.: 257). The aim of the teaching is final liberation, which supposes control of the mind, and 'to control his mind the yogī should control his breath. Three methods should be used simultaneously to master the breath: eating a controlled diet, assuming a particular posture, and stimulating Kuṇḍalini' (id.: 258).

Fragments of the *Gorakṣaśataka*, notably its central core, were later incorporated into many other works. Among them was the *Hathapradīpika* (or *Haṭhayogapradīpika*),[11] the best-known Sanskrit work on Haṭha Yoga, which was compiled by Svātmarāma in the fifteenth century and includes 28 verses from the *Gorakṣaśataka*. According to Mallinson, 'Svātmarāma valiantly tried to create a lamp (*pradīpikā*) to lighten the darkness [of many doctrines] by synthesizing into one coherent whole the doctrines in the texts he had at his disposal' (Mallinson 2012: 265). The later *Gheraṇḍa Saṁhitā* 'is a work very similar to the preceding, from which it borrows' (Briggs 1973: 254).

Worth mentioning among the works attributed to Gorakhnāth is the *Siddhasiddhānta Paddhati*, as it is regularly re-issued by the present-day Nāth authorities. It forms the basis of Banerjea's *Philosophy of Gorakhnāth*, who writes that 'among all the works of this school discovered so far, [it is] the most systematic and comprehensive presentation of [Gorakhnāth's] philosophical doctrines and it claims to be and is generally accepted as a gen-

[10] Our knowledge of the history of Haṭha Yoga will be greatly enhanced by the work in progress of 'The Haṭha Yoga Project' (European Research Council) which aims to provide critical editions and translations of selected Sanskrit texts at the basis of Haṭha Yoga; see also J. Mallinson and M. Singleton, *Roots of Yoga*, 2017.

[11] A translation with commentaries has been published in French by Tara Michaël (1974) and in English by G.P. Bhatt (2004).

uine work of the Master himself' (Banerjea 1962: 28). Chapter 3, entitled 'Knowledge of the body', has been translated and commented on by David White (2002 and 2011), who states that, 'while we cannot be certain that this is the work of a single hand rather than a compilation composed over several hundred years, the dates of the many identifiable sources, which it directly quotes, do in fact support a terminus ante quem of the twelfth century' (2011: 79). Mallinson, however, disagrees with this estimate, and points to the early eighteenth century as the most likely date of production (2011a: 422).

Besides these Sanskrit texts, which are more like 'technical guides to the theory and practice of haṭha yoga' (White 2011: 80), Gorakhnāth is credited with vernacular anthologies, including the *Gorakh Bodh*, a dialogue between Gorakhnāth and his guru Matsyendranāth,[12] and the *Gorakh Bānī*, a collection of poems that was first edited by Barthwal (1942). These metaphorical poems give a mystic and emotional flavour to the yogīc teachings.[13] Muñoz specifies that 'this poetry does not intend to systematically teach yoga techniques and physiology, but rather to express a spontaneous experience of the Absolute –the merging of the human yogī with Śiva, who is seen as the Primeval Nātha' (Muñoz 2011: 112). Often presented as aphoristic 'sayings' (*śabdī*), this literature had considerable influence on the Sants' traditions (Schomer 1987). The opinion of Barthwal that 'the Nirguṇīs are deeply indebted to the Nāth Pantha' (Barthwal 1978: 141) has been echoed in the works of Charlotte Vaudeville (1987a, b) and other *bhakti* scholars who believe that Nāth poetry must be included in studies on devotional Hindi literature (Callewaert and de Beeck 1991, see Agrawal 2011: 3-17). The thematic and stylistic proximity between Sant and Nāth poetry has a narrative parallel in the many stories (historically unfounded) relating encounters and religious debates between Gorakhnāth and, for instance, Nānak and Kabīr.[14]

[12] English translation in Mohan Singh 1937.

[13] See the English translation of a few poems in Djurdjevic 2008.

[14] According to the life stories of Guru Nānak as relayed in the *Janam-Sākhīs*, two such encounters took place at Mount Sumeru and

HAṬHA YOGA

As we have seen, Goraknāth appears in two very different lights: on the one hand, he is praised in legends for his purity and asceticism, while on the other he is known for the texts concerning Haṭha Yoga that are attributed to him, whether that attribution is accurate or not. He is even sometimes considered as the 'inventor' of Haṭha Yoga. Are these two portrayals of him contradictory?

Haṭha Yoga, or forceful yoga (*haṭha* literally means 'force'), is a later development, compared to what has been known as the classical or Pātañjala Yoga, the eight-limbed (*aṣṭāṅga*) yoga as exposed in Patañjali's *Yogasūtra* (350-400 CE).[15] According

---

Achal in Punjab. Additionally, a section of the Ādi Granth called the *Siddh Goṣṭ*, discusses a dispute between Nānak and a group of Nāth Siddhas. All this would seem to indicate a widespread familiarity with Nāth beliefs and legends (see McLeod 1986 and the translation of the *Siddh Goṣṭ* by K.E. Nayar and J.S. Sandhu 2007). Many verses of Kabīr's *Bījak*, moreover, have close parallels in the *Gorakh Bānī* (Offredi 2002, Lorenzen 2011).

[15] The section of the *Yogasūtra* on *aṣṭāṅga* recognizes eight stages or disciplines directed towards ultimate cessation of mental processes and final absorption into the Divine. The first two stages consist of the ethical and behavioural observances composed of five restraints (*yama*), or negative injunctions, and five positive observances (*niyama*). Together these serve as a prelude to the more specific yogic techniques, starting with the postures (*āsana*) and the control of the breath (*prāṇāyāma*). If the proliferation and the focus on the postures is a much later development of Haṭha Yoga (Alter 2004, Bühnemann 2007, Singleton 2010, Mallinson 2011b: 776, who specifies 'the 17th-century *Haṭharatnāvalī* is the first text to teach 84 individual āsanas', a listing which became an unquestionable reference in the twentieth century), the various techniques of breath regulation are considered to be fundamental or, in the words of Briggs, 'are esteemed for [their] great efficiency in producing occult powers' (1973: 267). The next step of *pratyāhāra* supposes the withdrawal of the mind from the sensory organs. These are the five external means preliminary to the three last stages: *dhāranā* or fixed attention and steadfastness of the mind; *dhyāna*,

to the seminal study of Jason Birch, 'the earliest occurrence of haṭhayoga is in [...] a Buddhist Tantra from eighth century' (2011: 535). Dividing the corpus he studied into an early Haṭha Yoga and a later one starting from Svetarama's fifteenth century compilation entitled *Haṭhapradīpikā*, he questions the meaning of *haṭha* and concludes that 'the force' of Haṭha yoga qualifies the effects of his techniques, rather than the effort required to perform them' (id.: 548), i.e. 'the force of Haṭhayoga refers to forcing what normally moves down (i.e., *apāna*, *bindu*) and what is usually dormant (*kuṇḍalinī*) to move upwards' (id.: 537).

According to Mallinson (2011b), who studied the history of Haṭha Yoga through a careful philological analysis of its various treatises, Haṭha Yoga as it became known around the fifteenth century with Svetarama's *Haṭhapradīpikā* is the result of the combination of two layers: an early Haṭha Yoga rooted in ancient ascetic practice aiming at preserving the *bindu* or semen as vital principle (the loss of which was said to bring weakness and death) and a later adjunction of tantric Kaula practices involving transgressive sexual techniques aimed at the union of female energy Kuṇḍalinī with Śiva.[16]

---

or one-pointed concentration; and the ultimate phase of *samādhi*, cessation of the mental process, dissolution of the self, and release (*muktī*). The Gorakhnāth tradition as found in the *Vivekamārtaṇḍa* teaches a sixfold yoga without the first two levels of *yama* and *niyama* (Mallinson 2011b: 771).

[16] As Mallinson explains (2011b): 'Haṭha is first referred to by name in Sanskrit texts dating to around the 11th century CE, but some of its techniques can be traced back at least a thousand years earlier [...]. In its earliest formulations, *haṭha* was used to raise and conserve the physical essence of life, identified in men as *bindu* (semen), which is otherwise constantly dripping downwards from a store in the head [...]. The preservation and sublimation of semen was associated with *tapas* (asceticism) [...]. The techniques of early Haṭha Yoga work in two ways: mechanically, [standing on one's head...], or by making the breath enter the central channel of the body, which runs from the base of the spine to the top of the head, thereby forcing *bindu* upward' (Mallinson 2011b: 770). The Kaula system overlaid its *kuṇḍalinī* conceptions over

Nowadays, Haṭha Yoga appears as a kind of synthesis of various currents largely referred to as Tantric, as exemplified by another etymology of *haṭha* 'given in the commentary to verse one of the Gorakṣa *Paddhati*, where it is stated that *ha* means the sun and *ṭha* the moon' (Briggs 1973: 274).[17] The aim of Haṭha Yoga is thus to facilitate the union of the sun and the moon, which correlates to the union of Śakti and Śiva.

Yoga, specifically Haṭha Yoga, stresses the importance of bodily techniques to attain the common goal of all spiritual disciplines, liberation. Haṭha Yoga allows one to experience a union with the Absolute within the body, which is thought of as a microcosm of the entire universe because the body and the universe are made of the same elements. The yogī's progressive control of his physiological and mental processes leads to a similar control of natural phenomena, which explains how he is thought to obtain superhuman powers.

The yogīc practitioner associates certain bodily practices (*mudrās*) with the control of the breath that moves through the

---

it, leading to the Hatha Yoga new formulation where 'the same [bodily] techniques [...] are said to effect *kuṇḍalinī*'s rise up the central channel (which is called the *suṣumnā* in these traditions) to a store of *amṛta* (the nectar of immortality) situated in the head, with which *kuṇḍalinī* then floods the body, rejuvenating it and rendering it immortal' (Mallinson id.). Thus we have, according to this theory, a synthesis between two somehow contradictory conceptions: the *bindu*-oriented early Haṭha Yoga practices to keep the *bindu* in the head and the Kaula *kuṇḍalinī* yoga whose aim is to flood the body with *amṛta* (Mallinson 2011b: 774). See also the critical edition and translation of the *Khecarīvidyā* of Ādinātha by Mallinson, 2010: 'The KV seems to be an attempt by a school of yogīns whose roots lay in Kaula tantrism at reclaiming the haṭhayogīc *khecarīmudra* from more orthodox *bindudhāraṇa*-oriented schools of haṭhayoga' (2010: 30).

[17] According to Birch, 'there is circumstantial evidence to support the possibility that this metaphysical definition was behind the name, Haṭhayoga' (2011: 533). However, we find it in only one text from the early corpus, the *Yogabīja*, the authorship of which has been attributed to Gorakhnāth without concrete evidence.

channels (*nāḍī*) of the mystical body (mainly, *iḍā* and *piṅgalā*, the two channels linked to breathing in and out, as to the Sun and Moon, or Śakti and Śiva). In this manner, he may succeed in awaking the *kuṇḍalinī*, or the cosmic energy viewed as a female snake sleeping and coiled at the base of the spinal cord. Once awakened, the snake-energy is thought to move up the central channel, or *suṣumnā*, along the way piercing the seven *cakras*, or 'centres' of spiritual energy distributed across the body, from the *mūlādhāra cakra* to the top of the head where is an aperture towards *brahman, brahmarandhra*. As described in many yogīc texts, and in particular in the *Yoga Upaniṣads*, the union of Śakti and Śiva, of Energy and Knowledge, leads the yogī to final illumination in a perfected and thus immortal body.

What we know of the evolution of the tantric Kaula system and what the Gorakhnāth's legends express is a transformation from overtly sexual practices to tamed or internalized practices (White 1996, Munoz 2010 and 2011, Mallinson 2011a). As quoted by Mallinson, the last verse of the *Gorakṣaśataka* stigmatizes the sexual rituals of the Kaula tradition.

> We drink the dripping liquid called *bindu*, 'the drop', not wine; we eat the rejection of the object of the five senses, not meat; we do not embrace a sweetheart but the *Suṣumnā nāḍī*, her body curved like *kuśa* grass; if we must have intercourse, it takes place in a mind dissolved in the void, not in a vagina. (2011a: 423)

Thus, Haṭha Yoga kept the same conception of the imagined Tantric body but turned the sexual practices of the Tantric Kaula into internalized ascetic disciplines. Furthermore, Gorakhnāth could be seen in the Nāth Yogīs' worldview as both a chaste avātar of Śiva and a Tantric propagator of Haṭha Yoga.

The Sanskrit treatises on Haṭha Yoga attributed to Gorakhnāth are currently published by the various Yogīs' presses (Dang Caughera until 1960, Varanasi, Gorakhpur, Haridwar) and the Nāth Yogīs authorities now claim Haṭha Yoga as their exclusive heritage, one that has been usurped by the thousands of flourishing Haṭha Yogīc schools all over the world. These leaders try to stimulate the practice of this kind of yoga in the monasteries and among the itinerant Yogīs. However, I have the impression that very few Nāth Yogīs can be acurately described as yoga practitioners, a fact that was already noted by Briggs in the 1930s: 'There seems to be a limited practice of Yoga among the Kanphatas' (1973: 251).[18]

LEGENDS AND POWERS

Much more than in theoretical treatises about Haṭha Yoga, the world-view and values of the Nāth Yogīs have been popularized through the medium of their numerous legends which have fascinated audiences for centuries. These narratives tell of a magical world full of heroic characters, changing appearances, wonderful deeds and excessive passions or disasters. The hero is not so much a dispassionate and otherworldly yogī as he is a wonder-worker. He is often a prince or a king and his meetings with Gorakhnāth or with a Nāth guru draw him into dangerous and fantastic adventures, leading him to ultimately reach true yogīc status. The yogī has some help in accomplishing his wondrous deeds due to support from the divine Gorakhnāth or other deities, combined with magical and alchemical practices, but most often the legends attribute the hero's feats to his *yogbal*, or his yogīc power. The yogī's progression on the path of the yogīc practice helps him to attain special superhuman powers, as detailed, for instance, in the *Yogasūtra*. This text also warns, however, against their danger and seductiveness. To control the inner physical processes of the body through yogīc techniques allows one to control outer natural processes; by experiencing the identity between the components of the body and of nature and by conceptualizing the body as a microcosm, the practitioner

[18] Some modern Nāth publications (cf. Narharināth 2025 vs: app. 1-21) try to link the two prestigious systems, the ancient references to the 84 Siddhas and the new successful postural yoga, giving the name of one Siddha to each of the 84 *āsanas*, and illustrating each with a small drawing. See their reproduction and analysis in Bühnemann 2007: 85-101.

of yoga gains the power to act upon nature as he wishes. These are the famous superhuman capacities, or *siddhis* (called *vibhutis* in the *Yogasutra*[19] and *guṇas* in the Haṭha Yoga texts) through which the Nāth heroes demonstrate their superiority. Even today, Nāth Yogīs are credited with such powers and are respected as well as feared. In popular belief, they are thought both to give boons such as helping women become pregnant, protecting against locusts or hail and diverting disasters, and to bring about calamities by cursing people and bringing them bad luck. However, the ultimate power that Nāth Yogīs sought was the ability to transgress the boundaries of the human condition and obtain immortality. Many foreign travellers gave colourful accounts of the way yogīs would bury themselves in underground pits for a few hours or a few days and then exit as if awaking from deep ecstasy. For these outstanding yogīs, death is just a state of profound meditation in which they will

[19] Vyāsa's commentary on *Yogasūtra* 3.45 lists the following as the eight major *siddhis:*

(1) miniaturization (*aṇiman*) [means] one becomes minute;
(2) levitation (*laghiman*) [means] one becomes light;
(3) magnification (*mahiman*) [means] one becomes huge;
(4) extension (*prāpti*) [means] one touches the moon with one's fingertips
(5) irresistible desire (*prākāmya*) [means] the lack of opposition to one's wishes — one dives into the earth and emerges as [if] in water;
(6) mastery (*vaśitva*) means one masters the elements and material things, but is not mastered by others.
(7) command (*īśitva*) [means] to govern manifestation, disappearance, and disposition [of the elements etc.];
(8) wish realization (*yatrakāmā -vasāyitva*) [means] making whatever is desired real — as one desires, so the gross elements and their natures (*prakrtis*) arrange themselves. (Pflueger 2012: 246, in Jacobsen 2012)

On the nature and interpretations of these superhuman capacities according to various religious traditions, see the volume coordinated by Jacobsen (2012).

eternally remain – this is why a single term, *samādhi*, designates the ultimate stage on the yogīc path and the tomb. The need to escape death and cheat Yama's messengers is a recurring theme of many stories and, as we shall see, also of the Nāth Yogīs' death rituals.

The motif of the heroic quest of the yogīs for the supreme good has influenced a huge corpus of popular literature, narratives, songs and epics in vernacular languages, the various versions of which can be found across north India. The foundational stories for the Nāth tradition include the epics of Bhatṛhari, the king of Ujjain, and his nephew, the unfortunate prince Gopīcand,[20] as well as the adventures of Gugā (Rose 1919, Lapoint 1978, Bouillier 2004) and Pūraṇ Bhagat.[21] We may add to this collection the numerous ballads of north India that draw a parallel between amorous quests and initiatory journeys, such as the adventures of the princess Sorṭhī and the hero Brijābhar, of Sāraṅga and Sādābrij, of Cāndā and Lorik, of Mālū Śāhī and Rājulī[22] in the Himalayas.

Moreover, specialists in early-modern Sufī poetry have long recognized the presence of Yogīc themes and metaphors in Sufī poems and romantic compositions, such as *Hīr* (by Vāris Shāh, see Matringe 1988), *Padmāvat* (by Jāyasī, see de Bruijn 2012) or *Madhumālatī* (by Mir Sayyid Manjhan, see Behl and Weightman 2000). This literary convergence echoed a deeper relationship on the philosophical and religious levels, in which Sufīs and Yogīs could meet and share the techniques of Haṭha Yoga, a fact attested by the popularity of texts like *Amṛtakuṇḍā*[23] or *Yoga-*

---

[20] See Grierson 1885, Grodzins Gold 1992, Servan-Schreiber 1999: 35-62.

[21] Also named Cauraṅgināth, cf. Temple (1884-90: vol. 1, pp. 2-65), Gill 1986 and Chapter 9 of this book.

[22] Cf. Champion 1989; Servan-Schreiber 1999: 65-87; Matringe 1988, 1992; Gaborieau 1974: 116-20.

[23] See the articles by Carl Ernst (1996, 2003, 2005) about the progressive Islamization of Yoga in the various Arab and Persian

Kalandar.[24] That both Yogīs and Sufīs met frequently in hermitages or sanctuaries is attested to in the Mughal paintings as well as in the *malfūzāt* of Sufī Shaykhs. These 'sayings', or records of daily discourses and conversations, testify to frequent encounters, even though they were sometimes competitive or hostile in nature. We see then how important the *siddhis* were in fuelling the confrontation between Yogīs and Sufīs as they competed for territorial domination. However, a Sufī would say: 'My miracle trumps your magic' (Burchett 2012) meaning supernormal deeds made possible through the power of devotion to God will always surpass human endeavours.

DEITIES

Nāth Yogīs place themselves in close relationship to Śiva: they consider their founder to be the god's *avatār* and they express the goal of their *sādhana* in Śaiva terms (to be united with Śiva, to attain his paradise and to experience the union of Śiva and Śakti). This Śaiva allegiance finds a more concrete and visible representation in the temples visited by the Yogīs, where they address their worship to a triad consisting of Śiva as Gorakhnāth, Bhairav and the Goddess.

Gorakhnāth as God

As we have seen, the Nāth Yogīs claim Gorakhnāth as the founder of their *sampradāya*. However, they also consider Gorakhnāth to be a divine being – specifically, a form of Śiva – whom they worship. Even though today the shrines owned by the Nāth Yogīs often have statues of Gorakhnāth on the altar, he was more traditionally represented by his *caraṇ-pādukā*, the footprints

---

translations of *Amritakuṇḍā* ('Pool of Nectar'), a Sanskrit text (now lost) about Haṭha Yoga.

[24] Or Yoga of the *kalandar* (a Muslim itinerant renouncer), a text copied many times, which France Bhattacharya translated in French from Bengali (2003-4).

inscribed on a marble pedestal, or by the *dhūnī*, the ascetic fireplace that burns perpetually.[25]

What the Nāth Yogīs worship, in accordance with a spiritual quest of a non-qualified absolute, is an abstract image of the quintessential Gorakhnāth, known as Gorakhnāth's *svarūp*. This *svarūp* is conceived as a mysterious *pātradevatā* or divine vessel, also referred to as *amritpātra*, meaning a vessel of liquor of immortality. It looks like a small bowl that always appears covered with many layers of cloth and topped by flower necklaces. It is publicly displayed on special occasions like the main festivals when the Yogīs gather for a common celebration. The *pātradevatā* is then made anew or taken from the safe place where it is normally kept and is worshipped by all the Yogīs. While it is displayed publicly during these situations, it is normally kept secret, to the point that until a few years ago, nobody knew what it was. When I was in Caughera, Yogīs liked to guess its appearance: was it a Śivaliṅga,[26] Gorakhnāth's begging bowl or even Brahmā's skullcap after his beheading by Bhairav? The common belief was that anyone trying to look under the many layers of cloth covering it would surely become blind.[27]

[25] There is, however, a statue hypothetically dated from the fourtheenth century of a standing Gorakhnāth in the Mañjunāth Temple of Mangalore, and two sculptures discovered by M.N. Deshpande in the caves of Panhale-Kaji (Deshpande 1986, caves 14 and 29; with many thanks to James Mallinson for this reference), which he also dates from the fourtheenth century. We also find mention of images of Gorakh (one in Gorakh Tilla and one in Gorakhpur) in the travel accounts of Pran Puri dated to 1792 (in *The European Magazine*, vol. 57, 1810), but ancient statuary evidence is very rare.

[26] A booklet published in Gorakhpur (*Yogvāṇī*, no. 1) sees in the *pātra-devatā* such a mysterious object that it quotes Briggs, who talks about 'a stone linga'; Briggs does not mention the term *pātradavatā* – he only alludes to its symbolism on the occasion of the pilgrimage of the Nepalese Caughera Yogīs: 'The [pīr] goes in front, carrying a stone liṅga, said to contain the spirit of Gorakhnāth' (Briggs 1973: 96).

[27] On the 'system of secrecy' as a way to maintain boundaries around corporate groups and on the necessity of 'advertising the presence of

However, in a 2004 videotape and a 2005 book published by Yogī Vilāsnāth, the authorities of the *sampradāya* chose to reveal the true nature of the *pātradevatā* and thus its symbolic character. The *pātradevatā* is indeed a clay vessel, or *pātra*, and it contains a few items which are the signs of the Nāth Yogī identity: round earrings made of clay (*kuṇḍal*), a long string made of thirteen threads of black wool (*selī*), a small whistle (symbolizing the primordial sound, *nād*), a rudrākṣa seed,[28] a *cilam* (clay pipe), and some ochre cloth. The *pātradevatā* takes on an esoteric meaning: the *pātra* contains the signs of the spiritual path, and this path itself is the *amṛit*, the elixir of immortality, thus representing the aim of the yogic practices. It is a metaphysical *mise en abyme* in which the true form of Gorakhnāth is none other than the yogic condition itself. As Yogī Vilāsnāth wrote, 'Through the practice of yoga, yogīs must install the *pātradevatā* in the temple which is their own body. Then, when in their yogic journey will come the time to reach the Kailaś, i.e. the *brahmarandra*,[29] they will drink the elixir of immortality' (2005: 550, translated from Hindi).

The Goddess

Gorakhnāth's legends insist on his chastity, his self-control and his restraint in the face of the diverse forms of feminine temptation. A story told by Yogī Vilaśnāth and inspired by the Bengali *Gorakṣa Vijaya*, gives a vivid illustration:

> Gorakhnāth was roaming through Calcutta. Mahākālī, the skull-bearing goddess, asked for alms but Gorakhnāth refused and instead offered to

secrets', see Robert I. Levy (1990: 335-8), who also points to the risk of 'loss of traditional knowledge', a risk that the revelation by the authorities was perhaps intended to prevent.

[28] The *rudrākṣa* seed (Elaeocarpus ganitrus) chosen in this case must be plain, without a 'face' (*mukh*), *nirmukhi*, symbolizing *nirākār niranjan*, the absolute without qualities, or it can have one 'face', symbolizing Ādināth.

[29] The last *cakra*, 'the place of final bliss' (Briggs 1973: 316), also called *sahasrāra*, the lotus 'with a thousand petals'.

give her the gift of his teachings. The goddess turned into a fly and entered into the body of Śrī Nāth, who went into deep meditation and thus heated up his body. Kālī Māī, in the form of a fly, was anxious and wanted to open the ten doors of the body to escape. She prayed to Gorakhnāth. Finally, Gorakhnāth produced from his nose the sound *jhīnk* (*chatr*) [*sic*] and helped her to escape.[30] They revealed their true nature to each other, the *devī* as Śakti *avatār* and Gorakhnāth as the *svarūp* of Śiva. Then Mahākālī said, 'Because I have been released by being ejected through a sneeze (*chatr*), from now on whenever someone does a *pūjā* of your *pātr*, they will also do the *pūjā* of my *chatr*. (Vilāsnāth 2005: 593-4, from Hindi)

The pun here is a little enigmatic. We have to suppose that *jhink* is a variant of *chink*(*nā*), which means to sneeze, and if the sound *jhink* is explained with *chatr*, it is because *chatr* is a kind of popular onomatopoeia for sneezing.[31] Thanks to a play on words, the goddess being expelled outside with a sneeze (*chink/chatr*) is worshipped with the use of an umbrella (*chatr*).

In fact, in some places we find both symbols together: the *pātradevatā* symbolizing Gorakhnāth is carried in procession, surmounted by a large multi-coloured umbrella symbolizing the Devī. This happens notably in the few places known as *śakti pīṭh* (places devoted to the cult of the goddess Satī Devī, where the parts of her dismembered body fell[32]), where the Nāth Yogīs act as *pujārīs*.

[30] In the *Gorakṣa Vijaya* version, as in the *Mina-cetan*, the goddess-fly is expelled through the anus and broke her loins on her way out! (with thanks to France Bhattacharya for her translation from Bengali).

[31] I am grateful to Dominique-Sila Khan and Ram Singh for the following explanations: 'When one sneezes for the first time, one says *chinkmā* (mother) and a second time *chatrpati*'. Chatrpati (Lord-umbrella) is the noise made by sneezing and is also the name of the deity, since one offers umbrellas to deities to ask for protection: sneezing is considered as dangerous, as it makes it possible for bad spirits to enter the body.

[32] See Sircar (1973) on the myth of the dismembering of Satī's body carried by Śiva after she killed herself, which informs the sacred geography of the Indian subcontinent.

We are here confronted with two opposite attitudes. On one side we know of Gorakhnāth's negative attitude towards women as demonstrated by the legends and by the harsh words of the *Gorakh Bānī*: 'during the day, the tigress sleeps//and at night she sucks from the body.//[man] does not understand the nature of sexual lust,//So he keeps and nurtures the tigress in his own house' (GB 48, trad. Djurdjevic 2008: 81). One can also observe a general avoidance of women by the Nāth Yogīs, who count very few women among their members.

On the other side we have ample evidence of the importance placed on the Goddess, under different names and forms, in the ritual and spiritual life of the Yogīs and in line with their Tantric background.

This is quite explicit in the figure of Yogmāyā or Yogśakti, who is so closely linked to the spiritual quest of the Yogīs that she is at the centre of the last rites of their life cycle, and thus presides over their final deliverance. Only the celebration of Yogmāyā after the death of the Yogī can assure his liberation, or *mokṣa mukti*, as Yogī Vilāsnāth says: 'Through the *pūjā* to Yogmāyā the soul of the dead Yogī can attain the abode of Śiva, the Kailās, i.e. obtain Liberation' (Vilāsnāth 2004: 47). And he explains, combining different levels: 'Where the Sadgurū (true Guru) is, so there is Liberation. The other name of Yogmāyā is Sadgurū, meaning liberation' (id.: 39).

During the last death ritual, known as *śaṅkhaḍhāl* (see Chap. 2), Yogmāyā, whose place is at the centre of the *maṇḍala*, is most often worshipped under the name of Bālā Sundarī.[33]

Bālā Sundarī is the child form of Tripura Sundarī, the goddess of the southern transmission of the Kula. Interestingly, the cult of the goddess Tripurā Sundarī is, according to Sanderson, the only one [with the Kubjikāmata] in all the Tantric traditions to include the system of the six power-centres (*cakra*) (1988: 687). The link between Bālā/Tripura Sundarī and the *cakra* system

[33] In Rajasthan, the *grihastha* yogīs may refer to her as Hiṅglāj Devī. Hiṅglāj Devī can also be associated with Bālāsundarī in the Nāth Yogī *śaṅkhaḍhāl*.

through which the *kuṇḍalinī* shall ascend is also mentioned by Briggs in his description of the *mūlādhāra cakra*, the first *cakra* at the base of the spinal column: this is the place where the *kuṇḍalinī* sleeps, 'coiled eight times and shining like lightning [...] She is to be meditated upon, here, as a girl of sixteen in full bloom (Bālāsundarī)' (Briggs 1973: 311). The ascent of the *kuṇḍalinī* from the *mūlādhāra cakra*, along the *suṣumnā*, and up to the last *cakra*, the *sahasrāra*, the lotus with the thousand petals where Śiva and Śakti are united, is accompanied with the sound *nāda*. It is this resonance, this *nāda*, that the small whistle worn by the Yogīs (also called *nād*), is supposed to produce when they blow it and at the same time make their internal *kuṇḍalinī* rise. For the Yogīs, the worship of Śakti is related to the rise of the *kuṇḍalinī*, her ascent to the *sahasrāra* where the union of Śiva and Śakti occurs as the joining of *bindu* and *nāda* that leads to spiritual liberation.

The importance of the Goddess for the Nāth Yogīs also takes on a public dimension when they act as officiating priests in Devī sanctuaries or when they gather at Devī pilgrimage places. Among the 51 Śakti *piṭhs*, the spots on which the dismembered limbs of Devī are said to have been scattered, there are three that are of special importance for the Nāth Yogīs: Jwalamukhi (where her tongue fell), Devi Patan (where her left shoulder fell), and Hing Laj (where the crown of her head fell). Jwalamukhi, a place devoted to the Devī with 'the tongue of fire' in Kangra, Himachal Pradesh, is still visited regularly by the Nāth Yogīs who are in charge of the Gorakhḍibbī ('box of Gorakh').[34] It is a kind of cave with a pool of bubbling under-ground water where the Devī manifests herself as 'tongues of fire', or blazing flames. The Yogīs, especially the roaming ascetics, gather there during the Autumn Nine Nights of the Goddess (*Navarātrī*). They perform the *pātradevatā puja*, during which they join the abstract

[34] According to the Nāth stories, Gorakhnāth used a small casket (*ḍibbī*) to beg because he had promised the Devī to come back with his own food.

form of Gorakhnāth with the abstract form of the Devī, her *chatr* (umbrella).

This is also the case during the spring *Navarātrī* festival held annually in Devi Patan (close to Tulsipur, Gonda district UP). Here the roaming Yogīs join a cortege arriving from Caughera in Dang Valley (Nepal); for the duration of this long journey made by the head (called *pīr*) and the Yogīs of Caughera (see Chapter 7), the *pīr* carries the *pātradevatā*.

The third place, Hing Laj, was certainly one of the most famous places for the cult of the Devī and for the Yogīs, but as it is located in modern-day Pakistan on the Makran coast with difficult access, Devī's cleft on the banks of the Hangol River is talked about much more than it is visited.[35] It was formerly considered to be a mandatory pilgrimage, especially for the wandering Yogīs. They placed great importance on the two symbols of their travels, the necklace made of small white mineral beads supposed to be the grains of rice prepared by Pārvatī for Śiva, and the branding on their arms of the *liṅga/yoni*, a reaffirmation of their Hindu Śaiva status after visiting a place that has been owned for centuries by Muslims.

These three places of Śakti worship are especially important for the Nāths, but even at a local level we notice that the Goddess is present in most of the temples and places owned or worshipped by the Yogīs. Names may be different according to the local form taken by the Goddess – she is called Jvālā Māī in places like Kadri and Jwalamukhi, and Bhagavatī in Nepal – but her shrine is included in the temple compound and her *pūjā* is made every day. She may also receive her special offering of animal sacrifices, as is still practised in some places during the *Daśahrā* festival.

It can be supposed that the importance given to the Devī, especially in Nepalese Nāth sanctuaries, denotes a particular connection with the centres of royal power. The Nāth Yogīs often have a connection to the political powers through their

[35] Cf. Briggs 1973: 103-10, Gold 1999c, and the forthcoming detailed study by Jürgen Schlaflechner.

roles as priests of the royal palaces and shrines. There, they worship the goddess as a bestower of power, the king's personal deity, and the one who protects his kingdom's prosperity. The small town of Gorkha in central Nepal is representative of this relationship. This small kingdom was the origin of the Shah dynasty that ruled over Nepal for more than two centuries. Its royal palace includes an important temple to the goddess Kālikā, whose huge festivals occur during the two *Daśahrās*. Beneath the palace complex is a cave dedicated to Gorakhnāth, where the Nāth *pujārīs* worship the tutelary and eponymous deity of the Gorkha kingdom. However, even though the palace and temple are located above Gorakhnāth's cave, worship ceremonies are performed separately by different officiants (Bouillier 1986).

The link between the Nāth Yogīs and the Goddess mediated by the king is most visible in public rituals such as *Daśahrā* as it is performed in the small Nepalese former kingdom of Phalabang (Krauskopff 1996), and during the huge *Daśahrā* celebrations in Udaipur in which the exchange of a royal sword kept by the Yogīs took on a spectacular dimension. A painting inside the royal palace depicts the crowd of Yogīs gathering in front of the temple of the Devī, where the Rājjogī kept the royal sword for nine days. Through fasting and remaining absolutely motionless, the Rājjogī recharged the power of Devī's sword through the power of his own asceticism (Tod 1983: I, 464-7). Rousseleau also reports a similar worship of the royal sword by a Yogī during *Daśahrā* in the small kingdom of Nandapur in Orissa (Odisha) (2008: 188-93).

The Nāth Yogīs' worship of the Devī conforms to their conception of Śakti. Devī is considered to be a form of Śakti, and she is the source of the power that Nāths hope to obtain through yogic practices and worship of her. This equivalence between Devī and Śakti is made evident in the function of one of the branches of the Yogīs, named Āī, who have the Devī as tutelary deity. The Yogīs from the Āī Panth, because of their link with the Devī, are often requested to exercise power (like leading unruly ascetics to their destination during the Kadri pilgrimage, see Chap. 5); they are said to have Śakti, or power, within them.

However the Devī still remains subordinate to Śiva; the Nāth Yogīs do not share the Śakta belief in the supremacy of the Goddess.

Bhairav

After Śiva/Goraknāth and Devī, Bhairav, the fearsome form of Śiva, is the third most important deity present in the rituals, invocations, and temples of the Nāth Yogīs. Bhairav, as viewed by the Yogis, appears to combine forms of Tantrism, of which he is the supreme deity,[36] and popular beliefs in which Bhairav is the chief of the terrifying spirits who escort Lord Śiva.

Let us note first how conspicuous Bhairav's altars are in the temples and monasteries of the Nāths. He may even be the most ubiquitous deity represented there; for instance, in Kadri, the two central shrines are dedicated to Bhairav and Jwālā Devī. Gorakhnāth, by contrast, is only represented by the symbol of the *pātradevatā* and by the ascetic fire of the *dhūnī*. In Nepal's Caughera monastery, Bhairav and Gorakhnāth are placed on an equal footing, with two parallel sanctuaries where worship is conducted with the same elaborate and lengthy procedures. However, the bloody sacrifices usually requested by this terrible deity are generally substituted with metaphorical offerings such as coconuts, vegetables and chickpeas covered by vermilion powder. The sacrifice of living animals may sometimes happen, especially in Nepal, during *Daśahrā* or for the *pūjās* called *cakra* performed by the Yogīs in the Kathmandu Valley (Bouillier 1986: 159-61). Bhairav may also receive alcohol, as in the Nāth monastery of Gogamedhi (Shekhavati), where bottles of local whisky are piled at the feet of a large black stone statue of Bhairav at the heart of the monastery.

[36] Cf. in Sanderson (2006: 62) the semantic analysis of his name by the non-dualistic Tantric tradition to try to make him a suitable 'candidate for the role of the Absolute', which overlies the literal meaning ('The Terrible') associated with cremation grounds and bloody sacrifices.

The importance of Bhairav for the Nāths' ritual life is particularly evident in relationship to the *pātradevatā*. This *svarūp* of Gorakhnāth rests under the protection of Bhairav, who is represented by a flag or a large round piece of bread, called *roṭ*. This *roṭ*, which is slowly cooked in the ashes of the *dhūnī*, is both the symbol of Bhairav and the specific Nāth offering to the god and to Gorakhnāth. When the *pātradevatā* has to be carried in procession, the group of Yogīs follows behind the Bhairav flag-carrier or the *roṭ*-carrier (he has the *roṭ* wrapped in red cloth on his head). Bhairav leads and protects the procession. Without him, the procession stops, such as when the *roṭ* reverts to the status of offering and is cut into pieces and distributed as *prasād*. The procession camps until a new *roṭ* is cooked in the *dhūnī* and can regain its symbolic function of being a protective Bhairav.

Bhairav is also the deity in front of whom the new initiates to administrative or ritual roles have to bow and take an oath to perform their duty. His fearsome personality is thought to prevent them from betraying their oath.

In some monasteries, such as in Caughera, Bhairav is present in his eight forms, collectively referred to as Aṣṭa Bhairav. Their small shrines form a protective circle around the place. However, most often Bhairav is worshipped in the Nāth Yogīs *maṭhs* in the form of Kāl Bhairav. Kāl Bhairav is the master of Time (Kāla): 'Because even Kāla fears him, he is called Kālabhairav (*Śiva Purāṇa* 3.8.47) [...] Bhairava is Śiva's integral form. It was Bhairav or Śiva as Bhairav who snipped off Brahmā's overweening head' (Kramrisch 1981: 284, see Chalier Visuvalingam 1989). The worship of Bhairav as the Master of Time fits with the Nāth Yogīs' quest to master Death and achieve immortality.

Is Bhairav's centrality in Nāth institutions a sign of a Kāpālika influence? Is it possible that the Nāth Yogīs succeeded these transgressive ascetics who disappeared from the Indian religious landscape about the same time that the Nāths appeared in the fourteenth century (see Lorenzen 1972)? The founding myth of the Kāpālikas' asceticism, the terrible penance made by Bhairav in order to atone for his crime of brahmanicide, is well known by the Nāth Yogīs, who regularly publish booklets (such as the *Bhairavanāthāvatar kathā*) giving a version of the legend similar to that found in the *Śiva Purāṇa*. However, today Nāth Yogīs do not seem to devote themselves to the extreme practices of what Sanderson calls 'the Kāpālika culture of the cremation grounds', practices which figure in the traditions of Svacchandrabhairav or the Vidyāpīṭha (Sanderson 1988: 668-70). But among the Aghorīs, the very small number of ascetics who still follow the Kāpālika practice of living near cremation-ground pyres and eating from a skull-bowl (cf. Parry 1985), some were Nāth initiates. Such was the case of Ram Nāth Aghorī, who was met by Ramesh Bedi (1991: 96-107), and for another Ramnāth Aghorī, disciple of Cetaṇāth and Dariyanāth, for whom the Pushkar Maṭh has recently built an impressive *samādhi* in front of its main entrance.

The rather curious case of the Kusles/Kāpālīs allows us to draw another link between Gorakhnāth and Bhairav, as well as between the Nāth Yogīs and the Kāpālikas. The Kusles/Kāpālīs are a low caste among the Newars of the Kathmandu Valley, who claim Gorakhnāth as a family deity and link their origin and special funeral duties they perform as part of their social role to the myth of Brahmā's beheading by Bhairav. The link to the beheading story is, in turn, a link to Gorakhnāth's intervention to pacify Bhairav, to cry with Brahmā and to cure him of his wound (Bouillier 1993).

The Nāth Yogīs' belonging to the current of Tantric Śaivism appears clearly from their pantheon which unites Gorakhnāth, the Goddess and Bhairav. The layout of the ritual premises, the daily worship ceremonies, and the festivals together demonstrate the complementarity of these three sides of the Divine; they may refer also to the three *guṇas*: Gorakhnāth is *sattva*, meaning purity, light, knowledge; Devi is *rājas*, meaning strength and activity; and Bhairav is *tamas*, meaning dark forces. Together they encompass all aspects of creation.

CHAPTER 2

Belonging to the *Sampradāya*

Until now we have looked at the Nāth Yogīs from a religious history perspective, examining their affiliation with a precise soteriological current. We shall now focus on their own organization as *sampradāya*, thus examining more specifically the relationship between the individual ascetic and the sectarian group, on the marks of belonging and on the internal structure of the sect.

How does one become a Nāth Yogī? What are the procedures for joining the sect and how do they elevate the initiate to the status of a full member?

Apart from the particular case of the Yogīs by caste that we shall examine later (Chapter 12), to become a Yogī requires a personal move to relinquish an ordinary social life and to choose a particular mode of salvation and way of life as determined by the principles of the sect. However, for the Nāth Yogīs, as for many other ascetics, the choice to belong to a given *sampradāya* is dictated less by soteriological or mystical considerations than by a personal meeting with a guru. The hagiographies of great Yogīs stress the importance of such encounters, which dramatically change the life of a would-be disciple. The personal relationship that follows between the guru and the disciple initiates the disciple into the guru's religious community. The disciple becomes a member of an ascetic group that has its own rules. The link between guru and disciple is marked by the initiation ceremonies.

INITIATIONS

Initiation into the Nāth Yogī *sampradāya* involves different steps determining different categories of initiates. These processes are called *dikṣā vidhi*, or consecration rites. They include five initiations grouped together in three steps, ear-splitting being only one among them, although that is the most spectacular step. Each initiation corresponds to a different guru.

The first initiation is the most important since it marks the 'admission into the sect' (*Nāth sampradāya mẽ praviṣṭ*). It includes the elements characteristic of a *dikṣā*: severing connections with one's former social condition and joining a new group with a new status. This first level of initiation is called *coṭī kāṭnā*, meaning the cutting of the tuft of hair (kept by the twice-born[1]). It is performed by the guru (the *coṭī-gūrū*), on a river bank. The disciple, whose entire head is shaved except for the one tuft of hair, bathes in the river and approaches his guru, who, while uttering the appropriate mantras,[2] presents him with an ochre cloth, brushes his forehead with ashes and passes a *śelī* around his neck. The *śelī* is a long black thread twisted according to precise rules and to which are attached a *rudrakṣa* bead, a small flat ring called *pavitrī* (symbolizing the Devī) and a small whistle or horn, called *nād*. Eighteenth century drawings and miniatures depict the *nād* as being made from a small twisted deer's horn. It was called *singnād*. This is no longer the case, as what hangs around the Yogīs' neck now is a small wooden whistle which makes a very soft sound.[3] The *nād* takes its name from the sound its produces, called the *nāda*, which is thought to be the sound of the *kuṇḍalinī* rising up in the body of the yogī. The union of

[1] Even though the Nāth Yogīs have recruits from groups other than the higher castes, they adopt the initiation rite for *sannyās* for the twice-born from the *dharmaśāstras*: the shaving of the brahmanic tuft of hair, symbolizing the severance of all links with the world.

[2] The text is given in Yogī Vilāsnāth 2005 (pp. 463 ff.).

[3] I have seen some roaming Yogīs carrying large deer horns that they blow during *pūjās*.

the *nād* and the *pavitrī* alludes explicitly to the union of Śiva and Śaktī, which occurs at the end of the *kuṇḍalinī*'s ascent: the *nāda* is the result of their union. Once a new Yogī is initiated, he will blow into the *nād* that he has just received at the beginning and the end of every ritual act and at each time he bows in front of a senior Yogī.

In addition to giving him the symbols of his new official status, the *coṭī-gūrū* cuts the last tuft of his *celā's* hair, thereby cutting his last link with his former status, and whispers the *gūrūmantra* into his ear. This step formally introduces the disciple into the *sampradāya.* The *coṭī-gūrū* gives the initiate a new name and passes his *panth,* the particular branch to which he belongs, on to him.

After passing this first level of initiation, the Yogī is called Aughaṛ ('misshapen') and he is supposed to continue his ascetic training with his guru and prepare himself for taking the subsequent steps. However, some Yogīs remain Aughars, either because the *panth* to which they belong advises them to do so (Briggs 1973: 10-11, 30-6, 65-6) or because they fear the pain and the ritual duties required by the next stage of initiation. This is the case for the majority of the householder Yogīs.

The next initiation rite is the most spectacular, and is the one which gave the Yogīs their name of *kānphaṭā*, meaning 'split-eared'. It consists of the *cirā-guru* (from *cirnā*, 'to cut, to split') splitting both ears in order to insert the large round earrings (called *kuṇḍal, darśan* or *mudrās*) that identify the *sampradāya* to which the initiate now belongs. The incision is done in the thick cartilage of the ear. It is said to open a channel of mystic physiology and allow the yogī to reach a superior state of consciousness.[4] However, as noted by Mallinson, all paintings and sculptures that depict yogīs prior to the end of eighteenth century show them with big earrings located in the earlobes,

[4] Or 'assisting him in the acquirement of yogīc power' (Briggs 1973: 6). An alternative explanation in Gold 1999a: 37: 'Some add that [...] there is a nexus of veins for subtle energy in the cartilages that is altered through the cutting. It is a seat of passion that is thereby diminished.'

rather than in the thick part of the cartilage (2011a: 418). The recurring mention of Yogīs with earrings in local pre-colonial reports and narratives as well as in foreign travellers' testimonies is a probable sign of their huge size rather than their way of wearing it. Since the tearing of the ears was equivalent to the social death of the yogī who was expelled from the *sampradāya*, it was perhaps considered safer to insert the rings in the cartilage rather than in the fragile lobes. An esoteric explanation based on the concept of the aperture of a mystic channel was added later[5] – the different texts attributed to Gorakhnāth or to the ancient Nāth tradition do not say a word about this practice: no mention is ever made of this particular *nāḍī* or the benefits of this type of cutting. The earrings were traditionally made of rhinoceros horn, a practice evidently discarded in modern times due to animal protection concerns. Today the choice of the material and the size of the ring depends on personal taste and one's financial means. Monastic leaders often have gold earrings that may be very discreet. Ordinary yogīs wear rings made of wood or white plastic that looks like glass. Yogī Vilāsnāth suggests an association between the material used to make the rings and various specific powers: clay is associated with knowledge, rhinoceros horn with meditation, sandalwood with medicine and plants, silver and gold with prosperity and bone with the Aghorī Nāth (2005: 472, 517).

The ear-splitting ritual is performed in private between the guru and the disciple and takes place either in the small underground cave (*guphā*) that is hidden in each Nāth monastery, or during a Kumbh Melā. The *cirā-gūrū* is a skilled specialist more than a spiritual master and many hagiographies tell of great yogīs who practice the incision themselves, either alone or near the tomb of the person they have chosen as their guide. The guru

[5] A legend of origin reported by Yogī Vilāsnāth (2005: 469) tells how Matsyendra asked Śiva for the right to wear earrings like him; Śiva granted him this right, which Matsyendra passed on to Gorakhnāth, who passed it on Bhartrihari, and so on. However, Śiva is always depicted with rings in his earlobes.

starts by testing the disciple by refusing three times to cut his ears and hiding the double-edged knife. Then finally he agrees to split the two ears while the disciple recites his initiatory mantra. Finally, he inserts sticks of nimwood into the slits he has just cut. Ten days later when the wounds are healed, the sticks are replaced by his guru with clay rings (called *yogdaṇḍa*) that the initiate has to wear for the forty-two days that he has to pass in seclusion. After that he is free to choose the earrings he wants. Yogīs say that in the past, the new initiate kept his clay rings for twelve years and was supposed to recite his mantra constantly.

This second step ends with two other initiations that complete the Nāth Yogī's process of training and are most often performed in conjunction with the ear splitting. They are the initiation of the ashes,[6] meaning the three parallel lines of *vibhūti* that the Śaiva ascetic draws on his body, particularly his forehead, and the initiation of the clothes (*bānā*), or the loincloth (*laṁgoṭ*) that symbolizes the vow of celibacy (*brahmacārya*).

After these four initiations given by four gurus, the initiate is now a proper member of the community and considered qualified to fulfil his role.

However, there is a fifth initiation given by a fifth guru that remains rather mysterious. It is called *updeśī* (from Skt. *upadeśa*, 'instruction, teaching'). The Yogīs refer to it, rather reluctantly, as a secret rite open to only the most advanced Yogīs in the practice of their *sādhanā*.[7] It is a Tantric rite devoted to the Devī

[6] On the symbolism of ashes, see Gross (1992: 357-61): 'the ashes and, hence, the *dhūnī* [fire-pit] as well, both symbolize the cremation grounds, physical death, transition from mundane to sacred realms, dissolution of ego-consciousness, and destruction of worldly attachments [...] also represent Śiva's transformative powers (id. 359-60).

[7] Curiously, this *updeśī* initiation is given secretly but without restriction among the Yogīs by birth, at least in Nepal and Rajasthan. It is considered to be an initiation into the caste that must be performed for everyone regardless of their age or status. This fact reveals the ambiguities pertaining to the castes of householder Yogīs who are considered Yogīs by birth; they are the topic of Chapter 12. This openness

as Yogmāyā, who is known as Bālāsundarī in north India and Nepal, and as Hiṅglaj in Rajasthan. This initiation is exceptional because it is inseparable from funerary rituals. As we shall see, liberation is imparted to the Yogī after death by a long ritual dedicated to Yogmāyā; this ritual, called *śaṅkhaḍhāl,* can only be performed by Yogīs initiated to the cult of the Devī in the *updeśī.* Thus a sort of mixing up occurs: the initiation ceremony, or *updeśī,* is celebrated just before a funeral ritual and uses the same ritual supports. The main officiant is an *updeśī gūrū*, who initiates the candidate with a particular mantra and thus entitles him to officiate for future *śaṅkhaḍhāls*, especially for his guru. *Updeśī* is thus a rite of consecration which is neither compulsory nor widespread and which is performed rather late in the life of an accomplished Yogī. This Yogī, having received the *updeśī*, becomes qualified to guide his own guru towards liberation during the funerary rituals, and to initiate a disciple who will do the same thing for him. The chain of spiritual succession, *gurū paramparā*, is rooted in a promise of liberation: the spiritual father begets a spiritual son and the son in turn gives deliverance to the father.

The succession of initiations creates a plurality of gurus. The importance of the guru is such that every Yogī finds his place and identity in the sect through his connection to his gurus, especially the one who first introduced him to his *panth*. Every time he has to present himself in an official religious setting, he gives his personal name, the name of his main guru and the name of his *panth*. Sometimes he even has to give the names of his five gurus, thus exemplifying the importance placed on lineage within the *gurū paramparā* tradition.

---

of the *updeśī* explains why I was invited to receive this initiation when I was among grihastha Yogīs in Nepal and at the time ignorant of the secret and dangerous character of the ritual, at least according to the ascetics whom I met later on. My invitation to this ceremony gave me the capacity to check the accuracy of the descriptions provided in the writings of Yogī Vilāsnāth (2004).

LAST RITES

Initiation is considered final: one who decides to become a Nāth Yogī remains a member of the *sampradāya* until the last moment of his life, when special rites are performed. He has chosen a spiritual path with the aim of being liberated from the cycle of rebirth. This liberation is supposed to be made possible by the strength of his *sādhana*, of his spiritual practices. However, Yogīs also believe in the efficacy of ritual action and think that they can obtain liberation through the rite of *śaṅkhaḍhāl*, thanks to the Devī: they will be liberated by asking for Yogmāyā's protection. As Yogī Vilāsnāth comments: 'The *pūjā* to Yogmāyā is *sātvik-pavitra* and śuddha, and through it, the soul of the dead Yogī, disappearing into Śiva's abode, the Kailās, obtains liberation (*mokṣa mukti*)' (2004: 47). He summarizes the rite, saying: 'In this rite to Yogmāyā all *updeśī* Yogīs pour Ganga water (*gaṅgājal*) with a conch on a small effigy (*putlā*, meaning *doll, puppet*) to which is given the name of the deceased. This is to secure liberation – *śaṅkha uḍhār*[8] for the dead Yogī [...] in *apabhraṁśa* one says *śaṅkhaḍhāl*' (id.: 43).

However, this liberation ritual is performed only a long time after a person has died – at least one and a half years, by most accounts. Before that time, the corpse has to be cared for: it has to be buried or, sometimes, immersed in water (*jal samādhi*). The practice of inhumation, at variance with cremation, is characteristic of the renouncers, because, as explained by the Dharmaśāstras and performed by the Dasnāmī Sannyāsīs, the rite of initiation into *sannyās* includes the absorption into the initiate's body of the domestic sacrificial fire that would be used to ignite his funeral pyre. The renouncer's body thus becomes a sacrificial altar and does not require the purification process

[8] *Uddhār* literally means 'raising' or 'removing', hence in a broader sense it can mean 'deliverance' or 'salvation'. This explanation, 'deliverance through the conch', is thus quite different from what Vilāsnāth gives as *apabhraṁśa* variant, śaṅkhaḍhāl, which means 'to pour out [*ḍhālna*] with the conch'.

of the cremation pyre. Moreover, before receiving the initiation mantra, the would-be Sannyāsī performed his own death rites, a symbolic marker of his death to society. Initiation rites of the Yogīs, as we have seen, are different, but they share the same ideal of breaking with former this-worldly sacrificial life and of longing for a new transcendental state. A true Yogī doesn't die – he is instead thought to be in a state of *samādhi*. His body buried in the grave is believed to not decay, while his soul is free to roam around, to go to Śiva's realm and to reanimate his body. Only the greatest of the Yogīs are credited with such powers, but the general practice of inhumation and the uncertainty about the real condition of the dead lead many people to confuse the deceased Yogīs with persons who suffered a 'bad death', unable to reach the ordinary world of the dead and condemned to wander in the world, unhappy and dangerous. Thus, believers remain uncertain about the precise state of these buried-yet-wandering Yogīs. The frightful image of these wandering souls in the popular imagination lends the word yogī a sometimes negative meaning, designating a bad spirit.

It is said that the most powerful Yogīs are able to decide the time of their death. They announce their death, which allows for organizing the funeral and inviting disciples, devotees, sectarian authorities and a Yogī officiant from the Satyanāth *panth* (cf. passim).

After the death has been certified, the corpse is cleaned, purified and dressed in the ritual paraphernalia of a Yogī, while the officiant utters the accompanying mantras. A bag containing some uncooked *roṭ* bread, sweets (*laddus*), a quarter of a rupee, and a pinch of cannabis is hung on his shoulder. Then the deceased Yogī is placed on a high seat and surrounded with a magic circle of protecting deities, so that 'they block the way to the *bhūt-pret*, *rakṣas*, and Yama's messengers (*dūt*)' (Vilāsnāth 2004: 9). The body is then sprinkled a last time with water (in which a *rudrakṣa* bead with one face had been placed). 'The Yogī, thus purified from the stains due to birth from a *yonī*, can go to Śivalok' (Vilāsnāth ibid.).

All those present pay homage by giving flower garlands,

clothes and, for the Yogīs, blowing their *nād*. The deceased is then carried on his seat in procession to the place where the interment will happen, which is often in the compound of the monastery. A square pit 7 to 8 feet deep has been dug. At the bottom, a hole is made where the deceased is placed on a layer of bricks, his legs crossed in *padmāsana*. The officiant (from Satyanāth Panth) goes down into the pit, puts a pot of water in front of the corpse, lights an oil lamp, throws a mixture of sugar and salt in the four directions, and places a clay bowl (*miṭṭī kā ṭhīkarā*) upside down on the deceased's skull. Right before this, the officiant has cracked the skull open with a swift blow to the head. People explained to me that this enables the soul to fly away faster, but this begs the question of why the officiant would then cover the skull. The explanation given by Vilāsnāth (2004: 11) is the following:

> a bowl is placed on the skull because once the skull has been broken, the soul (*haṁs*) flies up out of the body. At the last moment, the yogī uses yoga to make his breath (*prāṇ*) ascend to the *brahmānanda* – thus, if a bowl is placed on the skull, the breath is protected and, for the yogī lying in a *samādhi* state, liberation comes quickly. (ibid.)

As soon as the rituals inside the grave are finished, the officiant and the attendees throw a mixture of earth, sugar, salt, and ghee in the pit. When the pit has been filled, an oil lamp and a bowl full of ashes are placed on the soil. Later, a more permanent monument may be erected, in the shape of a *śivaliṅga*, a lotus flower or a sort of cylinder that evokes Muslim tombs (see Chapter 9).

The third day after the person's death, all the yogīs gather near the grave to share a feast consisting of many sweets and the favourite food of the deceased. A special gift is made to the Satyānāth officiant, who seems to take the part of the *mahābrāhmaṇ*, the specialized *brahman* funeral officiant, but without the social stigma attached to the *mahābrāhmaṇ*, as the death of an ascetic is not tainted with any impurity.

If the deceased was the head of a monastery, the ceremony

on the third day may also be devoted to the selection and consecration of his successor.

The last death rite, the *śaṅkhaḍhāl*, happens later – at a minimum, one and a half years after the death. Its performance at night during the dark half of the month when the moon is not visible emphasizes the dark and obscure side of the ritual. It is a secret rite performed only by Yogīs who have already had the *updeśī* initiation. There must be six of them. As I have explained already, the initiation rite *updeśī*, which introduces the Yogīs to the cult of the Devī who presides over the funerary ritual, is celebrated as the first part of the *śaṅkhaḍhāl*.[9]

Both rituals are performed in a secluded room. However, one can hear from outside the officiating Yogīs singing loud, lengthy hymns to Śiva, Gorakhnāth, the Nāths and Siddhas, and Devī, while performing the preliminary rites and drawing a large *maṇḍala* on the ground. In monasteries, the ritual generally takes place in the room devoted to the goddess in front of her statue. The room is set with a *maṇḍala* (which I will describe according to how it looked in the ceremony I attended), surrounded by six thrones (*gaddī*) made of squares of red and white cloth. Each throne corresponds to a precise charge that the Yogīs will assume: the *pīr gaddī* is the place of the head (*pīr*) of the ritual; facing him is the *joginī gaddī*, the seat of the Devī as Yogīnī Māī; close to the *pīr* is the *sākhya gaddī*, the throne of the 'witness' devoted to Brahmā; facing him is the *bīr gaddī* devoted to Hanumān;[10] *the ananta gaddī*, the throne of eternity, belongs

[9] My description will be based on the two ceremonies of *updeśī* and *śaṅkhaḍhāl* that I have observed in Nepal among the *grihastha* Yogīs. Since then, Yogī Vilāsnāth has published a book (*Śrī Nāth Siddhon kī śaṅkhaḍhāl*, 2004) that describes the rituals (accompanied by a few photos and drawings) and recounts the many mantras they use. He wanted to detail the rites performed, but the book seems to no longer be available for purchase.

[10] Hanumān has a place among the deities worshipped by the Nāths as the one who was miraculously begotten by Śiva. He embodies

to Gorakhnāth; and facing him is the *bhaṇḍārī gaddī*, which is occupied by the treasurer/cook. Each officiating Yogī takes his seat according to this fixed order.[11]

After each Yogī has taken his seat, a special assistant is put in charge of drawing the central *maṇḍala* dedicated to Bālā Sundarī. He starts by lighting a special lamp, and disposing the small cups of variously coloured rice flour that he will use. He starts his drawing with the centre; he first draws a star with eight branches, which he surrounds with a lotus flower with eight petals (*aṣṭadal*), followed by a lotus with sixteen petals (*soradal*). Everything is traced with white flour. On both sides, two lines like red and blue half circles coming out of the black mouth of a snake symbolize the two rivers Ganga and Yamuna, or also *iḍā* and *piṅgalā*, the two channels of the yogic physiology coiled up around the central *suṣumnā*. The symbolic reference to the rise of the *kuṇḍalinī* is clear. The lotus with eight petals corresponds to the fourth *cakra*, *anāhata cakra*: 'Within this *Cakra* there is [...] a fine lustrous lotus with eight petals facing downward. In the middle of this lotus, Śakti reveals Herself as shining in the form of an extraordinarily brilliant, beautiful and steady light in the shape of a Śiva-Linga' (Banerjea 1983: 177, quoting the *Siddha-Siddhānta-Paddhati*). 'It is in this *Cakra* that true spiritual enlightenment of a *yogī* really begins' (id.: 178). After the central motifs, the officiant draws the outlines of a few meaningful figures: the *AUM* mantra, the sun, the moon and a *svastika* in the upper part; the silhouette of Hanumān and various animals

---

strength and faithfulness and plays a part in the legend of Matsyendra. On Hanumān in the Nāth tradition, see Rose (1919: II, 391) and Gupta (1979: 135-6). Gupta mentions the cult in Rajasthan of 'Vir Hanuman, who is a Sakta god and is quite different from Das Hanuman, who is a Vaishnava deity [...] Vir Hanuman is a deity who keeps control over the Joginis, ghosts, and the spirits'.

[11] Briggs alludes briefly to this disposition (1973: 35). According to Vilāsnāth (2004: 140), each seat corresponds to a specific *panth*, *pīr* and *sākhiyā* being of the same *panth* as the one for whom the *śaṅkhaḍhāl* is made. The officiant, the *pujārī*, has to be Satyanāth.

(crabs, fishes, cows) on the right side; and the small outline of a man, the *kāliyuga ka manuṣ* (the man of our time, of the kāliyuga) on the left side.

Colours are then added. The various elements are covered with rice flour mixed with coloured powders. Each colour is said to be related to a god: black for Yama, yellow for the goddesses, green for Bhairav, red for Gaṇeś and Hanumān, and white for Śiva. The artist may also add colours or introduce variations to make his drawing as beautiful as he would like, as the aesthetic dimension is an important part of the ritual.

When the drawing is finished, the lamps are set. At the centre, in the middle of the eight lotus petals, is placed the biggest lamp, the *akhaṇḍa jyot*, or 'unlimited light' (one thinks of the brilliant light in the middle of the *anāhata cakra*); on the four corners are placed smaller lamps and a fifth lamp with five wicks is placed on the head of the snake.

During the drawing, the six Yogīs on their *gaddī* do not stop singing. Everything is now ready for the two ceremonies – first the *updeśī*, then the *śaṅkhaḍhāl*. Those who are to be initiated stand in front of the closed door. They will enter one at a time. The officiant calls one of the initiates, blindfolds him, places a coconut in his hands and leads him into the room. He asks him to name as his guru one of the six Yogīs present and makes him sit in front of the *maṇḍala*. The chosen guru moves near him, traces on his forehead the ashes symbol of Śiva (the three horizontal lines of the *tripuṇḍra*) and whispers the initiation mantra in his right ear. Then, putting the small whistle *nād* in the *pavitrī* ring, he blows lightly in the same ear. He does the same in the left ear and then removes the blindfold.

The initiate then discovers the beauty of the colourful *maṇḍala* and the majesty of the gurus, sitting motionless in the flickering light of the oil lamps, a red turban round their heads: a wonderful and mysterious atmosphere that heightens the experience. The initiate is now instructed to worship the deities and the gurus. He places a coconut, some coloured rice and flowers, and a little money in front of the *maṇḍala* and bows in front of it and before each of the gurus, referring to them by their ritual name: '*pīr gurū adeś,*[12] *ananta gurū adeś* etc.'. Then he stands up, spins around once (a substitute for a circumambulation of the room, which is impossible due to the small size of the area) then finishes by prostrating himself. He may be allowed to stay during any other initiations that are to follow.

At the end of the ceremony, the officiant brings a tray of sweets, which he offers first to the gods, then to the gurus and the initiates as *prasād.* The six Yogīs stand up and stretch a white cloth high above their heads, where the assistant draws the mantra AUM and a *svastika* with rice flour. The cloth is folded up again. The gurus go before the *maṇḍala* to bow in front of the gods.

The *updeśī* is followed by the *śaṅkhaḍhāl.* The arrangement of the room is kept the same but new preparations have to be made: the *pujārī* makes a small doll (H. *putlā*, Nep. *putāli*) of *kuś* grass and white cloth. This figure represents the dead Yogī and, by the power of special mantras, is supposed to receive a particle of the deceased's dead body that it incarnates. Then the officiant uses white threads to make a ladder with seven rungs that is about one and half metres long. Afterwards, he puts two bowls in front of the *maṇḍala* – one full of milky water containing a conch; and the other with the small *putlā.* He fastens the ladder: the top is hung from a sort of tripod supporting a water pot topped by a lamp, and the bottom is fixed around the bowl, which contains the puppet. The *maṇḍala* is now surmounted by this ladder, which will allow for the passage from this world to the other world. The ritual consists thus in making the small figure ascend the rungs of the ladder to attain the last step, Śiva's paradise, or Kailaś, symbolized by the lamp at the top of the tripod.

The six Yogīs play the part of witnesses. They chant the mantras and guide the officiating Yogī, who is preferably the disciple of the deceased.

The first part of the ceremony is a confrontation with Yama, the god of death, who has wrongly taken away the Yogī as his

[12] *Adeś* is the respectful greetings used by the Nāth Yogīs one to each other.

prey, a frequent motif of the Nāth epics. The gurus succeed in making the soul of the dead man come back and enter the puppet by repeatedly chanting the mantra *Gor gāyatrī* (Gor for Gorakhnāth).

The small figure, now reanimated, is bathed. This is the actual *śaṅkhaḍhāl*: the officiant pours water through the conch (*śaṅkha*) onto the figure 108 times, while the gurus chant the *amar gāyatrī*, the mantra for immortality (*amar*, 'immortal').[13]

The *putlā* is then fastened to the ladder and the officiant makes it slowly ascend each rung. At each rung he is supposed to make a different gift, using coins that represent gold, silver, copper, a cow, clothes, earth and rice. At every step, a Yogī repeats the *sarvajit mantra*, the mantra of universal victory. When the figure has reached the top of the ladder, it is made to circumambulate the water pot and lamp at the top: it has thus reached the Kailaś.

The officiant puts the puppet back in the bowl and shouts loudly: 'So-and-so (the name of the deceased), go now' (Nep. *jāū*) and he blows into the conch. He takes the figure, leaves the room and buries it close by and without any ceremony. When he comes back, the Yogīs question him. 'How many went out?' they say. 'Two', he answers. 'How many came back?' 'One'. 'Where is the other?' The officiant answers: 'He has gone to Kailaś!'

The *śaṅkhaḍhāl* ends the next day with a feast offered to the entire community and maybe with the erection of a monument on the grave.[14]

[13] The *amar gāyatrī* is called *mokṣa gāyatrī*, in Vilāsnāth (2004: 245) who emphasizes liberation, versus the more popular stress on immortality.

[14] The performance of the *śaṅkhaḍhāl* evokes the Śaiva 'Rite to Rescue the Dead' [from hell] (*mṛtoddhāraḥ*). 'In this ritual, the teacher makes a *maṇḍala* in front of him and places an effigy of the person, made of *kuśa* grass or cowdung or similar substance, and looks at it as if he is teaching his pupil. Then by means of the *jāla* [net] rite he draws the soul of the man towards him. The soul is saved from its present state and installed in the effigy, purified and initiated [...] and finally united with Śiva at the end of the ritual by oblation of the

Ritual action is thus considered necessary to ensure liberation.[15] The personal ascetic and spiritual path praised by the texts, the liberation at the end of the yogīc process of self-realization, is encompassed by the efficacy of ritual action. In a return to their Tantric Kaula roots, the Yogīs consider the Devī to be the presiding deity of such rituals and thus the provider of deliverance.

SECT ORGANIZATION

Once the individual Yogīs are initiated into the sect, they are part of an institution that has its own internal rules and modes of organization. However, the traditional organization with its various subdivisions is now also included in the modern administrative network that the pan-Indian Nāth Yogī Association has tried to build.

The Panths

As we already mentioned, the Nāth *sampradāya* is divided into various branches called *panth*, the membership within the *panth* being transmitted at the time of the first initiation: a Nāth Yogī belongs to the *panth* of the guru of his first initiation.

The Nāth Yogī *sampradāya* is also known as the Bārahpanthi *sampradāya*, or the sect with the twelve *panths*, a denomination that appears most often in administrative documents and

---

effigy in the sacred fire (*Tantrāloka* 21: 1-41) (in Goodall and Rastelli, *Tāntrikābhidhānakośa* IV, forthcoming).' The *mṛtoddhāraḥ* (the Śaiva counterpart of the *smārta nārāyaṇabali*) was performed for 'the benefit of individuals who had died impure deaths or in a state of impurity caused by unexpiated transgressions' (Sanderson 2006: 32), or as a liberating initiation for those who were not able to get full initiation. It seems that the Nāth Yogīs considered their initiatory *dikṣa* insufficient to ensure final liberation and thus in need of completion.

[15] On the question of ritual and its efficacy among Tantric practicians looking for liberation, see Sanderson 2006.

probably in relation to the need for various dispersed Nāth communities to appear as one unified body.[16] We find many similar occurrences of definition by counting among other ascetic orders: besides the well-known Dasnāmī Sannyāsīs, the Sannyāsīs with 'the ten names', we may mention the Bārabhāī Dāriyām, 'stick-holders who are twelve brothers', a Rāmānandī group from whom separated off the Terabhāī Tyāgī, 'renouncers who are thirteen brothers', followed by the Caudabhāī Mahātyāgi, 'great renouncers who are fourteen brothers' (van der Veer 1988: 110).

The number twelve is canonical even though the corresponding lists of names could be different. Some lists include more than twelve names, while others contain less. Briggs (1973: chap. IV) and Dvivedi (1981: 12) give detailed and comparative lists. My intention here is to look at the present situation and to try to decipher when and how these divisions are important.

According to the official list propagated by the present sectarian authorities and known by most of the Yogīs, the twelve names are the following: 1. Satyanāth, 2. Rāmnāth or Rāmke, 3. Pāgal, 4. Pāv Panth, 5. Dharmanāth, 6. Mannāth, 7. Kaplānī or Kapil Panth, 8. Gaṅgānāth, 9. Naṭeśvarī or Dariyānāth, 10. Āī Panth, 11. Bairāg or Bhatṛhari Bairāg, 12. Rāval (in Vilāsnāth 2005: 528-35).

This list does not correspond to those given by Briggs or Dvivedi but does include the names that are referred to most often today, even though their order may be different. There is no hierarchy between the *panths,* but rather a subdivision into two groups, which explains the rather enigmatic affirmation that 'inside the

[16] It is difficult to know when this organization in twelve panths and hence this denomitation of Bārahpanthis started. One finds a mention of 'the twelve sects (*panth*) of yogis (jūgīān)' in the *Nujūm al-'ulūm*, an Astrological Encylopedia from Bijapur dated 1570 CE (cf. Emma Flatt, 2011: 242), but few names correspond to what will be known later on. Other mentions of the twelve *panths* dated from the beginning of seventeenth are to be found in the Sikh writings (*Gurū Granth Sāhib*) and in the Dabistān (cf. Mallinson 2011a).

twelve *panths* (*bārah panths*), there are the eighteen (*aṭhārah*) and the twelve (*bārah*)', thus referring less to a count than to an origin. According to the Nāth tradition, which perhaps echoes a historical change,[17] there were eighteen *panths* using Śiva as reference and twelve Gorakhnāth. They fought each other and some of them disappeared. Only six from each affiliation were left. On Śiva's side, they were: Satyanāth, Rāmnāth or Rāmke, Pāgal, Pāv Panth, Dharmanāth and Mannāth. On Gorakhnāth's side they were: Kaplānī or Kapil Panth, Gaṅgānāth, Naṭeśvarī or Dariyānāth, Āī Panth, Bairāg or Bhatṛhari Bairāg, Rāval. This distribution into two groups finds some expression during ceremonies or in the group of wandering Yogīs (passim Chapter 3).

In the lists given by Briggs and Vilāsnāth, the *panths* are linked to certain places, certain tutelary deities and certain *sādhanās*, but I did not find any justification behind these connections. However, even today *panths* are important, as special duties are granted to particular *panths.*

As we shall see, when the succession within monasteries proceeds by election, certain *panths* are selected. According to the statutes of the monasteries, in some cases, the head and the main offices must be selected among the members of a certain *panth*, while in other cases a roll of succession is established between different *panths* in order to ensure an equal share of responsibilities among the *panths.*

Besides this role distribution, which is sometimes difficult to maintain because certain *panths* have declined in importance and number,[18] certain *panths* are permanently linked to certain functions. This is the case mainly for the Satyanāth *panth*, in which members act as *pujārī*, or officiants, for the Nāth rituals. We have seen them officiate at the funerals of Yogīs and also in the making of the *pātradevatā.* Besides these ritual duties, they can occupy other functions, like any Yogīs, and their role as 'the

[17] A passage from ancient Śaiva traditions (Pāśupata, Kālamukha, Kāpālika) to Gorakhnāthis (see Lorenzen 1972; White 1996: 97 ff.).

[18] Statutes may specify: if someone of the Gaṅganāth Panth is not available, choose Bhatṛharī Bairag, etc.

Brahmins of Yogīs', as it was described to me, does not involve any hierarchical position.

The Āī Panth is also special in the sense that it is the only one whose origin is feminine. The goddess Vimlā Devī, who was in Assam, a stronghold of śaktism, desired to unite with Gorakhnāth and to have his child. Gorakhnāth, who was always staunchly celibate, evaded her advances by giving the goddess some rice to husk. But the quantity of rice never diminished and from the two heaps of grain and husk appeared two children: Bhuśkaināth and Khaḍkaināth, from which the *panth* Āī originated. This *panth* is thus said to have a strong link with Śakti and to be able to cope with situations in which power is required. For instance, the head of a troupe of wandering Yogīs known as *jhuṇḍī* has to belong to Āī Panth.[19]

The Mahāsabhā

The traditional organization into twelve *panths*, Bāraḥpanth, is now included in the modern pan-Indian association, the 'Akhil Bhāratvarṣīya Avadhūt Bheṣ Bārah Panth Yogī Mahāsabhā', or Yogī Mahāsabhā, the purpose of which is to unify, control and promote the Nāth *sampradāya* across the entire Indian territory.

The Yogī Mahāsabhā was started at a time when, in response to both colonial census by caste and religion and reform movements within Hinduism, many new associations were created in order to reform and unify the practices of their members. Several organizations appeared at the same time in defence of Hindu orthodoxy and federated in 1902 in the Bhārat Dharma

[19] I wonder about the link between this Nāth panth and a peculiar tradition called Āī Panth that is related to the sanctuary of the goddess Āī Mātā in Bilara (Rajasthan), studied by Dominique-Sila Khan (1997: 175-86). I notice that, in a small booklet published by the Nāths for the Kadri pilgrimage, two songs are devoted to Āī Mātā, describing her legend and the specific rituals of the Āī Panthīs of Bilara (the eleven principles that correspond to the eleven knots on the ritual bracelet, as described in the title of the song: *Śrī Āī jī kī bel ke gyārah niyam*).

Mahāmaṇḍala. This association based in Varanasi had as its goal to 'promote Hindu religious education in accordance with the Sanatan Dharma, to diffuse the knowledge [of Hindu sacred books] and to introduce, in the light of such knowledge, useful reforms into Hindu life and society' (Farquhar 1967: 317). Many sectarian leaders joined the association, although it was soon undermined by internal contradictions and rivalries (Kasturi 2015).

Founded in 1906, probably following the Bhārat Dharma Mahā-maṇḍala, the Yogī Mahāsabhā was started by the heads of the two most important monasteries of the time: Kalānāth from Ṭilla (now in Pakistan) and Pūrṇanāth from Asthal Bohar (Haryana). Later on, in 1932, Mahant Dig Vijaynāth from Gorakhpur (U.P.) took the leading role and asserted his wish to unite all the Nāth Yogīs under the same authority. The importance of the Yogī Mahāsabhā has been constantly increasing, up to the present day when it successfully manages the entire sect. Administrative documents are issued under its name and its officials have to attend all local celebrations.

The Akhil Bhāratvarṣīya Avadhūt Bheṣ Bārah Panth Yogī Mahāsabhā has been 'registered as per the Indian act no. 21 of 1960' and published its *niyamāvalī*, 'rules and regulations', in Hindi and English. I will quote an English version from 1974 and a more detailed and augmented Hindi version from 1995.

Let us see what these statutes say regarding Nāth identity and proper behaviour. The text starts with a series of definitions. The aim is to decipher precisely to whom the rules are to be applied, to describe the diversity of the cases in listing them, and to codify behavioural norms.

The first article gives the name of the association and gives its localization: the headquarters are in Haridwar in the Gorakhnāth Mandir. One can see a change occurring between the two documents from 1974 and 1995, illustrating the intention to cover the entire community more efficiently: in 1974, only two sub-headquarters were mentioned – the Gorakhnāth Mandir of Gorakhpur and the monastery of Kadri in Mangalore, which thus constituted a distribution across two geographical zones, north and south. In 1995, only one sub-headquarter (*up kāryālay*) is left – the Gorakhpur Maṭh – but five provincial headquarters are added, in Karnataka (the Viṭṭal Maṭh, under the authority of Kadri), in Bombay (the Kāl Bhairav Mandir, also called Tānvā Kānṭā Pāvdhūnī, a very ancient Nāth place), in Saurashtra (the Bhīṛ Bhanjan Mahādev in Jaitpur), in Himachal Pradesh (the Gorakhḍibbī in Jwalamukhi) and in the Gonda district of Uttar Pradesh (Devī Pātan in Tulsipur, an important place for the Nepalese Nāth ascetics of Dang monastery, see Chapter 7). This geographic distribution of the administrative centers seems to exist more on paper than in real life, however.

After this institutional framework, the text gives the definitions (*paribhāṣā*) of the categories employed:

– '*Beṣ bārah panth*': a list is given of the twelve *panths*, without any explanation of the term *beṣ*; this word may have an ambiguous meaning. In Hindi the word *bhes* or *bheṣ* (from Skt. *veṣa*) means dress, appearance or disguise; in this context it designates the ascetic dress (ochre garment and bodily markers such as the ashes, the earrings, etc.) and was used in the Nepalese legal codes to qualify the category of ascetics as *beṣdhārī* (Bouillier 1978). However, the same compound in Sanskrit (*vesha-dhārin*) was defined as 'wearing the dress of a hypocrite or false devotee' (Monier-Williams 1988: 1019). This is evidently not the case here.

– '*Avadhūt*: to be naked (*nihang*, "naked, free of care"), i.e. free from the life of a householder (*grihastha jīvan se rahit*).' In the English version, it says 'a person who has renounced the worldly aspirations and who is not a *grihastha*'. The exclusion of non-celibate yogīs and Yogīs by caste is thus clearly asserted.

– 'Yogī: the followers of the Nāth *sampradāya* who are *darśanī* (who wear earrings, *karṇ kuṇḍal*) or *aughaṛ*' [those who are not fully initiated yet and thus do not wear the earrings].

– '*Sthan* [place]: the *maṭh, mandir, ṭillā, dargāh, dalīcā, samādhi, dhūnā,* as well as the statues of deities and *caraṇpādukā* settled by the Nāth *sampradāya*.' In this list, nothing is left out of the places belonging to the sect but also of the places where a wandering Yogī could stop or settle temporarily. A *ṭillā* is a hillock, a mound; this name was given to some Nāth institutions because of their setting. The *caraṇpādukā* are the sandals, however, the word also applies to the footprints (*caraṇcinh*) that were the most common representation of Gorakhnāth and are still often found before the statues or the tombs. We also find two Persian words: *dargāh*, the tombs of Muslim saints,[20] and *dalīcā*, which is peculiar to the Nāths; the term refers to the place where the Yogīs meet for special occasions, and by extension to the meeting itself: Yogīs are said to be 'in *dalīcā*' (*dalīcā men*), assembled for a meeting, in a special place, which can be a building or an open space.[21] The Yogīs assemble in *dalīcā* to make decisions regarding the community and generally perform there the collective worship of the *pātradevatā*. *Dalīcā* and *pātradevatā* go together as symbols shared inside the community to express its identity.

– '*Mahant*: *mahant, pīr, rājā, rājgurū, maṭhādhiś*, who are the managers, founders or those in charge of such places (*sthān*).' Here again all the possibilities are evoked, from purely administrative terms such as *maṭhādhiś* to exceptional designations such as *rājā* (only in use for the head of the Kadri monastery). The two most common terms are *mahant* and *pīr*, the latter being borrowed from the Muslim tradition.[22]

[20] The mention of *dargāh* in this context testifies both to the close relationship between Nāths and Sufis who could visit the same shrines and also to the religious continuum, which allows for some Nāth places to be called *dargāh-mandir* (see Bouillier and Khan 2009, Bouillier 2015).

[21] Ghurye (1953: 155) is the only one to mention the *dalīcā*, which he wrongly identifies as a monastic centre. The etymology is uncertain: is it related to the Hindi *dulīcā* (and to the Persian *gālīca*) meaning 'carpet,' or derived from the Hindi root *dal*, meaning 'group, band, or party'? It is mentioned in the *Gyān-tilak* and explained by P.D. Barthvāl as *āsan*, meaning 'seat' (I am thankful to Monika Horstmann for providing me with this information).

[22] At first I thought that the term was used in northern monasteries

– '*Janṭhī* or *jhuṇḍī*: *jhuṇḍī* is a sub-committee of yogīs appointed by the Mahasabha once every twelve years, during the Nasik Kumbha Mela, which with its Ista Deva, Patra Devatha [*sic*], goes on Dharma Prachar Pada Yatra to south India and installs Mahants, Raja, etc., at the southern region.' To this 1974 English entry is added in 1995 in Hindi:

> But it is only during this wandering that the *jhuṇḍī* has the power to hire and to dismiss the *mahants, rājā,* etc. At the end of the pilgrimage of the *jhuṇḍī*, the office of looking at the accounts of the *mahant, pīr, rājā, rājgurū, and maṭhādhiś* hired by the *jhuṇḍī*, and of dismissing the monastic heads who have misused the revenues or who are corrupt, this office will belong to the Assembly of Yogīs, the Yogī Mahāsabhā.

This entry is quite interesting in that it shows the Mahāsabhā's will to extend its authority over every Nāth institution. The *jhuṇḍī* is an old and peculiar tradition that had full power over the Nāths. The Mahāsabhā statutes make it a 'sub-committee' (of the much more recent Mahāsabhā), which it has never been, and specify its limited duration (only during the pilgrimage). However, the *jhuṇḍī* falls more and more under its control. For instance, the official appointment order issued by the *jhuṇḍī* when it nominates the monastic heads on its way, is now done under the name of the Mahāsabhā and specifies that the representative 'shall maintain proper accounts of the income and expenditure and send this statement every month to the Central Office of Akhil Bharat Varsheey Avadhoot Bhesha Baraha Panth Haridwar' (Appointment Order of the Representative for the Loki Maṭh, Chitradurga district).

A second part of the statutes concerns the aims of the Association. It comprises 23 articles in 1995, which can be summarized in this way:

---

where the Muslim influence was dominant; for instance, the Caughera legend was that Ratannāth got the title of *pīr* from a Muslim emperor who admired him. However, the appellation is widely used, especially for the most important collective (*pañcāyatī*, see passim) monasteries.

- The propagation of the knowledge and of the ideals of the *sampradāya*, especially the practice of yoga. It is even said 'to make the study of yoga compulsory for all the Yogīs'.
- Controlling behaviour: to banish bad and irreligious habits, to prohibit *gānjā, bhāng* (drink with cannabis), tobacco and alcohol, 'to remove any sādhu or mahant who disobeys the terms of the Nāth *Sampradāya* and becomes a householder (*grihastha*) or tries to become a householder [*sic*].' The prohibition of cannabis has little effect, at least on the roaming sādhus, and contradicts Śiva's tastes. Alcohol is sometimes needed for Bhairav's worship. But the puritanical trend of the Mahāsabhā does not encourage such traditions.
- Good management of the properties and revenues: the Mahāsabhā controls those in charge and replaces them if they misappropriate or misuse what belongs to the *sampradāya*.
- Public welfare (which is a 1995 innovation): to construct public buildings, to help the poor, to distribute food, etc.

The third part deals with the organization chart of the Mahāsabhā:

- The members of the Mahāsabhā are the Yogīs *avadhūt, nāth, tapasvī* [ascetic], *sthāndhārī* [residing in a fixed place], *darśanī* [with earrings], *aughaṛ* [novice] who observe the rules of the Sabhā and who are not excluded from commensality (*paṅkti bahiṣkṛit*).[23]

This community of Yogīs gathers informally during the

[23] *Bahiṣkṛit*, meaning 'excluded' and *paṅkti*, meaning 'line' or 'row', in this case the row of people eating together. The concept of *paṅkti bahiṣkṛit* is the most visible way to demonstrate who belongs to a given community of the ascetics and who does not. Another way to express exclusion, which is specific to ascetics who smoke cannabis, mentions the exclusion of some people from sharing the pipe (*cilam sāphī band ho jātī hai,* they are forbidden to use the small piece of white cloth – *sāphī* – that one rolls around the opening of the pipe prior to smoking.

great pilgrimages and festivals such as Kumbh Melās. At these occasions an executive committee of 24 members is elected, two for each *panth*, plus two nominated individuals. From among the members of this committee are elected a president (who since 1932 has happened to be the *mahant* of Gorakhpur Maṭh, Digvijaynāth, then Avedyanāth and now Adityanāth), a vice-president, a general secretary, a joint secretary, and five provincial secretaries. Other articles of the statutes specify the functioning of the committee: the meetings and the duties of the different offices. The provisions are rather vague and general. However, two articles are worth looking at for what they reveal regarding the sect's organization.

One article deals with the issue of succession:

> If in any sthan or Mutt a successor is not nominated by the Guru, then the Mahasabha will appoint a suitable person from among the disciples (shishyas) of his Guru. But if there is no suitable disciple, then a suitable person from the same Panth, or if there is no such person, suitable person from any other Panth may be appointed. (Article 17, 1974 statutes)

The normal system of transmission of power is from the guru to a chosen disciple. This is the most frequent case; however, as we shall see, it is not the only one.

A second article asserts the right to control all Nāth institutions:

> The president, General Secretary and Secretary will have powers to supervise the working and administration of the *nijī* [personal] or *pañcāyatī* [collective] *sthanas* spread throughout East, West, South and North India as well as other countries and to check their accounts and change or remove the officials.... (Article 11)

This dual mode of organization corresponds to a fundamental difference in the history, management and mode of succession of the Nāth monasteries. There is, on one side, the *nijī* monasteries and temples which are the personal property of a line of gurus/ monastic heads and thus belong to a particular *panth*, and, on the other side, the *pañcāyatī* monasteries, which are the common property of the Nāth *sampradāya* and in which the mode of succession is determined by election. It is evident and logical that this second category should be administered by the Yogī Mahāsabhā. But its right over the *nijī maṭhs* is often contested. Thus it is interesting to see the Mahāsabhā announce in the statutes its right to control even monasteries that are outside its direct authority.

The term *pañcāyat* ('a group of five people') refers to castes or village councils, and the term *pañcāyatī* refers to rule by assembly. The Nāth Yogīs are not the only sect to have such an institution; Van der Veer, for instance, mentions the organization of the *akhāṛās* among the Nāgā branch of the Rāmānandī ascetics: '[Hanumān garhi Akhara] is like all other akharas, governed by *panchāyatī* rule, that is by majority vote in the assembly of naga inhabitants' (van der Veer 1988: 153). The statutes of the *akhāṛā* specify: 'The whole responsibility to manage the akhara goes on the shoulders of the panchayat. The panchayat is the owner and manager of the temple. Each member has equal rights and in his turn he has a right to get a share of whatsoever' (id. 277).

The statutes of the Mahāsabhā understand *pañcāyatī* as a collective property, contrary to *nijī*, meaning the personal or private. This distinction matches with the Hindu law on religious endowments, based on the mode of governance of the monasteries. According to Paras Diwan (2002: 504):

'Broadly speaking, the maths fall into the following three categories:

(a) Mourushi *math*, where the office of *mahant* devolves upon the main disciples of the *mahant*.
(b) Panchayati *math*, where the office of *mahant* is elective, and
(c) Hakimi *math*, where the founder has reserved the right of nominating the *mahant*.'[24]

[24] This third category is seldom found. It perhaps corresponds to what Mukherjea is describing: 'examples occur where the founder may grant property to his spiritual preceptor and his disciples in succession with a view to maintaining one particular spiritual family or for perpetuation of certain rites and ceremonies [...] In such cases, the original grantor and his descendants are the only persons interested

The *nijī maṭh*, the personal monastery according to the Mahāsabhā, corresponds to the 'mouroushi' type, i.e. *maurūsī* (from the Arabic *maurūṣ*, meaning 'hereditary or ancestral'). These *maṭhs*, founded by a particular guru and often patronized by a local ruler or a successful businessman, are transmitted through the guru's spiritual lineage; they are linked to a precise *panth* and the succession is passed from guru to disciple within the *panth*. The guru usually nominates his successor and prepares him to take his place after his death; he works to ensure that his chosen successor is accepted by the other disciples and by the other sectarian leaders. If the guru has not secured his succession, the disciples have to agree on a successor after his death. The choice of the guru may be questioned,[25] but the principle of spiritual filiation and of a transmission rooted in the cult of the guru's tomb is never questioned. Often the monastery is known under the name of the founding guru. Regarding the issue of property, each monastery is independent. The properties are registered under the name of the monastery and the *mahant* is in charge of the management, sometimes with the help of an *ad*

---

in seeing that the institution is kept up for their benefit (2003: 385).' Briggs repeats these three categories but avows his ignorance on the mode *hākimī*, 'by authority or right. No definition of the third case has been discovered (1973: 38). 'A detailed analysis of the judicial precedents concerning the succession of the *Mourashi Mutt* is given in Mukherjea (2003: 347-55).

[25] I remember a case when the *mahant* on his deathbed nominated as his successor a disciple who had not yet completed his initiation; the other disciples contested this choice, which was finally ratified but led to a split among the devotees. Briggs writes about a similar case concerning the Gorakhpur monastery: the *mahant* Sundarnāth died without naming a successor; a conflict between the disciples followed and was taken to court; 'An interesting point was that one Nanhoo Singh, who was involved in the suit and who hoped to win the gaddi, was not a Yogī at all. He stated that if he had won his case at law, he had intended to undergo initiation, become a Yogī and have his ears split [...] Nanhoo Singh won his suit and is now [1928] mahant of Gorakhpur' (Briggs 1973: 37), cf. Chapter 10.

hoc committee. This regime of personal property does not mean that the *mahant* is free to act as he wants: he is an administrator and a usufructuary but he has no right to sell or misappropriate for his personal use the properties and revenues of the *maṭh.*[26]

The *pañcāyatī maṭhs* have a system of management that is quite specific to the Nāṭh Yogīs. They are under the authority of a head (called *pīr, mahant,* or *rājā*) who is elected by the community and who has no personal link with his predecessor; the head is elected for a limited period of time, which varies from case to case. The elections take place on a set date, according to the festive calendar of each monastery. Here the Nāth customs are specific, since ordinarily *mahants* are elected for life and in a different way; as Paras Diwan explains (2002 : 518), 'In most *panchayati maths*, it is the *mahants* of all the *maths* in a particular geographic area belonging to the same sect or school who assemble on the thirteenth day of the death of the *mahant* and elect the successor.'

The *pañcāyatī maṭhs,* governed by elections, do not belong to a particular *panth*. If it is prescribed to choose a head from a certain *panth,* it is with the idea of ensuring a rotation of the office. These

[26] As summarized by Paras Diwan (2002) quoting court cases concerned with the legal position of the *mahant*: 'The property belonging to a math is in fact attached to the office of the *mahant* and passes by inheritance to no one who does not fill the office. The head of the math, as such, is not a trustee in the sense in which that term is generally understood, but in legal contemplation he has an estate for life in its permanent endowments and a absolute property in the income derived from the offerings of his followers, subject only to the burden of maintaining the institution. He is found to spend a large part of the income derived from the offering on his followers, on charitable or religious objects' (2002: 507)... 'If there is a surplus he cannot spend the income for any purpose other than the purposes of math... He cannot use it for his personal use apart from the dignity of his office' (id. 509), which allows many conflicting interpretations on what constitutes this 'dignity': for instance, are mansions and luxury cars part of it? The cases reported by Mukherjea (2003: 341-3, 361-3, 371) testify to the ambiguity of these dispositions.

maṭhs are considered to belong to the Nāths as a community and they are in charge of the cult of the *pātradevatā*; these sacred vessels that are worshipped by the Nāths united in *dalīcā* are, as we have seen, kept in the *pañcāyatī maṭhs.* Is the presence of the *pātradevatā* linked to the restrictions placed on the movements of the monastic head? The superior is in fact forbidden to leave the precinct of his monastery for the duration of his service. This is quite peculiar since in many monasteries, notably among the Dasnāmīs, the chief abbots go on tours to visit the branch-*maṭhs* and their followers, often to collect donations. However, among the Nāgā Rāmānandīs, at least at Hanumangarhi, 'the chief abbot is appointed [according to *pañcāyatī* rule] for life and is not allowed to leave the temple of his own accord' (van der Veer 1988: 154). Perhaps the sedentary situation of the Nāga abbot and of the Nāth *pañcāyatī* head is made compulsory in order to contrast with the permanent wandering of the Tyāgis (in the case of the Rāmānandīs) and of the *jamāt* (in the case of the Nāth Yogī), as though in this way a structural equilibrum was reached.

Some of these *pañcāyatī maṭhs* divide the duties between the daily economic management, left to a caretaker (a *koṭhāri* in Pushkar, a *mānbhāū* in Dang), and the spiritual and ritual leadership that is centred on the worship of the *pātradevatā*; this is the case in Pushkar, where the *pīr* and his assistants are elected for a period of office, limited to the cult of the *pātradevatā*, of two-and-a-half days every year. In Jwalamukhi, the *pīr* is elected for six months, and in Dang Caughera for one year. In Kadri, the situation is more complex: the *rājā*, elected for twelve years, is in charge of both the material and the spiritual side of the institution.

The Mahāsabhā now supervises the *pañcāyatī maṭhs* directly. It is introducing a new sort of bureaucratic modern network of control over the Yogīs, codifying what it defines as good behaviour, registering institutions and individual ascetics.

Is this authority effective? We will see in a following chapter how the *rājā* of Kadri was punished for his misbehaviour and personal appropriation of the revenues of the monastery, but it was done only at the end of his term of office, even though the Yogīs' local associations had lodged a complaint against him. The town administration sent these associations to the Mahāsabhā, which waited till the end of his term.

Regarding the *nijī maṭhs*, the position of the Mahāsabhā is more ambiguous. In the case of the Vittal monastery (Karnataka), the Mahāsabhā was effective in persuading the *mahant*, guilty of cohabiting with a woman, to relinquish his monastery to the Association, and, thus, Vittal was transformed into *pañcāyatī*. However in a dramatic case where a pre-eminent *mahant* was, unjustly it seems, accused of murder, the Mahāsabhā replied that the monastery was managed according to the rules set by its founder and that it was absolutely independent from the Mahāsabhā, that no legal authority could turn the *mahant* away from his throne. Mahāsabhā's position may change according to circumstances. However, the present appropriation of the main offices of the Mahāsabhā, the office of president and vice-president, by two leaders who are both chiefs of *nijī maṭhs* (Gorakhpur and Asthal Bohar) and both 'political sādhus' competing for elections with a Hindutva programme, makes one fear an instrumentalization of this influential institution.

CHAPTER 3

Wandering Ascetics

The present volume deals mainly with monastic institutions since they offer the most visible part of the Nāth Yogīs' activities and represent the fixed and stable part of the *sampradāya*. However, the permanency of monastic institutions is to be understood in a dialectical relationship with the itinerant life that characterizes Hindu asceticism.[1]

The enduring image of a solitary roaming ascetic travelling through the Himalayan wilderness or the remotest places of India, free of any worldly possessions or interests, still inhabits the Indian religious landscape, as perennial wandering is a religious practice for renouncers, 'a way of learning about – and detaching from – materiality' (Hausner 2007: 95). An itinerant way of life in solitude and beggary is considered, both in texts and in common practice, as the sign and the requisite of any spiritual quest.

It is worth briefly comparing the high value given to wandering in the Hindu spiritual view to its condemnation in the Christian context. Very early in Christian monastic history, the *peregrinatio* was viewed in a negative sense and the monk was encouraged to settle in a monastery.[2] The rule of St. Benedict,

[1] See Bouillier, Enracinement monastique et itinérance, une relation dialectique au cœur de l'identité sectaire: exemple des Nāth Yogīs, forthcoming.

[2] See J.M. Santerre, 'Attitudes à l'égard de l'errance monastique en Occident du VI au XI siècle', in A. Dierkens, J.M. Sansterre, and J.L. Kupper (eds.), *Voyages et voyageurs à Byzance et en Occident du VI au XI siècle*, Genève, Droz, 2000, pp. 215-34. Also L. Mayali, 'Du vagabondage

for instance, which was promulgated in 540 CE and henceforth proposed as a model of monastic rule, severely condemns the practice of wandering and urges the monk to take the vow of *stabilitas (in) loci.* Similarly, the highest ecclesiastical authorities issued legislation against *monachi vagantes* and gyrovagues, who are considered to be refractory and insubordinate to the Church's authority.

By contrast, the Indian religious tradition of setting aside the world emphasizes the importance of itinerancy. Wandering ascetics have been part of the Indian religious tradition since antiquity. We can see this if we consider as the precursors to the ascetics the famous Keśins of the *Rgveda* hymn X, 136: 'The Munis, girdled with the wind [...] following the wind's swift course'. The tradition can surely be dated to the middle of the first millennium BCE. According to Olivelle, 'the earliest datable sources that attest to the existence of the renouncer tradition are the Aśokan inscriptions of the middle of the third century BCE' (Olivelle 2003: 271).

Significantly, in their description of the different stages of life (the four *aśramas*), the *Dharmaśāstras* link the last stages with wandering. The Āpastamba introduces both the *vanaprastha* (forest hermit) and the renouncer *āśramas* with the words: 'remaining celibate, he goes forth (*pravrajati*)' (Ap. Dh. 2.21.19, in Olivelle 1993: 163). And instead of referring to this latter *āśrama* with the current appellation of *saṃnyāsin*, the older *Dharmasūtras* (*Āpastamba*, Vaṣiṣṭha, *Baudhāyana*) use the term *parivrāja* or *parivrājaka* (Bronkhorst 1998: 13, 30-2), meaning wanderer.[3] Regarding Buddhism, we know that 'in the earliest phase of Buddhism, the teacher was peripatetic' (Tambiah 1981: 309), as well as are the Jain monks – thus the condition of the

à l'apostasie. Le moine fugitif dans la société médiévale', in D. Simon (ed.), *Religiöse Devianz*, Francfort, Vittorio Klostermann, 1990, pp. 121-42.

[3] From *pari-√vraj*, 'to wander about –as a religious mendicant', Monier-Williams, 1988: 602.

parivrājaka, the wandering mendicant, appears to be an integral part of the renunciatory quest.

Whatever the contested origins of the renouncer tradition (Bronkhorst 1998), can we see a Vedic heritage in the value attributed to the peripateric life? 'Vedic texts in general perpetuate the ideals of 'a society constantly on the move' [...]. In such a society despising sedentary life, the values of the adventurers probably dominated over those of the stability seekers' (Colas 2009: 102).[4]

Let us continue to explore the link between Vedic legacy and the value of wandering. Looking with Heesterman at the Vedic sacrificer who intends to perform the *śrauta* sacrifices, we find a distinction between two different types, the *yāyāvara* and the *śālīna*: 'the *śālīna* obviously is a householder with a fixed residence [...] The *yāyāvara* seems to be his opposite, a wanderer [...] Yet the *yāyāvara*'s way of life is consistently considered to be superior to the *śālīna's*.' This superior value is such that any householder wanting 'to perform the *śrauta* sacrifice [...] in order to qualify for the *śrauta* ritual [...] must set out from his residence, that is, he must conform to the pattern of the wanderer's life which is accordingly rated as superior' (Heesterman 1981: 254-5).

'The question of how asceticism fitted into Vedic religion remained, however, unanswered ' (Bronkhorst 1998: 1). Can we see a link in the itinerant way of life? Some theories see in the ascetic tradition a 'reaction originated with the Kṣatriyas, members of the warrior caste, who thus expressed their discontent with the ritualism of the Brahmins' (Bronkhorst, quoting Garbe, id.: 2). It is possible to read the 'archeology' of

[4] The settlement patterns of the Vedic groups find an expression in the use of the antonyms *yoga* and *kṣema*, 'with *yoga* paralleling 'expressions of moving [and] yoking up, while *kṣema* is parallel to expressions of standing still, repose at home, unyoking'' (White quoting Oertel, 2009: 65), thus 'the semi-nomadic existence of the Vedic peoples [is caracterized by] the *yoga-kṣema* distinction [that is] one that is obtained between periods of mobilization and settlement' (id. 75).

the renouncer traced by Heesterman as an entrance of Kṣatriya values, from 'the aggressive *yāyāvara* warrior setting out on his chariot' (1981: 268), to the *dīkṣita* and then to the ascetic, 'so at the end of the road [...] the *yāyāvara* emerges once more but now converted into the ultramundane ascetic wanderer. His *yoga* is no longer the yoking of his animals when he sets out on his trek. It has become the even more strenuous discipline for the no less precarious inner journey into the depths of the transcendent' (Heesterman 1981: 269).

Could the wandering ascetic be considered as the inheritor of the superior values of the nomadic Vedic warrior? This topic is at the heart of the motif of the 'warrior-ascetic'as studied by Dirk Kolff (1990: 74 ff.): in his account, these heroes of pre-modern Rajasthani ballads, described as 'fighters who go to war as yogīs, their bodies besmeared with ashes' (id. 81), come back and settle as victorious war-lords. Kolff insists on 'the common identity of the ancient Rajput and the Saivite warrior-ascetic' (id. 82) as exemplified in the songs and legends praising the Rānā of Mewar.

How do the Nāth Yogīs of today consider the itinerant way of life? As we shall see, not only do many of them still spend most of their time wandering, but they also claim the supremacy of itinerancy over the settled monastic way of life and asserts its primacy in the institutional framework of the sect.

Itinerancy expresses detachment from the world. It is described by the Yogīs as the choice of a life that is difficult to follow but is free from all mundane limitations and corresponds to the true purpose of being a Nāth Yogī.

Wandering is a choice – and the Nāth Yogīs, after their initiatory period, are free to adopt the way of life that they want or that is advised by their guru. Depending on the situation of their guru, they can wander alongside him if he is a roaming ascetic or settle with him in a monastery or hermitage if that is his choice. They can also travel alone or with other Yogīs in small groups. It as a personal choice – never compulsory – and wandering is never a permanent situation. Yogīs can freely alternate sedentary and itinerant ways of life if they so choose.

Most often, according to their narratives and to the biographies of greater ascetics, Nāth Yogīs choose to begin their ascetic life by wandering. They may go to the main pilgrimage spots, or prefer their own free wandering, dictated by chance encounters or by their visits to the Nāth monasteries. They often travel through Himalayan regions, and we may consider that many Śaiva cults and praises to Gorakhnāth encountered, for instance, in remote areas of Nepal are due to their long-lasting influence.[5]

Thus, when yogic texts such as *Haṭhapradīpika* recommend settling 'in a small room situated in a solitary place' (*HP* 1.12) to practise Haṭha Yoga and devote oneself to ascetic meditation, it is most often a pratice for yogīs having already attained true detachment through their previous wandering life.

The practice of wandering is common to all ascetics belonging to diverse *sampradāyas*. However, typical of the Nāth Yogīs is the existence of a constituted group of itinerant ascetics called the *jamāt*. The word *jamāt* (from the arabic *jamā'at*, group community) is employed among ascetics only to designate the groups of itinerant sādhus. Among the Rāmānandīs, a *jamāt* is a small group that unites around a sādhu who acts as their leader. As van der Veer explains: 'A disciple of a guru has finished his apprenticeship and goes wandering on his own through the country and starts raising funds for his own livelihood. If he is successful, he will also acquire more and more sadhus disciples who start raising funds [...] In this way he will have a successful group of itinerant sadhus, a *jamāt*' (1988: 112). Many *jamāt* can unite to form a bigger group called *khālsā*. Among the Nāth Yogīs, the *jamāt* is more organized and formal. Nowadays there is only one *jamāt*, consisting of a core of about a hundred Yogīs who continuously travel together. Some individual *ramtā* (or *ramat*, from *ramnā*, to wander) Yogīs can temporarily join this small circle, but they have to obey its rules.

The *jamāt* is well organized. It is run by two leaders, the *mahants*. As we have seen, the Nāth community is divided into two groups, the group of the eighteen *panths* known as

[5] See Bouillier, 'Mahādev Himalayen', 1992.

the *aṭhārah panth,* who claim Śiva as their tutelary deity, and the group of the twelve *panths* known as the *barāh panth,* who claim allegiance to Gorakhnāth. This division is reflected in the *jamāt*, which is run by the *aṭhārah panth ke mahant*, who is said to represent Śiva, and the *barāh panth ke mahant*, who is said to represent Gorakhnāth, each having authority over the sādhus of the corresponding *panths*. However, both *mahants* always act together and stay together during the *jamāt*'s travels. It is difficult to know the reason for this organization, as the sādhus are only rarely called by *panths* in the vicinity of their *mahant*: perhaps in earlier times there were two *jamāts,* each with its own *mahant* and its own route. Both *mahants* are nominated for a period of twelve years by the sectarian authorities of the Mahāsabhā during the Nasik Kumbh Melā. This nomination has to be confirmed by a vote of the community of the Yogīs who are present there. At the last Kumbh Melā in 2003, the two former *mahants* – Kriṣṇaṇāth, *mahant* of the *barāh panth,* and Somnāth, *mahant* of the *aṭhārah panth* – were again selected, as there were no other candidates. However, a few years later Somnāth was replaced by Sombharnāth for health reasons. And of course, the *mahant* of each group belongs to a *panth* linked to this group (Āī for Kriṣṇaṇāth, Ramke for Somnāth, Satyanāth for Sombharnāth).

The mode of travel of the *jamāt* has changed. While in earlier times Yogīs used to walk, they now travel by car. The *mahants* have Land Cruiser and the other Yogīs are packed into jeeps and a strange orange-painted, double-decker truck offered by the Jwalamukhi Gorakhḍībbī monastery. They often stop close to Śaiva temples or Nāth monasteries, where they camp in the open air. The centre of their camp is the big fire, or *dhūnī,* which they light at every stop and worship as Agni, the fire god. The *dhūnī* is the symbolic centre of the *jamāt*. It is the place where the Yogīs perform their ritual duties but also where are expressed all the ascetic values of their renunciatory way of life. As Gross has explained: 'the sacred fire which is continually being re-established corresponds to the sādhus' transient patterns of movement which in turn is linked to their ideology of world-renunciation' (1992: 356). The sight of the Yogīs standing in the darkness around the fire for the evening worship is quite impressive. Their appearance is much more wild, or *jaṅgli*, than that of the monastic Yogīs: they have long matted hair and beards, their bodies are half naked and covered with ashes, and some of them frantically play the *ḍamaru* (hourglass drum) and horns, especially the sinuous horn called *nāgphanī* (snake's hood), which is characteristic of the Yogīs. The *pujārī* makes the ritual offerings to the fire while reciting mantras and when he has finished, he bows in sudden silence in front of the fire and then blows his small *nād* whistle. This is the signal for all the other Yogīs to rush together to the fire with a big shout, to squat down and blow their *nād* three times, as they do to honour the gods and their gurus. Then they hurry to take some ashes and mark their foreheads with the three horizontal lines of Śaiva ascetics. Afterwards, they go to worship Śiva and their *mahants*.

At every stopping place, a low platform covered with carpets is fixed up for the *mahants* close to the *dhūnī*.[6] This structure constitutes the *gaddī*, or throne, of the two *mahants*. They sit on either side of a portable altar to Śiva made of a small table in gilded brass with a small silver statue of Śiva surrounded by the serpent-gods Nāgas. In front are the chromo paintings of Gorakhnāth, the nine Nāths, and Hanuman, all adorned with flower necklaces. The *mahant* of *aṭhārah panth* is on the left side and the *mahant* of the *barāh panth* on the right side of this altar, in front of which *pujārī* and Yogīs come to bow each morning and evening. The *gaddīs* are always set this same way, even when their occupant is away (which happens only for very serious reasons, as when Somnāth was taken to hospital). Usually the two *mahants* stay on their *gaddī* and do not mix with the rituals and activities of the monasteries and temples. They stay with a small

[6] Built in sand or mud, it may be also made in concrete when the Yogīs stop in a temple or *maṭh*. In Pushkar for instance, a space has been organized for the *jamāt* in a recently built temple to Śiva, with a central fire-pit surrounded by a gallery for the Yogīs and the *mahants*' platform.

group of close Yogīs; they do not speak much but they smoke a lot and they are evidently respected and feared by everyone. For example, the young sādhus of the *jamāt* who were one evening at Kadri watching a musical performance, immediately disappeared when they saw the *mahants* approaching.

Many elements of the *jamāt* – the function of *mahant*, the throne, the moving altar of the tutelary god, the rules – suggest we should consider it to be an itinerant monastery. However, like in a settled monastery, offices are distributed among *pujārīs*, *karbarīs* (accountants) and cooks, the other Yogīs without definite offices being free to join them for a short time. Richard Burghart has shown the meaning given to the notion of an itinerant monastery among the Rāmānandī sādhus (1996: chap. 4): 'This notion further entails the idea of pervading the universe. According to this conception, the universe has a moving centre and the ability of the centre to move is a sign of its liberation from the ties of conditioned existence. For the Rāmānandī Renouncers this moving centre which circulates within and pervades the Sacred Land of the Hindus is the autonomous itinerant monastery of liberated ascetics' (1996: 123). Wandering is thus both the way to, and the sign of, the state of liberation, and itinerant Yogīs like to feel superior to their settled counterparts.

The travels of the *jamāt* are regular and organized. Its standardized route helps to create a territorial integration of the sect – a way to link and build up a network between fragmented centres. Following Burghart's thesis, we can say that the *jamāt* when travelling delineates a sacralized universe. Like the religious geography designed by pilgrimages, the travels of the *jamāt* unite different areas, local or pan-Indian, in a space and time particular to the Nāth Yogīs, since they are decided according to a precise calendar. The *mahants* organize the itinerary according to the main festivals of the important monasteries or sacred places. They attend the four Kumbh Melās of Haridwar, Prayag, Nasik, and Ujjain – Nasik is the most important for the Yogīs since it is there that the two *mahants* of the *jamāt* are nominated and the huge procession of the *jhuṇḍī* (see Chapter 5) toward the Kadri monastery will begin. Besides this three-year cycle,[7] the *jamāt* has to visit some Nāth places every year, the most important being Pushkar for the Kārttik (October-November) full-moon festival,[8] Jwalamukhi for Navarātrī and Girnar in Gujarat for Śivarātrī. Every year for the past ten years the *jamāt* has also gone to Naida (close to Bikaner), where a rich devotee has built a new temple dedicated to the Nāths.[9] In addition to the regular travel cycle, the *jamāt* can also grace special events with its presence; I have seen the *jamāt* come for the anniversary festival of the Fatehpur Ashram (see Chapter 10); however, the sādhus stayed apart, attending only the feast at the end of the function (and receiving the *bidāī*, the generous departure gift, which the host monastery has the obligation to give to the visiting *jamāt*).

Until fifty years ago, the *jamāt* also went to Nepal to visit the Dang Caughera monastery for the annual festival of the election of the *pīr* (on the eleventh day of the dark fortnight of Phālgun, February-March). The group then accompanied the procession of the Yogīs to the Indian temple of Tulsipur Devi Patan (see Chapter 7). The *jamāt* was in charge of protecting the *pīr*, who carried the *pātradevatā*, during this potentially dangerous night-time journey.

The martial and protective function of the *jamāt* is symbolized by two swords held by the two *mahants*. When the group of

[7] Every twelve years in each place; there is thus a Kumbh Melā every three years but sometimes for astrological reasons the calendar is modified, for instance in 2003-4 the two Kumbh of Nasik and Ujjain succeeded each other after only nine months. There are also half-Kumbhs every six years in each centre but they are less well attended.

[8] Especially for the Rajasthani Yogīs and for the new initiates who have to be registered there by the Bhaṭṭa genealogist.

[9] With many thanks to Gildas Billet who shared with me this information and the images he filmed there for his documentary film on the Nāth Yogīs, *Babaji*.

Yogīs enters a place, two assistants posted close to the *mahants* brandish their respective swords which they then place in front of each *mahant* on the *gaddī*. During the collective solemn rituals such as the offering and cutting of the *roṭ*, the two *mahants* have to stand on either side of the officiating Yogī, brandishing their swords, which are crossed at the top like a kind of protective canopy over the *pujārī*. This symbolic apparatus explains why the sādhus of the *jamāt* are sometimes called the Nāga Yogīs. To my knowledge, the Nāth Yogīs do not have any Nāga branch, as the Dasnāmī Sannyāsīs and the Rāmānandīs do, i.e. specific branches of fighting ascetics (with initiation rites, martial training and separate monasteries[10]). However, one can understand how the *jamāt* could be considered as fearsome and easily confused by outsiders with the Nāgas because of the nature of this troupe of ascetics – they are scantily dressed, covered with ashes, often excited, smoke cannabis continuously and are equipped with tridents, fire tongs, walking sticks and swords.

The martial aspect of the *jamāt mahants* is also justified by their duty to examine the accounts and supervise the monasteries they visit. Wherever they stay, they are the highest authority. I have seen them in Pushkar, seated on their *gaddī* in the attic of the temple, looking at the books brought by the accountant, verifying incomes and expenditures, and presiding over a meeting restricted to the initiated Yogīs where, I was told, disciplinary matters were discussed and punishments were meted out for infractions.[11]

The authority of the *jamāt* is absolute, except for a few months every twelve years when the *jamāt* merge into the *jhuṇḍī*, the troupe of Yogīs who walk from Nasik to Kadri-Mangalore to

[10] On this topic, see bibliography in Bouillier 2003, Pinch 2005 and 2006.

[11] Unfortunately I could testify to their authority when they forbade me to attend a ceremony, which had previously been allowed by the chief of the monastery, who then told me that he could not do anything, that when the *mahants* have decided something, one must just obey!

escort the new head of the Kadri monastery (see Chapter 5). In this instance, the *jhuṇḍī* is an extension of the *jamāt*, where the Yogīs are more numerous and subject to a stricter ascetic discipline; it is under the authority of a special leader called *jhuṇḍī mahant*, who is chosen at Nasik. It is then up to the *jhuṇḍī mahant* to control all the Nāth places the procession crosses.

The superior value given to wandering in the world-view and organization of the Nāth Yogīs is also manifested in the successive steps that mark access to the throne of the heads of *pañcāyatī* monasteries: their obligation to remain in the monastery, or *stabilitas loci,* is preceded and followed by two phases of wandering that act as a legitimizing factor. We shall see that the *rājā* of Kadri, like the *pīr* of Caughera, are finally enthroned only after a long journey on foot (and by night in the case of Caughera). In other cases, the superior does not wander himself, but is elected only in the presence of the *jamāt* and, most importantly, he comes from another place. He arrives in the monastery to take office, and in a radical change with a former itinerant life, he is forbidden to leave the area. But as soon as his term is finished, he leaves the place immediately and disappears.

During the colonial period, the British authorities were suspicious of the roaming ascetics, whom they assumed were likely to propagate seditious ideas or a rebellious way of life. After having suppressed what was called 'the Sannyāsī rebellion', the British tried successfully to tame the uncontrolled wandering ascetics by encouraging them to settle, marry, and become householders. Many Yogīs followed the British lead, and in Rajasthan, for instance, one finds many *grihastha* Yogīs, or Yogīs by caste, who still have some religious or apotropaic functions and are perhaps the settled descendants of former itinerant ascetic Yogīs (see Chapter 12). However, the stigmatization of the vagrants was superimposed on a model which, on the contrary, viewed wandering as the only way to approach spiritual realization and attain the goal of liberation.

However, whatever the prestige and superiority of the wandering ascetics and their way of life, if they were not supported by an institutional framework, the different *sampradāyas* would have disappeared, merged into each other, or changed. The *sampradāyas* are not grounded on the peripatetic ascetics, but rather on the institutions and places that give them a collective existence and allow for the building of a community. That is the role of the monasteries, *maṭhs* and ashrams: to avoid the splitting of religious traditions, to facilitate gathering for communal worship and to allow for *stabilitas* of the places (if not in the places).

PART II

COLLECTIVE MONASTERIES

A life of free wandering, independent of such constraints as family, village and productive activity, is depicted by Louis Dumont as characteristic of the 'individual' as opposed to 'the man-in-the-world', whose being is predetermined by social paradigms. Drawing on the Dharmaśastras, Dumont has developed a model that organizes the values of Indian Brahmanic society around the two poles of the man-in-the-world and the renouncer. Even though the term renouncer should refer strictly to the Brahmanic Sannyāsī who has relinquished his sacrifical fire (or more precisely interiorized it) and with it his link to society, the values embodied by renunciation such as separateness from the world and the quest for the ultimate goal of liberation pervades all Hindu sects or traditions. For Dumont, the renouncer is characterized as an individual: 'In leaving the world he finds himself invested with an individuality which he apparently finds uncomfortable since all his efforts tend to its extinction or its transcendance. He thinks as an individual and this is the distinctive trait which opposes him to the man-in-the- world' (1960: 46). Dumont says also, specifying, as he usually does, his broad generalizations: 'He submits himself to his chosen master, or he may even enter a monastic community, but essentially he depends upon no one but himself, he is alone' (ibid.).

The 'monastic community' mentioned by Dumont in passing is an essential mediating term between the solitary ascetic individual and society. As a collective and organized institution, the monastery functions in society, but is composed of individual renouncers. As was said before, it is thanks to a monastic structure which ensures sectarian permanency that independent individuals can wander freely while maintaining their sectarian identity.

The dialectical relationship between the wandering individual ascetic and the collective institutions has been also of interest in Buddhist studies, S.J. Tambiah asking for instance: 'So what kind of individual is the quintessential Buddhist renouncer ?' (1981: 311). And he remarks that 'the logic of a renouncer's 'personal' quest [...] was thought to be best undertaken as a member of a collectivity subject to a communal discipline' (id. 303), since 'the Buddhist movement, which emphasised the teachings and the propagation of a certain knowledge or wisdom together with the attendant ethical practices, required as its basic grouping or cell a "master" [...] and a following of pupils whom he instructed' (309), thus was 'best undertaken in a monastic context' (id.). Patrick Olivelle goes as far as to say: 'Even though the ideal of homeless wandering is often maintained as a theological fiction, many of these renouncer groups such as the Buddhist and the Jain, organized themselves into monastic communities with at least a semi-permanent residence. These communities vied with each other to attract lay members, donors and benefactors, and for political patronage' (2003: 274).

Looking at Hindu ascetics, the link between the personal spiritual quest and the creation of monastic communities is not as intrinsic as in Buddhism. Slowly and informally, small groups of Hindu ascetics gathered around charismatic figures and constituted the core of communitarian institutions. The transmission of the guru's teachings required a minimum of organization and, as Romila Thapar described it, the relations with the caste society upon which the begging ascetics have to rely, led them to create an institutional base in order to be recognized as legitimate. As she explains, 'it was, therefore, necessary that they be organised as a group outside society and yet with some links – as a parallel group with its own norms. The Brahman could well regard them as outcastes and their legitimacy, therefore, depended on their receiving public support in terms or recognition of their parallel or alternate system' (1981: 292).

This is the sort of monastic communities that, I think, allowed for the continuation of the tradition of renunciation by organizing it around various value systems, philosophical or theological orientations. They most often gave rise to what might be called sects, which I define as a voluntary group of followers who share a certain religious orientation based on the transmission of exclusive teaching, practice or belief.

Today, most ascetics belong to different religious traditions, to sects generally distributed among Shaivites and Vishnuites and often focused around monasteries. It is these monasteries that serve as an anchor, places of education and often initiation, and centres of spiritual power and economy. That is where the religious authorities stay and where financial matters are managed.

However, Hindu monastic centres are quite different from the Christian or Buddhist models, even though the vernacular appellation *maṭh* is conveniently translated as 'monastery'. With neither strict regulations nor enclosure, these monasteries are open structures where ascetics come and go, and where sometimes only the head ascetic, the *mahant*, resides permanently. Here are the basic features of Indian asceticism: an overlap between an individual approach of standing outside the world and a monastic structure, a back and forth between wandering and life in the monastery.

The Nāth Yogīs offer a perfect example of this double movement, this fundamental relationship between a tradition that emphasizes a personal approach to asceticism and spiritual quest, and a collective organization anchored to the monasteries, which allows the sect to survive and adapt to the multiple socio-historical changes they face.

This duality is symbolized in the *pātradevatā*. This object, both secret and conspicuously displayed, containing ordinary items but with a high symbolic value, represents, as we have seen, the quintessence of the yogīc quest, the personal goal of every Yogī. And yet this *pātradevatā* is made, displayed, and worshipped during collective rituals that ensure the unity of the *sampradāya*.

It is with a complex ritual that the Yogīs pay homage to this sacred vessel that symbolizes their ultimate goal and the *raison d'être* of their *sampradāya*, and this ritual is performed when the Nāth Yogīs are all summoned for Kumbh Melās or for the renewal of monastery heads. The Yogīs are said to be in *dalicā*, in assembly, taking collective decisions under the direction of the sectarian authorities (*mahants* of the *jamāt*, of the *jhuṇḍī*, leaders of the Mahāsabhā). *Dalicā* and *pātradevatā* are linked: the Yogīs of the different *panths* assembled in the *dalicā* worship their tutelary deity, the *pātradevatā*, who is none other than Gorakhnāth himself, and they worship him under the form of their sectarian emblems. It is a sort of self-celebration of identity and community.

It is the function of the *pañcāyatī maṭhs* to maintain the sense of community and to guarantee the doctrinal, ritual and organizational continuity of the *sampradāya*. They are the basis of tradition as they are firmly rooted in the past; however, they are fragile because of their strictness. The other category of monastery, the personal or *nijī* monasteries, are much more flexible, as we shall see later; being transmitted from guru to disciple, they depend on personal factors but are more open to innovation and adapt more easily to a changing context.

The following chapters will be devoted to the functioning of the *pañcāyatī maṭhs*. They are few, no more than a dozen, but they play an essential part in the complex story of sect permanency.

We shall first look at Kadri monastery in the town of Mangalore in Karnataka. In the sect organization as conceived by the Yogī Mahāsabhā, Kadri Maṭh is its administrative seat in south India, the seat of the provincial assembly. But as we shall see, if Kadri is the southernmost and an essential centre of the sect, it has a long history, its importance being justified in the Nāth tradition by reference to a set of legends: the Nāth Yogīs have reinterpreted the legend of Paraśurām, well known on the coastal territory of Karnataka and Kerala, and depict the Viṣṇu's *avatār* as a devotee of Gorakhnāth. These are the founding references which legitimize the pre-eminence of Kadri monastery. Is it the reason why its head has the exceptional title of *rājā*, or *rājā*-Yogī, Yogī king ? His enthronement, which I will describe in detail (Chapter 5), follows a special procedure which involves and brings into play all the institutions and the identity markers of the sect. If the Kadri *rājā's* consecration rituals derive directly from royal models, they are preceded by a long sequence, a ritual cycle in which the Yogīs submit to six months ascetic wandering. However the dominance of the *rājā* is limited in time and more symbolic than real: as an elected king, he is the representative of the authority of the institution and the symbol of the community.

The other *pañcāyatī* monastery that I will present here is situated at the opposite end of the territory frequented by the Nāth Yogīs, in Nepal. It is considered to be less important by the Yogī Mahāsabhā since it is outside Indian territory, and thus economically and juridically independent. However, its history and functioning are quite interesting as they obey a traditional system* that was probably quite usual in former Indian and especially Rajasthani kingdoms. The Caughera monastery shows how interrelated and mutually dependent were kings and ascetics, kingship and monasteries. Caughera is linked to kingship through its foundation myth and through its functioning. Being a beneficiary of royal donations and being, in exchange, the protector of the kingdom, the monastery was endowed with a privileged tenurial status inside the Nepalese kingdom, while it was also subject to the rules which govern *pañcāyatī maṭhs*, such as the election of the monastic head and the handover of responsibilities, which occurs in this case every year.

* At least until the profound changes introduced by the Maoist insurgency and the end of the monarchy. The Caughera monastery is still in operation but its tenurial regime is not.

CHAPTER 4

The Kadri Maṭh: History

In the present situation of the Nāth Yogīs, the importance given to the monastery of Kadri near Mangalore in Karnataka may seem puzzling. Its many peculiarities such as the solemn enthronement of the superior invested with the unique title of *rājā*, and the long pilgrimage that surrounds the ritual, make us wonder: why Kadri? what part did this southern religious centre play in the Nāth Yogī tradition, which seems now much more important in northern India, and what is its role today?

Trying to answer these questions will take us into the past of the town and confront us with still controversial topics regarding rivalries between religious sects. Kadri is involved in recent polemics about Buddhism and Brahmanism and may give interesting clues to a highly conjectural history. What part did the Nāths Yogīs and the monastery of Kadri play in this complex situation?

MANGALORE, THE TOWN AND ITS TEMPLES

Capital of the south Karnataka district, Mangalore is now a small quiet town, bordered by the rivers Gurpur in the north and Netravati in the south. Sea access from this formerly very active port is now only through a narrow channel and the harbour activities have been shifted 10 km north. Nothing in the present town reveals the past grandeur and wealth of this trading centre with the Persian Gulf, a grandeur that inspired the novelist Amitav Ghosh (1992: 241-88) to narrate the commercial expeditions of the merchant Abraham ben Yiju in the twelfth century, and which was attested by the testimony of Ibn Battuta who counted more than four thousand Muslim merchants living in Mangalore in the middle of thirteenth century.[1]

Wealthy under the rule of the Alepa dynasty (seventh-fourteenth centuries), the town passed under the domination of Vijayanagar from 1345 to 1563, then suffered from the conflict between the Portuguese and the Keladi Nayakas, before being occupied by the Portuguese in the middle of sixteenth century. As described by the Italian traveller Pietro della Valle, who stayed in Mangalore in 1622, the town was still impressive, surrounded by high walls with a small fortress where the Governor stayed. However, the Portuguese control was limited to the heart of the town, the south being under the domination of the queen of Ullala,[2] and the north that of the king Keladi Venkatappa Nayaka. In 1763, Mangalore was annexed by the Mysore ruler Haidar Ali, after signing a treaty with the Portuguese. But new conflicts, this time with the British, followed by the victory of Tipu Sultan allowed him to impose on the British the humiliating treaty of Mangalore in 1784. However, Tipu's domination was shortlived and in 1799 Mangalore and its surroundings were annexed by the British.

Whatever its past glory, the town is now poor in architectural remains. However, we could till recently[3] credit its maritime commercial openness for the religious pluralism and tolerance

[1] *Travels in Asia and Africa, 1325-1354* (quoted by Ghosh 1992: 373).

[2] Divorced from Bangaraja, the king of Banghel allied to the Portuguese, the queen asked for help from the Keladi Nayaka, Venkatappa, who had an easy victory over Bangaraja and the Portuguese governor of Mangalore. Venkatappa ruled from 1586 CE to 1629 CE. On the ancient history of the south Karnataka or Tulu region, see Saletore (1936), Ramesh (1970), P. Gururaja Bhat (1975), Vasantha Madhava (1985), Veerathappa (1986).

[3] On January 2009 a right-wing activist group (Sri Ram Sena) attacked a group of young men and women in a pub, claiming that 'they were violating Indian values' and 'spoiling the traditional girls of Mangalore'. The attack and counter mobilization by women's groups were widely reported in the press.

which was its characterisitic. Before the present cohabitation between Hindus, Muslims and Christians, the town has probably seen many religious communities succeed one another: Buddhists, Shaivites, Lingayats, Jains, Vishnuites.

If ancient monuments are very few, we still find inscriptions, statues and mostly narratives that may talk about the past. Without entering the debate about the contested historical status of narratives or legends,[4] the impossibility of dating them precisely with regard to their composition or the facts narrated, nevertheless they may be considered as giving indications of the changes occuring in the local religious history or power relationships.

The foundation myths of Mangalore town are focused on two precise spots, two religious complexes that surround the town on the south and the north. And their divine images as well as the stories about them connect the places to the most ancient past of Mangalore and link this past to the Nāth Yogī tradition.

In the south, not far from the Netravati River, stands the temple of Maṅgaladevī, dedicated to the 'auspicious' (*maṅgala*) goddess who gave her name to the town. According to local legend, the origin of the place is extremely ancient and it was rediscovered and renovated in the tenth century by the Alepa king Kundavarma. The temple contains a *mūrti*, an effigy of the devī, which appears as an irregular and massive black stone stele, resembling a *śivaliṅga*.

In some legends, Maṅgaladevī is said to be the consort of the god Mañjunāth, whose temple constitutes the other religious complex at the northern limit of the town. The Mañjunāth temple sits at the foot of a small hill crowned by the Nāth Yogī monastery of Kadri. The complex, temples and monastery, are included in the same appellation of Kadri-Mañjunāth that attests their connection, even though the Mañjunāth temple is now in charge of the Vishnuite Madhva Brahmins. The temple follows the classical structure of Kannarese temple architecture and is currently dated to the fourteenth century, even though

[4] See Narayan Rao, Shulman and Subrahmaniam 2001.

constant repairs make the complex appear rather new. But the temple still includes beautiful statues, among which one is from the tenth century, making it one of the most ancient examples of the local statuary.

Legends, rituals, but also statues and inscriptions make this Mañjunāth temple the greatest centre of the south Indian Nāth tradition, but also evoke different religious currents. However, the history of this place is quite fragmentary and includes more polemical interpretations than in-depth studies.

My purpose here is to look at Mañjunāth from a Nāth Yogī perspective, taking into account the legends as well as the inscriptions found in the *maṭh* in order to grasp its complexity and importance.

A READING OF THE LEGEND OF PARAŚURĀM: MAÑJUNĀTH'S APPEARANCE

An old and common tradition relates the upheaval of the Deccan western coast to Paraśurām, Rām with the axe, the sixth *avatār* of Viṣṇu, who obtained from Varuṇa the territory that he could cover by throwing his axe towards the sea.

The legend of Paraśurām, mentioned in the *Mahābhārata* and many Purāṇas, is also quoted in several inscriptions 'dated from the first quarter of the 6th century to the first quarter of the 16th'.[5] It also, according to the historian Keshavan Veluthat, accompanied the migration of Brahman communities from Gujarat to Kerala.[6] Nowadays the whole coastal territory still

[5] Saletore (1936: 11-22), who devotes the first chapter of his book *Ancient Karnāṭaka* to this legend in Tuḷuva context, its variants and historical context. The most complete version is in the *Sahyādri-kāṇḍa* of the *Skānda Purāṇa*.

[6] 'The Paraśurāma legend originated in Gujarat, more specifically in the peninsula called Śurpāraka and it is likely that this legend also moved along with the moving people. In other words, the Brahman settlements of Kerala constituted the last link of a long chain of

considers Paraśurām as its patron deity;[7] this is especially the case in Karnataka because of the importance of the Saundatti temple where the couple Yellama-Jamadagni are worshipped (Assayag 1992), Paraśurām being the son of this problematic couple since Jamadgni is a Brahman renouncer considered as an *avatār* of Śiva, and Yellama-Renuka his Kṣatriya wife.[8]

The violent lifestory of Paraśurām, the Brahman warrior, makes him first a matricide: he kills his mother on the orders of his father, then resuscitates her. Later on, seeing his father persecuted then killed by the Kṣatriyas and their king Arjuṇa Kārttavīrya, he takes up arms and accomplishes his destiny as Viṣṇu's *avatār*: in twenty-one warlike expeditions he cleanses the earth of the violence and hubris of the Kṣatriyas.

The episode which makes him the hero of Mangalore, an episode that the Nāths have reinterpreted in order to give full legitimacy to their dominance in Kadri, happens after the fighting. Paraśurām has accomplished his duty and reestablished the Brahmanical order. However, according to the Nāths:[9]

---

migration moving along the west coast and carrying with them the tradition of Paraśurāma' (Veluthat 1978: 4).

[7] Cf. Vasudeva Rao (2002: 26): 'According to Puranic tradition [...] the region between the Arabian sea and the Western Ghats stretching from Nasik in Maharashtra to Kanyakumari at the southern end of the peninsula is known as the holy land of Parashurama.' The recurring mention of Nasik is surprising since it is quite far from the sea: is it because the Godavari region is considered as the territory of the Bhārgavas, Jamadagni's lineage ? Whatever the reason, this reference makes still easier Paraśurām's inclusion in the Nāth tradition.

[8] On Paraśurām see Biardeau (1976: 185-90, 1981: II , 239-41), Babb (2002: 133-54), Dejenne 2007.

[9] Summarized from oral narrative and from a Hindi booklet written by the head of Kadri monastery. The mode of Paraśurām's penance is most often the following: he must organize a huge sacrifice and offers the land he made emerge to the officiating Brahmans (Biardeau 1981: II, 240 ; Babb 2002: 141).

Paraśurām is full of remorse and crushed with grief and guilt. He wants to atone for his sin. He roams around in the company of several ascetics. One of them advises him to take refuge with Gorakhnāth, who alone can give him peace. Paraśurām then visits Gorakhnāth, who stands on Mount Kaulāgaṛh[10] in Tryambakesvar, and bows down at his feet. Gorakhnāth orders him to stretch out his arms and suddenly makes the *pātradevatā*, the divine vessel, appear between his two hands. Gorakhnāth then declares to Paraśurām: 'Go and worship this divine vessel in a place where nobody has ever practised any ascetic discipline'. Paraśurām goes all over the world and never finds any such place. Desperate, he comes back to Gorakhnāth who orders him to walk south without stopping till he finds a place which suits him. Paraśurām starts walking and finally arrives on the seashore close by modern Mangalore. There, anxious and sad, he thinks that he has reached the end of the earth and that the true meaning of Gorakhnāth's words is that he must go deep into the sea and disappear. He starts walking into the sea and the more he walks the more the sea recedes until a strip of land twelve *kos*[11] wide emerges, a land virgin of any previous occupation. Paraśurām here sets down the *pātradevatā* and begins to worship it. The mist (in Kannada *mañju*) which surrounded the *pātradevatā*, clears and Gorakhnāth appears in full glory. Paraśurām throws himself at his feet and worships him, calling him Mañjunāth, Lord of the Mist.[12] Gorakhnāth tells him that he has accomplished his penance and gives him his blessing.

For the Nāth Yogīs, Mañjunāth Temple has been erected on the

[10] I never found any other mention in Tryambakesvar or elsewhere of this mountain, whose etymology as 'the fort of the clan' suggests a link with the Tantric Kaula tradition. According to the Purāṇas, Paraśurām climbs a mountain from the top of which he throws his axe to the sea, or withdraws on a mountain after having given the land to the Brahmans. Generally it is mount Mahendra, sometimes mount Saṁya or Siṁha or Sahya (Saletore 1936: 24-5).

[11] A *kos* is about two miles. Saletore specifies: The *Grāmapaddhati* of Tuḷuva, based to some extent on the *Sahyādri-kaṇḍa* [...] gives the length of the province as one hundred *yojanas* from Nāsik in the north to Kanyākumārī in the south; and three *yojanas* in breadth from the Sahya mountain to the western sea (1936: 26).

[12] Local etymology juxtaposing Kannada (*mañju* as mist) and

very spot where Gorakhnāth appeared and the Kadri monastery still encloses the *dhūnī*, the ascetic fire where Paraśurām practised his meditation. The land is utterly holy and, as soon as it emerged, testified to the Nāth supremacy. Even Viṣṇu, under the guise of his *avatār* Paraśurām, was obliged to bow in front of Śaiva power. At least this is how the Nāth Yogīs want to see the situation.[13]

Is this reading of the legend influenced by the historical context? We shall now examine the interpretations given to this episode and more generally to the personage of Paraśurām.

THE *KADALĪ MAÑJUNĀTHA MĀHĀTMYAṀ*

Other versions of the legendary foundation of the Mañjunāth temple erase the Nāth connection, seeing Mañjunāth as a form of Śiva, without any mediation through Gorakhnāth.

This is the case in a local *māhātmya*, the *Kadalī Mañjunātha Māhātmyaṁ*, which testifies, however, to a strong Nāth influence. This text, written in Sanskrit, was published in a Kannada translation for the first time in 1956 (by a local scholar Kadav Shambhu Sharma with the patronage of the Yogī Mahāsabhā), then in Sanskrit in Varanasi in 1975. The Kannada version has recently been reprinted locally (2003).

Not reading Kannada I shall follow the English summary and comments made by the historian S. Nagaraju in a short article where he points out the ambiguities of the text and of the personage of Mañjunāth.[14] According to Nagaraju,

> the *Kadalī Mañjunātha Māhātmyaṁ* has been edited with the aid of two

---

Sanskrit-Hindi (*nātha*, protector, lord); *mañju* in Sanskrit means 'beautiful, lovely, charming' (Monier-Williams 1988: 774).

[13] On the relationships between Paraśurām and Śiva (Gorakhnāth here replacing Śiva) see Biardeau (1976) and Pinch (2006: 215) who, in the *Ramcharitmanas* see Tulsidas describing Paraśurām 'in terms typical of unruly Saiva asceticism', but for an opposite aim 'to subordinate ferocious Saiva asceticism to the devotional worship of Ram'.

[14] Its title is revealing: A rare Saivo-Buddhist work with Vaishnavite

manuscripts – one on paper and the other on palm-leaf. At the end of the palm-leaf manuscript there is mention of 1652 – Kali saṁvatsara. If 1652 refers to the Śakya year, the date of the manuscript would be AD 1730 (s.d.: 75).

The text, which consists of 2,600 verses and 60 chapters, praises the greatness and antiquity of Kadri. In Nagaraju's view, it is probably composed of different fragments, and 'with its easily recognizable additions and alterations is a fine indicator of the shifting influence of different religious denominations'.

The first part – Chapters I to XIII – relates the origin myth of Kadri and praises Mañjunāth (without any reference to Gorakhnāth's intervention). The second part (XIV-LX) refers entirely to the Nāth tradition, to the main Nāth Siddhas, the spiritual masters, without making any connection with Kadri. Nagaraju emphasizes two pecularities of the text which we shall come back to later: the link with Buddhism (traces of a Buddhist connection either with the holy place Kadri or early Nāthapantha could be seen to persist in certain passages), and the influence of Vishnuism: in several places we find eulogies of Viṣṇu and mentions of the ten *avatārs* (and among them of Paraśurām).

The *Māhātmyaṁ* begins with a dialogue between the two seers Bhāradvāja and Sumantu, examining who is the highest deity who can be worshipped in our world. Alluding to a similar discussion between the two ṛsis Kapila and Bhṛgu, they decide for Mañjunāth who then appears in a circle of light and declares himself to be the supreme *brahman* and Śiva himself. Viṣṇu appears afterwards and the seers ask him where Mañjunāth can be worshipped. Viṣṇu then tells them about his ten *avatārs* and says that, when he incarnated as Paraśurām, he worshipped the god Mañjunāth on the 'golden land of Kadalī' (*suvarṇa Kadalī kṣetra*, c.a.d. Kadri), which he won from the sea and where the divine architect Viśvakarma built a temple. Chapter XIII also includes an episode concerning the Devī which we shall come

interpolations, *Kannada Studies*, vol. 3, no. 1, undated, pp. 67-75 [I am grateful to Catherine Clementin-Ojha alerting me to this article].

back to later: 'When Paraśurām was living on this holy land, the goddess Vindhyāvāsinī came and settled as the goddess Maṅgalādevī'.

Thus, in this text as well as in oral versions told by the Madhva priests of Mañjunāth Temple, the god Mañjunāth is the form of Śiva as the ultimate God. The story keeps the link with Paraśurām as the first devotee, but no connection is made between Paraśurām and Gorakhnāth, which is astonishing since the text continues immediately with the evocation of the nine Nāths.[15] This is perhaps an indication that this *māhātmya* comes from the circle of the Madhva priests, who attempt to minimize the Nāth influence and to project retroactively into the past the present separateness of the two sanctuaries.

It is significant to find on the website of Mangalore town[16] a standard version of the legend which borrows from the two versions. As in the Nāth version, Paraśurām feels sorry for the murder of the Kṣatriya and asks for a land where he can do penance. However Paraśurām asks not Gorakhnāth but Śiva, who tells him that if he goes to Kadalī Kṣetra, he (Śiva) himself will incarnate in Mañjunāth. Paraśurām throws his axe towards the sea and makes a land appear that is suitable for his ascetic practices. Śiva settles here together with Pārvatī.

Mañjunāth Temple and its History

Leaving aside temporarily the legendary accounts of this hybrid *māhatmyā*, we shall look at the present Mañjunāth Temple and consider its enigmatic statues, with the many questions raised by the deities worshipped there.

[15] The evocation of the nine Nāths occurs in chapter XIV. Then chapters XV to XLV are devoted to Matsyendranāth, Gorakhnāth, and Cauraṅgināth, the following chapters to Kanthaḍi-nāth, Konkananāth, Ananganāth, and Jālandharanāth.

[16] A great deal could be said about these websites, which are often produced by tourist offices and propagate standardized and officialized versions without ever giving their sources.

The legends, the layout of the place, the statues, the inscriptions, the rituals all tend to attest to the strength and antiquity of the link between the Mañjunāth Temple and the Kadri Nāth monastery. The two complexes are a few hundred metres apart, the temple being situated at the bottom of the small hill crowned by the monastery. But historical changes and urbanization have led the monastery to create a separate entry. The main gates of the temple and the monastery are now quite far apart and the numerous visitors to the Mañjunāth temple rarely take the trouble to climb the steep staircase and take the small path that leads directly to the Kadri Maṭh from the temple.

The vast area of the temple complex contains many buildings intended for the pilgrims, such as festival halls or resthouses as well as small secondary sanctuaries including one dedicated to Durgā and another to Gaṇapati with a *śivaliṅga* and a probably very ancient statue.[17] There are also nine ancient pools, which play an important role during the main festivals. The Mañjunāth sanctuary, in the centre of the esplanade, is surrounded by a square gallery covered with a tiled roof. At the centre of this sort of courtyard, the *garbhagṛha*, the heart of the temple, contains the deity Mañjunāth represented by a *śivaliṅga swayambhū*, i.e. 'self manifested', a stone slab half buried in a little tank. The place has recently been topped with a whitewashed *gopuram*. And in the small rooms surrounding the *garbhagṛha* are now displayed the various statues that give the Mañjunāth Temple all its artistic and historical reputation. These effigies are the first historically datable elements of the temple and are subject to a controversy which curiously implies a religious group we never found mentioned in the legendary corpus: the Buddhists.

[17] The temple has published a booklet written by Gururaja Bhat, a well known historian of Tulunadu, in Kannada with some ten pages in English and photos. Bhat writes here (2000: 20) that the *śivaliṅga* of the Durgā shrine could be linked to an old Śakti cult and that 'the Durga shrine may be the earliest in Kadri'. For the Gaṇapati's statue, this sculpture may be ascribed to the eleventh century AD if not to an earlier date (2000: 20).

The Tenth Century Statues: Buddhists or Shaivites?

In a small chapel at the south corner is displayed a statue in gilded bronze about one and half metres high and of outstanding workmanship. It shows a deity with three heads and six arms, seated in *padmāsana* (lotus posture) on a high decorated pedestal. The details of the faces, the headdresses, and the ornaments are particularly delicate. In addition to its artistic qualities, this statue is extremely interesting because of the inscription engraved on the pedestal. This inscription of nine verses is written in Sanskrit and grantha letters and includes a precise dating since it mentions a planetary conjunction in the ninth month of the 4068 year of Kaliyuga (i.e. 968 CE).[18] The first five verses glorify King Kundavarma from the Alupa dynasty who is described, among other compliments, as 'a bee at the lotus feet of the one whose head is adorned with a crescent moon', thus a fervent devotee of Śiva. The last verse tells the reason for this dedication: King Kundavarma is organizing the installation of a statue of Lokeśvara in the *vihāra*[19] whose name is Kadri (*kadarikā nāmni vihāre*). The statue is thus dated and identified. But let us observe that actually the statue is locally described as figuring Brahmā. The inscription is the basis for many subsequent historical speculations.

On the other side of the main sanctuary, in a chapel on the northern side, we see two more bronze statues, equally outstanding and dating probably from the same period but without any inscription. The first, facing east, is known by the name

[18] Saletore gives the precise date of 13 January 968 (1936: 96). This inscription is considered by historians as the most important of the ancient history of Karnataka and is even used as a basis for periodization, Ramesh seeing king Kundavarma as representing the beginning of what he calls 'the medieval Alupas'. See the entire text in *South Indian Inscriptions*, vol. VII, no. 191, given in Saletore (1936: 95), and partially in Nagaraju (s.d.), Ramesh (1970: 97), Bhat (1975: 32-3).

[19] Buddhist establishment: for its original meaning of 'pleasure-ground' and our modern translations as 'monastery', see Gregory Schopen (2006).

of Nārāyaṇa. The god is figured seated in *padmāsana*, with one head and four arms. His rather high headdress has a small seated figure in its centre. The workmanship of the bronze is extremely fine, especially in the decorative details. Facing him is another statue, less adorned but with a high pedestal including three small figures, locally called Vedavyāsa.[20] Its simple and powerful treatment, the position of the two hands, the hair coiled up in small curls, resembles frequent representations of the Buddha. And indeed some of the Mañjunāth pilgrims give this name to the statue.

Still in the main temple but on the back, three huge statues express a completely different context: made of black stone, from another period and style, they take us to the world of the Nāth Yogīs and indicate the strong connection between Kadri-Mañjunāth Temple and this tradition. These statues, devoid of any inscriptions, are said to represent Matsyendranāth, Gorakhnāth and Cauraṅginãth. Matsyendra and Cauraṅgi are seated in *padmāsana*, Gorakhnāth is standing. All three wear large earrings and Gorakhnāth has a *rudrākṣa* necklace. The statues have been hypothetically dated from the fourteenth century (Bhat 1975: 299) and thus represent a successive layer in the occupation of the Mañjunāth Temple, which corresponds to the many legends related to Matsyendra and Gorakhnāth.[21]

[20] Vyāsa or Vedavyāsa, the *ṛṣī* traditionally considered as the author of the *Mahābhārata*.

[21] I did not come across any local mention of or story about Cauraṅginãth, sometimes called Śārṅganāth. Saletore mentions a 1279 CE inscription from Mysore state, which gives the names of eight Nath gurus, Caturaraginātha (Cauraṅginãth) being the second one (Saletore 1937: 18). Cauraṅginãth figures in the third place in many lists of the Nine Nāths (see Dwivedi 1981: 29), but he is absent from the lists given by Briggs. He is mostly known in north India under the name of Pūraṇ Bhagat, as the brother of Rājā Rasālū alias Mannāth, founder of the eponymous *panth* (see Chapter 9). About the importance of Cauraṅginãth or Śāraṅgadhara in south Indian traditions, especially Nāyaka, see Narayana Rao, Schulman and Subrahmaniam (1992: 125-

Based on the Kundavarma inscription and on the style of the gilded bronze statues, some historians see in Kadri an ancient Buddhist site. In addition to the use of the term *vihāra* which applies to Buddhist establishments, the iconography clearly evokes Buddhism: the hand position and the attributes of the two statues known nowadays as Brahmā and Nārāyaṇa are currently those of Avalokiteśvara; Vyāsa has the pose ordinarily associated with Buddha; several small Buddha-like figures can also be seen on the headdress, the nimbus and the pedestal of the three statues. And finally the name Lokeśvara in the Kundavarma inscription is the same as those of the Boddhisattva Avalokiteśvara whose cult spread all over the Mahayanist world from the second century CE. Known as Lord of compassion, one 'who looks down' (*ava-lok*, to look downwards, to observe) and takes care of the people, Avalokiteśvara has been strongly associated with kingship. Thus it is no surprise to see his cult patronized by king Kundavarma.[22]

Another enigma concerns the name of Mañjunāth given to the main deity of the temple, to this black *svayambhū liṅga* kept in the *garbhagṛha*. Mañjunāth, 'the charming Lord' is one of the appellations of the Boddhisattva Mañjuśri (id. 296) whose 'beauty is charming'. He is known in the southern Buddhist schools as the teacher of the Buddhas but is mostly worshipped in Tantric Buddhism, especially in Nepal where he is said to be at the origin of the Kathmandu Valley in making the water covering the valley flow out. 'One attributes him the power to take any form in order to help living beings to attain Salvation' (Frederic 1987: 720), which is however also a quality of Lokeśvara.[23] But in my

---

43), and on his importance in the iconography of the Srisailam Temple, see Linrothe (2006: 99-105).

[22] Concerning the link between Avalokiteśvara and kingship, see a summary in Locke (1980: 410-14). On Avalokiteśvara, de Mallman 1948.

[23] Cf. Locke 1980: 408: 'Two of the most important characteristics of Avalokitesvara were his compassion and his assumption of different forms according to the needs and dispositions of people in various places and various ages, which facilitates his inclusion of different

view Saletore goes a little too far when he presents Mañjunāth as evidently a name of Lokeśvara (1937: 19) and thus draws a link between the two deities in the temple.

Despite these Buddhist parallels, we have seen that the inscription on the pedestal of the Lokeśvara icon tells of Kundavarma as a devotee of the God with the crescent moon, Śiva. This is the main argument of the advocates of the other thesis, the Shaivite Hindu thesis.

An ideological conflict appears to set a first generation of historians, such as Saletore, in favour of a strong Buddhist influence and thus certain to identify the tenth century statue with Avalokiteśvara, against the following generation represented by Bhat and Ramesh who affirm the Hindu character of these icons. 'There appears to have been much exaggeration about the Kadri hill as a Buddhist centre' asserts Bhat (1975: 371). As for Ramesh, he describes the inscription without even giving the term *vihāra* (1970: 97). Mukunda Prabhu, a local historian, remarks that the *yajñopavīta* that crosses the chest of the so-called Lokeśvara has a little ornament that could be the small whistle worn by the Nāth Yogīs,[24] and that the bun is typically Shaivite. Bhat (2000: 14) thinks that the pearls on Nārāyaṇa's *mālā* could be rudrākṣa seeds and that these are clearly visible on the headdress of the Brahmā-Lokeśvara. All these details concur in supporting the thesis that Lokeśvara is just another name for Loknāth, one of the appellations of Śiva. This is the opinon of Ramesh, who adds: 'This identification of Lokeśvara with Śiva is further supported by an inscription of AD 1215 from Mundkuru, Mangalore taluk, which refers to Śiva as Lokeśvara' (1970: 294). Also according to Bhat: 'This image of Lokeśvara is neither Buddhistic or Jaina as contended by scholars but Śaivite, to be identified with Śiva or Matsyendranātha himself in accordance with the philosophy of Nāthism' (1975: 292). However, he is less assertive in the

deities: New deities brought into a Buddhist environment could be accepted as manifestations of Avalokitesvara' (id.)

[24] Such an assertion regarding the tenth century figures is clearly an anachronism.

booklet he wrote about the Kadri-Mañjunāth Temple and even contradicts himself when, after having explained the Buddhist iconographic elements and affirmed that all the places all over the country called Kadari or Kadarika have been Buddhist centres, he maintains that 'unless proved to the contrary, we may tentatively identify Likesvara [*sic*] with Siva or Matsyendranatha himself who had his incarnation in Adinatha according to the mythology of the Natha Pantha' (2000: 19).

Keeping the Hinduistic bias but unable to find any other exemple of the epithet Mañjunāth applied to Śiva, Bhat tries to explain it linguistically: 'It could also be reasoned out that the name Matsyendranātha took the form Macchi(e)ndranātha which, later, got altered into Manjinātha and then into Manjunātha' (Bhat 1975: 296). The *Kadalī Mañjunātha Māhātmyaṁ* goes further, seeing in Mañjunāth 'the ultimate Brahman, Śiva and everything in the universe' (Chap. VI, Nagaraju: 70).[25]

Lokeśvara: A Transitional God

The key to these contradictions is the figure of Lokeśvara. Here Nepalese data can help us, which is not too farfetched since Nagaraju himself notes that 'the image of the tenth century AD has some stylistic features of the Nepalese bronzes' (s.d. 69). I see in Lokeśvara a transitional figure, a pivotal god whose characteristics are suited admirably to a fusion of Buddhism into Shaivism, such as occurred in the Nāth tradition. John Locke, in his work on the cult of Avalokiteśvara-Matsyendranāth in the Kathmandu Valley (1980), describes at length this blurring of

[25] We may add the opinion of Jaini (1980: 90) who sees in Mañjunāth an expression of the Trimurti. He mentions local Kannaḍa legends according to which, after Paraśurāma's penance, 'the members of the divine Trinity, Brahmā, Viṣṇu and Maheśvara, came together and were spontaneously manifested in the form of the Mañjunātha (i.e. the Śivaliṅga)'. And he adds: 'Does this unusual coalescence of the three deities perhaps reflect a confused reference to the three-faced Lokeśvara image ?' Personally I didn't hear this interpretation locally.

religious borders, well illustrated in the following myth (from the Nepalese chronicle known as 'the Buddhist chronicle', written for the English resident D. Wright):

The fourth Buddha was the son of Amitabha. He was named Lokesvara and given the task of creating the world [...] He instructed Siva in *yoga-jnana* which Siva then taught to Parvati one night as they dallied by the sea shore. Parvati fell asleep during the explanation and Lokesvara, in the form of a fish, took the role of listener [...] When he finished, Siva realized that Parvati was asleep and that someone else had actually been listening and responding. He was angry and threatened to curse the interloper until Lokesvara revealed himself. Siva fell at his feet and begged for forgiveness. From this incident Lokesvara became known as Matsyendranatha – 'the Lord of the Fishes'. (Locke 1980: 288-9)

Historically, the study by John Locke shows clearly how the cult of the deity known under the Newar name of Bunga-dyaḥ[26] was introduced by the Mahāyāna Buddhists, probably around the seventh century, then modified under the dominant Vajrayāna influence and finally borrowed by the Hindus at the end of the fourteenth century when the Nāths benefited from royal patronage. The continuity of the Buddhist presence in the Kathmandu Valley explains the present interweaving: the deity is both Lokeśvara and Matsyendranāth; the cult, while mainly Buddhist, includes Nāth elements; and devotees worship the god with the name they like, without bothering about his mixed identity.[27]

[26] As John Locke says (1980: 328): 'The cult of Bunga-dya: was entirely Buddhist from its inception [...] however, it is entirely possible that the cult is the result of a metamorphosis of a local animist god, Bunga-dya: into Avalokiteśvara by Buddhist monks who settled in the area [...] It is equally possible that the cult began with Buddhist monks who settled in Bungamati and propagated the cult of Avalokiteśvara to foster the devotion of the Buddhist laity.'

[27] A remarkable inscription dating from 792 Nepal Samvat (AD 1672) commemorating the gift by the king Srinivas Malla of a golden door and a *toraṇa* [archway] for the temple of the glorious Lokanātha, begins with the following formula: 'Praise to that deity bearing the form of

The situation in Kadri was apparently different. It seems – but we lack documents – that Buddhism left few marks in the region. This is one of the arguments advanced by Ramesh to deny that Lokeśvara belongs to Buddhism: 'It will otherwise be very difficult to explain away the prevalence of Buddhism at Kadri alone and during Kundavarma's reign alone and its absence elsewhere in that region before and after' (1970: 295). He adds: 'The Buddhistic iconographical features in these Kadiri images are to be taken not as evidence for the prevalence of Buddhism in South Kanara but as evidence of the influence of Buddhist iconographical prescriptions on the works of the sculptors who made those images' (id. 294) ... strange to argue for a pervasive Buddhist influence which imposes its norms on artists, without any Buddhist presence!

Looking at these various indications, it is clear that the Kadri *vihāra* represents a turning point and Lokeśvara a liminal deity, able to be linked to successive and different religious groups. Such is also the thesis of Jaini, who deals with the disappearance of Buddhism (and survival of Jainism) and bases part of his argument on the Kadri monastery. Despite some factual uncertainties[28]

---

brahman, whom the Sāktas, best of ascetics, call Matsyendranātha and the Bauddhas Lokeśvara' (Bühler 1880: 192). Locke who does not know this stone slab from Bungamati, quotes its mention in the modern Chronicles according to which 'above the door was a Sanskrit inscription that said that the yogīs call the deity Matsyendra, the Saktas call him Sakti, the Buddhists call him Lokeśvara and his true form is Brahma' (1980: 307). The detailed list given by Locke of all the documents concerning the cult of Lokeśvara-Matsyendranāth shows well how the denominations are juxtaposed. The same fact is made explicit in a poem composed by a Buddhist priest around 1890; he describes first the Matsyendranāth festival then explains 'that the Vaisnavas call [Matsyendranāth] Visnu, the Saivas call him Siva, the Saktas call him Sakti, some call him Bhaskara, the twice-born call him Brahma, the munis call him Matsyendra, the Buddhists call him Lokesvara. Everybody invokes him daily as the merciful (*karunamaya*) Lokesvara' (Locke 1980: 323).

[28] These include a eventual dating of the Kundavarma inscription to

his argument seems convincing and especially that 'the doctrine of the heavenly *bodhisattvas* made Buddhism uniquely vulnerable to the assimilating tendencies of the surrounding Hindu cults' (1980: 88). If, as Vasantha Madhva says (1985: 2-4), Buddhism lost its importance in coastal Karnataka after tenth century, if the Alepa kings protected primarily Shaivism and if Nāth influence was present from the thirteenth century onwards (Saletore 1937), Kadri is clearly a religious centre where Buddhism and Hinduism succeeded one another.

KADRI OR KADALĪ *VAN*: THE PLANTAIN FOREST, THE GODDESS MANGALĀDEVĪ AND THE NĀTH ANCHORAGE

We shall now look at the name Kadri itself and at the Nāth Yogīs, not only through the legends which link Kadri and Mangalore to the traditional Nāth corpus, but also through the inscriptions that allow us to date more precisely their arrival in the local religious landscape.

We have seen the name Kadri first occuring in the 968 inscription: *kadarikā nāmni vihāre* (in the *vihāra* called Kadari). Kadri can be related to *kadalī*, the plantain banana tree, as is made explicit in a 1386 Kadri inscription which refers to 'Kadaliya-Mañjunātha'.[29] We may think that this is just a common appellation for a place planted with banana trees. However Bhat states that 'it may be recalled that all the place-names called Kadari or Kadarika have been Buddhist centres all over the country' (2000: 21) but does not give any source nor justification for this assertion.

However, in the Nāth context the term is quite meaningful. *Kadalī van*, the plantain forest, which is called also *Kadalī rājya*, the plantain kingdom, is no other than the *Strī rājya* or the

1068 CE (Kaliyuga 4168) instead of the currently accepted 968 (Kaliyuga 4068) and the belief in Nāth Yogīs presence at such an early date.

[29] The written forms Kad(a)rī and Kad(a)lī both exists also, the retroflex ḷ being preferred in Kannada.

kingdom of women, a place of pleasure where Matsyendranāth loses himself, according to one of the most popular legends of Nāthism. As shown by David White, *Kadalī van* can be read at different levels (1996: 238) and refers to a place identified with the sensual life (as in the legend of Matsyendranāth), but also [to] a grove of yogīc realization and immortality (1996: 238). White evokes the alchemical metaphor – 'a Forest of Mercuric Sulfide, identified with bodily immortality' as well as 'a land of death and darkness, identified with the failure to attain superhuman goals' (id. 239) — and the bodily association – 'a forest of women's thighs ... [which] can lead to the death of a Yogīn, but can also constitute a "boat to immortality"' (id.). This Kadalī Van has been situated in various locations according to narratives, the most common being Assam (Kamrup) but also Ceylon and, in our context, the Indian Ocean shores, Kerala and Karnataka.

The local account of the episode of the kingdom of women as told by the Kadri Nāth Yogīs has some particularities:[30] it allows the Kadri Nāth monastery to be rooted more deeply in the legendary complex of Mangalore town and to annex the eponymous deity Maṅgaladevī to its tradition, after a few distortions:

The kingdom of women has Piṅgalā Devī[31] for queen. She asks Hanumān to give her a child, a son, by bodily union. Ordinarily, Hanumān was giving children by blowing a sound in the ear of the asking women but she could beget only a daughter. Such is the origin of the *Strī rajyā*, the women's kingdom.[32] Hanumān answers Piṅgalā Devī that he is bound

[30] See various versions of the legend in Grierson (1885), Temple (1885 vol. 2), Dvivedi (1991: 49 and 55), Grodzins Gold (1989 and 1992: 265-301), Digby (2000: 160-80), Muñoz (2010: Chap. III).

[31] The name is usually for the trustful wife of another Nāth hero, the King Bhartrihari. The queen of the women's kingdom is generally known as Kamalā, but the name Piṅgalā allows a phonetic parallel with Maṅgalā. Iṇ Dvivedi, the seductress of Matsyendranāth is even called Maṅgalā from the beginning (1991: 49).

[32] Simon Digby mentions equally the intervention of Hanumān, but with a few differences: 'They say that all the time the Son of the wind

by his vow of *brahmacārya* but that he will send her a yogī as attractive as himself. Later on he persuades Matsyendranāth to experiment the yogīc power to enter into another body[33] and to choose the body of a king in order to unite with Piṅgalā: 'Be the king of this queen and enjoy her with the body of someone else'. Everything happens as wished by Hanumān and Matsyendranāth and Piṅgalā have two children, Nemināth and Parśvanāth.

Gorakhnāth, Matsyendranāth's disciple, discovers the sad situation of his guru, who is forgetting himself in pleasure, and tries to bring him back to his former self. Thanks to the power of his yoga, he takes on the body of a woman, enters the kingdom of women and brings Matsyendranāth back to consciousness by playing on his drum the rhythmic sequence: 'Awake Matsyendra, Gorakh has come'. Matsyendranāth comes back to his true nature and, according to the local variant, starts to leave but accompanied by Piṅgala and their two sons.[34]

Matsyendra and Piṅgalā reach the bank of the Netravati (the Mangalore river on the south) where Gorakhnāth is waiting for them, leaning on his staff as a local statue represents him. Matsyendra declares: 'We both shall be released from the world, what shall we do with Piṅgalā ?' They decide to set her in an auspicious place and transform her into a liṅga, which would be worshipped under the name of Maṅgalā, the auspicious one. Because of that, the stone which is at the heart of Maṅgalādevī temple, has the vague shape of a woman's body.

Matsyendranāth and Gorakhnāth stay in Kadri, meditating. But they regret not having a Śivaliṅga to worship and Matsyendra sends Gorakh

---

Hanumān comes there and makes a noise of thunder. A man when he hears that noise cannot remain alive. The women become pregnant when they hear the noise of the thunder. All their children are girls, never boys' (2000: 161).

[33] *Parakāyapraveśa*, see David White 2009, especially Chapter 4.

[34] The queen's presence is an innovation justifying the episodes which follow. The two sons for their part have an unhappy experience in a Banya house where they are begging and are deprived by Matsyendranāth of their Nāth status, becoming then the two Jain Tirthankaras Nimnāth and Parasnāth! A similar version is reported by Anne Grodzins Gold (1992: 291-6), see also Muñoz (2010: 159-60).

to Kaśi (Varanasi) to obtain one in the holy city. Matsyendra stays in Kadri, where Śiva appears to him and reproaches him for having sent his disciple far away since he, Śiva, is always close to him and that there is a Śivaliṅga in the tank where he bathes every day. Matsyendra then discovers in the tank a liṅga *swayambhū* (self born) and worships it. This liṅga is now at the heart of the Mañjunāth temple. When Gorakh comes back from Kaśi, the liṅga he brought back is set in a small pool close by.[35]

A local scholar, Tuluvite (1966: 41-2), gives a shortened and more 'rational' version of the same story where the Kerala queen is a staunch devotee of Matsyendranāth. The deity is presented as Pārvatī's son who took the shape of a fish. He decides on a pilgrimage, which leads him to Rameshvaran.

Thence he continues his journey from the south to Kerala where one Parimale was reigning as the queen of Kerala. She becomes a disciple of Matsendranatha, in whose honour she puts up a mutt in Kerala. After some time, Gorakhnatha ... invites Matsendranatha and Parimale for a religious exhibition in Nasik. Before starting ... Matsendranatha changed the name of Parimale and called her Mangale. On their way they halted at Bolar in Mangalore. Matsendra requested Mangale to stay on at Bolar until his return ... Mangale employed her time in instructing the local people on the worship of Shiva... She passed her life in doing good to all and finally closed her virtuous and exemplary life in the same place. The people ... put up a small temple in her honour which was subsequently enlarged and embellished by one of the Alupa rajahas who also erected a beautiful statue of Mangale in the temple. In remembrance of Mangale, the temple was named Mangaladevi and the country surrounding it Mangale-uru.

Today the small booklet in English sold at the Maṅgaladevī Temple and grandly titled *Shri Mangaladevi Mahatme and Sthala Puranam*, tells the legend in order to integrate logically the

[35] This liṅga is said to be now in the inner sanctuary of the Mañjunāth Temple of Dharmasthal (70 km from Mangalore). A local Nāth legend explains the Śaiva Nāth presence in this Jain complex.

Goddess, Paraśurām, the Nāth heros and the King Kundavarma in an effort of historico-puraṇic reconstitution:

The text begins with a story inspired by the *Devī Māhātmya* which relates the victories of the Goddess on the demon devotees, blessed rather lightly by the gods, and especially the demon Anda.[36] Then follows the story of Paraśurām, the link between the two passages being provided by a goddess's declaration: 'The spot where I killed Andasura will be the spot that Bhargavarma [i.e. Paraśurām] will choose for his penance' (p. 9). Thus after fighting against the Kṣatriyas, Paraśurām obtains land by threatening Varuṇa and does penance. The goddess Maṅgaladevī appears to him and tells him that he may find a liṅga 'which is the symbol of Shiva Shakti' (p. 13) at the convergence of the rivers Netravati and Phalguni, and that he has a temple made with the help of Viśvakarma. The third episode happens at the time of the king Kundavarma, 'the most famous king of the Alepa dynasty [...] At that time there came two sages named Machhendranatha and Gorakhnatha from Nepal. They reached Mangalapura [...] The place were they crossed the river Nethravathi came to be known as "Gorakdandi"' (p. 14). They settle on the river bank and are greeted by the king Kundavarma who offers them land and patronage. They reveal to the king the antiquity of the place and the former existence of a temple dedicated to Maṅgaladevī. The king has the place dug up and discovers the liṅga symbolizing Maṅgaladevī. He builds a great temple, 'the two sages themselves guided and supervised the execution of the work'. (p. 15)[37]

[36] Andāsura, a local variant of Andhakāsura, who in the classical puranic mythology is rather chastized by Śiva. He is not mentioned in the *Devī Māhātmya* and the Mangalore booklet makes a synthesis of disparate elements, which is now replicated on all the websites linked to Mangalore town.

[37] On each side of the temple gate two panels illustrate the legend. On the first is written in English and Kannada: 'Lingaroopa of Srimangaladevi who appeared before Parashurama who seeked the blessing of Lord Shiva', and on the second: 'Kundavarma-King of Tulunadu worshipping the renovated goddess Sri-mangaladevi according to the blessings of Sri Machendranatha & Gorakhshanatha'. Paraśurām is depicted on the seashore, his axe thrown on the ground

We see that, whatever the narratives, they all attest to a strong relationship between the Nāth Yogīs and the eponymous goddess of Mangalore. The Nāth traditions see in Maṅgaladevī the queen of the kingdom of women. The traditions coming from the Brahman priests of the temple see in her a form of Durgā but they acknowledge the Nāth connection, their main problem being to make legend and history coincide. The name Mangalapura predates clearly both Kundavarma (tenth century) and the Nāths. As Bhat says (1975: 302): 'The name of Mangalapura occurs in the 7th century AD in a Tamil epigraph'. He adds: 'based on an examination of the sculpture of Devī installed in the temple of Maṅgalādevī and also the representation of Gaṇeśa in the sub shrine of the same temple, we have sufficient ground to believe that the temple must have existed in the 7th or 8th century AD'. He sees in the 'beautiful statue' (according to Tuluvite) an icon of the goddess in *padmāsana*. The paintings of the Maṅgaladevī temple are closer to the present effigy (at least when it is not adorned, see the pictures in Bhat 1975: 137c): a rounded black stone, a *linga* vaguely feminized by two bulges.

HISTORICAL HYPOTHESIS

Can we see behind these changing and contrasting religious affiliations a change in society? The conjunction of religious vagueness, of blurred and uncertain appellations and identities of the gods, with the myth of Paraśurām is significant. Is not the myth of Paraśurām, the Brahman warrior who has repeatedly to ride the world of the excesses of the Kṣatriyas, irrespectuous of Brahmans' superiority, a metaphor of a recurring fight against those who opposed the Brahmanic orthodoxy, i.e. the Buddhists and the Jains?

Close to this perpective, Verardi (1996: 234) describes the

and dressed like a Śaiva ascetic. He worships a black rock surrounded by radiant rays, at the same time Śivaliṅga and idol of Maṅgaladevī: Mañjunāth is not mentioned and the legend is thus modified in a sense which infuriates the Yogīs.

violent confrontations between Brahmanism and Buddhism and shows that 'the Buddhist buildings in Deccan that were replaced by Shivaite temples are numerous' (he mentions Kadri-Mañjunātha in a note) and that Shivaism, which was the interpreter of the Brahmanic *revanche*, will later be metabolized by Vishnuism, destined – thanks to its upper hand in the Deccan – to become the winning ideology of Brahmanism in the whole of India (ibid.). In this context,

> once again it is a myth that helps us in understanding past events. In the *Mahābhārata*, the mirror of Vishnuite neo-orthodoxy, Rāma is depicted as repeatedly slaying the Kshatriyas. He does so a good twenty-one times... The insistence on the struggle against the Kshatriyas in the late-ancient and medieval sources show that it did not take place in an indistinct period projected into a little known past. Besides, Rāma is the characteristic hero and avatār of the region in which the clash between the Brahmans and Kshatriyas was paradigmatic, tougher and more protacted in time: eastern Uttar Pradesh and Bihar. (Verardi 1996: 236-7)

Could we read a similar history in Karnataka ? Could we draw a parallel between the effective presence of a Buddhist place and the mythic presence of Paraśurām, such as the one noted again by Verardi for Bhubanesvara: 'One of the most ancient temples dedicated to Paraśurāmeśvara is the one at Bhuvanesvara, a place that had been controlled by the Jains and Buddhists for a long time' (id. 237)?

This thesis has to remain conjectural in the absence of any document allowing us to date the beginning of the Paraśurām cult. Bhat (1975: 334 and 373-6) assumes that this cult developed under the influence of the Dvaita Vedānta philosopher born in Udupi (Karnataka), Mādhvācharya (1238-1317), who is credited with the boom of Vaishnavism in the area. Further, Bhat remarks that the *Sahyādri-Khaṇḍa*, the foundation narrative, which is referred to and quoted by the Brahmins and in which the story of the creation of this land by Paraśurāma is mentioned, is [...] not more than 300 years old (1975: 334). Undubitably between the fourteenth and the seventeenth centuries the influence of the Mādhva Brahmans grew to the extent of creating a violent conflict with the Nāths of Kadri. According to their tradition (but without any formal proof), the Mādhva succeeded in appropriating the Mañjunāth temple at the end of the seventeenth century and took away financial control of it from the Nāths (with a few ritual accommodations).

In this complex religious landscape, we also have to take into account the importance of the Śaiva sects and particularly of the Kālāmukhas. As the study by David Lorenzen (1972) has shown, many inscriptions concerning the Kālāmukhas come from Karnataka. It seems that between the eleventh and thirteenth centuries the Kālāmukhas received many donations from ruling powers, especially in the Mysore region. The inscriptions present them as Brahmans keen to study the Vedas as well as to practise yoga. More orthodox than the Kāpālikas, they seem particularly fit for a takeover of Buddhist or Jain domains by the Brahmans (if it ever happened). No trace of their presence is to be seen in Mangalore but we may imagine that they played an important role in the history of the Nāthism in the area. This is attested by an inscription dated 1030 CE found in Mysore State (Nelamangala taluk) and studied attentively by Saletore. The text associates a Kālāmukha priest and a series of gurus whose names end in nāth(a). It commemorates the erection of a Siddheśvara Temple by the Chief Minister Vāmanyaya on the occasion of the death of his guru Maunināth (who is also at the beginning of the record called Mauni Bhaṭṭāraka). He entrusted the temple to the charge of Rupaśiva.

The text gives the spiritual genealogy of Vāmanyaya: 'At the root of big sacred tree in Candrapuri, situated by the Western Ocean,[38] was stationed Ādinātha [...] His disciple [...]

[38] Saletore adds in footnote that Candrapuri said to have been situated on the shore of the western ocean, cannot be identified and he proposes some eventual localizations without deciding. Bhat astonishingly localizes the inscription itself in Candrapuri (which is mentioned only as the dwelling place of Ādināth) then identifies Candrapuri with Chadāvara from Honnavara taluk (North Kanara),

was Chāyādhinātha [...] An intoxicated bee at his lotus feet was Dvīpanātha, the world renowned. His disciple, invicible by other disputants, was Mauninātha, in the form of Rudra' (Saletore 1937: 20-1).

What is striking in this inscription is that among the four gurus whose names end in nāth(a), and who are given as the spiritual genealogy of Maunināth, only Adināth belongs to the Nāth canonical list. No mention is made of the celebrated gurus of the sect: Matsyendra and Gorakh. It is thus rather difficult to link this inscription with the Nāth Yogīs, as clearly as Bhat seems to think (1975: 293), all the more so at such a remote time (1030 CE). I would rather agree with David White in seeing in these 'Nāths' who worship Śiva Siddheśvara one of the numerous Śaiva movements which he groups together under the name of 'Siddha tradition'. The Kālāmukhas mentioned as experts in magical powers (*siddhis*)[39] were part of this tradition as well as the Tantric *kula* school about which White tells an anecdote which resonates with the Kadri context:

> According to the *Kubjikānityāhnikatilaka*, one of the canonical texts of the western transmission of the Tantric schools, we are told that Śrīnātha [another name for Ādināth] – with the aid of three Siddhas named Sun, Moon, and Fire – founded the Tantric *kula* tradition at a site called Candrapurī, located in Koṅkana, in coastal western India. The original core of this new *kula*, the text continues, was composed of nine Nāths who, originally Buddhist monks, had converted when, through a miracle produced by Śrīnātha, the roof of their monastery had collapsed! (White 1996: 73-4).

One may think that Buddhism was followed by an intermediate

---

without explaining why, and finally concludes rather lightly: 'This epigraph clearly testifies to the fact that the Nātha-Pantha was strongly rooted in Chandāvara in the eleventh century AD' (1975: 293).

[39] See Lorenzen regarding the special powers of the famous master Bonteyamuni (inscription of Hombal in Dharwar district dated 1189 CE) or those of Bhujanga, ācārya from Bijapur (inscription of 1074-5 CE, Lorenzen 1972: 131 and 156).

stage during which Tantric Śaiva and Śakta sects flourished, some of them fusing later in the Nāth Yogī tradition.

The first inscription in Karnataka that relates undoubtedly to the Nāth Yogī movement dates from 1279 CE (Saletore 1937: 18-19). It was found near the Kalleśvara Temple in Mysore State and attests to the gift of a village by a general of the king Hemmaḍi Deva to a Yogī, whose spiritual lineage includes eight Nāth gurus; among them are mentioned the names of Ādināth, Cauraṅgināth and Gorakhnāth (plus a Lonanāth assimilated by Saletore to Lokanāth in seventh place). Other inscriptions follow (see Bhat 1975: 293-4), and in one inscription of 1372 CE in the Koteśvara Temple of Barakuru,[40] the donors are Nāths (Bhat 1975: 294).

What about Kadri? The oldest document found in the monastery consists of two small copper plates dated 1251 of the Śaka era (1329 CE): on one is mentioned 'Kadire Mañjunātheśvara' and on the other 'Basali Kadre Śrī Mañjunāth'.[41] The next is the one already mentioned, dated 1386 CE referring to Kadaliya-Mañjunātha (Bhat 1975: 292, *S.I.I.* vol. 7, no. 189). The link between the Mañjunāth Temple and Kadri monastery is there established but not explicitly the one with the Nāth Yogīs.

The most ancient inscription referring explicitly to the Nāth Yogīs' dominance over Kadri is on a slabstone, still in the monastery today. It is dated 1397 Śaka era (i.e. 1475 CE) and records the land donation to Maṅgalnāth Oḍeya, disciple of

[40] A coastal town and a provincal centre 10 km north of Udupi (thus 65 km from Mangalore). According to several inscriptions related to Barakuru, it seems that it was an important Śaiva then Nāth location (see Bhat 1975: 293-4 who specifies that there was even a temple dedicated to Hiṅg Laj or Hiṅguladevī, a Devī and Nāth pilgrimage place on the Makran coast).

[41] This is according to late Ānandanath Jogi, member of the Jogī community of Mangalore, secretary of one of their associations and historian of the monastery; he published a small book in Kannada in 2003 (the title trancribed in English on the first page is '*Nāthapanthakshetra Jogimatha*') which he explained to me very patiently. His help has been immeasurable. The photo of the two plates is on the back cover.

Candranāth Oḍeya, *arasu*[42] of Kadariya, by the ruling mahārājā of Barakuru, Viṭharasa Oḍeya[43] for the welfare of his family. It is stipulated that the revenues are to finance offerings of food and light.[44]

Two other slabstones are to be found in the monastery but their poor condition allows only a few words to be deciphered. Both register a land donation by Vira Pratapa Vijaya Bhupati Maharaya, the Śaka year being 1345 (1423 CE).[45]

More interesting is the mention in a 1490 CE Barakuru inscription of the following incident: 'When Subhuddhinātha-Oḍeya, disciple of Anupamanāth-Oḍeya was being taken to Kadre, perhaps for the *paṭṭa* (chiefship) or pontificate of that place (*arasutanada paṭṭakke*), he was deterred from going by the five chiefs of Chauliya-keri and a gift of land was made to the *maṭha* of Anupamanāth-Oḍeya for the worship of Gorakhnātha' (Bhat 1975: 294).[46] Is this the first allusion to the very peculiar Ḳadri enthronement ceremony where the monastery head to be is brought from outside following a long journey ?

In sum we may note the importance of Kadri as a regional religious centre, one that was from early times linked to the Nāth Yogī tradition. Karnataka appears as a crucial place for

[42] *Arasu* designates the king in Ṭulu language, we see then the title already given to the head of the monastery.

[43] An important ruler during the Vijayanagar domination, Vitharasa was the governor of both the provinces of coastal Karnataka, Barakuru and Mangaluru-rajya, a joint governorship which was quite exceptional. He is mentioned in a few inscriptions between 1465 and 1477 (see Ramesh 1970: 180-3).

[44] According to Ānandanāth Jogi (2003: 21). The inscription (see *SII*, vol. VII, no. 194) figures also in Bhat (1975: 293).

[45] Ānandanāth Jogi (2003: 20-1). Inscription mentioned also by Ramesh (1970: 166): Vijayarāya would have ruled over Mangalore province for five years.

[46] According to the Annual Report of South Indian Epigraphy, 1931-2, no. 269.

the propagation of the *sampradāya* whose main centres were commonly considered north Indian.[47]

A sign of the entrenchment of an ancient yogic tradition in Karnataka and especially in Ṭulu region can be seen in the few *bhūtās*, these local heroic deities, who bear the name of Jogī Puruṣa. They are represented by wooden statues of standing or seated figures with huge earrings, matted hair and a *rudrakṣa* necklace.[48] Even though it is quite impossible to date these figures, their integration into the local pantheon testify to the Yogīs' long and pervasive presence.[49]

The Maṅgaladevī myth reveals how the Nāth Yogīs have succeeded in including a locally celebrated goddess in their own universe. They gave Maṅgaladevī a place in the legendary corpus which is constitutive of the Nāth identity, the story of

[47] Perhaps Kadri is the southern most centre? I have never come across Nāth Yogīs current centres in Tamilnadu and none is mentioned in the list established by the Yogī Mahāsabhā. Regarding Kerala, R. Freeman (2006) mentions a caste of householder Yogīs or Coyis which he relates to the Jogī caste of Karnataka.

[48] See the pictures in Bhat 1975: plates 324b and 326d.

[49] See the articles of the volume *Coastal Karnataka* (ed. U.P. Upadhyaya, 1996) dealing essentially with the Bhūtā cult, particularly the article by Chinnappa Gowda who writes: 'It is accepted that the *Naatha Pantha* has influenced the Bhuta worship of Tulunadu. There are traces of *Naatha* traditions in the costumes, weapons, ornaments, and the convention of offerings to *Puruṣa* spirit' (1996: 277). Another proof is to be seen in the dance drama of the ethnic group Gauda entitled *Siddaveeṣa*: the main character is called Sannyāsī but he is rather a Yogī. According to Bilimale (1996: 286), '*Siddaveeṣa Sanyaasi*'s external detail of dress, movements, style of talk and his caste of character as such [...] resemble the medieval Karnataka's most popular *Paaśupata Sanyaasis* of *Lakuliiśsa* tradition.' After a study of the songs and of the tradition *Naathasiddha* [i.e. Nāth Yogī], the author concludes: 'We perceive that *Naathasiddha* and *Laakula śaiva* traditions meet in the *Siddaveeṣa* performance [...]. What is preserved in the so-called 'folklore' of the Gaudas sheds light on the secrets of medieval leftist sects (*Taantrika pantha*) of Karnataka' (id. 290).

Matsyendranāth and the kingdom of women. The goddess and her territory have been incorporated into the Nāth world and, still today, even if the link with the Nāth Yogīs is not acknowledged explicitly by everybody, the idea that Matsyendranāth and Gorakhnāth 'rediscovered' the goddess is quite common among Mangaloreans.

However, the rereading by the Nāth of Paraśurām's story is less well known outside the sect. By this alternative version where the Viṣṇu's *avatār* submits to Gorakhnāth's advice , the Nāth Yogīs try to claim Nāth superiority over the Vishnuites (and the Mādhva priests of Mañjunāth) and to change the course of history during which they were led to lose their control over the Mañjunāth Temple and to limit themselves to their monastery. Their ritual performances, the pilgrimage and the coronation of the *rājā* every twelve years enact a symbolic process of territorial reconquest of their lost supremacy.

THE KADRI MONASTERY IN MODERN TIMES

Since we have very little ancient evidence concerning the Kadri monastery, the report given by the Italian traveller Pietro Della Valle in 1622 is very precious. His testimony shows clearly that the Mañjunāth Temple was at this time part of the monastery, included in the vast compound over which ruled 'the king of the Gioghis'. Again the mention of this royal title we already found in the 1475 CE inscription under the Ṭulu form *arasu* resonates with the modern appellation of *rājā* given to the head of Kadri and only to him.

> On December the eleventh [1623] I went in the morning about half a league from Mangalor to see the Hermitage, where lives and reigns the *Archimandrita* of the Indian *Gioghi*, whom the *Portugals* (usually liberal of the royal title) style 'King of the Gioghi' perhaps because the Indians term him so in their language; and in effect he is Lord of a little circuit of land, wherein, besides the hermitage and the habitations of the Gioghi, are some few houses of the country people and a few very small villages subject to his government [...]
>
> On the edge of the plain, where the ascent of the hill begins, is a

great cistern, or lake, from which ascending a flight of stairs, [...] you enter into a gate, which has a covered porch, and is the first of the whole enclosure, which is surrounded with a wall and a ditch like a fort. Having entered the said gate, and going straight forward through a handsome broad walk, beset on either side with sundry fruit trees, you come to another gate, where there are stairs and a porch higher than the former. This opens to a square piazza, or great court, in the middle whereof stands a Temple of indifferent greatness, and for architecture like the other Temples of the Indian Gentiles [...] also in two, or three, places of the court, there are little square chappels for other idols [...] The gate of the Temple looks eastward, where the hill begins to rise very high and steep. From the front of the Temple to the top of the hill are long and broad stairs of the same black stone, which lead up to it, and there the place is afterwards plain [...] The Temple [...] walls were covered with large plates of brass; but that Venk-tapa Naieka carryed the same away [...] This temple is dedicated to an Idol called *Moginato* [...]

Having viewed the Temple, I ascended the hill by the stairs [...] and came to the habitations of the *Gioghi* and their King; the place is plain, planted with many trees [...] There are an infinite number of little square chappels with several idols in them and some places covered over head, but open round about, for the *Gioghi* to entertain themselves in. And, lastly, there is the King's house, which is very low built. I saw nothing of it, (and believe it is nothing more) but a small porch, with walls round about, coloured with red and painted with Elephants and other animals, besides in one place a wooden thing like a small square bed, somewhat raised from the ground, and covered with a cloth like a tent; they told me it was the place where the King used to reside and perhaps also to sleep.

I believe it was built by the king of the *Banghel* whilst they flourished, for it lies in their territory, and that the place and the seigniory thereof was given by them to the *Gioghi*; and as they had no wives, the dominion of this hermitage and the adjacent land goes not by inheritance but by elective succession.

I thought to find abundance of *Gioghi* here, as in our Convents, but I saw not above one, or two; and they told me they resort not together, but remain dispersed here and there as they list, or abide in several places in the Temples where they please, nor are subject to their King in point of obedience as ours are to their Superior, but only do him reverence and honours; and at certain solemn times great numbers of them assemble here, to whom during their stay the King supplies victuals. In the hermitage live many servants of his and labourers of the earth, who till these lands, whereby he gets provisions. They tell me that what he possesses within and without the hermitage yields him about five or six thousand Pagods yearly, the greatest part whereof he expends in feasts and the rest in diet, and in what is needful for the ordinary service of the Temple and his idols: and that Venk-tapa Naieka had not yet taken tribute of him but it was feared he would thereafter.

At length I went to see the King of the *Gioghi*, and found him employed in his business after a mean sort, like a peasant or villager. He was an old man with a long white beard, but strong and lusty; in either ear hung two balls, which seemed to be of gold, I know not whether empty, or full, about the bigness of a musket bullet; the holes is his ears were large, and the lobes much stretched by the weight; on his head he has a little red bonnet [...] From the girdle upwards he was naked, only he had a piece of cotton wrought with lozenges of several colours across his shoulders; he was not very dark, and, for an Indian of colour, rather white than otherwise. He seemed a man of judgement, but upon trial in sundry things I found him not learned.

He told me that formerly he had horses, elephants, palanchinos, and a great equipage and power before Venk-tapa Naieka took away all from him, so that now he has very little left. That within twenty days after there was to be a great feast in that place, to which many Gioghi would repair from several parts [...]

At my going I was told [...] that the hermitage and all the adjacent place is called Cadira.[50]

This description, while it attests to the former importance of Kadri monastery, attests also to its dilapidated state following local conflicts. As supposed by Della Valle, the monastery was patronized and the land donated, as was usual with the Yogi monasteries, by the local rulers, the rājās of Banghel or Baṅga, who 'were the most powerful and influential of all the chiefs of the district of South Kanara. By diplomacy, war and matrimonial alliances they extended their sway over the whole of present

[50] English translation by Edward Grey for the Hakluyt Society, 1892, pp. 345-52.

Puttur taluk and parts of the Mangalore taluk' (Bhat 1975: 66). They were defeated by Venkaṭṭapa Nāyaka, allied to the queen of Ullala. Venkaṭṭapa Nāyaka (1586-1629) from the Keḷadi dynasty was very powerful. He was considered a protector of the Liṅgayat Viraśaiva tradition, perhaps at the expense of other religious traditions. We may suppose that if the Kadri monastery was protected by the vanquished Baṅga dynasty, its defeat entailed unhappy consequences for the *maṭh*.

Della Valle's description is still very accurate: even though the murals which surrounded the huge domain of the temple-monastery complex have disappeared, and the separation between the Mañjunāth Temple and the Kadri monastery is manifested physically by the separate entrances, the general topography of the place is still visible. From the temple one may still take the flight of stairs ascending the hill and reach the 'the habitations of the Gioghis and of their king'. One discovers there the same general arrangement of the buildings on the top of the hill with platforms, chapels, and 'the King's house' of which Della Valle says he 'saw nothing', describing however what is probably the throne. The layout does not seem very different, although these buildings have been renovated, cemented and painted anew for the ceremony of the last king's coronation.

The hill is a large forested area, cut on the eastern side by a public park recently purchased by Mangalore town from the monastery. The remaining 'jungle' contains a impressive number of small tumuli or stone heaps, the graves or *samādhis* of the Yogīs, that surround the sanctuaries as it is often the case in the Shaivite monasteries. Here the *samādhis,* half buried in the ground and so numerous, suggest an impression of great antiquity and holiness. This impression is reinforced when one discovers, behind a more formal old cemetery, the entrance to a subterranean rock sanctuary, locally called the Pāṇḍav *guphā.*[51] Its style and the local tradition may allow it to be dated

[51] This cave evokes the numerous caves discovered in Tamil lands. Decorated with inscriptions they were places of retreat for ascetics during the rainy season. Unfortunately there is no such inscription in

to the fourteenth century. The Yogīs still use it for meditation. This 'jungly' area contains a few other remarkable spots: a stone platform where Mastyendranāth was supposed to sit to look at the sunset and a small shrine containing the altar of the Mallarāya *bhūtā*. This Tuḷu deity is linked to the territory, worshipped by priests of low status (Billava toddy-tappers), but his cult is patronized by the monastery's *rājā*. Down the hill on the eastern side, a pool called Chilimbi *kuṇḍ* is overlooked by a small temple to Pātāl Kāl Bhairav ('Infernal Black Bhairav').

The *maṭh* proper is surrounded by an old brick enclosure with two entrances: the old one from the Mañjunāth Temple, is now surmounted by a new statue of Paraśurām. The new entrance has been created on the opposite side and is accessible by cars. Let us take the old entrance. In front of us a cobbled path is lined on the left side with a large platform where the Yogis could easily camp and on the right side by small chapels. The first two look very old: called Rām and Lakṣmaṇ's caves, they include underground stairs supposed to lead to the Paṇḍav *guphā*. Three more recent shrines are dedicated to Cauraṅgināth, Matsyendranāth and Gorakhnāth, represented by modern statues in black marble. Matsyendranāth's statue replaces an old one now in the Mangalore museum (dated the tenth century) where Matsyendranāth is represented seated in *padmāsana* on a fish and wearing all the attributes of the Nāth ascetic, the earrings, the cord with the whistle, the *rudrakṣa mālā*, the begging bag, and the meditation staff. Gorakhnāth's statue shows him standing, the chin resting on a staff in the attitude

---

Kadri. Why such a name from *Mahābharata*, the cave of the Pāṇḍava? The legend says that they hid here from the Kaurava. It is a common feature all over India to give names taken from the epics or the *Purāṇas* in order to sacralize the local geography, to multiply the connections and to make from every sacred place an image and a part of the whole. 'Sitā's well' farther along the same hill or the the caves of Rām and Lakṣmaṇ in the monastic compound partake of the same logic.

that the legend says he took on the bank of the Netravati at the place called Gorakhdaṇḍ.[52]

One sees also a few tombs built like small shrines with a *śivaliṅga*. Often in the Nāth monasteries these well-constructed and impressive *samādhis* shelter the remains of former deceased superiors, but the situation is different in Kadri, as well as in other *pañcāyatī maṭhs*, since the head has a temporary mandate; but it may happen that a *rājā* dies before the end of his term, or chooses to be buried alive in deep meditation, like Jwalanāth here in the 1870s.[53]

Following the path, one enters the monastery buildings. They constitute two close but separate compounds: the western part for the *rājā* and the eastern for the temples, each part made of a courtyard surrounded by galleries.

The temples in the eastern part are situated in the middle of the courtyard whose gallery was till 2001 traditionally made of bricks and covered by tiles. An unfortunate renovation has plastered the walls with cement, flattened the roofs, and built a pink pyramid on top of the sanctuaries. These sanctuaries, two square adjacent rooms, are dedicated to Kāl Bhairav represented by a black marble statue, and Jwālā Māyā Māī, by a small white statue. Facing the Devī's shrine is the *dhūnī*, the ascetic fire said to have been lit by Paraśurām; its clean rebuilding in coloured marble makes it difficult to perceive its great antiquity ! The platform in front of the temples has also been recently refitted to accommodate the crowd of the Yogīs and devotees, and the *nagārā* drum players for times of *pūjās*. There is also another small chapel with a *śivaliṅga* surrounded by three statues of the goddesses Durgā, Candragutti and Mātaṅgī.

[52] He could be close to Lakulīśa, the ascetic with a club, the founder of the Pāśupatas but his attitude is different, Lakulīśa being most often depicted 'seated in the *padmāsana*, with his penis erect, and with a citron in his right hand and a club (*daṇḍa*) in his left' (Lorenzen 1972: 177).

[53] They are said to take a 'living *samādhi*' (*jivit samādhi*, see Vilāsnāth 2005: 622-3).

A shrine devoted to Bhairav is a common feature of Nāth temples where usually the triad of Gorakhnāth, Bhairav and the Devī are worshipped. However in Kadri Bhairav is given pre-eminence, his shrine is the main ritual place and Gorakhnāth seems conspicuously absent, only represented in a cryptic way by the holy vessel, the *pātradevatā* which remains hidden in a small cupboard between one procession and the next. Is this central importance given to Bhairav a trace of the former influence of the Kāpālikas? I don't know.

A short passage leads from the temple courtyard to the Yogīs' courtyard. In the middle of the passage is the altar of the *bhūtā* Jumādi; it is noteworthy to find at the core of this Nāth sanctuary the figure of this Ṭulu deity, well-known for ensuring soil fertility. However, the Nāths foreign to Karnataka call her Dhūmavātī[54] and, as Jumādi is a *bhūtā* half male and half female, they see here also an image of Śiva/Śaktī. Jumādi is depicted like many *bhūtās* by a round golden mask, resembling a sun with a large mouth, and set on a wooden swing, flanked by two long swords. These local *bhūtās*, regularly worshipped in the *maṭh*, tend to be associated with pan-Hindu deities or considered as the escort of Śiva, who guides them, being Bhūtānāth or Lord of the *Bhūtās*.

The Yogis' courtyard is surrounded by a gallery in which has been recently set a white marble throne, a *siṃhāsan*, for the *rājā* to sit on. In his absence a coconut signifies his perpetual presence. Onto the gallery open the private apartments of the *rājā*, the kitchen and two rooms, for the only permanent residents in the *maṭh* with the *rājā*, the *pujārī* and the caretaker.

THE MONASTIC STRUCTURE

As Delle Valle aptly remarked, in normal time the monastery is quite calm and the ascetics very few. Ultimately only the head

[54] In Tantrism one of the ten Mahāvidyā, form of the Goddess as Supreme Knowledge: the one 'who makes smoke', dark deity also called Kālārātrī, Dark Night, Night of Death which symbolizes the obscure

and the officiating priest are requested to stay permanently. Delle Valle was quite surprised ('I thought to find abundance of *Gioghi*, as in our convents'), as we may be since we know that Kadri is the most important Nāth establishment for south India.

This situation gives clear evidence of the nature of Hindu monasticism. Monasteries are not considered as permanent residences except for the ascetics who have managerial or ritual duties. The other ascetics roam freely and are not subject to any kind of control or formal discipline, they may come and go at will or according to the indications of their guru but they are not dependent on a monastery head. Here again Della Valle is quite correct when he writes: 'Nor are [they] subject to their king in point of obedience as ours are to their Superiors, but only do him reverence and honour' (1892: 350). And the only duty of the chief of any monastery, regarding his fellow ascetics, is to provide them with food and shelter for three days, and to give them what they need for their journey to their next stop. However, these monastic leaders, *mahant*, *pīr*, or *rājā*, can also initiate disciples, who then come more frequently and regularly and may eventually stay with their guru. They consider the monastery as 'theirs' and give its name when they are obliged to register, since the State asks for a fixed address to give an identity card. But that does not oblige them to remain there all the time. This informal situation explains why monasteries most often seem empty of ascetics and why festivals are so important. They are the time and place of gathering for the ascetics of the whole community, meeting places where the idea of belonging makes sense. This cyclical rhythm offers such a stunning contrast between the ordinary appearance of a monastery, which looks half deserted, and festival time, when huge crowds of ascetics and lay devotees reveal its true importance. Kadri *maṭh* which, by its location, stands apart from the most common pilgrimage routes of the Yogīs, is usually absolutely quiet, reduced to the close companions of the *rājā*, himself a foreigner to the place.

---

forces of the Creation. However she has been explained to me in the *maṭh* as a form of Piṅgalā/Maṅgalā Devī!

But as we shall see, every twelve years the *maṭh* is the set for a huge ritual performance that attracts hundreds of people and constitutes a foundational event for the Nāth *sampradāya.* It is difficult to imagine how sudden and drastic is the change: in a couple of hours hundreds of *sādhus* and visitors sweep into the monastery, town and district authorities show off, various committees take to organizing activities and loudspeakers resound with devotional music or advertisements, often both together.... But already the next day after the *rājā's* enthronment, the monastery is back to its former solitude and tranquillity.

CHAPTER 5

Kadri *Rājā's* Enthronement

Kadri monastery is the southernmost establishment of the Nāth *sampradāya* and for the sect's authorities it represents a main administrative centre, the seat of the south provincial assembly. But its past importance far exceeds this organizational position. As we have seen, Kadri's history goes back to the beginning of Nāth Yogīs' establishment, to the many changes that allowed the *sampradāya* to emerge from the many locally attested Śaiva currents. However, beyond its multi-layered nature made up of conflicting legends and historical testimonies, the present monastery's paramount importance for the sect also lies in the complex process by which its head is selected. As we shall see, this process involves all the components of Nāth identity, and its performance gives the sect a particular cohesiveness.

In accordance with the title of *rājā* given to the head of the Kadri monastery, and only to him, the nomination and coronation processes appear also rather unusual. They combine three models whose elements take precedence alternatively: the model of royal consecration codified in well known ritual treatises; the model of Nāth consecration, which applies to other monastic heads, *mahants* or *pīrs*; and the local model for which Kadri inherits a long history rooted in the Paraśurām legend.

The specificity of the *rājā's* coronation is also based on its rare but regular performance every twelve years since it is done in concordance with the Nasik Kumbh Melā, during which the selection of the new *rājā* is made, followed by a six-month-long pilgrimage to Kadri, to perfom the enthronement rituals on the day of Śivarātrī.

SIṀHASTHA KUMBH MELĀ: TRYAMBAKESHVAR

Counted as one of the four huge gatherings of ascetics and devotees known as Kumbh Melā,[1] the Nasik Melā on the bank of the river Godavari takes its name, Siṁhastha Melā, from the conjunction of the Sun and Jupiter in the zodiacal sign of Leo (Siṁha), usually at the beginning of August. The pilgrimage is made at the two places of Nasik and Tryambakeshvar, which is 30 km from Nasik at the source of the river, at the very spot where, according to one version of the legend, Śiva made the divine Gaṅgā, under the name of Godāvārī, flow down to allow the sage Gautama to cleanse himself of the murder of a cow. The water gushed forth where there is now the Gaṅgādvāra Tirtha. And Śiva promised Gautama to stay there always as a *liṅga svayambhū* – one of the twelve *jyotirliṅgas*, *liṅgas* of light, which map the sacred geography of Shaivism. The vast temple of Tryambakeshvar, which contains the *jyotirliṅga*, is thus dedicated to Śiva as 'the three-eyed Lord' (*tri-ambaka-iśvara, ambaka* referring to Śiva's eye).

Among the other sanctuaries of Tryambakeshvar (notably one dedicated to Paraśurām) is the Gorakhnāth Akhāṛā. Briggs visited it in 1924 and described it as 'roomy but unsubstantially built. On the large, stone platform, which faces the monastery, is a huge, three-sectioned stone, painted red and representing Bhāiroṁ' (1973: 121). The place 'possesses some fields and considerable grass land. The resident monk claimed that the land was granted to the monastery by "the Peshwa"' (id.). The pattern of residence reported by Briggs agrees with what we know of monastic life: 'three or four Āughars, one Kānphaṭa, Narbadnāth, and a wandering Rāwal' (id.), the Āughars being probably the disciples of the only resident ascetic, who is surely the head.

The monastery today looks new and not very impressive. But every twelve years it becomes the core of the Nāth *sampradāya*.

[1] On the construction of the tradition of the four Kumbh Melās, see the ground-breaking study by Kama Maclean 2008.

All the Yogīs have to gather there and celebrate a succession of rituals, which parallel the Kumbh Melā ceremonies. And for them the Nasik Kumbh Melā is, together with Haridwar Melā, the most important of their periodic meetings.

The link between Tryambakeshvar and the Nāth Yogīs is well established. Even the Nasik town website alludes to the sacrality of Tryambakeshvar as 'a place of the first Nāths of the Nāth *sampradāya* consisting of Gorakhnāth and others' and describes 'a place where Nivrittināth was made to imbibe his holy knowledge by his guru Gahinināth', thus enrolling the place in the sacred landscape of Maharashtra and linking it to the medieval Sant tradition with their Nāth affiliation.[2]

However, for the Nāth Yogīs, Tryambakeshvar's pre-eminence is due first of all to its place in Gorakhnāth's legends and its link with Kadri Maṭh's legendary corpus.

According to the Nāth tradition in Kadri,[3] after establishing the nine Nāths and eighty-four Siddhas, Gorakhnāth went to the Mount Kaulāgarh in Tryambakeshvar, 'at the middle of the earth', and sat on the *anupān śilā*, the *anupān* rock,[4] to give his teachings. It is there that Paraśurām went to ask for his help, as we have already seen. At the time of Kumbh Melā, all the Nāths and Siddhas gathered on this spot to hear their master's words, but could not find him. Gorakhnāth was not on the *anupān śilā*. They meditated and thanks to their inner vision,

[2] Since Jñāneśvara or Jñāndev (1275-96), the famous Marathi poet of the Krishnaite bhakti, 'claims Nivrittināth as his guru and Gahanindruāth as his grand-guru' (Vaudeville 1987b: 218) and 'traces his spiritual lineage to Adināth, followed by Matsyendranāth' (id.).

[3] I translate and summarize here the legend as it is written in a small booklet entitled *Cet Machandar* published by the new Kadri *rājā* for his enthronment.

[4] I am uncertain of the etymology of *anupān*; Sanskrit *anu-pāna* means 'a drink taken with or after medicine' (Monier-Williams 1988: 35) ; *anūpa* would have been more understandable, signifying 'situated near the water' (id. 42), an allusion to the position of the rock near Godavari source ? or is it simply a misspelling of *anupama*, excellent, incomparable?

discovered Gorakhnāth under his quintessential form of *pātradevatā* worshipped by Paraśurām on the Oman seashore. To get the *darśan* of Gorakhnāth, they set off and from Tryambakeshvar reached the place where Gorakhnāth appeared as Mañjunāth, in Mangalore. There the Nāths and Siddhas took *darśan* of Gorakhnāth, who then declared to Paraśurām:

You have done your penance. Thanks to your example, someone who, like you, has killed a human being would be able to atone for his sin by touching the feet of the nine Nāths and eighty-four Siddhas. The earth will be freed from sin. After each Siṁhastha, every twelve years, the Nāth Siddhas will have to walk to Mañjunāth's place, and the earth will be relieved from sin for twelve years, and everybody could be happy. Myself I shall stay with you in your group, in your *jhuṇḍī*.

Since then, every twelve years following the Siṁhastha Kumbh Melā, the *jhuṇḍī* of the Nāths and Siddhas make this pilgrimage in order to free the earth from sin. Gorakhnāth asked Matsyendranāth, as his guru, to lead the procession. Matsyendranāth agreed and, taking the *pātradevatā* in his hands, became the 'king of the *jhuṇḍī*' and started walking.

This origin myth somewhat artificially links various elements such as Tryambakeshvar, the Kumbh Melā, the pilgrimage to Kadri, the *pātradevatā* and Matsyendranāth, but it succeeds in giving a proper etiology to this astonishing long pilgrimage from Tryambak to Mangalore and gives an interpretation of the title of *rājā* given to the head of Kadri who, like Matsyendranāth, will lead the procession.

THE SELECTION OF THE *RĀJĀ*

I will now describe what happens in Tryambakeshvar, taking for example the Kumbh Melā of August 2003.[5]

[5] I could not participate in the Kumbh but had access to a DVD made there by a Kadri Yogīs' Association who filmed the main rituals as well as an interview with Ānandanāth, the general secretary of the Yogī Mahāsabhā by a Bengalore University researcher, Dr. Rahamath Tarikere. I also questioned some participants in Kadri and read the description given by the *rājā* in the booklet *Cet Machandar*.

Officially the Kumbh Melā started on 23 July with an inaugural ceremony in Tryambakeshvar but the first auspicious bath, for which the different sects fight to be first, was not until 8 August. The Yogīs' calendar started on the eve of Nāg Pañcāmī, the fourth day of the clear half of Śrāvaṇ (July-August), 2 August. The celebrations were held in three main stages: the election of the officials, the cult of the *pātradevatā*, and the departure of the *jhuṇḍī*.

On 2 August, all the Yogīs who had arrived in Tryambakeshvar – there were about two thousand of them – gathered inside the Gorakhnāth Akhāṛā according to their *panth*. This gathering, called *dalīcā*, was presided over here by the Mahāsabhā General Secretary Ānandanāth. Its task would be to proceed to the election of several officials: first the heads of the main monasteries in southern India, then the main people in charge of different tasks in the *jhuṇḍī*, and finally the two heads of the roaming Yogīs (the *jamāt*).

The first election concerned the Kadri *rājā* as the head of the monastery that has authority over all other monasteries south of Narmada. The central part played by the *rājā* and its unifying character appear clearly from the fact that formerly the *rājā* was elected alternately among the twelve *panths* on a particular rotation basis: this eminent leadership was by its very essence open to all Yogīs and rules were established to ensure proper alternation. However, a rule has recently been promulgated to exclude from the succession role the *panths* that did not send any members to any one of the Tryambakeshvar Melās. Nowadays only four *panths* have succeeded in being present at every Kumbh Melā, and thus it is from the Gaṅgānāthī, Bhartṛharī Bairāg, Naṭeśvarī, and Kaplānī *panths* alternately that the *rājā* is elected. In 2003, it was the turn of the Gaṅgānāthī Panth.

The election is through a show of hands by a simple majority: a name is mentioned (with the agreement of the candidate) and all the *sādhus* present vote. The chosen *rājā* in 2003, Sandhyānāth, was elected in the second round. Born in 1972 in Rājāsthan in the Raibāri caste,[6] an orphan from a numerous family, he was entrusted to his guru's care and initiated very young. He had already taken part in two Nasik Kumbh Melās and two *jhuṇḍīs*: the first time he was eight, and the second time, in 1991-2, he was in charge of his *panth,* Gaṅgānāthī.

After the *rājā's* election the gathering proceeds to the election of two other monastery heads: the *pīr* of Sunharī Bhairav, a place 30 km west on the Bombay Road, who is chosen also from among the same four *panths* (with a different succession role), and the *pīr* of the Tryambakeshvar Gorakhnāth *akhāṛā*, who must belong to the Satyanāth *panth.*

Every elected superior receives a ceremonial headdress, a turban made of orange material in which is intertwined a black wool thread twisted with thin silver and gold thread and coloured pompoms. He has to wear this turban, *pheṭā,* at every solemn occasion and especially for the cult of the *pātradevatā.*

After these three elections are completed, the Yogīs proceed to the selection of the chief of the *jhuṇḍī*, the *jhuṇḍī mahant*. He has to be from the Āī Panth since this *panth* is under the protection of the goddess Bimlā Devī, a form of Śakti and since the *jhuṇḍī mahant* is given absolute power during the six month pilgrimage, he has to be endowed with *śaktī*, with spiritual strength. If no possible incumbent from Āī Panth is present, the *jhuṇḍī* cannot get under way. The chosen *mahant*, Surajnāth, had already been elected in the last *jhuṇḍī* in 1991-2. Quite an impressive figure, he is very tall, has a long gray beard and has the reputation of being an alchemist; his natural authority makes him a true leader for the difficult task of leading a troupe of *sādhus* who have to obey him and walk together during a six month journey.

After him are selected the ascetics in charge of different tasks during the pilgrimage: the *koṭhārī* (keeper, steward) from Satyanāth Panth, the *kārobārī* (accountant) from Dharmanāth Panth, the *śrībhaṇḍārī* (in-charge of food supplies and meals) from Bhartṛharī Bairāg Panth, the *pujārī* from Naṭesvarī Panth, and the *roṭbhaṇḍārī* (in charge of cooking in the *dhūnī* and of carrying

[6] A pastoral nomadic caste also called the Raikā (see Chapter 11, p. 283).

the *roṭ*, the thick bread that is both the symbol and the offering to Bhairav) from Rāmke Panth. Then each *panth* elects one of its members as *pañc* in charge of managing his fellow ascetics during the journey.[7] Among the ascetics in charge during the *jhuṇḍī*, the *paṅkh* (herald) has the important duty of standing close to the *rājā* and *pātradevatā*, holding a long silver mace, to sing hymns to the glory of Gorakhnāth, and to announce in a loud voice the names of the worshippers and the sum that they are offering to the *jhuṇḍī* which the accountant will inscribe in his register and put in the heavy trunk he is carrying.

The Tryambakeshvar assembly is finally the moment to elect the two *mahants* of the itinerant troup or *jamāt*, the leaders of the twelve (*barāh*) and eighteen (*aṭhārah*) *panths*. The *jamāt* takes a leading part in the pilgrimage. Even though the Yogīs of the *jamāt* are less numerous than the 'ordinary' ascetics taking part in the *jhuṇḍī* and the two groups kept separate, it is their behaviour, their rules which become the norms for all the Yogīs. No special *panth* is prescribed for being a *mahant* (except the respective belonging to a *panth* included in the group of the 'twelve' or the 'eighteen'), but as it is a difficult and strenuous duty, there are few candidates and this time the two same *mahants* have been re-elected for the next twelve years: Krișṇanāth from Āī Panth as *mahant* of the 'twelve' and Somnāth from Rāmke Panth as *mahant* of the 'eighteen'.

This process of election testifies to a very democratic way of functioning, where everyone can compete, where all voices are equal and debates can be heated. Parallel to this egalitarian individualistic trend, the division of the tasks and their alternation according to the *panths* gives the sect its cohesion and allows for a balance between the right to personal expression and collective duties. We may add that these duties are not easy ones, and that the Yogīs in charge have to carry them out for

[7] If a *panth* is not represented or if nobody from the *panth* is suitable, a Nāth from another *panth* may be elected, according to a fixed permutation table in order that the twelve *panths* figure at least symbolically.

several months. To arrange the travel of a few hundred *sādhus* requires good logistics: besides the purely material organization (lodging and meals), it is necessary to check the performance of the rituals, to welcome the numerous visitors and devotees, to enquire on the management of the dependant monasteries on the way and to maintain discipline over a troupe of unruly *sādhus*.

THE CULT OF THE *PĀTRADEVATĀ*: THE MAKING OF A COMMUNITY

This first part of the Tryambakeshvar meeting, the elections, has been reserved for initiated Yogīs. However, the next ritual, on the day of Nāg Pañcamī, can be observed (and even filmed) by non-initiates. Called *pātradevatā kī sthāpanā*, the installation of the pot-deity, the ritual unites those recently elected with all the Yogīs around the cult of their common deity. But even though the symbol is unique, three *pātradevatās* have been made in great secrecy by Yogīs of the Satyanāth Panth, since every new head has to carry one back to his monastery.

Let us describe the ceremony. In the main hall of the Gorakhnāth Akhāṛā, on the left side of the main altar adorned with a plaster statue of Gorakhnāth, carpets have been set out for the *pātradevatās* and the dignitaries. Close by is standing the *pañkh*, the herald, and in front, the group of the Nāth Yogīs. Then in a rush comes first the *pīr* of Tryambakeshvar surrounded by *sādhus* holding hands. He carries his wrapped *pātradevatā* on his turbaned head. The *jhuṇḍī mahant* gives instruction and helps the *pīr* to put the *pātradevatā* on its carpet throne, after having rotated it violently a few times. The receptacle is freed of one of its red wrappings, allowing its round and hollow shape to appear, into which some money is put. The Sunharī Bhairav *pīr*, then the Kadri *rājā* do the same and the three new heads take their places behind their *pātradevatā*, close to the *jhuṇḍī mahant*. The *roṭ bhaṇḍārī* also brings a *roṭ* carrying it on his head and places it near the *rājā's pātradevatā*.

The *pūjārī* now worships each of the *pātradevatā* just as he will do morning and evening during the following six months of pilgrimage. He starts by blowing his small *nād* whistle, while the *nagārā* drummers and the Yogīs blowing the *nāgphani*, the serpentine trumpet typical of Nāth rituals, play. Then he honours the *pātradevatās*, the three monastic heads, the *jhuṇḍī mahant* and other officials, with a vermilion *ṭika*, a flower necklace and water sprinkling. Now he worships successively each of the *pātradevatā* and of the dignitaries rotating one hundred times an incense burner, then an oil lamp and finally a fly-swatter. With the left hand he shakes a small bell whilst the standing Yogīs beat drums or brass discs, blow trumpets or horns, and shake bells in a holy cacophony. When the worship finishes, all the Yogīs hold hands and the Yogīs in charge surround the *pātradevatās* with a large cloth. They form a close group, a corporate group in the literal sense, around their *pātradevatā* and in this way express their worship in common. Hidden behind the cloth screen, the *pujārī* takes the *roṭ*, shakes it violently, unwraps it, and cuts it into pieces according to a fixed model: the central square part called *nābhi* (navel), is offered to the *pātradevatā*. This cutting of the *roṭ*, always very important in the Nāth rituals, is called here *roṭ muktā*.[8] The cut *roṭ* will be made in small pieces and distributed later by the *paṅkh* as *prasād* to the Yogīs and devotees. The *pūjā* ends with the officiant presenting to the Yogīs a large plate where camphor pieces are burning: the Yogīs pass their hands above the flames then over their faces in order to absorb its

[8] *Muktā*, the adjectival and feminine form of *mukta*, 'loosened, set free, liberated' (Monier-Williams 1988: 820). My informants did not see any allusion to a 'liberation' but only a formal way to mean offering (*roṭ arpaṇ karnā*, make offering of the *roṭ*). Are the use of this word, the strange shaking movement given to the *roṭ*, its furtive and very codified cutting up, the link with Bhairav, alluding to a simulacrum of animal sacrifice? The ritual manual *Śrī Nāth Rahasya* (Yogī Vilāsnāth 2005: 409-11) does not explain it but describes the cutting up: the central part has to be cut square, then separated into three layers, the upper one for Śrī Nāth, the middle one for Gaṅgā (put in water), the lower one for Bhairav and given to a dog (or a cow).

benefit. During this time the *paṅkh* recites a long invocation to Śiva, Gorakhnāth and the nine Nāths. When he has finished, the dignitaries squat down, touch the earth with their joined hands holding the thread, *śelī*, and the small whistle, *nād*, then blow three times in their *nād*, still touching the earth with their left hand. The whole body of Yogīs does the same afterwards. One hears a murmur of quick muffled whistling. The same sequence is done another time, then all shout together with loud voices: '*Mahāraj ki jay*'. Every newly elected Yogī approaches the *pātra-devatā* and makes an offering, which the *paṅkh* announces publicly, giving the name, *panth*'s and guru's name of the donor, establishing in this way his spiritual filiation. The *rājā* comes first and offers a pile of notes, the substantial sum of Rs. 11,000 (in 2003 approximately 200 $) that he had promised to give (and which some say helped his election).

Then the two *mahants* of the *jamāt* arrive, followed by two assistants each carrying a sword. The *mahants* bow in front of the *pātradevatās*, the assistants unsheathe their swords and brandish them when the *roṭbhaṇḍārī* arrives carrying on his head a second *roṭ* wrapped in red cloth. Their group leaves the room and proceeds towards the large stone platform, which they call *anupān śilā*,[9] in front of the monastery. All the Yogīs follow and take their places in two groups, the 'twelve' and the 'eighteen', depending on which group their *panth* is attached to. The three elected heads, who were carrying their *pātradevatās* on their heads, put them on a carpet-throne and stand behind. The two *jamāt mahants* stand on either side and cross their brandished sword above the *pātradevatās*, the *pujārī* takes the *roṭ*, shakes it violently and puts it down, the two *mahants* touch the centre of the *roṭ*, the *nābhi*, with the points of their sword then resume their initial posture while the *pujārī* again worships the *pātradevatās* as previously with lamp and incense burner. And hidden behind cloths, he proceeds to the cutting of the second

[9] This stone, which figures in the Gorakh legend (see fn. 4), has, say the Yogīs, the capacity to expand in order to accommodate all of them, whatever their number.

roṭ. All the Yogīs who are going to take part to the *jhuṇḍī* come, bow, and receive a *roṭ prasad*.

THE ASCETIC PILGRIMAGE

The next day is the departure day for the long procession called the Navnāth *jhuṇḍī*, 'the group of the Nine Nāths', an allusion to the journey the Nine Nāths made looking for their guru Gorakhnāth and an entrenchment of the modern pilgrimage in the identitarian legendary corpus of the Nāths.

The following rules are stated to the *jhuṇḍī* Yogīs, which they have to swear to follow for the next six months on pain of exclusion:

- The main authorities have to walk barefoot and the others should not wear any leather;
- No Yogī should get in any vehicle;
- No Yogī should walk in front of the *pātradevatā*, no Yogī should eat or drink alone, accept personal gifts, stay aloof. If a Yogī is late to the point of being absent for three *ārti* cycles (morning and evening worship), he is excluded from sharing the (cannabis) pipe (verbatim 'to him the *cilam* cloth is closed', i.e. he is banned from the community of those Yogīs who share the small clay pipe whose base they wrap with a thin white cloth).
- The Navanāth *jhuṇḍī* lasts from Nāg Pañcamī to Mahāśivarātrī. If the *jhuṇḍī* has not reached Kadri for Śivarātrī (the 14th day of the dark half of Phālgun, February-March), it has to continue walking south of Narmada for another twelve years and no Yogī could be free of his commitment before the end of that period.

Of the 2,000 Yogīs in Tryambakeshvar, 373 (in 2003) had taken the formal commitment to join the *jhuṇḍī* and to respect its rules. They were of all ages and all origins, a majority being from north-west India. Among them were three or four very young boys already wearing the earrings of initiated Yogīs, and a tall

Yogī in black leading a black dog nicknamed Bhairav (and which the Brahmans do not like to see entering their temples!) As I have already noted for previous meetings, there are no women.[10]

The procession started in the early morning (on 4 August 2003) after a final homage to the *pīr* of the Gorakhnāth Akhāṛā, who will stay in Tryambakeshvar till the next Kumbh twelve years later. The marching order, as well as the daily rituals, are strictly regulated. First walked the *roṭ bhaṇḍārī* with the Bhairav *roṭ* wrapped in red cloth on his head: Bhairav is leading the group and without him, without the *roṭ*, everything stops. Alongside him came the *pañkh*, the herald, carrying the silver mace adorned with a red flag. Close behind walked the *rājā* carrying the *pātradevatā* and the *jhuṇḍī mahant*. The other Yogīs in charge followed, among them the accountant carrying on his head a metallic trunk containing the money necessary for the journey and the offerings. The two *mahants* of the 'twelve' and 'eighteen' were accompanied by their sword carriers. Behind came the bulk of the Yogīs, trying to cope with the quite rapid walking speed. The procession took the main roads, which somewhat disrupts the traffic: on this first day it was raining, the Yogīs were not yet used to this fast pace, they tried to hurry, sheltering under umbrellas or plastic sheets and the trucks and buses tried to pass them, hooting their horns violently.

On this first day, the Yogīs have to cover 35 km in order to reach Nasik, where they will stay for 17 days, taking part in the main Kumbh Melā events and auspicious baths (*snān*). They camp inside the Kālārām Mandir. According to the Yogīs, this temple belonged to them in the past and was called Guru Gorakhnāth Maṭh. At that time, they say, the Yogīs had the privilege of bathing first for the *mahāsnān*, the great bath of the Kumbh. But in 1770 as a violent conflict broke out between the Śaivas and the Vaiṣṇavas for the second place, the then *mahant* of the

[10] Only once during the Pushkar *dalicā* I saw two yoginīs: distrustful and silent, kept aloof by the others, they have not been allowed to attend the general meeting of the Yogīs which then was held. They refused to talk to me.

Gorakhnāth Maṭh, Santoṣnāth, declared that if the two parties could not come to an agreement before three days had passed, he would take a living *samādhi*. Three days passed without any agreement and Santoṣnāth was buried in a grave close to the *maṭh* (and still visible). Then the conflict vanished and both parties agreed to accept any settlement proposed by the Nāth *sampradāya*. The Vaiṣṇavas agreed to bathe second and the Nāths gave their right to first place to the Śaiva Dasnāmīs.[11] I found no other report regarding this dispute, but the story as told by the Nāths is a very noble way to justify their present exclusion from the bathing order.

Their stay in Nasik for the Kumbh over, the *jhuṇḍī* Yogīs resumed their journey towards the south, towards Kadri where the new *rājā* is to be enthroned on Śivarātrī (on 18 February 2004). The journey will take six months, the Yogīs will cover approximately 1,300 km crossing ten districts. The itinerary is fixed in advance and includes 87 stops in monasteries or temples, 19 of which still belong to the Nāth *sampradāya* while 10 have been recently shifted to other sects or to lay trustees. In some important places, the *jhuṇḍī* stopped for a few days and made trips around the area. In Pune region for instance, the yogīs spent almost one month but changed residence twelve times.

At every stop in a new temple or *maṭh*, the procession is welcomed by the authorities of the place. The *rājā* carrying the *pātradevatā* and the *jhuṇḍī mahant* salute the local deities and then take their places. Helpers set carpets and cushions, the *rājā* puts down the *pātradevatā* and takes his place behind it. The *jhuṇḍī mahant* sits on his left, then the caretaker and the accountant. On the right side stands the herald. In front of the altar supporting the *pātradevatā*, a Yogī makes a floral decoration, writing some short mantra or the letter *aum*. Devotees come to worship the gods and the Yogīs and make offerings, the amount of which is announced by the herald and registered by the accountant. Often rich devotees or famous *mahants* offer special meals to the

11 As written in *Cet Machandar* (2004). Regarding other sectarian conflicts in Nasik Kumbh Melā, see Pinch (2006: 236).

jhuṇḍī and organize *bhaṇḍārā* or feasts. The caretaker and the cooks organize and supervise the meals, the food is of course vegetarian, rich, plentiful, and varied.

A striking fact is that every night the *jhuṇḍī* divides in two: the ascetics from the *jamāt* leave the precinct of the place and settle their camp in the open air, what they call 'the jungle' since, as truly roaming ascetics, they are not supposed to sleep under a roof. They prepare a huge fire, their common *dhūnī*, and their two *mahants* take place on their thrones on either sides of their small portable altar to Śiva.

At night time, then, two different worship ceremonies take place: one to the *pātradevatā* by the *pujārī* of the *jhuṇḍī* and the other to the *dhūnī* by the *pujārī* of the *jamāt*. The first ritual in front of the *pātradevatā* follows the sequence we have already described with the successive offerings of lamps and incense to the *pātradevatā*, the *rājā* and the other dignitaries. Few Yogīs are present since they gather outside, close to the huge fire light by the *jamāt* officiant. There, everything is dark except for the flames fed now and then with ghee. One can make out the figures of the Yogīs in the darkness, some blowing horns or beating drums or gongs, the two *mahants* seated in their place. The *pujārī* squatting before the fire worships it with incense, light, water and flowers while chanting mantras. Then he bows in front of Śiva's altar, and in front of the two *mahants*, goes back to the *dhūnī* to take some ashes and mark his forehead with the *tripuṇḍra*, the triple Śaiva line. It is now the turn of the Yogīs to bow down, to blow their *nād* three times, and to mark their foreheads with the *tripuṇḍra*. After that they join the last part of the *pātradevatā pūjā* for which briefly the two *mahants* of the *jamāt* arrive: their reserved attitude, their dignity, and their evident authority arouse respect. Later on the Yogīs gather to sing devotional songs to Śiva and Gorakhnāth, or the pan-Indian *ārtī*, *Om Jay Jagdiś Hare*.

Once a week on Sunday there is the ritual of worshipping and cutting of the *roṭ* bread, the *roṭ muktā*. This day the *jhuṇḍī* does not move since there is no *roṭ*, no Bhairav to take the lead of the procession. During the night another *roṭ* is cooked in the ashes of the *dhūnī* and is prepared for the departure the following morning.

During the whole period time of the pilgrimage, the two swords which the helpers of the *jamāt mahants* brandish while walking are put in front of the throne of the *jhuṇḍī mahant* whenever the cortege stops. It is a sign of his absolute power, which encompasses and surpasses the power of the two *jamāt mahants.* According to the statutes of the Mahāsabhā, which evidently recall an old tradition, the *jhuṇḍī* has full authority over the monasteries on its way. The *jhuṇḍī mahant* must check the account books and organize the election of new heads when the system of succession follows a twelve years cycle. This has been the case in Tryambakeshvar with the elections of the two heads of Tryambak and Sunhāri Bhairav, then a few other times on the road, for example for Bhairavnālā in Pune (where no suitable *mahant* was found and the decision postponed to the next Ujjain Kumbh), the Chandragupti (district of Shimoga) and Loki Maṭh (district of Chitradurga), and finally in Kadri (with the rājgurū of Vittal, a monastery dependant on Kadri).

As we have already suggested (see chapter 3), what the *jhuṇḍī* expresses is the necessity and the superiority of itinerance. The troup of itinerant Yogīs, who have vowed to observe ascetic constraints, have control and authority over the established institutions they go through. But this troupe is not made of free-roaming ascetics. They constitute a well-structured group where cohesiveness and obedience are strictly enforced but which promotes values of mobility and non-possession. Their walking is the ultimate outcome of their asceticism and the expression of their detachment from the world, the true values which justify their enrolment among the Nāths.

The head of the Kadri monastery, even though he is selected in Tryambak, is only consecrated after the long *padyātrā*, the long walk which takes him to Kadri, as if only this ascetic journey entitles him to exercise his leadership. Moreover the journey is set in legendary surroundings that contribute to establish the head's legitimacy and his particular status: he is likened to Matsyendranāth who led the procession of the 9 Nāths and

84 Siddhas when they were looking for Gorakhnāth. And like Mastyendranāth he is the king, the *rājā* of the *jhuṇḍī* and the *rājā* of Kadri.

In the same way, in accordance with the title of *rājā*, there is an analogy between the different steps and rituals by which the head of Kadri monastery is consecrated and the royal coronation. The *rājābhiṣeka* or royal consecration, as well as the solemn sacrifice made by the king or *rājasūya*, are divided into different phases: 'not only are unction and inthronization separated but, more importantly, the interval is taken up by an interesting rite, the chariot drive. This rite is clearly a symbolic war expedition [...] In other words, after the unction the king should go abroad' (Heesterman 1998: 26). And this journey represents also a symbolic integration of his kingdom into the king's person (Heesterman 1957: 135). The procession led by the Kadri *rājā* after his nomination and his coronation (with a royal turban) and before his enthronement is not a war expedition, but it evokes nevertheless the triumphal royal tours, the crossing over territories submitting to his domination, the symbolic 'world conquest' (*digvijay*).

THE ENTHRONEMENT OF THE KADRI *RĀJĀ*

The Arrival of the Jhuṇḍī

The *jhuṇḍī* has kept to its plan and a few days before Śivarātrī 2004 comes close to Mangalore. The Yogīs have spent the last Sunday resting in a temple some 8 km from the town. Early on Monday morning the procession starts walking, accompanied this time by many devotees, lay or ascetic, who came for the occasion. At the ourskirts of the town they are solemnly welcomed by the town authorities led by the Mayor, who is himself a Yogī by caste. A profusion of flower garlands are given to the *rājā* and *jhuṇḍī mahant*. Music bands play and the cortege, now much enlarged, walks around the centre of the town, stopping in different places to let the people worship the *pātradevatā* or themselves to worship the town deities. One longer stop is made at the Veṇkaṭarāmana temple owned by the Gauḍ Sārasvat Brahmans. The leading Yogīs bow in front of the main deity, Viṣṇu Viravenkaṭeśvar, and take their places in the courtyard where the temple priests come to worship and give donations to the *pātradevatā*.[12] Afterwards the *jhuṇḍī* starts out again towards the north to reach the Mañjunāth Temple, then the Kadri Maṭh. A newly erected stucco arch marks the entrance in the old domain of Mañjunāth. Two lines of auspicious women carrying water pots on their head escort the *rājā* as far as the entrance. The procession circumambulates the temple and then enters the inner courtyard. The *rājā* stands at the entrance of the *garbhagṛha*[13] while the main officiant marks him with a *ṭikā*. He sits with the *jhuṇḍī mahant* in the gallery where the temple trustees offer the *pātradevatā* Rs. 1,000. The bulk of the Yogīs and devotees stay outside. Then all start out for the last stage of the journey, the ascent of the hill to the Kadri Maṭh: they climb the stairs then take a small lane which surrounds the *maṭh* till they reach a small platform on its northern side called the *bārah panth kaṭṭa*.[14] There a final ritual takes place which marks the arrival of the *jhuṇḍī* and mirrors the first ritual on the *anupān śilā* in Tryambak.

The dignitaries ascend the platform and set up the *pātradevatā*

[12] According to informations given by the temple, in 1804 a 'peripatetic Sannyasi' the possessor of a beautiful statue of the god, gave it to the merchant's family who built a temple, later consecrated by a Dasnāmī Sannyāsī. According to the Nāths, the peripatetic Sannyāsī is a Nāth Yogī from the Bairāg Panth, and this is the reason for the long stop made by the *jhuṇḍī*.

[13] Christopher Fuller (1984: 58) remarks also that the Srngeri Śaṅkarācārya does not go inside the sanctuaries in the Minakṣi Temple: 'He stood near the entrance to the two main sancta [...] but did not enter any of them, nor claimed any privileged access'.

[14] As explains Gnanambal (1973: 106) *kaṭṭa* or '*katte* means a raised platform. It is generally built round a shady tree' and was used for the meetings of the caste councils which were called '*kattemane*'. It is the same use here.

and the *roṭ*. The two *jamāt mahants* holding their swords stand one at each end. Down below is the crowd of the Yogīs, devotees, journalists and cameramen. The *pañkh* receives the order from the *jhuṇḍī mahant* to call loudly each of the *panth*: the *panth* leaders (elected at Tryambak) check their members' presence and press close to the platform, whose name of *barāhpanth kaṭṭa* takes here its proper meaning. This is another sign of the importance of the ritual for the sect in expressing and maintaining its identity.

A main difference in this final act of worship is the meeting of the two *rājās*. When the *jhuṇḍī* officials take their places on the platform, the Kadri *rājā* who is still in office arrives with his *bhaṇḍārī*, carrying on his head a *roṭ* that he puts in front of the *pātradevatā*. Then the former *rājā* worships the god and proceeds to cut the *roṭ* that he just brought, protected by the two *mahants* brandishing their swords and hidden from view by cloth hangings. Afterwards he goes back to the monastery and his private quarters, while the *jhuṇḍī pujārī* finishes his usual worship. As soon as the last word is said, everybody hurries up to the *maṭh*, a few hundred metres away. The *jhuṇḍī* authorities with the new *rājā* bow in front of the *maṭh* deities, Bhairav and Jwālā Māyā, and take their places in the main courtyard, facing west, the direction of the Mañjunāth Temple. Their positions are the same as during their journey, and they perform for the last time the offering and cutting of the *roṭ* that the *jhuṇḍī bhaṇḍārī* was carrying; since they don't walk anymore, they no longer need the protective presence of the *roṭ*-Bhairav.

All other Yogīs settle freely within the monastery precincts except for the *jamāt* whose two *mahants* take positions in an open air area close to the path leading to Mañjunāth Temple. They sit on their throne-carpets on either side of the small portable altar and in front of the huge fire where the act of worship will be performed morning and evening. During the few days that remain before the *rājā's* enthronement, they will seldom quit their place, resting, smoking *gaṅja*, and talking with their closest disciples. Bare-chested, their very long hair wrapped around their heads, they are looked at with respect and awe by the many lay devotees who visit the monastery. Further grounds for amazement are the two *sādhus* who took the vow to always remain standing (*khaṛeśvarī*): one did it for twelve years and just renewed his vow for another twelve years, the other started during the pilgrimage. Both never sit but can be supported during the stops by a system of ropes, which allow them to rest the upper part of their body on a small plank.

Visitors and organizers continue to arrive daily and make preparations for the coming festival. Leading Yogīs from big monasteries are coming, among them the vice-president of the Yogī Mahāsabhā, Cāndnāth, the head of the Ashtal Bohar monastery in Haryana who will preside at the *rājā's* investiture, being the highest authority present. Many visitors gather in the evening to participate in the worship and devotional singing and then watch the performances and listen to the public speeches given on the podium. Each evening performance starts with a lengthy invocation to Śiva sung in Sanskrit, then with teachings in Hindi given by the *jhuṇḍī mahant*, by the vice-president of the Mahāsabhā, by both *rājās*, or by a yoga teacher. Local political leaders or well-known figures take turns giving speeches, distributing or receiving flower garlands. Finally come the artistic performances: sitar and saxophone[15] performances, Bharatanatyam performed by the children of the local Jogī community and for the final evening a performance lasting the whole night of Yakshagana, a typical Karnataka theatre form, in which were enacted the legends of the Nāths and of Paraśurām.

On the eve of the new *rājā's* consecration, the time comes to settle the accounts of the preceding period. All the Yogīs of the *jhuṇḍī* gather in the main courtyard and close the gates. Those who did not participate in the *jhuṇḍī* are excluded, even Cāndnāth, the Mahāsabhā vice-president. The Yogīs meet together in *dalīcā*, in an assembly representative of the whole of the *bārah panth*, in order to make decisions which are issued by the collectivity. Evidently the proposals are made by the *jhuṇḍī mahant*, in agreement with the Mahāsabhā, but they are

[15] A member of the Jogī community is one of the leading saxophone players in India. He has made many donations to the monastery.

accepted or refused by the assembly which expresses itself with loud exclamations. This time the atmosphere appears tense: it seems that the *rājā* still in-charge had been obliged to stay on his feet for five hours during which the *jhuṇḍī mahant* examined his account books and listed a long series of grievances; for every reproach the whole of the Yogīs kept crying out and their indignant shouts made us jump, we who were trying from outside to guess what was happening! At the end of this quasi trial, the *jhuṇḍī mahant* announced the sentence in three points; each time he asked if any Yogī disagreed and was answered only with a profound silence, a sign that all suscribed to what was considered as a collective decision, as the 'democracy of the Yogīs'.[16] The first point concerns the transgression of the interdiction for the *rājā* to leave the area of the *maṭh* and especially to cross the Narmada: he did it 41 times and was fined the regulation amount of Rs. 11,000 for each, thus Rs. 4,51,000 all told. The second grievance concerned misappropriation of funds: the revenues from Kadri were said to have been transferred to the *rājā's* personal *maṭh* in Rājāsthan and he was condemned to repay Rs. 1 crore to Kadri (out of the 8 he was rumoured to have misappropriated). The third decision obliged him to pay back this sum of Rs. 1,04,51,000 before two years had elapsed; if not his new Rājāsthani monastery would be taken back by the sect's authorities and considered as a *pañcāyati*, or common property, *maṭh* and would be managed by the Mahāsabhā.

A final decision made by the *dalīcā* concerns the neighbouring monastery of Vittal whose head, who bears the title of *rājgūrū*, will be renewed in his post and reconsecrated at the same time as the Kadri *rājā*.

[16] The same rule applies for the *dharma pariṣad* (assembly on dharma), which requires not just a majority but unanimity (many thanks to C. Clementin-Ojha for this information). The Yogīs insist also in their assemblies on the importance of an unanimous decision.

The Vittal Monastery

Before describing the consecration ceremonies, I shall make a short digression to explain the joint presence of two recipients on the coronation platform. Moreover the Vittal Maṭh is of great interest since it shows how a monastery can change status. At first a private monastery, *nijī maṭh*, linked to the history of the local kingdom, the Vittal Maṭh became *pañcayatī* after some conflicts and problems and is now managed by the Mahāsabhā.

The small town of Vittal, 20 km south of Mangalore, was the centre of a small kingdom, whose king in the seventeenth century, Domba-Heggade, was visited by a prodigious Yogī from north India, Meharnāth. Filled with wonder at his powers, the king invited Meharnāth to stay and made him his guru. He gave him and his fellow Yogīs 101 acres of land to build a monastery, still very beautiful with its traditional buildings surrounded by areca palms. After Meharnāth, the succession went from guru to disciple as is the rule in *nijī maṭhs* and the monastery was autonomous. But four generations ago, the eighth successor of Meharnāth broke his vow of celibacy to the point of producing four sons; it took some time for the authorities of the Mahāsabhā to sanction him but finally he was obliged in 1955 to 'make a gift' of his monastery to the *Bārah panth*. The Vittal Maṭh then became *pañcāyatī* and its head selected by the assembly of the Yogīs, in agreement with the Kadri calendar; however, the ancient title of *rājgūrū* is still in use. Some conflicts appeared between a few disciples and the Mahāsabhā, until the nomination of Lālnāth who was to be re-enthroned in Kadri in 2004 for another twelve years despite his great age.

THE CONSECRATION OR *PAṬṬĀBHIṢEK*[17]

The final day of the long ritual cycle, which had begun seven months earlier in Tryambak and finishes with the *rājā's*

[17] *Abhiṣek(a)*, 'anointing, inaugurating or consecrating by sprinkling water', *paṭṭa*, 'slab, tablet ... copper plate ... bandage ... frontlet, turban

consecration in Kadri, is composed of several steps that I shall describe before examining their signification and making comparisons with other consecration rituals.

The first ritual is done secretly and before dawn. Called *sampradāyik pūjā*, sectarian worship, it is only attended by the initiated Yogīs. From 3 to 6 a.m. they gather in front of the two sanctuaries of Bhairav and the Devī and worship the gods with an abundance of offerings: coconuts and flower garlands cover the place when I am finally allowed to approach.

The unction itself or *abhiṣek*, the next part of the ceremony, is said to be '*vaidika*', based on vedic texts and in the charge of the Tantrī,[18] the officiating priest of Mañjunāth Temple. Still young, having recently graduated from the Udupi *gūrūkūl*, Vittal Das Tantri will preside over the rituals, under the supervision of his aging father who officiated for the last coronation, twelve years ago. Both arrive from the Mañjunāth Temple around 7 a.m. and Vittal Das takes his place on the platform in front of the Gorakhnāth shrine outside the *maṭh* buildings. He starts the preparations for the *havan*, the fire offering, with an auspicious worship of Gaṇeś and of the nine planets.

A few minutes later he joins the two *rājās* and the Vittal *rājgūrū* in front of the Bhairav Temple in the *maṭh*. While they give offerings of coconuts and flowers, he sings Sanskrit verses. Bhairav's blessing assured, they all go back to the *havan* platform. The Tantrī sits on the northern side, facing Gorakhnāth's shrine. On the opposite side sit the two *rājās* and the Vittal *rājgūrū*. Using rice flour the Tantrī draws a square diagram on the ground and

... tiara, diadem' (Monier-Williams 1988: 71 and 579). I shall discuss these terms and their context at the end of this chapter.

[18] On the role of the Tantri in Kerala temples, see Gilles Tarabout (1986: 96-7): 'In the big temples, the ritual activity is supervised by a member of a Nambudiri Brahman family who is specialised in tantric cult – he is called then *tantri* [...] The power of the Tantris is clearly assimilated to the power of the yogīs' (translation from French). The priests of Mañjunāth are also Nambudiri Brahmans from Kerala. They are specialized in Śaiva Āgama (more precisely the *Vatulāgama*).

places the small dishes, heaps of rice, waterpots embodying the deities, and a short dagger, which will play an important role in the second part of the ceremony and which he sprinkles with water, flowers, and grains of rice. On the eastern side of the diagram are placed two large earthenware jugs that contain the water to be consecrated for the *rājā's* aspersion. After the first invocations from the *Yajur Veda*, the Tantri prepares the central fireplace: he lays a thin layer of sand, sets down two open tiles, a few logs and lights the fire. He throws grains of rice in the fire then circles the fire with various oil lamps. Finally the Tantrī and the *rājās* and *rājgūrū* stand up, gongs and drums play fast and loud, the Tantri throws into the fire a full ladle of ghee, after which the three monastic superiors do the same. The *havan* finishes in this way after two hours of rituals during which the Tantrī continuously recited texts from the *Yajur Veda* (*Subhoda Saṃhitā*).

The attention shifts now to the *piṭh* or 'seat', a narrow podium[19] with two levels adorned with a canopy of flower garlands and areca nuts. The courtyard is full of people, the notables of Mangalore, the *grihastha* Yogīs, the devotees, and the journalists for whom a higher platform has been erected. Music bands rival each other in enthusiasm and volume. And the Yogīs scramble to get close to the podium and see the unction of their *rājā*. An armchair has been prepared for Cāndnāth, the vice-president of the Mahāsabhā, who made quite an entrance, followed later on by the two *mahants* of the *jamāt*.

The Tantri prepares the podium. He lays a plank down on each step on which he draws a diagram that he covers with a white sheet adorned with flower petals. In front he puts the two water jugs with consecrated water and a few small pots topped by leaf plates with coconuts and flowers. The *rājā* and the *rājgūrū* arrive, accompanied by musical bands. Both are bare chested,

[19] The former *rājā* had prepared a new podium in a larger space but the *jhuṇḍī mahant* rejected this innovation and ordered the podium to be reinstalled at its former place, any change in the tradition being proscribed.

the *rājā* has taken off his royal turban and wrapped a simple strip of orange cloth around his head. Both climb up the small podium and sit, the *rājgūrū* a little lower. Both face north and face the Tantri who will proceed to the ablutions, helped by his expert father and singing verses from the *Ṛg Veda* (the *puruṣasukta*, the hymn to the Puruṣa).

The Tantri first purifies the *rājā* and the *rājgūrū* by sprinkling a few drops of water over them and putting a small triangle made of *kuś* grass on their heads. Taking each of the small pots successively, he sprinkles both men with the consecrated liquids, using a *bel* leaf as sprinkler. Then he takes the first big jar and pours the consecrated water all at once over the *rājā's* head, and does the same with the second jug, pouring the contents over the *rājgūrū*'s head. All the Yogīs stand up and acclaim their *rājā* with great excitement. Quickly the Tantri waves a lamp around the podium, and the former *rājā* applies a *ṭikā* on the forehead of his successor, and both *rājā* and *rājgūrū*, drenched, leave the podium to change clothes. The *rājā* comes back shortly after to receive a flower garland from his predecessor.

Then everybody goes back inside the monastery's courtyard, while a group of Raibari villagers, who came to honour the first *rājā* born from their community, bow in front of the podium which is still soaked with the sacred waters of the *abhiṣek*.

The *abhiṣek*, the sprinkling, has to be performed with nine different liquids or products mixed with water: yoghurt, honey, milk, red sandal powder, clarified butter, sugar, perfume and two sorts of pure water: *gaṅgājal*, the Ganges water (here some running water flowing in the monastery tank) and *tīrthajal*, water from a holy spot [here taken from a well and sanctified by a *tulsi* (holy basil] leaf).

Adhikār, *Entitlement: Enthronement and Coronation*

Only the *rājā* is now involved in the installation rituals. The throne of Kadri is just for him and the *rājgūrū* is now only a mere attendant. A few months ago the former *rājā* had ordered the construction of a new throne, a marble impressive *siṃhāsana*, but here again the *jhuṇḍī mahant* has refused the innovation and it is at the old place, where is now the swing of Dhūmāvati *bhūtā*, that sits the *rājā* cross-legged. Besides him stand the *rājgūrū* and the Kadri *pujārī* on his left side and the Tantrī and the former *rājā* on his right. The new *rājā* takes the solemn vow to respect his charge and to follow its obligations.

He is then crowned, i.e. he receives a new turban, which is then called *mukuṭ*, crown. As a matter of fact, this *mukuṭ* is very similar to the turban worn by the *rājā* since he was in Tryambakeshvar. The only difference is that the black thread is longer and thicker and has been twisted specially by a group of Yogīs the previous day.

The Tantrī applies a red *ṭikā* (the *rājtilak*) on the *rājā's* forehead, then proceeds to the transmission of the dagger (*kattī*), the same dagger he consecrated during the fire offering. He is joined by the former *rājā*: both take the dagger together and give it to the *rājā* seated on his throne. Together they hold the dagger which the *rājā* places afterwards on the throne. From now on, when the *rājā* quits his throne, he will instead place the dagger there as a visible sign of his office. And people will bow in front of the dagger as they would in front of the *rājā*. Here again royal symbolism prevails in the installation of the head of a monastery.

After this enthronement, the Tantrī takes the *rājā* to worship the gods and the *pātradevatā*, then leads him outside again, onto the *abhiṣek* podium. The *rājā* sits and, for the first time, Cāndnāth, the Mahāsabhā vice-president, takes part in the ritual. He garlands the *rājā* with flowers, marks him with a *ṭikā* and presents him with a brocade shawl (*cāddar*). With this gesture he recognizes, in the name of the sect's authorities, the installation of the new monastic head. After Cāndnāth, the two *mahants* of the *jamāt* tie a black thread (*selī*) around the *rājā's* neck and all the Yogīs follow, bowing, offering flowers, *ṭikā* and, for some, a shawl.

According to the Tantrī, this consecration ritual follows the *Kāmikā āgama*[20] (or the *Tantra samuccaya*, a 'collection of Tantras',

[20] Core texts of the southern Śaiva tradition, the āgama are

a kind of summary of tantras).[21] It is not specific to the Yogīs and we shall return to its characteristics at the end of this chapter.

Parting with the Pātradevatā

One last time the *rājā* takes his place behind the *pātradevatā* he brought with him during the long journey and a final act of worship is performed by the *pujārī* in front of a huge crowd which gathers together all the Yogīs of the *jhuṇḍī* and all the devotees who came for the enthronement. The herald is busy announcing loudly all the donations that devotees and visitors make to the *pātradevatā*, before it disappears from view.

The *pātradevatā* is intrinsically linked to the person of the *rājā*, and so it remains with him during his twelve year 'reign', not

---

generally said to be 28 in number. Traditionally each temple was linked to a particular āgama (Brunner-Lachaux 1977). At the beginning of the twentieth century, manuscripts of āgamas started to be collected and published for religious purposes. 'The tradition of editing religious treatises for the temple officiants continues to the present day: for instance the *uttarakāmikāgama* with a Tamil translation was published in 1999 by the Ministry of Hindu Religious Endowments of Tamil Nadu Government who gave a copy to each temple under its control' (Ganesan, Barois 2003: 257). In parallel to this, since 1955 the French Institute of Pondicherry has been collecting all the religious manuscripts from South India and possesses no fewer than 1890 manuscripts of the Śaivāgamas (id.: 259). The *Kāmikāgama* is 'among the āgamas the one whose name is the most well known [...] The Kāmika is a voluminous treatise [...] which teaches all what is needed about the life of the temple, since its construction till the exceptional rituals [...] Modern ritualists still refer to it [...] The common rituals described there are still close to those performed in modern India [...] which does not seem to caracterise a very ancient text' (Brunner 1985: VII-XIII, my translation from French).

[21] Perhaps because of the Nambudiri identity of the Tantrīs' family: 'Priests in Kerala (Nambudri) ... perform rituals in temple to all three deities – Viṣṇu, Śiva and Devī – so they follow the *Tantra Samuscaya*, which gives instruction for all three' (Venkatachari 1996: 187).

on view, but locked up in a small cupboard in the *dhūnī* room. The arrival of a new *pātradevatā* is necessarily accompanied by the removal of the previous one, just as the installation of the new *rājā* entails the removal from office of the previous *rājā*, a removal which is also a sort of liberation.

Early in the afternoon of the coronation day, all the doors of the *maṭh* are closed. The two *rājās* join the *jhuṇḍī mahant* in the *dhūnī* room and the former *rājā* takes out of the cupboard his *pātradevatā,* which he covers with red cloth and flowers, while the new rājā puts his *pātradevatā* there instead. Then, suddenly, the old *rājā* with the *jhuṇḍī mahant* and a group of Yogīs leave the monastery by a back door and start walking very fast across the 'jungle' towards the seashore. Half an hour later, the group reaches the mouth of the Gurpur River, a place called Sultan Battery where there is an old fort attributed to Tipu Sultan, half sanded up, amongst dilapidated wooden boats and a few poor fishermen's huts. A few boats are waiting there to take the Yogīs across the river to the sea which lies just beyond a low sandbar. The Yogīs are quite excited and go on board among shouts of laughter and applause. When they disembark, they surround the *rājā* carrying his *pātradevatā* and the *jhuṇḍī mahant* and walk towards the sea. The *jhuṇḍī mahant* refusing at that point to be followed any further, I can just see from a distance the Yogīs taking their clothes off and moving forward into the sea. It is an explicit reference to the Paraśurām legend as it is depicted on the *maṭh* walls. Like Paraśurām, the *rājā* carries the *pātradevatā* and moves forward deep into the sea; like him, the *rājā* appears ready to give up his life.[22] But the sea receded in front of Paraśurām, and here the *rājā* returns finally to the

[22] A version of the Paraśurām legend in Kerala (see Tarabout 1990: 230) allows for an interesting parallel: Paraśurām gives authority to the Brahmans, but 'later on, these Brahmans, seeing that they are unable to rule, call in foreign princes, each of them allowed to exercise power only for twelve years'; and another legend specifies that the legitimacy of one of the local rulers 'was based on his duty to cut his own throat after twelve years' (id. my transl.).

sea shore; however, only after he would have immersed the *pātradevatā* at the farthest possible point.

If nowadays the scene looks playful and the Yogīs seem to be enjoying themselves, people say that, in former times, it happened that the *rājā* took a *jal-samādhi* (a *samādhi* in water) and went into the sea until he disappeared in a death which was a final liberation. It was why the *rājās* chosen were old ! The complete assimilation between the *rājā* and the *pātradevatā* required that they disappear together.

This time the *rājā* did not drown but he does not go back to Kadri. He leaves immediately for his own monastery in Rājāsthan, while the Yogīs and *jhuṇḍī mahant* return to the *maṭh*.

This was the final dramatic ritual of this months-long performance.

Now in the Kadri monastery comes the time to settle the accounts of the *jhuṇḍī*. The *jhuṇḍī mahant* and the accountant check the expenditure and distribute the cash surplus to the Yogīs according to their office during the *jhuṇḍī*. As for the *rājā*, he personally gives some money to all the Yogīs who accompanied him during these six months.

The Yogīs are now quite eager to leave, to regain their freedom and eventually their solitude. But they still have one night to spend in the monastery since Śivarātrī, Śiva's night, is not finished and the officiants have to perform the three ritual cycles of homage to the God. The Yogīs divide into three groups: one with the officiants, one close to the fire of the *jamāt* and one with the lay devotees who spend the night listening to religious speeches and watching a long performance of Yakshagana enacting the story of Paraśurām.

The next morning a small group with the *jhuṇḍī mahant* and Cāndnāth, accompanies the *rājgurū* to Vittal to take his office. This time they travel by coach: the *jhuṇḍī* is finished.

The completion of the liminal period represented by the itinerant *jhuṇḍī*, by the six-month-long installation, also shows on the body of the *rājā*. He had kept his hair and beard long as a sign of asceticism; this first morning, he shaves completely before starting to perform his duty as a monastic head. The many Yogīs who surrounded him now leave, but for a very small group of close followers. And the local community of *grihastha* Yogīs waits anxiously to see how the new *rājā* will adapt to this very different environment and to this region, the language of which he does not even understand.

COMPARISON WITH OTHER CONSECRATION RITUALS

In order to better understand the sequence of events during Kadri *paṭṭābhiṣek*, it would be useful to look for comparisons with other monastic or royal rites of consecration.

Comparison with other Nāth Monasteries

Compared to the Kadri *paṭṭābhiṣek*, the investiture ceremony I attended in Dang-Caughera monastery is simpler. Called *pīr-sthāpana*, or 'installation of the *pīr*', it is performed every year, the monastery being *pañcāyati* but the *pīr* being elected by the Yogī community for one year only (see Chapter 7).

The ceremony is purely yogīc and does not include any fire ritual, nor any sprinkling or *abhiṣek*. It starts early in the morning with a private cult to the *pātradevatā* by the *pīr*, who afterwards carries the deity-pot to the central hall where the ceremony will be held. All the Yogīs who came for the occasion take their places in this hall, called the *dalicā*, and proceed, by common agreement, to the election of the new *pīr* and of few other ritual specialists. As soon as he is elected, the new *pīr* is taken in front of a Bhairav altar where he receives the headdress which marks his new status. In Dang it is not a turban but a conical cap in red velvet (explained as the typical headdress of the monastery's founder, Ratannāth), a thin black thread (*śeli*) being wrapped around its border. Crowned before Bhairav, the new *pīr* then goes back to the hall and the carpet-throne (*gaddī*) in front of the *pātradevatā* where his predecessor is waiting. As soon as he reaches the *gaddī*, the former *pīr* wraps him in a large white ceremonial shawl. Other Yogīs and lay authorities and devotees come to bow in front of the group constituted by the two *pīrs* and the *pātradevatā* and give a money offering which the herald announces loudly. The former *pīr* then teaches his successor the complicated gestures required for the worship of the *pātradevatā*, some of which are done under the secrecy provided by the shawl. Finally the monastery's *pujārī* pays homage to the *pīr*.

This ceremony of installation is centred on the transmission of a ritual expertise required by the worship of the *pātradevatā* which is here the *pīr's* main duty. However, some elements belong to a more general framework: a 'coronation' with the presentation of a particular headdress (in the Caughera case a bonnet, elsewhere a turban, or even a crown as we shall see), and an 'investiture' with the transmission of a special garment, a shawl given by the predecessor.

This first consecration is followed by a long journey made together by the two *pīrs* to the Devi Patan sanctuary (in Gonda district in Uttar Pradesh), where the ritual process ends with the withdrawal of the last *pīr*.

George Weston Briggs was the only author to give some details about the procedures in some Nāth monasteries. He mentioned 'the mahant of Tulsipur (Devī Pātan) [who] is chosen by vote of twelve Yogīs representing the twelve sub-sects of the Gorakhnāthīs. He is placed upon the *gaddi*, given a *janeo* and a special dress, and offerings of *prasād* are made before him' (1973: 38).

He gave more details about Gorakhpur:

> The mahant at Gorakhpur nominates his successor, invariably choosing a member of his own sub-sect [...] The rule as stated at Gorakhpur is that, upon the death of the mahant, representatives of the twelve sub-sects of the Gorakhnāthīs meet to choose a successor. They invariably elect the person named by the late mahant [...] After a mahant has been chosen, the electors proceed to the District Officer of Gorakhpur and announce their decision [...] The mahant is inducted into office with the usual form of worship, the *prasād* and a feast [...] Part of the services of installation take place while the mahant is seated in a niche in the wall of the main shrine. The Yogīs worship him, present him with a new garment and mark his forehead with the *ṭikā*. Afterwards

he is seated on the *rājā gaddi*, or royal seat, outside the veranda of the main shrine. Then the priest at the monastery gives him a garment and marks his forehead with the *ṭikā*, and makes other presents. There is of course a large number of Yogīs and others including prominent men of the community present. In connection with the ceremonies there is a protracted worship of *Pātar Deo*, covering seven days.[23] (1973: 36-7)

Regarding other places, Briggs specifies that at Dinodhar, in Kacch, 'the pīr is chosen, from among the Yogīs at the monastery by the Rāo of Kacch and holds office for life' (id. 38).

The differences between Gorakhpur and Dinodhar on the one hand and Tulsipur, Dang-Caughera and Kadri on the other are those between *nijī* monasteries, where succession passes from guru to disciple in the same *panth*, and *pañcāyatī* monasteries where the head is elected among the Yogīs from all the twelve *panths*. But whatever the procedure, the community of the Yogīs is symbolically represented as well as the civil authority which sanctions the nomination. The ceremony seems to consist essentially in an enthronement – in the literal sense: seating on the *gaddī* – and a homage (with a *ṭikā* and the gift of a piece of cloth: a 'new garment' in Gorakhpur, a 'special dress' in Dinodhar, and always a shawl or a scarf).

Other Monastic Investitures: The Nimbārkī Vishnuites of Salemabad and the Dasnāmī Sannyāsīs of Sringeri

Here again the comparison with the few descriptions we have from the investiture of monastic heads in other *sampradāyas* will allow us to put Kadri rituals in perspective. As analysed by Catherine Clementin-Ojha (2006), the investiture of the head of the Rājāsthani Nimbārkī monastery of Salemabad is as follows:

> The investiture comprised two distinct parts: (1) an aspersion (*abhiṣeka*) and (2) the conferring of a shawl (*cāddar satkār*). The first

[23] Briggs ignores the specificity of the *pātradevatā*. He explains Pātar Deo with 'Patel Deo, the spirit of the ancient (village) proprietor' (id.: 37).

part was performed [...] by the domestic priest of the monastery: the boy sitting on the monastic seat (*ācārya-pīṭha*) was sprinkled with consecrated water while the appropriate mantra was recited. Then the priest ceremoniously placed on his head the sacred stone-emblem [... The second part] was performed by [...a] prominent Nimbārkī ascetic of Vrindavan (...] Standing close to the teenager who was still sitting on the monastic seat, he first applied the sectarian mark (*tilaka*) on his forehead with some sandal paste, then tied a rosary (*mālā*) of sacred basil (*tulsī*) beads around his neck and finally wrapped him up into the ceremonial shawl [...] Afterwards, other ascetics of note came to pay their respects and garlanded him with flowers as he sat in public for the first time, giving his blessed vision or *darśana* (2006: 546-7).

Till the end of eighteenth century, the mahārajā of Jaipur had to approve the choice of the incumbent by giving him a 'dress of honour' which included a turban, a gift which marked the later's entitlement to administrative reponsibilities.

The ritual of investiture of the head of the great Shankarian monastery of Sringeri has been well documented by Glenn Yocum, who attended Śrī Bhāratī Tirtha's enthronement in 1989. The ceremony has also been filmed under the supervision of the monastery in *Avichinna Paramparā: The Unbroken Chain*. It lasted two days and was performed mostly in the temple of the main deity (the Sharada Temple) where the throne is placed.

On the morning before the pattabhisheka, an elaborate *homa* lasting over two hours was performed in the south corridor. Ten to twelve priests were involved in chanting and making oblations. At about noon Bharati Tirtha came to the temple in procession. [...] he sat on a low silver throne [...] Various pujas were performed in front of him. [Afterwards he went round the monastery temples then gave a press conference to a group of thirty journalists]. The pattabhisheka itself was celebrated in the Sharada Temple's south *prakara* close to the site of the previous day's homa [...] where the throne has been placed [...] Shortly before the jagadguru arrived, a curtain was held in front of the throne. Behind a ritual called *mangalashtaka* was performed. Soon Bharati Tirtha arrived and [...] ascended the throne to shouts and applause. This was the climactic moment of the ceremony [...] A number of rituals followed, all performed by the matha's purohit [...]

The abhisekha proper consisted of the priest sprinkling the swami with water by means of bundles of grass that were dipped into small metal pots [...] mantras were intoned, not only by the purohit but also by the sannyasis and anyone else present who knew them [...] After the abhisekha proper, a silk cloth was held in front of the swami for a period of about twenty minutes. When this cloth was removed, the guru was wearing his gold and gem-incrusted crown as well as other jewels and a splendiferous gold-thread and silk shawl. (Yocum 1996: 72-7)

Watching the film one sees, when the cloth is removed, Bhāratī Tirtha standing close to the throne with his splendid shawl and his crown, then ascending the throne where he sits while the officials and devotees pay homage to him. Later in the night he crosses the town in a palanquin amidst enthusiastic cheers.

The sequence of events at Sringeri evokes the Kadri rituals but on a much larger scale considering the religious and sociological importance of Sringeri. The royal pomp symbolized by the gold crown shows *a contrario* the Nāth dimension of the Kadri enthronement. However, the consecration and transmission of the dagger in Kadri represent an important element of royal symbolism, which is absent in Sringeri.

Installation Ceremonies of the Kings

Let us follow Ronald Inden's description of the main parts of the royal consecration, or what he calls 'affusion (*abhiṣeka*) into kingship (*rajya*)', according to the *Viṣṇudharmottara Purāṇa*[24] (1998: 53-82).

[24] 'The second book [of the *VdhP*] containing 183 chapters on kingship, is the most extensive treatment of this subject in early medieval India, especially in its elaborate description of the rituals to be performed by the king' (Inden 1998: p. 83n.9). 'In 1674, the *VdhP* rule provided the basis for Śivāji's coronation; and in the present, it appears to have been the main source for the coronation of the kings of Nepal' (id. 56).

The *rājyābhiṣeka* itself is binary in its structure. The first-half, the *abhiṣeka* proper, consists of a series of baths of which the king is the passive recipient. The second half, often referred to as the *paṭṭa-bandha*, the 'fixing' or 'tying on' (*bandha*) of the 'headband' or 'crown' (*paṭṭa*), consists of the crowning, enthronement, and a series of other rites by which the king acts out his royal role. (id. 61)

The first half, *abhiṣeka,* takes place in the *abhiṣeka-maṇḍapa* (bathing pavilion) and is performed by the royal domestic priest who 'begins [...] by making homa oblations of clarified butter into the fire to the chanting of formulas (*mantras*), and places the remainder of the offering in a golden jar (*kalaśa*)' (id.). Then 'the priest "bathes" (*snā*), but here "daubs" is more accurate and "purifies" fifteen parts of the king's body with "clays" from appropriate parts of the earth's surface' (id.): it is at the same time a purification and a union of the person of the king with the earth.

This is followed by different aspersions considered as Vedic or Puraṇic according to the symbols and texts recited. The king is seated on a special throne, in the centre of the pavilion like an axis mundi. The rituals and effusions of this Vedic sequence make the king 'a microcosmic form of the Cosmic Man, Puruṣa' (id. 64). In particular the first sprinklings are made by four Brahmans who embody the four *varṇas*, an allusion to the myth of the *varṇas* generated out of the body of the Cosmic Man (Puruṣa).

Even though the Kadri sprinkling of the *rājā* does not include this quadripartition between four officiating Brahmins, the mention of the recitation of the *Ṛg Veda* hymn to the Puruṣa by the Tantrī clearly refers to it and finds here its justification.

The puraṇic sequence of the *abhiṣeka* appears as parallel to the vedic one, but more encompassing, involving all segments of society. The main officiant is the royal astrologer who makes aspersions onto the king's head from a golden jar full of different liquids and previously consecrated substances. Says Inden, 'the ritual enactment of Puruṣa's creation of the king by drawing together portions of the gods is now completed. The recipient had earlier been made into an independent, regional king by the vaidika segment of the rite, the *rājasūya*; here he has been made into an imperial, universal king, a replica of Viṣṇu, the Cosmic Man of the *VdhP*' (id. 71).

The second part of the ceremony, or *paṭṭa-bandha*, 'tying of the head-band', establishes the new power of the king which he acquired through *abhiṣeka*.

The king, clad in a white garment, comes back to the throne, and after having looked at his image in a mirror, proceeds to auspicious rites and offerings to the gods. Then the priest honours him with the *madhu-parka* offerings. 'The king, welcomed as a god to his kingdom [...] is next presented with his *paṭṭa*, a kind of plate or band resting on the forehead, and *mukuta*, or crown, both of which are fixed on his head [...] The king is now ready for his enthronement' (id. 73-4).

The king goes to the audience hall (*sabhāmaṇḍapa*) where his throne has been brought. He sits there solemnly while the priest recites mantras invoking firmness and steadiness (*dhruva*). The king is thus offered to the full view of his subjects. The ritual ends with the distribution by the king of the *dakṣiṇā* or sacrificial fees to the Brahmans.[25]

The final episode is a triumphal procession through the town's streets.

This detailed description shows that many elements of the king's installation are present in Kadri and even more in Sringeri. However, one may remark that some essential parts of the royal *abhiṣek* are missing in the monastic rituals, like the unction-union with earth, the foundational role of the four *varṇas*, all elements which inscribe kingship in the world. The *paṭṭābhiṣek* of monastic heads represents a compromise between the other wordly tendency of one who dedicates himself to an ascetic life, and the obvious this-wordly involvement of someone who has

[25] Heesterman (1998: 27) adds that the *rājābhiṣeka* cycle ends with a hair-cutting ritual accompanied by mantras, and that it can be done immediately after enthronement, the king being thus still seated on the throne.

to manage a religious institution and sometimes even a huge estate.

Another Model: The Consecration of a Spiritual Master

One last comparison supports this point. The *ācaryābhiṣeka*, according to the passage of the *Somaśambhupaddhati* translated into French by Helène Brunner-Lachaux (1977), is performed on a Śaiva initiate in order to allow him to accede to the highest function of spiritual master. She insists on 'the solemnity of these ceremonies which have similarities with the consecration of kings' (1977: XI).

This consecration has to be prepared with some observances that 'the candidate should respect preferably during a pilgrimage' (id. 456), which reminds us of the Kadri *jhuṇḍī*.

The ceremony itself comprises three stages:

- The installation of the jars in the sacrificial pavillon or *yāga-maṇḍapa*. These nine jars are filled with water mixed with beneficial substances and placed on a *maṇḍala*.
- The sprinkling in the bathing-pavilion (*snāna-maṇḍapa*), which can be adorned with a canopy, flags and flower garlands. A seat can be prepared: a wooden plank covered by a cloth. The initiate takes his place and is sprinkled with the water of the nine jars by the guru who recites the appropriate mantras to the sound of auspicious roars and music.
- The initiate comes back wearing white clothes and the guru honours him, then gives him several objects 'as a sign of his new authority', among them 'a turban, a crown, an umbrella', all symbols of kingship, but also 'a water-pot, a rosary [...], books' (id. 482). By these gifts, the guru confers on the initiate the *adhikāra*, the habilitation.

The text of the *Somaśambhupaddhati* elaborates next on the fate of the former master who, as soon as his successor has been initiated, can – and sometimes must – disappear, stripped of his privileges.

BACK IN KADRI: AN ORIGINAL SYNTHESIS

This comparative excursus has made it possible to draw parallels between the Kadri *rājā's* investiture rituals with those of other spiritual authorities and with their model, the king's coronation. But first we have to think about the vocabulary employed.

Abhiṣek, 'anointing, consecrating (by sprinkling water), royal unction, etc.' (Monier-Williams 1988: 71), applies to the ritual action and to its consequence: the entitlement of the king (in *rājābhiṣek*), of the spiritual master (*ācaryābhiṣek*), to the exercise of his function (his *adhikār*). The expression *paṭṭābhiṣek* employed for the coronation ceremony is also used for the investiture of the heads of monastic institutions.[26] However the meaning of *paṭṭa* in this context is rather ambiguous. As Clementin-Ojha says, '*paṭṭa* [is] a polysemous term which refers to anything that is flat, such as a length of cloth or a slab. It seems that it stands for a headband (or a turban) in the expression *paṭṭābhiṣek*. Yocum translates the latter as "coronation"' (2006: 550).

The Monier-Williams Sanskrit dictionary (1988: 579) is rather wordy regarding *paṭṭa* as turban or strip of cloth and gives many compounds among which *paṭṭābhiṣek* as 'consecration of a tiara' or *paṭṭa-bandha*, 'binding or crowning the head with a turban'. And effectively turban and crown seem equivalent: if, in Sringeri the abbot receives effectively a crown, in Kadri as well as in other Nāth monasteries his headdress is more like a bonnet or a turban on which is interwined a black thread, a *śeli*, as a reminder of ascetic Nāth identity.

However to complicate the situation, the name by which the Nāths refer to this turban is *mukuṭ*, crown! And when I asked

[26] Clementin-Ojha mentions that it 'is also the name given to ceremonies of consecration of some deities' (2006: 551 n. 32) and she remarks that references to the investiture of Salemabad Abbot as *paṭṭābhiṣek* are rather recent, perhaps in an attempt 'to raise the prestige of the lineage of Salemabad' (id. 550). To my knowledge the term *paṭṭābhiṣek* is employed among the Nāth Yogīs only for the investiture of the Kadri *rājā*.

for explanation, I was told that the word *paṭṭa* refers to what the administrative authorities call in their English documents 'appointment order'. Clémentin-Ojha arrives at the same conclusion: 'But today in Sringeri itself *paṭṭābhiṣeka* is associated with the notion of deed (conferring a right) or with that of a seat (conferring a position), and *not with a crown*' (2006: 550). Some people even told me in Kadri that *paṭṭābhiṣeka* signified 'anointing to the throne' and that *paṭṭa* referred to the throne in Kannada! Let us add that the word *paṭṭa* is currently used by the Nāth Yogīs in the compound *yogapaṭṭa* for referring to the long strip of cloth used by meditating yogīs to maintain a sitting position.[27]

The Kadri *paṭṭābhiṣeka* or investiture ceremony presents a fascinating combination of elements which come from different traditions or influences and explain the heterogeneous aspects of the Kadri abbot's sovereignty.

First the closeness of the *paṭṭābhiṣeka* to the general basic structure or royal consecration is striking.

- Even though the stages can develop with a different temporality, it fits with the cycle of the royal ritual of *rājasūya* described by Jan Heesterman (1998: 26-7) which includes four phases: unction, war or raiding expedition, enthronement, and hair cutting. We have already mentioned the *padyātrā*, the pilgrimage of the *jhuṇḍī*, as a victorious journey over a territory submitting to the *rājā's* authority. However in case of Kadri, the conquering expedition precedes the unction, which is split into two phases: the formal investiture made in front of the *pātradevatā* in Nasik, and several months later the aspersion performed by the Brahman priest after a 'vedic' *pūjā*.
- Regarding the enthronement itself, the binary structure

[27] Clementin-Ojha refers to another meaning of *yogapaṭṭa* as meditation shawl: in the ritual of initiation into *saṁnyāsa* among the Daśnāmī, the last step is the conferring of a 'meditation shawl' by the guru (2006: 562).

exposed by Inden is obviously there: on one side the vedic rites with fire offerings and vedic mantras followed by the sprinkling, and on the other side the presentation of the symbolic attributes of royalty (headdress, throne, public homage). And in Kadri the royal theme is reinforced by the solemn transmission of the dagger (*kattī*).[28] The association between sword, or dagger, and kingship is quite well documented, especially in the Nepalese kingdoms where the sword, *khaḍga*, was often ritually considered as a substitute for the king's person.[29] And as mentioned by Adrian Mayer (1985: 209) during *darbārs*, when the king goes absent, 'a sword might be placed on the *gaddi* to signify his presence, for the *gaddi* could not be left empty'. It is exactly what is done in Kadri.

However, as in the *ācāryābhiṣek*, the royal elements are reinterpreted in an ascetic context and more precisely in this case Nāth Yogī. The distinctive features of this Nāth performance are: the succession by election and the part played by the egalitarian community of the ascetics, the *pātradevatā* as a symbol of this community considered as a superior authority, the asceticism or physical hardship of the pilgrimage, the approval given by the Yogīs to the *rājā's* investiture in giving him the traditional shawl and the black wool thread, and finally the haircut modified into complete shaving. All these elements contribute to making the *rājā* not just the Kadri *rājā* but the representative of the entire sect with authority over all of south India.

[28] Even though Kadri is an exception and there is no mention of a dagger, or a sword, in the other various investiture rituals we have mentioned, be they monastic or royal. However Heesterman (1957: 142) mentions that during the *rājasūya*, the periodic royal sacrifice, the king sits ceremoniously on the throne and receives from the hands of the *adhvaryu* priest, a sacrificial sword, with the words: 'You are the Vrta killing bolt of Indra, thereby be subject to me'.

[29] This substitution being grounded in a common relationship to the deity, most often Durgā (see Toffin 1993: 67-70, 182 and Lecomte-Tilouine 1996).

CHAPTER 6

Caughera Maṭh (Dang Valley, Nepal): Legends of Foundation

A second example of a *pañcāyatī* monastery introduces a new theme: the part played by a monastery which is important both for the Nāth *sampradāya* and for Nepalese kingship. In my view, the monastery of Caughera in the Dang Valley of Nepal Terai provides a clear illustration of the type of relationships existing between monastic establishments and traditional Hindu monarchy. Anchored both in Nāth identity and in relationships of mutual legitimation with royal powers, the Caughera Maṭh presents a configuration that was probably rather common in the former small kingdoms of Rajasthan and Nepal (Bouillier 1989).

YOGĪS AND KINGS

As we mentioned before, the yogīs were supposed to have ascetic and yogic practices that allowed for control of natural processes and surpassing the ordinary limits of the human condition. Credited with exceptional powers, they were sought out by kings: they figure in numerous foundation myths as allies of conquering kings, giving help both in mastering natural obstacles and subjugating enemies. Usually nothing moral or dharmic was involved in these conquests, rather it was a simple confrontation between opposing powers. And when the conquest or the domination was ensured thanks to successful actions on the part of the Yogīs, a cult to Gorakhnāth would be instituted, a temple or a monastery founded where the spiritual successors of the first miracle-worker could settle.

Let us take a few examples before dealing with the case of Caughera. The Himalayan area was divided during the pre-modern period into numerous little kingdoms, often at war with each other. Powerful Siddhas and Yogīs are often mentioned as protectors of these kingdoms: Charpaṭnāth in Chamba, where, according to the chronicles and records reported by Mahesh Sharma (2009), the Siddha Charpaṭnāth[1] was instrumental in helping the ruler Mahilla Varman to assert his power and build his township;[2] the kingdom of Tehri with Satyanāth;[3] Kumaon Almora with Nāgnāth and the Chand dynasty;[4] Doti with the renouncer-king Dipayal; Jumla with both Candannāth and Baṭuk Bhairav (Unbescheid 1980); Dang with Ratannāth as we shall see; Gorkha with Gorakhnāth.

The example of the small kingdom of Gorkha in central Nepal is particularly illustrative of the close relationship between kings and yogīs, both in the legendary world and in the historical context. The eighteenth century chronicle known as

[1] Charpaṭnāth seems to have been a quite original figure. He is credited with subversive songs, which mock the apparence and habits of the Nāth Yogīs (even their earrings) according to a 1654 CE Lahore manuscript published by Mohan Singh (1937), see also M. Sharma 2009: 91-2.

[2] However, there is a huge gap between this legend whose facts would date from the tenth century and the first landgrant to the yogīs as priests of the temple dedicated to Charpaṭnāth, dated 1783 (Sharma 2009: 79).

[3] According to Atkinson (1974: 815) it is in the Tehri capital, Dewalgarh, 'that one of the ancestors of the present Raja met the Siddh [Satyanāth] and so pleased the god by his devotion [...] that the Siddh raised him up in the hollow of his hand and promised him the entire country as far as he could see ... [In Dewalgarh] we have the oldest and most honored temple of Satyanāth. The service of the temple is now conducted by Jogis and their chief has the title of Pir' (ibid.).

[4] The Siddha Nāgnāth helped King Kirati Chand, giving him 'a whip with which he will scourge [his enemy] as a man doth scourge a vicious horse' (Atkinson 1980: 534). 'Naturally Nāgnāth acquired great influence' (ibid.).

Gorkhā Vaṁśāvali recounts the many apparitions of Gorakhnāth to successive rulers, beginning with Dravya Shah, the conqueror of Gorkha crowned in 1550, to whom Gorakhnāth announces his future sovereignty over Gorkha and the future dominance of his lineage over the whole of Nepal following the conquest of his seventh-generation descendant, Prithvi Narayan.[5] The constant protection granted by the Siddha finds visible expression in the sanctuary built close to the palace by the king Prithvipati Shah (1667-1716) where Nāth Yogīs give ritual service.[6]

A similar configuration can be seen in Rajasthan where many of the former kingdoms originated in a marvellous encounter between a would be king and a yogī: the encounter between Jodha and the Yogī Ciṛiyānāth at the origin of Jodhpur (Nagar 2001: 19-26), between Bappa and the hermit Harita then with Gorakhnāth (Tod 1983: I, 185), between Deoraj of Jaisalmer and the yogī Baba Ritta (id.: II 188).

Encounters did not only happen in a legendary past. Yogīs have been priests of royal temples, officiated in kingship rituals, and played a part during the consecration and renewal ceremonies of many sovereigns in Rajasthan,[7] Nepal (Bouillier 1989, Krauskopff 1996), and Orissa (Rousseleau 2008). Yogīs can also be instrumental in giving more material help, like

[5] Gorakhnāth, looking like an ordinary yogī, appears in front of Prithvi Narayan, who then is still a child. Asking him for curd, he drinks then vomits it and orders the child to drink. Shaking, the child Prithvi Narayan drops the curd on his feet and the Siddha laughingly tells him: 'since it is your feet which received the blessed drink, you will only reign on the land you have walked on' (Narharināth, *Gorkhā Vaṁśāvali* 95). However, after the royal massacre of 2001 a number of people (relayed by press and websites) echoed this episode, adding that Gorakhnāth was enraged and laid a curse on the proud king, saying that his dynasty would last 10 generations, one for each of his toes, after which it would lose power.

[6] On these Yogīs, their settlement, and their ritual duties, see Bouillier 1986.

[7] See Tod 1983, I, 464-8 (Mewar), II, 107-15 (Jodhpur), 188-92 (Jaisalmer).

Bhagavantanāth who assisted Prithvi Narayan thanks to both his supernatural and diplomatic skills (Bouillier 1991, 1992b). This closeness went as far as identification in the famous case of the Jodhpur kingdom at the beginning of the nineteenth century, when the Yogīs became the effective leaders of the state, the rājā Man Singh having relinquished all power in their favour and decided to renounce the world (Sharma 1972, Gold 1995). Although nowadays the huge Jodhpur Mahamandir Temple is no longer in Nāth hands, the monastery founded by Man Singh in Pushkar is, like Caughera, an establishment both founded by a royal power and belonging to the Nāth community, since it is now an important *pañcāyatī maṭh*.

We shall see from the Caughera example how a relationship of patronage and mutual support between kings and yogīs works in a practical way. We shall explore first the legendary corpus related to the foundation of the monastery, where the king and the ascetic merge in the person of Ratannāth, a prince who became Gorakhnāth's disciple. In addition, we shall discover the complex references made in the narratives to the whole Nāth universe and also to the surrounding north Indian Muslim context. Then, after studying how the monastery reveals, through its rituals and organization, how it belongs to the Nāth tradition, we shall come back to the relationship with the political powers. We shall mention the historical foundations of the link between Caughera and the Dang kingdom then with the Nepalese kingdom that succeeded it, through the donations made by the kings and the consequences for the monastery's status of the privileges and obligations that accompany the donations. Even though the land tenure system is rooted in the particular Nepalese situation, the mode of relations it supposes between the sovereign power of the king and the patronized religious institutions can be generalized.

CAUGHERA MONASTERY: THE PLACE

The small valley of Dang, in south-west Nepal, not far from the Indian border, is nested between the two parallel hill chains of the Mahabharat and Siwalik. Considered as inner Terai, this Dang Valley was densely forested till the beginning of the twentieth century and mostly inhabited by the tribal group of the Tharus (Krauskopff 1989). However, since probably the fourteenth or fifteenth century, control was exercised by feudal powers claiming a Kṣatriya origin and caste people slowly became pre-eminent, installing their social order of which the Nāth monastery was a part.

Situated close to the small administrative and commercial town of Ghorahi, the Nāth monastery is nevertheless located in a quiet and green setting. Its various buildings are of moderate height, whitewashed, in north Indian style with verandas, arcades and its temple surmonted by a shikhara roof. The entrance gate leads into the garden in the middle of which is a square pillared hall open on all four sides. Its name, the *dalicā*, tells of its function. It is the place where the Yogīs assemble on festive or solemn occasions like the ceremony for the renewal of the head. Thus, most of the time, the place is empty, visitors only sometimes entering to look at the few wall paintings representing some Shaivite landscapes.

The living quarters of the Yogīs include a small Nepali-style house which is the residence of the administrative head of the *maṭh*, the *mānbhāu*, who has the long-term employment of managing the *maṭh* properties. On the ground floor of the main building are situated the small rooms where resident or visiting Yogīs may rest. Close by is the kitchen. Behind the *mānbhāu*'s house, a small room contains the numerous booklets which remain from the printing press that was very active during the term of Narharināth, Nepal's most famous Yogī, historian and politician.[8] There was also during his leadership a Sanskrit school,

[8] Besides many pamphlets on Nāth beliefs and legends and texts on haṭha yoga, Narharināth published there the historical results of his many years of gathering inscriptions and documents from all over Nepal. He also was a close advisor and sometimes an opponent of the Shah Kings, notably Mahendra; he spent some time in prison, involved himself in pro-Hindu and pro-monarchy movements; he was a member

which was closed some years ago, even before the emergence of Dang as a staunch Maoist bastion during the civil war.

The main part of the monastery is dedicated to ritual activities. First, outside the inner low wall surrounding the *maṭh* buildings, there is a sort of graveyard which encloses many *samādhis*. This graveyard, in close proximity to the *maṭh* as is always the case in Nāth compounds, is dominated by a temple dedicated to Kāl Bhairav. A painting on the door represents the fearsome god holding in his right hand a severed moustachioed head whose blood drops into the cranial cup (*kapāl*) he holds in his lower right hand. His two left hands held a mace and a hourglass-drum (*ḍamaru*). Inside the temple, there is a small statue of Bhairav surrounded by a forest of tridents. Other small platforms scattered here and there represent the seat of the eighth Bhairavs, the Aṣṭa Bhairavs whose duty is to protect the monastery against any malevolent incursion. Dogs run here and there especially at *pūjā* times since they know they will receive the leftovers from the offerings.[9]

Bhairav is not only guarding the *maṭh* from the outside. He is also at the centre of the *maṭh*. The main sanctuaries are to be found on the first floor of the main building. Surmounted by a single shikara roof, two dark square rooms house the deities, on one side the Nāth Siddhas, on the other Kāl Bhairav. Nobody except the officiating priests is allowed inside the rooms, which are closed off by heavy wooden doors during the long *pūjā* hours. However, the many worshippers freely enter the *maṭh* compound during day time; they walk in the garden, climb the stairs, sit on the veranda to chat, smoke and devote themselves to menial tasks with the Yogīs and when the *pūjā* is finished and the doors open, they worship the gods.

---

of the Raj Parishad (the king's privy council) and he died in February 2003. His *samādhi*, his grave turned shrine, has been inaugurated (on Śivarātrī 2006) in the courtyard of the Nāth monastery on the hill of Mrigasthali in Pashupatināth.

[9] Bhairav's leftovers are not usually eaten as *prasād* by the devotees, as they are considered too dangerous, too impure.

The devotees remain standing in the doorway outside each sanctuary room. They may bow down, throw a few coins and flowers, perhaps mark their forehead with ashes and silently revere the gods whose statues in black marble have been beautifully adorned during the *pūjā*. The first statue to be seen, alone, facing the door is of Ratannāth; he is represented seated in *padmāsana* with his characteristic curious pointed headdress and both hands cupped around a begging bowl. Behind him a small platform carries many small lamps, thin cotton wicks placed in small cone-shaped piles of rice. Farther in, a second row of statues has Gorakhnāth at the centre with Matsyendranāth on his right and Śiva-Ādināth on his left (smaller and in white marble). None of the statues seem ancient but I have no information about the date of their installation. And finally at the far end of the room, on a raised platform covered with yellow silk, one can make out a sort of round casket wrapped in silk scarves and flower necklaces. It is said to contain the *pātradevatā*, or *amritpatrā*, the vessel of nectar given by Gorakhnāth to Ratannāth according to the local legend, but which also marks the *maṭh* as *pañcayātī*.

Next the worshippers move on to the doorway of the adjacent room, Bhairav's shrine. The only statue here, also in black marble, represents Bhairav standing, brandishing a sword. In front of the statue are the usual offerings of flowers and lamps and a small table which holds a water ewer and a silver dish in the form of a skull (*kapāl*). The third sanctuary they visit is on the same level but in a more remote corner. It is dedicated to the Goddess: two small statues of Bālā Sundarī and Durgā and a *Śivaliṅga* are surrounded with the usual *pūjā* utensils: lamps, bells, incense burner, water pots. Thus one finds in Caughera a clear demonstration of the 'pantheon' of the Nāth Yogīs, a spatial representation of their deities with equal importance given on one side to the sampradāyic affiliation with Śiva, on the other to fearsome Bhairav, with a subsidiary place given to the Goddess, who, however, is preeminent during the life cycle rituals of the yogīs. It is in this small shrine, which is for this occasion designated as *maṇi*, jewel, that the Goddess under the form of Bālā Sundarī presides over the initiatory and funerary rituals.

A last ritual space is seldom visited by anyone other than Yogīs. It is the *dhūnī*, a large fireplace kept in a room on the ground floor. Constantly burning, it is the symbol of their ascetic status for the Yogīs who use its ashes every morning to rub on to their bodies and mark it with the three horizontal lines of the *tripuṇḍra*. It is also in the *dhūnī* that the *roṭ*, the thick bread offered to Gorakhnāth, is cooked once a week, on Monday night.

Visitors are finally most welcome to visit a sort of art gallery set in front of the sanctuaries, where the paintings of the late Prabhatnāth, the yogī painter whose works can be seen in many places owned by the sect, are hung in long rows. His successors continue to adorn the walls of the monasteries with visual depictions of the foundational legends, but with less aesthetic skill (at least in my opinion!). Some twenty canvases represent the various episods in the life of Ratannāth, many with captions written on the painting itself. This visual enactment of the legend has a didactic purpose, making visitors aware of the grandeur of the place and its traditions. It contributes also to fixing a 'canonical' version among the many variants of the legend.

THE LEGENDS OF RATANNĀTH

When we look at the legends surrounding the figure of the Siddha Ratannāth, as they are narrated and depicted in Caughera, we may be surprised by the evident complexity of their references and by the discrepancy between the two main episodes of the hagiography. The version proposed in Caughera appears as a palimpsest, whose composite elements refer to different levels of the Nāth Yogī religious universe.

Ratannāth appears as a paradoxical figure, both rooted in the local landscape of the Terai valley, and legitimized by his travels in the northwestern Indian subcontinent, less well known in the purely Nāth context than in the hybrid religious world of Muslim dominated areas.

In the Dang monastery his hagiography takes the form of pamphlets written and published locally, which claim to be inspired by two Sanskrit works published in Jodhpur: the *Megh-mālā* ('cloud Necklace')[10] and the *Śrīnāth Tīrthāvalī*, both kept in the Jodhpur palace library and possibly composed by the Jodhpur Rājā-*cum*-Nāth, Man Singh. These pamphlets, especially the *Siddha Ratannāth Caritāmrit* (2043 vs) and the *Siddha Ratannāth* (2013 vs), have been the main inspiration for the paintings and their captions, which represent the episodes of Ratan's life.

Ratan's Initiation: Local Roots

The first episode of the Ratannāth's legend establishes him as a Siddha whose true identity is hidden behind his royal status. The story follows the well-known Nāth model of the renouncer-king, which describes the initiatory quest of a hero of princely lineage who ends up embracing the yogī's condition. Its archetype is Gopicand. Like him and like many Nāth renouncer-kings, Ratan is satisfied with his status as a king and does not think *a priori* about becoming a yogī. The initiation is created and imposed by the guru. However, Ratan accepts his initiation easily and does not experience the moral crisis, the heartbreak, the revolt, which render Gopicand's story deeply moving, and rich in human dilemmas (cf. Grierson 1885, Grodzins Gold 1992).

The scene of his initiation, his encounter with Gorakhnāth is rooted in the local landscape, the densely forested area of inner Terai, rich in wild game and governed by a true Kṣatriya ruler, a wise king whose subjects are happy.

According to the *Siddha Ratannāth Caritāmrit* (my translation from Nepali):

> In the North of our country is the sacred land of the Himalayas where lived Ṛṣis and Siddhas, as mentioned in the Vedas and Puraṇas and where the Siddha Yogīs accomplish their deeds and miracles for the

[10] I was able to read the part of it which has been translated into Nepali by Yogī Narharināth (IPS, 2022 *vs*: 514-22).

welfare of humanity. To this holy lineage belongs the great Siddha Ratnanāth, disciple of Gorakhnāth who is the deity of the kingdom and the true form of Śiva. For the whole of his life, Ratnanāth tried to bring peace to the people. He manifested himself in the place called Caughera, in Dang, in Western Nepal. There, he founded a great and beautiful monastery.

There are different traditions dealing with his coming, his initiation and his actions. It is said that in the lowlands, at the foot of the hills of Dang Deukhuri, Māṇikya Parīkṣaka was king. His son, Ratna Parīkṣaka, had all good qualities. When he begun to rule, the country was flourishing. Nobody went naked, nobody was hungry.

One day the king Ratna Parīkṣaka went hunting with his companions. Seeing a deer which was going slowly past, he shot an arrow at it. The deer fled, the king ran after it and thus went deep into the forest where he lost his escort. The deer had disappeared but the king saw a pool of blood and looked for the animal. Not far off, in a deserted spot, he discovered, seated on a throne in front of a fire, a meditating Siddha of radiant beauty. His side was wounded and at his feet was an arrow. The king understood: 'The one who took the appearance of the deer is Gorakhnāth, who dwells in a hermitage in the forest. It is at Gorakhnāth that I shot the arrow !' And very contrite, he continued standing. After a while, Gorakhnāth awoke from his meditation and he, the radiant one, looked at the king. Seeing his remorse, he granted him the gift of safety[11] and told him: 'King, non-violence (*ahiṃsā*) is *dharma*, is the greatest *dharma*, you should not take life, it is sinful'. But the king, intoxicated by hunting, replied: 'Lord of life, when one living being kills another one, there is neither sin nor merit. It is the law of nature (*prakritiko niyam*)'. Gorakhnāth then said the following verses: 'This swan (*haṁsa*) without breast, without hoof, without beak nor wing, this living being, kill him, O king, that is Ratan's flesh'.[12] Saying that, he gave the king initiation to *haṁsagāyatrī*. Then he gave him the vessel

[11] *Abhaya*, absence of fear, security, peace. The term is closely related to non-violence, *ahiṃsā* and to renunciation, the renouncer, the Sannyāsīn, having to utter the following vow: 'I shall not cause any injury to any creature in thought, word or by the body ; may all creatures have no fear of me' (Kane 1930-62: II, 2, 960).

[12] I choose here the older Nepali version of the book *Siddha Ratnanāth* but in the more recent *Siddha Ratnanāth Caritāmrit*, *ratan* is changed in *rakat*, blood, (followed by the negative *na*) and the commentary in

of ambrosia (*amritpātra*), identical to his own self. Gorakhnāth gave the king the name of Yogī Ratnanāth. Ratnanāth had built in Caughera the seat of the *pātradevatā* and worshipping it, he became a Siddha.

The forest and the jungle are spaces outside the social world which are common to king and ascetic. But if the ascetic chooses wilderness to practice meditation in harmony with local environment, the king enters the forest to hunt. His violent and predatory behaviour stands in profound contrast with the peacefulness which surrounds the ascetic, a contrast that an oral version of the legend transforms in rivalry:

After shooting at the deer, the king follows it deep into the forest. There he discovers a meditating ascetic. In front of him lies a dead deer. The king says to the ascetic: 'Mahārāj, I shot an arrow at this deer, it belongs to me'. The ascetic gets very angry: 'Bastard, this is the deer I kept ! Why did you kill it ?' The king replies: 'You kept a deer ! Deer are wild and they live in the jungle. I am the king of this jungle, the deer are mine !' Gorakhnāth says: 'It thus your function (*adhikār*) to kill deer. Whoever takes life must then have the power to give life back'. The king: 'I don't have this power. You, can you do it ?' Gorakhnāth exclaims: 'Little one, stand up !' The deer stands up and the king becomes Gorakhnāth's disciple.'

Whatever the versions of this first encounter between Gorakhnāth and the future Ratannāth, they all praise *ahiṃsā* and deny the king the right to hunt, to kill. This is a feature common to many Nāth legends, which is not widely shared in the Hindu context. *Ahiṃsā* is a supreme value for renouncers but the king's duty may include violence. As developed in the *Arthaśāstra*, the king's nature and vocation are to be 'imbued with the desire to conquer'.[13] War as well as hunting are part of his *dharma* and both can be considered as sacrifices.[14] However,

---

Nepali develops: 'The swan who keeps moving day and night, O king, kill this animal, in him there is no blood, there is no flesh'.

[13] Cf. Charles Malamoud (2003: 209-18).

[14] Cf. Francis Zimmerann (1987: 184) 'Hunting, like dueling to the death on the battlefield, can be assimilated to a sacrifice [...]

even though a growing value given to *ahiṃsā* finds its most articulate expression in the *Bhagavad-Gītā*, in the condemnation of selfish desire, in the acceptance of war if guided by non-attachment, the ideas expressed in Ratnanāth's legend seem closer to Buddhist ideology. The very words of the text present a striking similarity with an episode from the life of the famous Tibetan saint Milarepa (twelfth century) which, according to the pilgrims of his Nyeshang hermitage at the border between Nepal and Tibet, happened the following way:

> A hunter in Nyeshang with his dog was trying to hit a deer with his arrows but failed. He chased the deer up a steep hillside and arrived at a hermit's cave. The deer entered first and saw Milarepa meditating. [...] The deer [...] sat beside him [...] The hunter charged into the cave, became enraged by what he saw and shot an arrow at Milarepa. It could not touch him. Then Milarepa sang to the hunter asking him to kill the passions within rather than to kill sentient beings without. He invited the hunter to remain and practice the dharma. The hunter threw down his bow and repented of the sin of killing sentient beings. (Mumford 1989: 74)

As was said earlier, the condemnation of hunting is a familiar topic in many Nāth epics: for instance, in the well-known epic about the king Bhartṛhari, the king went hunting and killed a stag despite the supplications of his seventy hinds. 'On his return the Raja was met by Gorakh who said he had killed one of his disciples. Bhartari [*sic*] retorted that if he has any spiritual powers he could restore the stag to life, and Gorakh, casting a little earth on its body, did so. Bhartari then became a Jogi' (Rose 1919: II, 404, see also Muñoz 2010: 165). A similar example occurs in a Bhojpuri song where the king Nihal De killed a male

---

Warfare and hunting provide so many opportunities for the *kṣatriya* to accomplish his function as sacrificer' and Madeleine Biardeau: 'The *kṣatriya* is justified in his violent actions. It is thus not surprising that kings practice hunting and that a parallel be drawn between the murder of animals and the murder of enemies' (Biardeau and Malamoud 1976: 134, my translation from French).

deer and, cursed by his females, was obliged to become a yogī (Champion 1989: 67).

In all these cases hunting appears as a path leading to a yogic condition, taken on more or less voluntarily. Initiation is a sort of atonement, the consequence of a transgression. However, both Ratannāth's and Milarepa's stories use also the motif of hunting as a metaphor – to kill one's own passions rather than an innocent animal. If generally in the yogic texts the metaphor is rather to ensnare a wild elephant[15] than to kill, one finds it nevertheless in the *Haṭha-Yoga-Pradīpikā*: '*Nāda* [the Sound] becomes a snare for binding the mind, like the spotted antelope; and it can also slay it, as the (snared) antelope is slain' (HYP 4: 93, transl. in Briggs 1973: 346).

This context throws some light on the paradoxical reference to a *haṁsa* to be killed in Gorakhnāth's formula, since the *haṁsa*, a goose, or with more dignity a swan 'is since the Veda a symbol of the Supreme Reality as it is also of the individual soul identical to this Reality' (Padoux 1987: 145). If this *atman*, this soul, is compared to a *haṁsa*, a migratory bird, it is 'because it flies from body to body [...] It is like such a bird kept captive with a thread attached to one leg' (Varenne 1971: 24). This constantly moving *haṁsa*, this *atman*, has to be liberated by making it consider its true nature, and realize its identity with the *brahman*.[16] In

[15] *HYP* 4: 90: 'The mind, wandering in the garden of the objects of sense, like a rutting elephant, can be brought under control by the sharp elephant goad of the *anāhata nāda* (unstruck sound)' (in Briggs 1973: 346). The same 'elephant of the mind' appears in Bengali yogic texts quoted by Dasgupta where Khemāi [personification of *kṣema*, safety, tranquillity) 'pierces the undisciplined and unsteady elephant of the mind with the hook' (1976: 233). And we find it in the hagiography of Mastnāth, the founder of the Asthal Bohar monastery in Haryana. The narrative, which seems to summarize and assign to Mastnāth many deeds of other Nāth heroes, tells how Mastnāth having taken the form of a stag, was chased by a hunting Sikh prince. The moral is similar: 'The true hunter was he who was capable of ensnaring, through haṭhayogīc practices, the wild elephant of the mind' (White 2001: 149).

[16] In the *Nārada-parivrājaka Upaniṣad* (9.6): 'In this great wheel of

Plate 1: Wandering Yogīs.

Plate 2: Yogīs of the *jamāt* in front of their truck.

Plate 3: Yogīs of the *jamāt* making a stop at the Pushkar monastery.

Plate 4: A rest at Pushkar monastery.

Plate 5: Kadri monastery: the *pūjā* to the *pātradevatā* by the members of the *jhuṇḍī.*

Plate 6: Kadri, the consecration of the *rājā*.

Plate 7: The previous *rājā*, accompanied by the *jhuṇḍī mahant*, carried his *pātradevatā* to the sea.

Plate 8: Caughera monastery: painting figuring Ratannāth visited by Kājī Narudīn of Khorasan.

Plate 9: Caughera monastery: a group of Yogīs in front of the shrine.

Plate 10: Caughera monastery: the *pīrsthāpanā*. The former *pīr* showing the gestures of worship to the newly elected one.

Plate 11: Kathmandu, Mṛgasthali monastery: inauguration of Yogī Narharināth's memorial (Śivarātri 2006). In front, a portrait of the last king.

Plate 12: Fatehpur: *pūjā* to the *śivaliṅga* and to the *samādhi* of Amritnāth by the *mahant* of Amritnāth Ashram.

Plate 13: Fatehpur Amrit *mahotsav*: the *mahant* worshipping Śiva on the *mūlvedi*. Next to him a couple of lay devotees and a few of the officiating Brahmins.

Plate 14: Gorakhpur: the main temple.

Plate 15: Gorakhpur: a gallery of stucco effigies of the famous Nath Siddhas.

Plate 16: Asthal Bohar: one of the two *mahants* of the *choṭī dhūnī*.

classical texts there is never mention of killing the *haṃsa* but rather of freeing it: the aggression is for the bonds that trap the soul and that have to be cut 'with the knife of Yoga'.[17] However, looking at the Nāth use of the metaphor of the wild elephant may suggest, among Ratnanāth's followers, a peculiar use of the swan metaphor to refer to *manas*, to the mind whose restlessness has effectively to be 'killed' with yogic practice in order to find quietness.[18]

Afterwards Gorakhnāth initiates Ratannāth to the *haṁsa gāyatrī*. Here we have the usual meaning of *haṁsa* since in the yogic speculations, the *haṁsa gāyatrī* is the supreme formula, the ultimate mantra which states the identity between the individual soul and the cosmic Self – *Ham Sah*, I am Him. And this formula is none other than the breath itself.

In the words of Akshaya Kumar Banerjea (1983: 165):

> Now Gorakhnāth teaches us that every time we breathe out, air passes from within with the sound *Ham*, and every time we breathe in, air from outside passes into our body with the sound *Sah* [...] This means that every creature is naturally and inconsciously repeating the Mantra '*Ham-sah*', '*Ham-sah*' with every breath [...] The sound *Ham* implies *Aham*, i.e. I or the individual self, and the sound *Sah* implies 'He' or the Cosmic Self, –*Brahma, Paramātmā, Śiva*. Thus with every out-breathing the individual self (*jeeva*) frees itself from the bodily limitations and goes forth to the Cosmos and identifies itself with the Soul of the Cosmic body (Śiva); and with every in-breathing He, -the Soul of the Cosmos, *Śiva*- enters into the body and reveals Himself as *Aham* or the individual soul. If [... breathing out] precedes breathing in, the *mantra* is *Hamsah*; and if it is the opposite way [...] it becomes *Soham*. Both mean the same, i.e. the identity of *jeeva* with Śiva.

As stated in the *Gorakṣa śataka* (44): The *gāyatrī* called *ajapā*

---

brahman which is the life of all, the support of All, the swan roams as long as she thinks she is cut from the one who incites; but by his favor she attains immortality'.

[17] As suggested by the *Kṣurikā Upaniṣad*.

[18] A comparison that appears also in the *Amanaska Yoga* 85 (cf. Tara Michael 1992: 206).

[the unrecited, name given to the mantra *haṁsa*] is the giver of liberation to yogīs. Thus Gorakhnāth, by bestowing the *haṁsa gāyatrī* to Ratannāth, makes him a perfect yogī, freed from the bonds that tied him to the phenomenal world and made him mortal.

Thus this narrative of the initiation of Ratnanāth inscribes the history and the ritual practice of the Caughera monastery at the heart of an esoteric approach deeply rooted in the Nāth mystic tradition.

Nāth Legitimation: Ratannāth as Kanīpā

Differently rooted in Nāth tradition, a version of the legend published in the *Meghmālā* makes Ratannāth an *avatār* of the famous Siddha Kanīpā. It presents the advantage of integrating Ratannāth into a prestigious genealogy, thus enhancing the prestige of the monastery. As we shall see, Ratannāth is not exactly an orthodox figure, he is not one of the famous Siddhas mentioned in the canonical lists, thus the attempt to standardize him as Kanīpā is well received and has found a new impetus in the devotional art gallery: of twenty new canvases, eight show the Kanīpā legend, never previously illustrated.

Here is the *Siddha Ratnanāth* version, adapted from the *Meghmālā*:

The two guru brothers Gorakhnāth and Kanīpāv were quarreling. Gorakhnāth cursed Kanīpāv, who was scared and asked him when the curse would be lifted [...] Seing Kanīpāv fearful and sad, Gorakhnāth was moved with compassion and told him: 'If you keep your devotion towards me, you will recover your Siddha condition at your third rebirth, if you are rebellious, it will be at your second rebirth.'[19] Hearing these words, Kanīpāv, thanks to his yogic powers, abandoned his body, took a body made of light and flying through the sky went to the forest country (Dang, the country with twenty-five thousand

[19] I have no explanation for this weird clause – opposition preferred to submission- that the rest of the story will demonstrate.

bushes).[20] There ruled the great king Māṇikyaparīkṣak. Kanīpāv went to the palace and thanks to his yogīc powers he took the form of a child and, without coming from a womb, appeared in front of the king and queen. Since they were childless, they treated him as their son and named him Ratnaparīkṣak. Long afterwards when his father died, Ratnaparīkṣak became king and continued worshiping Gorakhnāth. He did that for twelve years without Gorakhnāth ever manifesting himself. Saddened by this, he remembered Gorakhnāth's words about the best way to lift the curse and gathered by force all the Yogīs, requiring them to work at digging wells and ponds. Thus Gorakhnāth, seeing hundreds of Yogīs so unhappy, went near to them in order to soothe their sufferings and stop the digging work.[21] Ratnaparīkṣak learned about it from his spies and went immediately to the spot. Even though he knew the person here was Gorakhnāth, he started to shout abuse at him. The verbal battle lasted seven days. [...] Ratnaparīkṣak was relieved of the curse and blessed by Gorakhnāth. He became famous under the name of Siddha Ratannāth'. (2025: 9-10, my translation from Nepali)

The rivalry between Gorakhnāth and Kanīpā is a well-known topos of the Nāth tradition. Kanīpā is the worthy disciple of Jālandhari, also known as Haḍipa, who, like Matsyendranāth, has been directly initiated by Ādināth. Kanīpā's adventures are mostly narrated in relation to Gopīcand's stories in which Kanīpā's main deed is to get Jālandhari out of the well where the reluctant disciple Gopīcand had thrown his guru, and then to protect Gopīcand, his *gurubhāī* (guru brother) from the anger

[20] *Savā lākh jhaṛ khaṇḍa*, the traditional appellation of the Dang Valley.

[21] The trick used by Ratan to oblige his guru to come evokes a similar stratagem employed by Gorakhnāth to obtain the *darśan* of Matsyendranāth; in the words of the Buddhist *vaṃśāvalī* published by Daniel Wright (1983: 141), '[Gorakhnāth] thought that his life was worthless unless he saw Matsyendra-nātha. However, he thought of a plan to bring Matsyendra-nātha before him. This was to catch the nine Nāgs and confine them, so that they could give no rain. There would thus be a great drought, and the people would cry out, and surely Matsyendra-nātha would appear for their relief'.

of their common guru. But the rescue of Jālandhari is preceded by two episodes dealing with the enmity between Kanīpā and Gorakhnāth. They are vividly enacted in the Rajasthani tales translated by Ann Grodzins Gold (1992: 265-77, 306-10). The first episode deals with Kanīpā (or Kannī Pāv) and his fourteen hundred disciples in the Chapala Garden, begging food from queen Maṇāvatī, Gopīcand's mother; she sent carriages full of treats and sweets, which were turned into stones by Gorakhnāth appearing seated on the way. Kannī Pāv sent his troop to fight him but Gorakhnāth made twice as many disciples rise up. Finally the two gurus reconciled and collaborated in the rescue of their respective gurus (Jālandhari in the manure pit and Matsyendra in the women's kingdom). But the enmity was not dead, and later on when Gorakhnāth offered a wish-feast, a feast where everyone gets whatever he desires, Kannī Pāv and his disciples asked for 'improper things [...] to spoil his honor' such as snakes, lizards, goats' heads, which they got, together with the curse[22] of Gorakhnāth and of both gurus Jālandhari and Matsyendra (see Grodzins Gold 1992: 307-9)

Kanīpā also appears in the list of the Tantric Buddhist Mahasiddhas under the name of Kṛṣṇācārya.[23] Hence Simon Digby sees in the enmity between Gorakhnāth and Kanīpā an expression of the rivalry between Nāth Yogīs and Buddhist Vajrayānas: since 'the Vajrayāṇa affiliations of Kṛṣṇācārī/Kāṇhupā/Kanīpā are particularly strong, we may be confronted with a situation [...] in which Vajrayāṇa Yogīs and Gorakhpanthīs have been involved in a contest to take over the cult of Jālandharī' (1970: 29).

The presentation given in Caughera of Ratnanāth as an embodiment of Kanīpā does not erase his initial hostility towards Gorakhnāth. However, the following narratives as well as the paintings lay stress on his later devotion and worship towards

[22] Kannī Pāv's disciples would be the ancestors of the Kalbeliyas, a Rajasthani caste of snake charmers who claim Nāth connection, or of the Sepalas (Briggs 1973: 59-61).

[23] As in Taranāth (Chattopadyaya 1970: 412-13). See also Dasgupta (1976: 393) on his mention in Caryā songs of Tantric Buddhist Sahajiyās.

the Siddha, a worship that justifies the existence of the monastery. Thus Ratnanāth's legend seems to consist of two layers: an encompassing and prestigious Nāth identity and a local rootedness. We shall see now how a third layer makes Ratnanāth a very complex character indeed.

RATNANĀTH, RATAN BĀBĀ, HAJJI RATAN

Ratannāth's Travels as Narrated in Caughera

The local hagiography takes on a very different style when narrating the second part of the life of Ratannāth following his initiation. It consists of a succession of brief episodes that highlight the many miracles performed by the Siddha during his travels in Muslim lands or under the authority of the emperor, the Badshah. The striking feature common to these stories is an effort to entrench the biography of Ratannāth in a reality defined by a specific geography and history. Names, dates, events and famous historical figures appear in the story of his adventures, in a somewhat confused way.

The first miracle done by Ratannāth, the miracle of the blossoming garden, is well known by devotees and abundantly illustrated in the monastery. It happened to be very effective since it instantly achieved its goal: the subjugation of the Muslim emperor and the recognition of the power of yoga.

Gorakhnāth [having initiated Ratnanāth] sent him to foreign countries.[24] Ratnanāth came to a Muslim country. There was a devastated

[24] There is no mention in Caughera of what is known elsewhere as the reason for this exile: the way Ratannāth made a show of his powers in creating his 'double', Kāyānāth, from the ashes covering his body and was then scolded by his guru Gorakhnāth. This legend is at the origin of a curious tradition called '*Har Śrī Nāth*' which developed in Khorasan before shifting to post-Partition India; their main centre is now the 'Dargāh Mandir Pīr Bābā Ratan Nāth' in Delhi and they claim to belong to the Nāth *sampradāya*, whatever their many pecularities. On this tradition and more generally on the Islamic side of Ratan see

garden, where he sat under a withered tree. Thanks to his ascetic powers, Ratnanāth made everything bloom again. The trees bore fruit and the birds sang wonderfully. The gardener saw this miracle, went to the Emperor (the Badshah) and told him in detail, but the Emperor did not believe him. When Ratnanāth, by the force of his yoga, saw that the emperor did not believe in his miracle, he sounded his horn (*sringnād*). And Badshah and all the Muslims of the palace were turned into women. Frightened, they all went to Ratnanāth to ask for forgiveness. Ratnanāth took pity on them and in his melodious voice he said to the emperor and courtiers: 'Now do not disturb the Hindus anymore, welcome them as guests, here's my order'. It is said that after doing this to teach the emperor a lesson, he returned to Caughera. (*Siddha Ratnanāthcaritāmrit*, p. 8)

The miracle of the blossoming garden is a frequent topos of Nāth hagiographies[25] and exemplifies their power over nature. Transforming the unbelievers into women (or into eunuchs in a popular version) evokes the frequent transformations during magical confrontations between wonder-workers of different creeds.

The following miracles, as they are told or depicted in Caughera, are occasions for Ratannāth to show his powers. And like many other Nāth Yogīs, if angered, he can be quite aggressive.

On the way to Kabul he had to cross the Indus at the famous ford of Attock. Since he had no money, the boatmen refused to ferry him across, which he did finally flying on his shawl. But he transformed the two boatmen into rocks, still visible on the shore. The rocks are called Jamal and Kamal!

At the same ford, another miracle is this time performed only out of compassion. Ratannāth, seeing an old woman constantly crying on the river shore, asked the reason for her sorrow. Hearing that twelve years ago the wedding party of her son

---

Bouillier and Khan, 'Hājji Ratan or Bābā Ratan's Multiple Identities'. 2009.

[25] For instance the deeds of Pūraṇ Bhagat (Gill 1986: 136) or Gorakhnāth in Gugā's story (Rose 1919: I, 179-80).

drowned in the river, he resuscitates him and makes the boat carrying the whole bridal procession reappear on the river.[26]

The hagiographic pamphlet continues with scattered mentions about Ratannāth's travels in North-Western Provinces of South Asia (from Punjab to Afghanistan) and his many Muslim devotees.

While Ratnanāth was returning home after demonstrating his yogīc powers [the miracle of the blossoming garden], the emperor gave him the title of *pīr* and built for him temples and monasteries in Peshawar, Kabul, Kandahar, in Rajasthan, Kurukshetra and Delhi. So far the tradition is still respected and Hindus and Muslims go there to honour him. Muslims called Siddha Ratnanāth 'Hājī Ratan'. (*Siddha Ratnanāth Caritāmrit*, p. 9)

In Khorasan there is a famous place of pilgrimage related to Ratnanāth, Śamśer Gaha, in the mountains. There are seven lakes. At the entrance, there is a huge circle (*cakra*) at the middle of which hangs a sword.[27] Behind this circle is the cave of the philosopher's stone (*parasmaṇī*).

'The Emperor of Kabul, impressed by the miracles of Siddha Ratnanāth, built a temple in Jalalabad and asked him to stay in the fortress,where his shawl[28] is still an object of veneration.' (caption on a painting)

A more precise but enigmatic caption on a painting showing Ratnanāth with a small, apparently Muslim, devotee, reads:

[26] According to the caption on one of the paintings. Astonishingly the same miracle in almost the same terms is found in a hymn glorifying 'Abdu'l-Qādir Jīlānī, the founder of the Qādiriyya order in the eleventh century (Temple 1885: II, 153-62). See details in Bouillier 1997: 70-1 n. 37.

[27] A mention, enigmatic as well, of this place in Pran Puri's travels in 1792: 'Fourteen miles from Candahar we went to Shumsheer where there is a circle of swords in constant motion, with the cause of which I am not acquainted' (*The European Magazine* 1810, vol. 57: 341).

[28] With many thanks to Xavier Hermand who carried out some wonderful research around Jalalabad and told me that the memory of Ratan and the legend of the shawl was still well known.

Sri Ratnanāth predicted the birth of Sri Muhammad Śāh [Muhammad] in an Arab country. In the sixteenth century [*sic*], Ibn Hajar in his book *Iṣāba* [cf. passim] mentioned those who had the Darsan of Ratnanāth. By learning from them the fame of Baba, Kaji Narudin Khorasan also visited Ratnanāth, who told him that he was then 600 years old.

The final miracles mentioned in Caughera make Ratnanāth a protector of the two most feared Muslim conquerors, Mahmud of Ghazni[29] and Muhammad Ghori, a fact which does not provoke any comment in Caughera.

To show the Muslim king the power of yoga, he refreshed with water from his *kamanḍalu* (water pot) the whole army of Mahmud Gajnavi.

Another brief mention in the pamphlet takes us to almost two centuries later, and makes Ratannāth instrumental in ensuring the victory of Muhammad Ghori[30] in the second battle of Bhatinda (also called Tarain or Tabarhind), which opened the road to Delhi to him.

Mohammed Gori [*sic*] came to seek the blessing of Ratannāth to be victorious in the battle which was to take place in Bhatinda against the king of India, Prithvi Rāj. Ratannāth said to Sahabuddhin Gori: 'Thanks to the bravery of two brothers, you will be victorious at the Battle of Bhatinda, but you, you will die'. The Ghoris won the battle and the two brothers died. Their graves are located north of the *samādhi* of Ratannāth. This event would have happened in 1191 AD [*sic*, in fact 1192].

If limited to the information given in Caughera, the story is very ambiguous as to the identity and function of the 'brothers';

[29] Mahmud of Ghazni (997-1030) is credited among the Hindus with a very bad reputation as a ruthless invader and plunderer of the temples of Mathura and Somnāth. He raided India many times but did not try to occupy its territory.

[30] After his victory over Prithvi Raj Chauhan, Mahmud Ghori established the Muslim domination over north India (even though he transferred power to his general, Aibak).

they tend to be confused with the two Ghori conquerors, Ghiyas-ud-din Mahmud and Shihab-ud-din, but neither of them died at Bhatinda. The battle was fought against the Rajput coalition led by Prithvi Raj Chauhan, the last Hindu Raja in Delhi, who was captured in Bhatinda and executed in Ghazni.

The blessing given by Ratannāth to Mahmud Ghori who went to visit him in Bhatinda where the Siddha was settled is considered in Caughera as a proof both of his reputation among the Muslims and of his extensive power.

Contrary to what was written on the previous painting mentioning Ratannāth's *samādhi* in Bhatinda (close to the tomb of the two brothers), the caption on a nearby painting says:

> After spreading the dharma for 700 years Mahasiddha Ratannāth disappeared thanks to his yogīc powers in front of thousands of people. They waited for days, hoping to see him, but they did not obtain his *darśan*.

This disappearance is in accordance with the absence of any tomb in Caughera. The monastery is not founded on Ratnanāth's tomb but on his legacy, the *pātradevatā*. No information is given about the possible location of his tomb in the Bhatinda town in Punjab.

Ratan and Gogā Pīr: A Samādhi *in Gogamedhi*

Ratannāth is not well known in Nāth lore, hence the attempt to make him a form of the famous Kanīpā; however, he appears in another Nāth context, in relation to the widely celebrated north Indian hero and disciple of Gorakhnāth, Gogā. But the part he plays in the life of Gogā alludes to quite a different background.

According to the many epics that proclaim the fame of Gogā all over north India,[31] he was a Chauhan Rajput whose birth

[31] The Legend of Gogā, an epic sung by bards, enjoyed considerable success throughout northern India, and variations are endless. Mentioned in all reports and gazetteers (the most complete narrative, detailing the regional variations, is that of Rose, but see also Tod,

was due to the blessing of Gorakhnāth. He grows up like a true Rajput hero, marries a princess, fights many battles, has many adventures but then is obliged to kill his cousins in battle. Cursed by his mother, he took refuge with Gorakhnāth asking for his help. According to the version recorded by Richard Temple (1985: I, 208), Gogā looked for death, and begged the Earth to swallow him up. But Earth replied: "Ay, my son, I tell thee how is it that you does not know? Musalmans are buried below; Hindus go to the pyre [...]. Go to Ratan Hājji and learn the Musalman's creed. When thou hast done this, I will take thee to myself.' Other versions, like those of Rose (1919: I, 181) state more precisely: 'Earth bade him to learn yogā from Ratn Nāth, Jogī at Bhatinda'.

The small town of Gogamedhi in northern Shekhavati holds the mausoleum of Gogā which embodies this final part of the hero's life, since it is in the form of a mosque. And the officiating priests are both Muslims and Hindus and worship successively according to their creed.[32] Near the *samādhi* complex of Gogā there is a small whitewashed building which bears the inscription: *Śrī Ratan bābā jī kī samādhi.* Inside there is a white marble tomb, similar to that of Gogā and engraved with a bust of Ratan. But the place is new (1950 CE). The present caretaker, whose sectarian affiliation is unclear, claims to have received in a dream the divine order to build a memorial tomb to honour Ratannāth. But, he says, the real grave is in Bhatinda.

Hājji Ratan of Bhatinda

This small Punjabi town, site of the famous battle between Mohammad Ghori and Prithvi Raj Chauhan, houses the complex

---

Temple, Crooke, Nevill), this legend is distributed locally by quantities of booklets, audio and now video tapes. We should also mention the studies by local historians and folklorists and the article by Lapoint (1978), whose analysis of this corpus focuses on the themes of power relationships and family conflicts.

[32] For more details I refer the reader to my 2004 article 'Samādhi et dargāh: hindouisme et islam dans la Shekhavati'.

of the 'Dargāh Bābā Hājjī Ratan', the most conspicuous building of which being Ratan's tomb, a square building crowned by a hemispherical dome surrounded by four green turrets. On its wall, a few inscriptions are related to repairing work, the earliest being dated 1603 CE. According to the archeologist Subash Parihar (2001: 109-10), the style of the tomb and the calligraphic style of the inner inscriptions allow us to date the monument from the beginning of the thirteenth century. The date agrees with a tale about Sultan Raziyya (the daughter of Iltutmish) who briefly reigned over Delhi (1236-40) and was said to have worshipped at Ratan's grave when in Bhatinda. A small mosque in the compound is said to have been built by her.

Among other graves in the compound (I had no information about the 'two brothers' of the Nepalese legend), a curiously-shaped tomb is said to hold the remains of the camel given to Ratan by the Prophet Muhammad, which takes us to the foundational legend of Ratan's fame in the Muslim context. According to a legend collected at Bhatinda by Horovitz,

> Bābā Ratan belonged to the class of Chauhān Rājputs. His knowledge of astrology told him that a prophet called Muḥammad would be born in Arabia [...] He set out to Arabia in order to meet him. In Mecca he embraced Islam and lived with the Prophet for thirty years, so that he was numbered among his 'aṣḥāb' or companions. Later on he returned to India [...] and stayed at the place where his shrine is now [Bhatinda] and devoted himself further to the practice of restraining his breath. (1914: 99)

By other accounts supposedly from the mouth of Ratan, he was given six dates by the Prophet and blessed by him with 'May God bless thy life'. 'The prayer was accepted by God who lengthened my life by a hundred years for every one of his prayers so that today I am more than six hundred years old' (id. 108).

Exceptional longevity is meaningful in both the Nāth and Muslim contexts. For the Nāth the most evident proof of the powers acquired by Ratan, and thus of his yogic skills, rests on this longevity mentioned in all hagiographies. As we know, Nāth Yogīs practice various haṭhayogīc and alchemical techniques in their quest for bodily perfection and immortality, and great Siddhas even when they do not simply disappear like Ratan in Caughera, take only the appearance of death, being in the perpetual ecstasy of *samādhi.* If immortality is the goal of Nāth Yogīs' practices, longevity is also quite an important motive in Islamic hagiography, which accepts the idea of saints living a few hundred years or disappearing temporarily. This belief rests on the strong wish to have encounters with the Companions of the Prophet, those who could transmit directly the true words of Muhammad. Ratan was believed to be one of them.

Ratan al-Hindī: Muslim Polemical Accounts

If the legendary accounts we had till now were rather confused or imprecise in their dating of Ratan, we find in Islamic hagiography commentaries attributed to Ratan's contemporaries who visited him usually in Bhatinda or heard about his fame.

The first critical opinion is found in Al-Hasan al-Saghānī (577-650 H /1181-1252 CE) who considered him as the author of a fake compilation of the Prophet's sayings (Ishaq 1955: 224-7).

Horovitz, in his ground-breaking study, summarizes the many subsequent mentions he found in Muslim records and most specially in the '*Iṣāba*, by Ibn Ḥajar of Askalon, one of the great theological authors of the ninth century H.' In this text Ibn Ḥajar gives biographies and critical judgements on all those people who were believed to have given testimonies on the Prophet. 'In his article on Bābā Ratan, Ibn Ḥajar quotes the accounts of various travellers whom the fame of the saint has induced to undertake the pilgrimage to Bhatinda' (Horovitz 1914: 106), and from these testimonies, Horovitz concludes: 'We cannot doubt that there lived at Tabarhind, towards the end of the sixth and the beginning of the seventh century of the Hijrah, a man called Ratan, who claimed to have intercourse with the Prophet at Medina and to have been granted through the power of his blessing a lease of life exceeding six hundred years; further that these claims had attracted a good deal of attention even outside India' (id. 110). However, following again Ibn Ḥajar, Horovitz mentions the many critical and polemical discussions related to Ratan's wondrous deeds and even to his mere existence: 'In the seventh, eighth and ninth Islamic centuries his claims were hotly discussed, some of the most distinguished authorities on Ḥadīth dismissing them. One of them, Dhahabī (673-748 H.) wrote a monograph, *Kasr Wathan Ratan* (the breaking of the Idol Ratan), the title of which is sufficiently suggestive of its aims' (id. 110).

These many discrepancies in the records and opinions relating to Ratan also find expression in the *Ā'īn-i-Akbarī* (around 1590), where Abul' Fazl 'Allāmī names Ratan among the saints of India: 'In the time of Ignorance he was born at Tabrindah and went to Hijāz and saw the Prophet, and after many wanderings returned to India. Many accepted the accounts he related, while others rejected them as the garrulity of senile age. He died at Tabarindah, in AH 700 (AF 1300-1)' (Jarrett 1978: 401).

BACK TO CAUGHERA: HINDUS AND MUSLIMS

Even though the hagiography of Ratan in Caughera gives some clues as to his importance in the Muslim context, local oral narratives show a certain uneasiness about this closeness. An example would be this local account which comments humorously on the link between Ratan and his Muslim devotees:

> Having been honoured by the Kabul king, Ratannāth stayed a long time in this region and started to behave like the people there, and in particular to salute with a *salam*. When he came back to Caughera, he made a *salam* to Gorakhnāth who was angered: 'You acquired bad habits! Stay twelve years underground!' Ratannāth thus stayed underground and when he came out, he again made a *salam* to Gorakhnāth, who cursed him: 'You will not get my *darśan* anymore! Worship the *pātradevatā* which is my representation for a hundred thousand years and then you shall see me again!' Since then we always make the *pūjā* to the *pātradevatā*. And the *pīr* embodies Ratannāth, so if he changes every year, it is a way of counting the years before the moment when one will see Gorakhnāth again.

The multiple layers of Ratannāth's legend give an insight into the complex background of many Nāth institutions. A local hero, an emblematic *kṣatriya* converted by Gorakhnāth, becomes an authentic yogī, in accordance with the well-established model of the renouncer-king. His Nāth identity is reinforced by the reference to Kanīpā but this identification of Ratan/Kanīpā introduces also the theme of the rivalry between the two Siddhas, Gorakhnāth and Kanīpā, and thus complicates the situation. Moreover, the scattered references to Muslim devotees and the subsequent discovery of Ratan Hajji as an important figure in the Sufī world of north-west India add another dimension to the foundation myth of Caughera. As a charter for the multiple Nāth universes, it shows how intertwined identities were a dominant feature.

CHAPTER 7

The Yogīs in the Kingdom: Ritual Services and Worldly Possessions

Besides the legendary corpus, which includes Ratannath in the pantheon of the Nāth figures and testifies to his encompassing influence, we shall now consider another variant of the foundation legend which makes a clear link between Ratannāth, the Dang kingdom and the community of Yogī officiants, thus legitimizing the monastery's local enrootedness and socio-economic status.

This variant, written in the locally printed booklet *Siddha Ratannāth*, gives to Ratannāth the part played by Gorakhnāth in the preceding version:

The King of Dang, whose capital was Caughera, went hunting. He shot an arrow at a black deer, followed the deer, and deep in the forest found the Siddha Ratannāth meditating with the arrow in front of him. Deadly scared, the king asked for forgiveness and the Siddha granted him a boon. He gave him sovereignty over a huge territory but the king refused, uncertain he would be able to protect such a large kingdom. Thus Ratannath gave the king a vision of the Dang kingdom, which the king accepted. Ratannath gave him the arrow, saying : 'As long as you keep the arrow you will keep your kingdom'. The king took the arrow and became Ratannāth's disciple. All the king's successors worship this arrow for six months of the year, and during the six other months the cult is carried out by the Yogīs. And always the king offers half of the kingdom's annual revenue to the Yogīs. (summarized from the *Siddha Ratannāth,* 2013 vs : 14-15)

There is no longer an arrow in the monastery of Caughera. However, the idea that the worship performed by the Yogīs in the monastery of Caughera is a necessity for the kingdom, that the Yogīs contribute to its permanency and that they are entitled to receive part of the revenue in exchange, is the common ground on which the *maṭh*'s ritual and economic activities rest.

CAUGHERA RITUALS

The main characteristic of the Caughera monastery is the centrality given to the worship of the *maṭh* deities, Bhairav, Ratannāth and the *pātradevatā*, and the Devī. The whole of the *maṭh* organization and daily schedule revolves around these acts of worship, the *pūjā* lasting eight hours daily, in two parallel sequences at dawn and late afternoon, and requiring the service of four officiants, exclusively Nāth Yogīs, who are elected every year together with the monastic head.

In Caughera the head, called *pīr*, is mainly the first of the officiating priests. The title of *pīr* is currently given to monastic heads, especially in the *pañcāyatī maṭhs*, but Caughera Yogīs consider the title as specific to their place; they claim that this current appellation of Sufi spiritual masters was granted to Ratannāth by the Muslim emperor and that each successive *pīr* is Ratannāth's embodiment. In this way the Siddha continues to be in charge of the cult of the *amritpatrā* he founded. The sign of this identification is expressed in the headdress characteristic of the Caughera *pīr*; as in the paintings depicting Ratannāth, the *pīr* wears a conical bonnet in red velvet, which may appear similar to the caps of dervishes or Muslim renouncers. Around its base is wrapped a thin black thread, which may also evoke the turban wrapped around Muslim headdresses; however, because of its thinness and black colour, it is said by the Yogīs to evoke the snake (*nāg*), wrapped around Śiva's matted hair. The handover of the cap (called *ṭopi*, Nep.) is an essential part of the *pīr*'s investiture.

The main duty of the *pīr* is to perform the worship of the Nāth Siddhas and *pātradevatā*. He thus spends most of his time in their shrine where he also has his sleeping arrangements. He is forbidden to leave the monastery (except for the annual procession), must remain barefoot and live a secluded life. Even though the office is prestigious, it is considered taxing and, at the time of elections, the candidates are not numerous.

The second elected officiant is called *pujārī*. He assists the *pīr* and, like him, is in charge of the cult in Ratannāth's sanctuary. He prepares the place and the ingredients necessary for the *pūjā* and obeys to the same restrictions as the *pīr*.

The third and fourth officiants are in charge of Bhairav's cult, inside and outside the precints of the *maṭh*. The main officiant is called *bhaṇḍārī* (the term generally signifies the treasurer, store-keeper) and his assistant *sirāne* (perhaps from *sir*, Nep. head, since he carries the 'throne' of the *pātradevatā* on his head during processions).

The ritual service of the monastery rests on these four Yogīs, supposedly chosen by their fellow *sādhus* for their spiritual and moral qualities. They are elected for one year with no immediate re-election possible; however, since suitable candidates are few nowadays, the turnover is compulsory only for the *pīr*.

In official documents the four offices are always mentioned together, as representing the spiritual authority in the *maṭh*. Specific also to Caughera is the division between these spiritual officiants and the administrative head of the *maṭh*, called *mānbhāū* (from *mahānubhava*) or *maṭhādhyakṣa*, who is responsible for the economic and political management of the *maṭh*. He has to survey the properties and revenues of the *maṭh* to make sure that the necessities for the rituals, the building maintenance and the Yogīs' living expenses are covered. He is the true head of the monastery as he ensures its continuity: he remains in post while the *pīr* changes every year. However, his nomination has to be ratified by the State authorities and the Nepalese archives possess quite a number of confirmatory edicts, like this edict issued by Jang Bahadur Rana in 1926 VS (1869 CE): 'Hail to *mānbhāū* Harināth from Caughera temple. Hiranāth, the *mānbhāū* having died, we establish by this royal edict the charge of *mānbhāū* in your name and order you to take good care of the *maṭh* properties and to look after the *pūjā* in accordance with traditions' (Narharināth, *IPS* 484).

A number of other functions are carried out by residents or passing Yogīs but not submitted to elections, such as the *dhūnī* Yogīs who take care of the fireplace but mainly have to participate in rituals in playing the huge drums, *nagārās*, and ringing the bell at the prescribed moments. Among them, one, the *maṇidār*, is especially in charge of the daily *pūjās* in Devī's sanctuary.

The *pankha*, herald, plays his part of public announcer essentially during the yearly ritual of the *pīr's* renewal. The *koṭhārī* is in-charge of the daily supervision of the items necessary for the *pūjās* and the feeding of the Yogīs. Adding on the other functions such as those of accountant, cook, gardener, and so on, around fifteen people are needed for the maintenance of the monastery, which makes it a big establishment according to Nāth standards. This is made necessary by the complexities of the rituals, which are quite exceptional in the Nāth context.

THE *NITYA PŪJĀ*: DAILY RITUAL

The daily *pūjā* is described as '*viśuddha sāttvik tāntrika*' in the monastery booklet, which corresponds to the Tantrik ritual manuals, in which 'the *nitya-pūjā* is classified as the purest form of *pūjā* (*sāttvika*)' as it is 'a manifestation of the Tantric's devotion to his *iṣṭadevatā* and is performed without any ulterior motive' (Gupta 1979: 126).

The two parallel four-hour rituals of dawn and late afternoon contain more or less the same sequences, which I will describe according to what I have seen or been told when rituals were done secretly.[1] Tantric ritual texts describe very precisely the numerous and complex rituals to be performed as well as the mental attitudes of the officiant.[2] The rites I looked at were

[1] The *pātradevatā pūjā* performed behind closed doors was done publicly once a year during the *pīrsthāpanā*. The Bhairav *pūjā* was also done in a closed room but I was allowed to look through the window!

[2] See for instance the details given by Senjukta Gupta, mainly from the *Paraśurāma Kalpasūtra* (1979, Chap. V). See also the volume edited

much more simple, first because of my own inability to grasp the esoteric meaning of gestures and attitudes and also because of the ignorance of most of the officiating Yogīs on the meaning of these gestures, the sequence of which they learned by heart.

Let us start with the afternoon ritual. Quietly, the Yogīs prepare the *pūjā* by tipping flowers into the garden and making flower garlands to adorn the statues later on. The two assistants, *pujārī* and *sirāne*, make for the nearby river to fetch water, considered as Gaṅgājal (Gaṅgā water). They fill two silver pitchers (*jhārī*) with water and come running back, their mouths covered with a white scarf so that their breath does not pollute the water; they carry the pitchers set on the palm of their right hand while they handle their *nād* whistle with the left hand. They take the water into their respective sanctuaries, bow in front of the deities and awaken the *pīr* and the *bhaṇḍarī*, who are dozing inside.

One of the Yogīs beats on the *agavānī* drum ('the one who goes first', a smaller *nagārā* which always plays first) to mark the beginning of the *pūjā*. While *pujārī* and *sirāne* gather the necessary ingredients (ghee, oil, incense, camphor, *pañcagavya, akṣatā*, flowers and leaves), the *pīr* and *bhaṇḍarī* go to the well to purify themselves and prepare for the cult.[3] Returning to their sanctuaries to the Nāths and to Bhairav, they close the heavy wooden doors and prepare for the *pūjā* by cleaning the ritual instruments (bells, lamps, fly-whisk, incense burner) and clearing the statues of the former offerings, bathing them

---

by André Padoux, '*L'Image Divine*' (1990), and the works of Hélène Brunner-Lachaux with the translation of *Somaśambhupaddhati* (vol. 1 on daily ritual, 1963).

[3] Regarding the importance given by the Yogīs to this bath (*snān*), see also Gupta (1979: 130-1): 'The bath differs from the usual Hindu bath, in that the Tantric takes several forms of bath, one after another'. After the usual ritual bath with oil, river-bed clay and bathing in deep water' he takes a '*mantra-snāna*', i.e. he sprinkles different parts of his body with consecrated water while evoking the deities with appropriate mantras and *mudrās* (gestures). Then he marks himself with consecrated ash (*bhasma-snāna*). On the very elaborate cleansing and bathing practices of the Vaiṣṇava *sādhus*, see Gross 1992: 382-6.

in water and *pañcāmrit*. From now on the *dhūnī* Yogīs play continuously on the five huge *nagārās*, the sound of which can be heard many kilometres around. Having washed the statues, the officiants adorn them with sandalwood paste and vermilion, flower garlands and small oil lamps: they 'make the deities beautiful' (*śṛiṅgar garne*, Nep.). Then the *pujārī* leaves the Nāth temple, his mouth covered with a white scarf, and an incense burner in his right hand, quickly reaching the outside of the temple of Kāl Bhairav. He enters and closes the door; then, for almost an hour, he stands in front of the altar where is a small statue of Bhairav, the incense-burner in his right hand and a small bell in the left. Slowly, he folds back his stretched right arm onto his chest and unfolds it, while ringing the small bell with the left hand. Echoing this light tinkling, the *nagārās* and the huge bell up in the monastery are played loudly and rapidly. During this time, the *pīr*, alone in the Nāth sanctuary, worships Gorakhnāth according to Tantric forms. Wearing his conical Ratannāth cap, seated on his throne, he begins by blowing three times into his *nād*, as all Yogīs do before any worship, then enters in a deep state of concentration and follows Tantric ritual inner procedures in order to identify with the god he worships.[4] He invokes the nine Nāths and eighty-four Siddhas and repeats Gorakhnāth's name while slowly moving the flywhisk from right to left. Then he moves the lamp and the incense burner around the different statues, ringing a bell with his left hand. He makes flower offerings and sits on his *gaddī* to repeat Gorakhnāth's mantra 108 times.

When the *pujārī* has finished worshipping Kāl Bhairav outside, he also worships Bhairav in the compound and comes back into the Nāth sanctuary.

The *bhaṇḍarī* and the *sirāne* similarly worship Bhairav in the

[4] See A. Padoux, '*nyāsa*' (1980: 59-102) as well as the festschrift dedicated to him (Goudriaan ed. 1992), particularly the articles by Davis ('Becoming a Siva, and Acting as One, in Saiva Worship', pp. 106-19) and Dwiveda ('Having Become a God, He Should Sacrifice to the Gods', pp. 121-38).

inner sanctuary and the *maṇidār* does an *ārtī*, an offering of lights in the Devī's room.

Suddenly the drummers stop playing, the *pīr* and the *bhaṇḍarī* open the doors of the sanctuary: the dark rooms appear brilliantly illuminated by dozens of small oil lamps and the statues beautifully adorned, covered with flowers, are exposed to public worship. All the Yogīs gather; one after the other, their heads covered, they bow at the entrance of the sanctuaries, they blow their *nād* three times and turn around (a symbolic circumambulation). They do the same in front of Bhairav's and Devī's temples then salute each other repeating the standard Nāth formula 'Ādeś'. A musician from the Damāī caste arrives to play the flute and Yogīs and lay devotees remain for some time in front of the sanctuaries to sing hymns to Gorakhnāth, to Śiva and the Devī. The atmosphere is very peaceful and serene. The night falls.

The officiants enter the sanctuary rooms to take some rest and the doors remain open. However, only an hour or so later the *pujārī* and the *sirāne* get up while the *pīr* and *bhaṇḍarī* continue resting. They go to bathe, then, until midnight, again make preparations for the *pūjā*; they spend a long time crushing sandalwood to make a sort of white paste, which, once diluted, will be used to adorn the statues. Again they wash the statues with water, milk, *pañcāmrit,* then adorn them in the *śṛiṅgar pūjā.* One Yogī starts beating the *agavānī* drum, the sign for the *pīr* and the *bhaṇḍarī* to stand up and prepare for the worship,which they again perform behind closed doors, in the same way as in the afternoon. At 4 o'clock in the morning, they open the doors and offer the beautifully adorned deities to public worship.

Another moment of the daily ritual concerns food. Nobody can eat anything before Bhairav has received his due. It is the duty of the *sirāne* to provide Bhairav with his *bhog* ('enjoyment, eating, feeding on', Monier-Williams 1988: 767), some rice mixed with saffron placed in the *kapāl*, the vessel in the shape of a skull (*kapāl*) that is placed on his altar. The process of giving is rather peculiar: the *sirāne* comes back from the kitchen carrying the full vessel on the palm of his right hand and, with his left hand he carries a water pitcher, touching it with his *nād-selī* and running a trickle of water. He puts the *bhog* on Bhairav's altar, makes three circles with the water, takes the *kapāl* back and goes to Bhairav's outside shrines, still trickling the water. There in the graveyard, having 'nourished' the various Bhairavs, he gives the food to the waiting dogs. He goes back with the empty vessel and the pitcher and at the entrance of the Nāths' sanctuary makes seven circles with the water. He does the same in the inner sanctuary of Bhairav, and, having put the vessel upside down on the altar, bows in front of the deity.

Bhairav having been fed, the Yogīs can have some tea, then around 10 o'clock their lunch, which consists of rice, lentils, vegetables. Afterwards they busy themselves with whatever occupation they like: some rest, chatter with visitors, prepare incense and wicks for the *pūjās*, read or meditate in their cells, others go outside walking, doing some shopping in Ghorahi, even playing cards in a small teashop. Of course the *mānbhāū* and other administrative officers continue their work.

And again, in the early afternoon, the worship cycle starts anew with the fetching of the river water.

PĪRSTHĀPANĀ

The main ritual event of the monastery, which is both a re-enactment of Ratannāth's legend and a performance on Nāth identity, occurs during the month of February-March, on the 11th day of the dark half of Phālgun. *Pīrsthāpanā* ('the installation of the *pīr*') is the public selection and acceptance of the new *pīr*, as the embodiment of Ratannāth, especially in his duty of worshipping the *pātradevatā*. The *pīr* reenacts the performance of Ratannāth as it is depicted on the many paintings in the monastery: seated cross-legged, with his ritual paraphernalia, he makes *pūjā* to the *pātradevatā*.

The *pīrsthāpanā* is divided into the following sequences:

- first, the *amrit pātra* is solemnly taken out of the sanctuary by the current *pīr* and brought to the ceremonial hall, *dalicā*, where the *pujā* will be performed in front of all the Yogīs and visitors. The *pīr* lays out the ritual objects and makes a first *pujā*.

- Then, all the Yogīs are gathered and consulted about the new nominations. The four offices of the four officiants have to be filled: *pīr, pujārī, bhaṇḍarī* and *sirāne*. After they have been chosen by common agreement, they take an oath in front of Bhairav, and the *pīr*-to-be receives the conical bonnet typical of Ratannāth; the *pīr*, as soon as he receives it, is supposed to represent the Siddha.
- The third part consists of the progressive replacing of the last year's *pīr* by the newly selected one. The old *pīr* is still seated in front of the *pātradevatā* in the ceremonial hall; the new one, after receiving his cap in the Bhairav temple a few yards away, climbs the stairs in a sitting position (in *padmāsana*) and gradually takes the place of the former one, progressing in small jumps; the seat of Ratannāth, the throne of the *pīr*, must never remain empty. When he reaches his place, his predecessor wraps him in a huge shawl. Now that the new *pīr* has been installed, all the Yogīs and the important local people come to pay their respects to him, bowing in front of him and giving some rupees as a ceremonial offering. This is the official enthronement of the *pīr*.
- Then, for the first time, the new *pīr* makes the *pūjā* to the *amritpātra*. Helped by the former one, who teaches him all the gestures, he makes a series of *mudra*, sometimes with his hands hidden under the shawl. He waves the fly-swatter one hundred and eight times in front of the *pātra* and mutters mantras. When he has finished the *pūjā*, all the objects are collected and the new *pīr* carrying the *amritpātra* leaves the hall and proceeds to the main temple where he puts the 'recipient-god' back on its throne.

After this ritual installation, the *pīr* is introduced to his new responsibility as an administrator of the *maṭh* property. The account books, and the various objects that constitute the treasure of Caughera are taken out of the temple room, presented to the administration committee under the leadership of the *mānbhāū* and counted in front of the old and new *pīrs*.

However, the consecration of the new *pīr* as a new Ratannāth in his local dimension as the founder and head of Caughera is not completed until the journey to Devi Patan has been made. This sanctuary in the Gonda district of Uttar Pradesh is dedicated to Durgā Bhagavatī and is under the control of the Nāth Yogīs. We do not know much about the origin of this place and still less about the Yogīs' pilgrimage.[5] Local tradition says that a temple – the third one following the first erected by Karna and the second by Vikramaditya – was built there by Ratannāth but that this one was destroyed by Aurangzeb or some captain from his army, who was then killed by the Devī.

Ratannāth's hagiography tells us of a special relationship between him and the Devī. Either they had the same guru and were spiritual siblings (*gūrū-bhāī*), or she helped him and he promised to visit her once a year. Another interpretation would be in terms of power, the Devī being considered as the *saktī* of Ratannāth, and her support necessary to the new *pīr*. The local Tharu population, not considering the Gorakhnāth's and Nāth Yogīs's vow of celibacy, considers it a conjugal relationship!

The *yātrā* takes one month altogether, but the journey itself requires five days – more exactly five nights – each way. The departure is on the first day of the month of Caitra (15 days after *pīrsthāpanā*), then after a one night's walk through the Siwalik Chain, the procession stops for fifteen days in a place called Deopur in the district of Deukhuri. Settled near a temple

[5] If we look at the history of the Dang Valley, we see that Devi Patan is close to the town of Tulsipur where the king of Dang, Nawal Sen, took refuge when he was driven out by Gorkha armies in 1786. One interpretation would be to link the origin of the pilgrimage to Devi Patan to this removal of the king, but it does not seem right. It seems, according to the documents we have, that the journey occured prior to this event, particularly since one edict from 1789 (only three years after the conquest) says 'not to give trouble to the Yogīs for the Patan Devi *yātrā*'. The tradition seems to have been already well established.

of Ratannāth, the Yogīs receive homage from the local people and gather offerings – a tribute called *kaṭālā* that they have been entitled to collect from the houses of Deukhuri for at least two hundred years. They restart their journey on the night of the new moon and stop at three places (with Devī temples) before reaching Devi Patan on the 5th day of the clear half of Caitra, where they are welcomed by the *mahārāja* of Balrampur. They stay there till the tenth day. Their stay coincides with the main festival of the temple, Caitra *Daśahrā*, which was until recently the occasion for thousands of animal sacrifices. In Devi Patan, the newly elected *pīr* makes the *pūjā* of their *pātradevatā* four times in front of the Devī temple, and then takes leave and starts his journey back to Caughera with the other Yogīs of the cortege, the former *pīr* being free to go wherever he wants. The return to Caughera is celebrated with a public *pūjā* in the ceremonial hall, to show everybody that Ratannāth and the *pātradevatā* are back.

The procession is carefully organized: the two Damāī musicians who usually play for the *pūjās* go first, one blowing the *sahanai* (oboe), the other carrying a *nagārā* drum. Then come Yogīs carrying a silver mace, a pitcher, a brazier which is used as *dhūnī* – the fire which the Yogīs keep constantly burning – and a red flag which represents Bhairav. Then comes the *pañkha* carrying a mace, followed by the *sirāne* carrying on his head the carpets and cushions that will be the throne of the *amritpātra*. Behind them, the *bhaṇḍarī* takes charge of the *roṭ*, the symbol of Bhairav, which must always precede the *pātradevatā* during ritual outings. Then come the two *pīrs* both wearing a huge shawl and the red cap that indicates their function. The former *pīr* carries a torch and the new *pīr* carries the *pātradevatā*, wrapped in white cloth, and flower garlands. He is followed by the *pujārī* carrying a huge ceremonial umbrella. Then come other Yogīs with the ritual objects for the cult, the brahman officiant and – until a few years – ago about thirty Tharu carriers, the tenants of the monastery lands required to provide this ritual service. They carry wood, food, and goods to be traded during the *melā*, the fair which follows the Devī festival.

We see here again the value given to itinerancy in the ritual sequence. The *pīr*'s enthronement is only confirmed after a ritual journey made by all the Yogīs who constituate the spiritual core of the monastery, and who escort the *pātradevatā*. The sedentary life of the *pīr* takes place between two compulsory itinerant episodes: a first journey as a would-be *pīr* and a second one to mark the end of his year of duty. As in Kadri the theme of the ascetic journey is entertwined with royal parallels: the *pīr* covers the territory like a king his domains, receiving homage and tributes, which echoes both the legend of Ratannāth as a former king of the Dang Valley, and the close relationships with the real kings of the place who have to be present, at least symbolically, at the key moments of the journey. The umbrella which is carried on the head of the *pīr* also takes us back to royal symbols, and also as we have seen in the case of the Nāth Yogīs, to the Goddess, when she is worshipped together with the *pātradevatā*. The importance given to the Goddess, the fact that the journey is to a temple of Devī, particularly to a *pīṭh*,[6] a 'seat of power', is characteristic of Caughera particularities; it shows openly what has been alluded to for instance in the Kadri *yātrā*, the necessary presence of the Śaktī which in Kadri manifests itself only in the belonging of the *jhuṇḍī mahant* to the Āī Panth, the feminine *panth*.

CAUGHERA MONASTIC PROPERTIES

This ceremonial devotional life cannot be separated from its profane context. The service of Goraknāth, the 'lord of salvation', is only possible with the backing of a worldly institution. The monastery is integrated into a sociological, economic and political space; its functioning depends on society, on the king who as 'lord of the land' is the sole authority empowered to make

[6] A *pīṭh* is a place where a part of Devī's body fell; in Devi Patan, it is said to be her left shoulder. However Briggs who sees the etymology of Patan as 'deriving from the Sankrit *pāt*, meaning to fall, to sink' refers to 'a right hand' (1973: 90).

gifts of land, and on the dependent peasantry who produce the commodities necessary for the cult. The monastery is a 'worldly' institution managed by individuals who are 'unworldly' and the paradox is that far from remaining ascetics set apart from worldly business, the Yogīs become genuine landlords and feudal rulers, governing their domains and people like many other managers of monasteries of various religious persuasions.

The history of the Caughera monastery is linked to the history of the Dang kingdom. But information is scarce before the end of eighteenth century and Nepal's unification. Local tradition tells how this tribal area of Inner Tarai was conquered by a Rajput king fleeing from India and we may imagine a joint arrival of this rajputized king together with the Yogīs (as was narrated about western Nepalese kingdoms after the downfall of the Malla empire). The last independent king of this dynasty, Nawal Singh or Nawal Sen, ruled from Caughera. The settlement of the Yogīs and their relationship with the king was well established since an edict (unfortunately incompletely dated) mentions a meeting between the king and the Bārahpanthīs (among them Bhagavantanāth) in Caughera *dalicā* to discuss a taxation problem. The same king had a throne made for the *pātradevatā* by a goldsmith in 1768 CE and offered it to the *maṭh*. Political vicissitudes then led to the eviction of Nawal Singh and his replacement by the king of the neighbouring state of Sallyan and finally by the Gurkha Shah dynasty. However, whatever the changes in political sovereignty in the Dang Valley, the status of the Caughera monastery remained unchanged. Letters of successive kings confirm the rights of the Yogīs. For instance an edict signed by the Sallyan king in 1789 CE mentions that: 'Sri Kriṣṇa Śāh warns the people not to create any trouble in the collections of funds for the porterage and the food intended for the Yogīs going to Patan Devi for *pātradev yātrā*.'

Caughera monastery had various rights and privileges since it was the beneficiary of land grants bestowed by the kings. These land grants were made under the tenurial regime called in Nepal *guṭhi*, where lands were endowed 'for the establishment or maintenance of religious and charitable institutions' (Regmi

1976: 17). This type of tenure implied certain consequences such as a general surrender by the giver of all sources of revenue that could come from this grant. Only then was such a gift thought of as alms and a source of merit for the donor.[7]

Gift giving was a religious duty for the king (Burghart 1987, rpt. edn. 1996, chap. 7). Moreover since the landgrants were made to ascetics such as the Yogīs who were close to the king, being disciples of a renouncer-king like Ratannāth, or being wonder-workers and worshippers of a divine protector of the kingdom such as Gorakhnāth was for the Shah kingdom, the grants were beneficial for the king in terms of supernatural insurance. Yogīs' blessings were a much desired consequence, which the donation and the confirmation formulas evoke: 'Perform the *pūjā* without fear of confiscation and celebrate our triumph' (Nep. *hāmro jaya manāu*) – such is the dedication formula that concludes the confirmation of the property of Ratannāth by king Rajendra in 1883 VS (1826 CE) (Narharināth 2022 VS: 493). The Yogīs, devotees and priests in the service of Ratannāth are thus entrusted to propitiate the god for the benefit of the king in exchange for the possessions they can enjoy: 'Let the Bārapanthīs [the Yogīs] make use of what remains [after the necessities of the worship]' (Narharināth id.). The king thus surrenders a material possession in exchange for a spiritual one.

In addition to making the Yogīs into what has been called 'an army of prayer'[8] in charge of insuring his welfare and the

[7] Cf. Burghart (1996: 54): 'In order that a gift be classified as alms the donor may not partake the fruits of his gift. Hence when the king bestowed rights over land in alms to Brahmans and ascetics, he waived the payment of all gifts of fealty, fees of obeissance, rents, levies and duties over that tract of land, hereby alienating that land from the jurisdiction of the intermediary revenue officers and acknowledging the ritual or spiritual superiority of the recipient'.

[8] By Jahangir about the 'men of Allah' (Eaton 1978: 219) or Muhammad Adil Shah, who in a farman dated 1636 that surrenders land to the priests in charge of a particular sanctuary (*dargāh*), states very explicitly: 'The Imperial Court [...] expects that they, living on the

prosperity of the kingdom, the king also makes a political gift. Caughera monastery was situated in Tarai in a forested area, uncultivated, close to the border and inhabited mostly by tribal communities outside of the caste society. The monastery was supposed to develop cultivation as it says clearly in a donation deed of 1837 to the monastery of Srigaun, also located in the Dang Valley, which states: 'This uncultivated land of 50 *muris* is given to you; harvest it, put fencing around it, construct irrigation canals and reservoirs, perform the *pūjā*, distribute food and bless the rulers' (Narharināth 2022 vs: 462). Moreover, the monastery was also conceived as a tool to propagate Hindu beliefs and rituals and Hindu normative behaviour. As the Nepal Tarai was till the nineteenth century a region difficult to tame, open to military incursions and individual infiltration, and especially vulnerable to expansionism from the south – Muslims of the Mughals and the Nawabs of Oudh or Bengal, and lately Christians of the East India Company – the Hindu monastic model functioned in just this way, 'as a permanent bastion of Hindu civilisation [...], as a Hindu line of defence' (Burghart 1978: 184) and as a guarantor of the Hindu conception of kingship.

Were these land grants and the proprietary rights they involve opposed to the religious ascetic ideology of non-attachment and non-possession (*aparigraha*)?

It should first be noted that the vow of non-possession is an individual one. The monastery's wealth is collective. Furthermore the Hindu monasteries are by definition not proprietors since endowments, as we have seen above, are usually made in the name of the god, the ascetics being only managers. This is evident in the case of Caughera where the grants and endowments refer only to Ratannāth or to Bhairav. The *guṭhi* belongs to the gods,

---

income of the state, will pray for the long life of the king' (quoted in Eaton 1978: 218). A similar mention figures in a landgrant to Yogī Udan Nāth from Jakhbar (end of sixteenth century) 'so that he may remain occupied with praying for the permanence of the Conquering Dynasty (while) sustaining himself year after year with the entire produce from that (land)' (Goswamy and Grewal 1967: 51).

the Yogīs are only in their service. The collective and divine possessions forbid individual appropriation at least in theory, but it is equally obvious that some Yogīs have used their position as a means to acquire private titles to land.

This wealth is legitimized by the necessities of the rites, the demand that the divine service be done according to the proper rules and with the required splendour. The harvest of the *guṭhi* land is destined to supply the ingredients for the *pūjā*, 'the incense and the lamp' (*dhup-batti*) as it is stated in the edicts. If the religious commodities are not supplied or if the lands are not cultivated, the *pūjā* cannot be performed. Thus the Yogīs have repeatedly remonstrated against, for example, poor irrigation: 'The water has been diverted, the village of the Ratannāth *guṭhi* has turned barren and we the Yogīs, we ask ourselves how to serve Ratannāth properly?' (Narharināth 2022 vs: 495).

The prosperity of the monastery is necessary to the proper accomplishment of the rites. But also it is a sign of divine grace, a sign that the cult has pleased the god and that he, in return, is dispensing favour upon his devotees. 'Abundance and prosperity were signs of being the beneficiaries of divine grace' writes Richard Burghart (1978: 196) in reference to the spiritual heads of the Mahottari monasteries.[9] It is not very surprising that the power of a god should be judged from the splendour and prosperity of what touches him.

The wealth of these ascetic monasteries is equally justified by the value attached to the charitable gift. The Hindu monastery has the duty to offer accommodation and food to travelling ascetics, to the poor and more generally to all those who come. The inability to give appropriately is invoked by the Yogīs in

[9] One can discern a similar tendency in the Sufi *dargāhs*: 'In the devotee's eyes, there may have been no necessary contradiction between the sanctity of the building and the material prosperity of its in'amdars (beneficiaries of donations, generally the descendants of the *pīr*). Indeed the devotees may have considered it appropriate that the spiritual power of a deceased saint be expressed in the material prosperity of his descendants' (Eaton 1978: 237).

order to reclaim from the State their right to fully enjoy the possession of their lands. In 1895 vs, the king Rajendra replied to the *pujārī* of the Chilli Ratannāth Temple: 'With the produce of the lands you possess as *guṭhi*, do the *pūjā*. Proclaim our glory, feed your visitors and enjoy the remainder'. On another occasion, the Caughera Yogīs complained that revenues were drying up and deplored the fact that, 'we can only skimp on the feast that we used to offer to the Yogīs who come for the Ratannāth festival'. This charitable duty is obviously ritualized and limited. It is not intended to redistribute the possessions of the *maṭh* to the destitute but merely, on special occasions a few times a year, to entertain certain chosen visitors (conveniently defined as 'poor' [*garib*]) to whom a meal and a few symbolic coins or goods are distributed.

CAUGHERA'S STATUS VIS-À-VIS ITS DEPENDANTS

Through the donation, the king is delegating a part of his sovereignty. The donation of land is accompanied by a series of rights and privileges that invest the monastery with a global authority over its dependants. The monastery thus finds itself not only in the middle of a network of economic activities but is also involved in relationships of authority. It is thus doubly involved in the worldly sphere. The ascetics are not merely in proximity to the Power, but they represent this Power within the boundaries of the land allotted to them. Their autonomy vis-à-vis the state compels them to take on a number of its functions. As lord of his fiefdom, the head of the monastery does not usurp the honorific title of 'Mahārāj' that his subordinates use to address him. But how was this relationship between the monastery and its 'subjects' put into practice?

I will first examine the archival evidence concerning the relations that the Caughera Maṭh has maintained with the villagers working for it, primarily Tharus, and then look at how the state intervenes in those relations.

The oldest edict mentioning the *guṭhi* of Caughera dates from about the 1790s. In fact it confirms a previous donation of which we have no record but that pre-dates the conquest of the independent kingdom of Dang by the Gorkha armies. The document reads as follows: 'We confirm what has always been given in houses, fields and villages by the king of Dang to the monastery. Let the Yogīs eat what is theirs. Let the king eat what is his. No difficulties should be created for the *guṭhi*. The *pūjā* should be done according to the tradition' (Narharināth 2022 VS: 659).

Thereafter, in 1883 VS (1826 CE), a *lālmohar* granted by King Rajendra enumerates in detail all the land properties of the *guṭhi* of Caughera. Recently it amounted to 1,250 *bighās* or 840 hectares, which is a considerable holding when we know that the land reform of 1964 fixed the ceiling at 28 *bighās* (18.5 ha) per family in the Tarai area. The *guṭhi* holdings were exempted from this land ceiling.

The majority of the land is located around five villages in the Dang Valley, approximately a dozen kilometres from Caughera. These villages are surrounded by fields which are meant for paddy cultivation in the summer time and for mustard in winter time – fields that require a good irrigation system. But this has always caused problems. During the whole of the nineteenth century complaints, requests and conflicts came one after another in relation to the distribution of the river water, which was diverted by a canal that supplied water to a number of villages, out of which five belonged to the *guṭhi*. Apparently, the management of this canal and the relations of the monastery with the villages adjacent to those on the *guṭhi* land were far from good. We have the records of ten different requests dated between 1811 CE and 1895 CE addressed to local or state authorities concerning water sharing. For example, in the first one from 1868 VE [1811 CE] the following order is given to the Tharu authorities by the lieutenant (*subedār*): 'Do not close the canal of Hapurkhola, the *pujārīs* have complained against it. Be kind and let the water flow, the Yogīs need it' (Narharināth 2022 VS: 492).

Apart from these water problems, neighbourhood discords can also relate to boundaries, in particular in the recently cleared border district of Deukhuri. For instance in 1852, the Yogīs came to complain that 'land attributed to the *guṭhi* remains uncultivated because the boundary of the *guṭhi* holdings that was to be defined in agreement with the *caudhari* and *mahaton* [village authorities] was not agreed upon. In this case, how are we to perform the *pūjā*?' (id.: 483).

Such conflicts sprang from the landholdings themselves and became the focus of confrontation between the monastery dwellers and their neighbours. The State was called upon to act as an arbiter and its duty was to defend the interests of the *guṭhi.* But the relationships between the monastery and the farmers who tilled the *guṭhi*'s land could also be quite conflictual, often as a result of the double burden, for these farmers, of paying agricultural rent and taxes.

The monastery's land was farmed following two systems. The first one was applied mostly on the land surrounding Caughera where the land was tilled by hired labourers, paid on the basis of an annual and renewable contract. The second system applied to the remaining 1,000 *bighās* which were cultivated by registered tenants (*raiti* or *mohi*). Most of the land holdings of the five villages of the *guṭhi* were tilled by the farmers for an annual payment of a rent paid in kind plus some services rendered to the monastery. The system called '*potet*' or '*potayat*' was in application during the entire nineteenth century and more or less till 1960.

These payments in kind and labour have often provoked protest. For instance, in 1812 a conflict rose between the Kumal porters and the Yogīs concerning the earthenware to be supplied for the *Daśahrā* rituals. The *faujdār* (magistrate) took the Kumals' side and wrote to them, 'Give the Yogīs five pots, but not the ten that they are coming to get!' (Amatya s.d. 90). Ten years later in 1879 VS (1822 CE), the conflict was caused not by the number but by the carrying of the earthenware: 'Last year you supplied the earthenware as required by the custom but to your great dismay, you were required to pay a portage tax. You are not to carry the earthenware. Let the Yogīs take care of the carrying themselves' (Narharināth 2022 VS: 493).

It is around this compulsory labour that opposition to the

existing system has crystallized. On the one hand, its undefined nature made exploitation of the tenants easy; on the other hand the supposedly dharmic nature of the task would mask the purely financial side and make it difficult to shirk such labour. As a royal order once put it, 'The Bārapanth want to build a temple in Caughera (...) It is a labour for *dharma*, all of you unite yourselves and donate your effort, donate wood that you may have on your land, donate lime' (id. 494).

From the 1960s, the power struggle between the monastery and its tenants intensified. The tenants wanted to maintain the *potayat* system of paying in kind but not to supply labour, while in that case the monastery wanted to modify the rent and demanded one third (*tinkur*) or even half of the harvest (*adhiyā* system). The Land Reform Office became the intermediary between the monastery and its tenants and managed to impose an agreement, often with difficulty. Long is the list of petitions from both sides, of convocations, of summons and of agreements which were never endorsed.

Apart from the agricultural rents and services, the monastery used to receive tax payments, usually levied by the State, on all sorts of activities (taxes on weaving, on fishing, custom duties, etc.). Furthermore, the monastery used to collect amounts corresponding to judicial fines as well as unclaimed inheritances. In short, the State would surrender to the *guṭhiyār* all the sources of revenue which could come from his grant. The multiple taxes that the peasants had to pay were levied by ordinary collectors, thereafter to be handed over to the monastery, usually in the form of an item that the collector commissioned. Thus a letter of the *ḍiṭṭhā* (justice officer) Jagu Kavar, dated 1907 VS (1850 CE) informs the monastery: 'It seems that, according to custom, the officer in charge of collecting the taxes on block-printing [on cloth] (*chapāiko rakam*) for the territory of Ratannāth, had an item made, therefore as per the practice, I have a sandalwood bowl made at the cost of 24½ rupees and offer it in front of the Ratannāth's pavilion' (id.: 497). But it happened that the tenants could be subjected to double taxation: For example, the *mānbhāū* (administrative head) complained twice (1930 VS and 1932 VS) that the customs duties collectors had unfairly taxed the shepherds of the Ahir caste, who had migrated from India and had settled on the *guṭhi* lands in Deukhuri whereas 'the Yogīs had already taxed them previously saying that it was for the *pūjā*'. As a result, the Ahirs left and the monastery got no revenues.

According to the Nepalese *guṭhi* system, the *guṭhiyār* was responsible for administrating ordinary justice on his land, a duty that was often perceived as amounting to the right to collect fines. The income derived from the exercise of justice could be considerable. It included the fine imposed on the offender or on the losing party, as well as the fees paid by the winning party. The monastery was also assigned to enforce the social order. It intervened in matrimonial matters, prohibited unions or adulteries, and in general ensured the proper implementation of inter-caste regulations. Violations of law were lucrative for the monastery since it pocketed the fines. This is the case also with a curious tax called '*sarva candrāyaṇā*', which appeared in the Caughera documents *c.*1858 CE, shortly after the promulgation of the *Muluki Āīn* (Civil Code) by Jung Bahadur Rana which was intended to unite the diverse populations of Nepal under a single legal regime based on the Hindu code of conduct (Höfer 1979). For caste-purity related misdemeanours, the culprits were most often fined and received a purification certificate, delivered by one of the Court Brahmans, the *dharmadhikār*, a specialist in religious law. The *sarva candrāyaṇā* was levied in each house supposedly to erase any past or future transgression resulting from accidental contact with an untouchable. It was said that the merit obtained by paying this amount was equivalent to the *candrāyaṇā* fasting, i.e. a fast regulated by the moon. This was thus a collective and annual fine, intended to purify any possible future transgression, and very lucrative for the *dharmadhikār*. However, in the case of Caughera, the money bypassed the Royal Brahman and was transferred directly to the *maṭh*, at least in normal proceedings. For instance, following some dispute the justice officer wrote in 1890 CE to the Yogīs:

I confirm that the *sarva candrāyaṇā* was always handed over to Ratannāth. [From] 1948 vs onwards, the annual *sarva candrāyaṇā* for the Caughera Yogīs and the *guṭhi* villages will be levied by the *mānbhāū* to be entrusted to the Ratannāth treasury and my duty is to have a spear made with the name of Sarkār [the Government, i.e. the King] on it, which I will present to Ratannāth. (Narharināth 2022 vs: 485)

Conflict with the *dharmadhikār* occured also on purity matters, the Yogīs claiming their autonomy and refusing to pay the fines. One such case occurred in 1908 vs (1851 CE), during which the *dharmadhikār* Laksmiraman Pandit sent the following letter to Caughera:

Mangali, the daughter of Baijanāth[10] of Malneta, had sexual relations with a Kami ['untouchable' caste blacksmith]. Therefore the Yogīs of Malneta are polluted by acceptance of their rice: You [...] have eaten with them during a feast in Salyan, you are therefore polluted. I had sent a letter asking you to come for your purification, you did not obey and furthermore you insist that you do not need to be purified (since you are directly purified by Ratannāth). In this matter, you cannot disobey. If you have supporting evidence of Śrināth that you do not need the purification, come and show it. (id.: 497)

THE MONASTERY AND THE STATE: CONTROL AND CONFLICTS

The royal gift and the mode of ownership that results from it made the monastery an autonomous realm, an enclave that escapes the authority of the royal administrators.

However, the growing concern of the State to control and appropriate revenues was in contradiction with the fiscal autonomy accorded to the land surrendered as *guṭhi.* Hence the conflict between State and monastery. The State tried sometimes to revoke the status of the *guṭhi.* At other times it tried to control it; it wanted to check the monastery's mode of operation and to nominate its head. The tax collectors encroached upon the

[10] On the caste Yogīs and their relationships with the Caughera Yogīs, see Chapter 12.

monastery's privileges and the luckless farmers were burdened by double taxation. The *dharmadhikār* refused exemption from the law of common purification to the monastery. Conversely, Caughera tried to increase its possessions illegally or abuse its right to forced labour and thus entered into conflict both with the State and with the peasantry.

One sees, in the first place, the unfolding of the State's intention to retain control in matters regarding the succession of the head of the *maṭh*. According to the practice, each co-optation or election of the monastery head should be ratified by the king who issues a *lālmohar*, the red-seal edict, in the name of the new head of the *maṭh*, confirming his duties and privileges.

The legal documents concerning Caughera showed clearly the tendency towards reinforcement of State supervision, a tendency that intensified in 1910 CE with the creation of a *guṭhi* management agency (the future *Guṭhi Samsthan*) by the then Prime Minister Chandra Shumsher, following a series of scandals in the monasteries. Caughera was not spared, as evidenced by the indignant denunciation of a tax collector who accused the monastery as follows:

> Fields and villages were given by *lālmohar* to Ratannāth to ensure the *pūjā*. But the *pīr*, the *mānbhāū*, the *pujārīs* and the Bārapanths met and reached an agreement with the farmers and those cultivating the land [for the Yogīs]; they stole, lied, encroached upon and annexed the Crown land, extending along *guṭhi* land. These lands, which were thus misappropriated, equal 7,000 Rupees of State revenue.

In view of this conflict, the government officials made a minute inventory of the possessions and of the obligations of the monastery and imposed upon Caughera a *lāgat*, a convention that detailed resources and expenditures in a very restrictive way. The monastery was no longer free in its expenditures; the quantity and the amount to be devoted to each ritual and each festival were all fixed.

In sum, the relations of Caughera with its peasants, on the one hand, and with the State on the other were characteristic of those that we find in general between the ruling power and the big landowners to whom the former has mandated rights and duties. However, we have seen that, even though the consequences of the grants are not limited to religious ownership, their motivation was of a true religious nature and lay within the general framework of a relationship of mutual legitimation between politics and religion. The king desired the favour of the gods and the intercession of their priests. He followed his *dharma* and in this way defended his status of *kṣatriya*, his status as king-protector of religion and of the Hindu order that legitimated his position of dominance. He made 'his army of prayers' the spiritual and at the same time the worldly defender of his kingdom's integrity. The Yogīs as recipients of the *guṭhi* would therefore ensure the order of the kingdom through the efficiency of their worship and the fulfilment of their duties. These religious references, this recourse to *dharma*, was put forward whenever the need arose to protect the right of the *guṭhi* owners, to oblige the subordinates to provide their service, or to make government officials respect the privileges of the monastery. Whoever assaulted the autonomy of the *guṭhi* land jeopardized the *dharma* and thus risked supernatural sanctions, as the donation formulas clearly specified.

The recent political turmoil and the collapse of monarchy have evidently affected the status of the monastery. But even though Dang Valley was a Maoist bastion, the buildings and its inhabitants were preserved and Caughera still counts among the important *pañcāyatī* monasteries, keeping its ritual agenda and strong Nāth traditions despite the loss of most of its landed property and fiscal privileges.

PART III

PERSONAL MONASTERIES

The two monasteries discussed in the earlier chapters, the monasteries of Kadri and Dang Caughera, are two examples of *pañcāyatī* monastic structures: collectively owned by the sectarian institutions, led by heads elected from among the entire community of the Nāth Yogīs, devoted to ritual performances celebrating the unity and singularity of the sect, they ensure the permanency of the sect's values and structures. But they are not numerous and not very active except at festival times. Much more numerous and varied are the *nijī maṭhs*, or privately owned monasteries. However, although all are privately owned, the *nijī maṭhs* vary greatly in size and antiquity. Some of them are just small hermitages, while others may claim an ancient history, have impressive buildings and are influential institutions. However, whatever their differences, all the *nijī maṭhs* function independently and their succession and headship are not decided by the sectarian authorities, which does not mean that they are beyond the sect's control.

The context and the problems faced by the *nijī maṭhs* are specific. Their legitimization is a major issue: how are these monasteries included and recognized in the Nāth tradition? How do they ensure their continuity and secure their transmission? And looking at the way they function as economic and financial institutions, how do they succeed in attracting patronage and how do they cope with their lay devotees? All these questions can be asked in similar terms for all the *nijī maṭhs*; the importance and longevity of the monastery depend on the answers. Alongside ancient and still important institutions, many remains of destroyed former Nāth establishments, especially in Rajasthan, testify to their inherent frailty. Even in such a place as Varanasi the huge Gorakhnāth Maṭh, built by the Jodhpur Rājā Man Singh, now seems rather neglected, even though its ownership is now claimed by the Gorakhpur monastery.*

Thus, the Hindu monastic network can appear as fragile, depending on the personal aura and support of the various *mahants* and lasting as long as their memory is alive, as Dana W. Sawyer writes regarding monasteries of Daṇḍī Dasnāmī Sannyāsī in Benaras:

> Dandi monastic complexes originate and develop around charismatic gurus rising with their brotherhood. The guru is the pivot and foundation of the entire monastic structure, *maṭhs* (monasteries) forming and dissolving as gurus come and go. The effect of guruism (having the living guru at the top of the monastic hierarchy) is a very volatile, ephemeral, and plastic monastic structure. (1998: 159, 162)

The three monasteries that I will describe now, Fatehpur, Gorakhpur and Asthal Bohar have been able to retain their importance and prosperity.

The Fatehpur monastery in Rajasthan is an example of a successful new implantation and is expanding rapidly. Founded at the beginning of the twentieth century, it locates itself both in the Nāth tradition and in the 'modern era'. We shall see what is intended by this 'modernity' and how innovative it may be, compared to the Nāth main paradigms. Gorakhpur monastery in Uttar Pradesh tends to be seen as the main Nāth establishment while encompassing pan-Hindu deities and festivals in a Hindutva attempt for leadership. Asthal Bohar in Haryana offers a particular synthesis of the various components of the Nāth identity.

* See the precise description of its buildings made by Briggs (1973: 83-5), who already (in 1924) deplores its decayed state, and its confirmation by Sinha and Saraswati (1978: 113-14).

CHAPTER 8

Fatehpur Ashram

The Nāth monastery of Fatehpur is situated on the northern edge of this small town of the dry Shekhavati region of Rajasthan. It is called Amritnāth Ashram, a name which attests to its main characteristics: a strong link to its founder Amritnāth and a modernist orientation implied by the choice of the word 'āśram' (or *ashram* in the anglicized form). Even though the word 'āśram' has since Vedic times referred to ascetic hermitages, it seems that in modern parlance the word *maṭh* is preferably used to refer to monastic institutions of established sects and the term 'āśram' to designate the diverse residences of new gurus who attract mainly lay followers. Amritnāth Ashram is characterized both by respect for a traditional guru-disciple relationship and by modern surroundings which favour innovation and openness to society. We are in a very different structure there from the *pañcāyatī* monasteries we have studied so far.

Many deserted places, decayed buildings or shifts in sectarian allegiance testify to the difficulty with which personal or private monasteries outlast and develop beyond the life of their charismatic founder. However, Amritnāth Ashram is a model of success. How has it maintained its influence and prosperity? Its growth in Fatehpur combined with the creation of branch-monasteries in order to put down roots both in the Nāth sectarian tradition and in the social context of Shekhavati. How did this institutionalization happen, how was the charismatic authority of the founder transmitted and continued, how did what Max Weber (1964: 363-73) called the *routinization of the charisma* function?

HAGIOGRAPHY: AMRITNĀTH AND THE MONASTIC FOUNDATION

The founding of the Ashram, its growth and popularity are rooted in the prestige and deeds of the charismatic and heterodox figure of Amritnāth (1852-1916 CE). To keep his memory alive was thus essential and it was the task chosen by one of Amritnāth's close devotees. Durgāprasād Śarmā Trivedī (pen-name Śankar), a lay devotee born in Amber, wrote in Hindi a first version of Amritnāth's life and teachings, Śrī Amritānurāg, which was published in 1932. The book was republished in 1942 under the title of *Śrī Vilakṣaṇ Avadhūt* with a foreword by a well-known pandit of Jaipur,[1] which tells of the growing reputation of Amritnāth's tradition. The book was republished in 1990 by the present *mahant* Narharināth with a short biographical note on his three predecessors on the throne of the Amrit Ashram.

This book has acquired canonical status and for the devotees constitutes the 'Truth' about Amritnāth and his tradition. It is composed of three different sections aimed at meeting the different needs of its readers. The first part describes the events of Amritnāth's life which Durgāprasād heard of or lived through himself. The author presents himself, describes his personal relationship with his guru and his sorrow at his own absence at the moment of Amritnāth's death. He had been warned by his guru to return to the Ashram before the 15th of the month of Asvin. However, his business in his village took him longer than expected and in the middle of the night of the 15th, when the moon was full, while half-asleep he suddenly saw his guru smiling at him through the window. Disturbed by this vision, he quickly returned to Jaipur where he learned of Amritnāth's death in Fatehpur. He was thunderstruck by the news. Remorse and sorrow led him to write about the life of his guru.

The second part of the book contains the teachings of Amrit-

[1] Purohit Harnārāyaṇ Śarmā, with many thanks to Monika Horstmann for this information (see 'Two sides of the Coin: Santism and Yoga in Rajasthan', Paris, 2005, unpublished).

nāth as he gave them orally to his disciples. As well as being a classical development on Haṭha Yoga, Amritnāth's message claims to be simple and good for all. He stresses the importance of a disciplined life, of correct eating habits and of what he calls *sahaj yoga*. We shall see later how simple this yoga is (*sahaj* as natural, instinctive) and how novel Amritnāth's teachings were.

The third part is written directly by Durgāprasād and consists of poems inspired by the 'energy of Amritnāth'. Durgāprasād tells how he showed Kabīr's poems to Amritnāth; Amritnāth told him that all the poems had been authored by Kabīr's disciples and that he himself, Durgāprasād, could write as well with his guru's inspiration. Quite astonished, Durgāprasād 'discovered that he was able to compose rapidly songs about yoga, bhakti, detachment, devotion, inspired by *nirguṇ bhāv*'.[2] This corpus of poetry constitutes the third part of the book and inspires the many *bhajan* or devotional songs dear to the lay worshippers.

Durgāprasād's book had a great influence. It made it possible for a community to form around a shared memory. It also served as the basis for subsequent narratives dealing with Amritnāth and in particular the book of the local historian Sāgarmal Śarmā, entitled *Śekhāvatī ke Sant*, which contributed to the diffusion of the Ashram's reputation. The facts related by Durgāprasād, especially the supernatural deeds of Amritnāth, were later illustrated by Prabhātnāth who, in the 1980s, was the creator of the majority of paintings illustrating the foundation legends of the Nāth monasteries. He used the same technique as in Dang Caughera, depicting the scene in a colourful naïve style and adding captions on the canvas itself. These 60 paintings formed a kind of hagiographical gallery in front of the Ashram sanctuaries, but very recently a huge showroom has been built

[2] (Trivedi 1990: 59). According to Monika Horstmann, 'it is not astonishing that it took him a bare twenty minutes to compose a song, for what he wrote was deeply rooted in the regional poetic and religious tradition [...] he followed the special regional mood which did not find it essential to distinguish between doctrinal yoga and doctrinal bhakti' (2005: unpublished mss., p. 14).

with the walls covered with new paintings more in the style of mythological comics, with English captions. New episodes have been added which incorporate the memory of the devotees' families; for instance one painting shows Amritnāth teaching Durgāprasād about celibacy.[3] The same paintings figure on the website of the Ashram (amritnāthashram.org) which now has both Hindi and English versions.

The desire to reach a foreign public[4] led the Ashram authorities to commission an approximate English summary of Durgprasād's book. With the title *The biography of Shri 1008 Vilaxan Awadhoot*, it limits itself mainly to the miraculous deeds of Amritnāth. Without any author's name, it merely mentions in the text: 'At that time Shri Durga Shankar the writer of Shri Vilaxan Awadhoot book was also sitting with Baba' (p. 36).

The personal memory of Durgāprasād and his authorship tend to disappear or be put to one side in favour of a collective appropriation of Amritnāth's personage. The personal charisma of the saint has been preserved and its memory nourished by a hagiography which has acquired the status of a canon and became 'the stabilizing factor that served to consolidate religious group identity in terms of theology, ritual and moral conduct'.[5]

[3] The image explains that 'The wife of Durgāprasād Trivedi died in 1914 and he planned to remarry'. Amrithnāth's words to him are: 'Brother! Do you want to live in enlightenment or darkness? Do you like stench or fragance? Tell me quickly'. The comment under the canvas is: 'The insinuating questions of Babaji had such pure and deep effects on Durgāprasād that his desire for remarriage extinguished. Living in abstinence, he pursued the path of self-realisation and later authored the book titled *Shree Vilakshyan Avadhoot Parahans Shree Amritnāthji Maharaj*.

[4] 'It will be more beneficial for the foreigners who are unfamiliar by the miracles, preachings and yoga knowledge performed time to time by almighty great saint Shri Amritnāth' (foreword of B.L. Bhinda to the 2002 English translation). However, interested foreigners were only two in those days, myself and a Scottish devotee who built the first website.

[5] See Introduction to the volume *Charisma and Canon*, edited by

As Stietencron explains (2001: 16): 'Drawn from the memory of elders who were themselves witness to the life, words and deeds of a charismatic leader, this canon draws its legitimacy partly from actual experience or memory of charisma, and partly from the collective consent of learned religious leaders of the community'. And Françoise Mallison states (2001: XV):

> A saint is made from the way the others look at him [...] A hagiography exists only when acknowledged from outside [...] A saint is not for a single disciple but for a collectivity that projects its dreams or fantasies into the hagiographical narratives that the authors-narrators transmit. The community, substituting for the author, suggests its desires to him and appears as the true collective author of the hagiography, the writer simply fulfilling the demand (my transl. from French).

The religious biography of Amritnāth is thus to be considered as a hagiography in the way it includes the many life episodes in a narrative on which the community of disciples and devotees is founded. The rather recent process of its elaboration allows for a better understanding of the process of standardization of memory, of the collective appropriation of real personal events and their integration into the hagiographical mould. In studying the details of Amritnāth's life as recounted by Durgāprasād, we shall see how it corresponds to certain stereotypes, to a model of saintliness built around Amritnāth's character of miracle-maker. Durgāprasād and other disciples knew very well the multiple sectarian and devotional traditions and the many hagiographies told in Rajasthan;[6] the references to Kabīr's songs also shows how Durgāprasād's work is anchored in the Sant tradition.

However, what makes the narrative very lively is its rootedness

---

Vasudha Dalmia, Angelika Malinar and Martin Christof (2001: 3) and in the same volume the article by Heinrich von Stietencron (pp. 14-38).

[6] As Winand Callewaert, editor with Rupert Snell of one of the ground breaking books dealing with hagiographical writings (*According to Tradition*) wrote: 'The desert and jungles of Rajasthan are full of life, with a great variety of small insects and numerous large animals. Such too are the manuscript collections in that dry region, preserving scores

in the local landscape, both geographically and sociologically. The places where Amritnāth travelled, the kind of people he met, are the same as those linked today to the Ashram. Despite insistence on miraculous events, the descriptions have an air of familiarity, of day-to-day life in a shared environment.

I will now summarize the main episodes of Amritnāth's life relying on Durgāprasād's account, on Sāgarmal Śarmā's abstracts, on the paintings in the monastery, and on the oral narratives given by the disciples.

AMRITNĀTH'S YOUTH

As is the rule for this kind of text, Amritnāth's hagiography begins with his birth where bodily marks and supernatural appearances announce his exceptional destiny.

Amritnāth was born into a peasant family of the Jāṭ caste. He was the fourth child of a pious family who had migrated from Bau village[7] (Sikar district) to Pilani, close to Bisau.[8] In this village, at a favourable time, on the first day of the clear half of the Caitra month of the 1909 VS year (i.e. 1852 CE), he whose name was initially Yaśarām was born. He was born smiling, looking like a one-year-old child and already having all his teeth. For five days he refused to drink his mother's milk to his family's dismay. But his father Cetarām consulted astrologers, who told him that a divine being had been born in his house, and Cetaram saw in a dream his son as a divine being teaching him the essential frailty of the human condition. The child was so advanced for his age that, when he was eighteen months old, he played with children of six and ran faster than them. Sometimes he stayed quiet, silent, lost in profound meditation and nobody dared to disturb him. A passing *sādhu* even told his father: 'Ram was born in your house!' When he was six years old,

---

of small Bhagatmāls and half a dozen huge works of hagiography' (1994: 87).

[7] A place where is now an important monastery in the Amritnāth tradition.

[8] Another place with a monastery which was managed from 1908 to 1915 by Campanāth, Amritnāth's guru (see passim).

his parents and some other people of the village decided to go back to Bau. The child walked at the front of the procession of carts but walked so fast over a distance of 23 *kos* (50 miles) distance that he arrived three hours before everyone else. (This episode is dear to all in the Ashram, often depicted on canvas and retold repeatedly.)

From Amritnāth's youth the hagiographer selects the details which show his exceptional capacities: control over nature and detachment.

Yaśarām/Amritnāth had a sister who became a widow at a very young age. He cultivated the fields for her; at harvest time, when the people thought the production would be something like 9 or 10 mounds (360-400 kg) of paddy, he alone collected more than 70 mounds. People were very amazed. Another time, when he was bringing water from far away (as it is often the case in Rajasthan), his jar full of water broke. He declared that, if it did not rain on his fields that very night, he would cease breathing and leave his body. During the night, the rain fell so heavily that everyone was amazed.

According to the hagiography, he got his powers thanks to his inner spiritual qualities: compassion, simplicity, detachment. He used to say that 'wordly possessions were a mere illusion, that we should not be attached to wordly goods but should restrict our needs and desires, and then we will enjoy life happiness'. He was satisfied with the most simple diet, a theme repeated throughout his biography. He mostly ate curd and *rābrī*,[9] carrots and turnips, sometimes in huge quantities and sometimes fasting for several days. He had refused to marry but lived at home till his mother's death in 1945 vs.[10] As soon as he had put her ashes into the Ganges at Haridvar, he started roaming as *sādhus* ordinarily do. He was thirty-six years old.

[9] A local dish made of barley flour, millet flour and buttermilk, boiled and cooled.

[10] A similar link to a mother is mentioned in the life of the Bengali mystic Caitanya 'who, in order to stay not too far from his mother, choose to settle in Puri because he had promised to never abandon her' (France Bhattacharya 2001: 189).

HIS LIFE AS AN ASCETIC

He travelled all over Rajasthan and Gujarat looking for a guru. In the Bikaner area he met a large group of *sādhus* gathered around Motināth, a Nāth from the Mannāthī Panth. Motināth was very learned and advised the newcomer to first learn how to read and write. The future Amritnāth asked if studying would improve his concentration but Motināth answered negatively, that concentration comes only from training and patience. 'Why then learn writing and reading?' asked Amritnāth.[11] This episode and the contempt for studies and script it reveals are often remembered today in Fatehpur, where in contrast the stress is on the value of discipline and practice, the respect for rule and duty.

Among Motināth's followers, Campanāth immediately recognized the particular radiance of Amritnāth and gave him his protection. He gave him his first initiation by cutting his hair tuft. Campanāth was then Amritnāth's *śikhā* guru and gave him his name and his *panth*, Mannāthī. Shortly afterwards Amritnāth performed the second step of initiation: the ear-piercing and the wearing of earrings. His guru was Jwālānāth and people said that in front of Amritnāth, and despite his experience, his hands were shaking so much that Amritnāth was obliged to finish the incision himself.[12]

Afterwards he continued to travel throughout Shekhavati[13] and visited many places which are now locations of branch ashrams of the Fatehpur tradition. Everywhere he went he gave

[11] Is this an echo of a similar episode in the *janam-sākhī* of Guru Nānak? As he was sent to a Brahman for study, Nānak told him: 'These subjects which you have studied are all useless [...] He then sang a hymn: 'Burn your worldly affections, grind [them] and prepare ink; let [your] mind be as paper of excellent quality" (McLeod 1994: 31).

[12] The fact of cuting one's own ears is told in Nāth folklore about great Siddhas, as a proof of their exceptional courage and self control.

[13] The chauvinistic hagiographer comments: 'No area in India is worth Shekhavati; nowhere else are the food, the water, the air, and the ordinary way of life comparable. Its qualities are beneficial to human beings and particularly to *sādhus*' (Trivedi 1990: 11).

speeches and met people whom he impressed with his austerities and his miracles. However some were troublesome and thus had to suffer the consequences of his wrath.

As he was meditating near Lakshmangarh, a man attempted to distract him. Amritnāth told him to stop and leave him alone but the man kept on bothering him. Amritnāth threw a staff in his direction, the man fled but the staff followed him like a bird! Another day, as he passed close to the police station in Fatehpur, he didn't answer the policeman who was calling him. The policeman struck him a blow, Amritnāth said only: '*śābās*' (very well) and the policeman suddenly became mad. People brought him to Amritnāth to apologize, Amritnāth gave him buttermilk and the policeman returned to his normal state.

Sometimes his opponents were the Brahmins.

In Churu the Pandit Jaisā asked him with mistrust: 'What is special about you? What kind of miracles can you do?' Amritnāth answered: 'I can perform miracles. Go and prepare your shroud, here is my miracle!' When Jaisā arrived home, he died. Another Brahmin in Lakshmangarh reproached him for not washing his hands properly and thus being polluted. Amritnāth replied that his purity was inside and putting his mouth at the end of a water pipe, he let the water run through his body and come out of his anus.

Let us note that Amritnāth's display of contempt for socio-religious rules is revealed by means of a bodily feat.

Other ascetics could be envious.

A group of *sādhus* went to challenge him, asking if he knew the mantra of the *kappar* (skull/begging bowl). He answered that he knew all the mantras and all the Vedas and could recite whatever they wanted.[14] The *sādhus* were quite impressed and bowed at his feet. But in Rajpur in Bikaner district, Hiranāth was reluctant and challenged Amritnāth

[14] As explained by Snell (1994: 5-6), the Saint – and his hagiographer have to prove their link to tradition, before suggesting a new interpretation: 'Hence the commonplace portrayal in hagiographies of the infant bhakta's enviably precocious command of an entire standard corpus of traditionnal texts, and a complete mastery of its wisdom'.

to eat some drugs which were supposed to give him great pleasure. Over a period of twelve days Amritnāth ate almost 6 *ser* (6 kg). These products were *siṅgiṅ, mohrā* and *hiṅglu* (the first two being a certain kind of poisonous plant and the third cinnabar[15]).

A few other mentions in the hagiography may allude to an interest in alchemy often associated with Amritnāth: his taking of *saṅkhiyā* (arsenic?[16]) is mentioned but whatever the nature of these experiments and their motives, the hagiographer retained only the physical prowess, i.e. not being affected by poisons. As was explained in the English version: 'All these performances of Baba put Baba equal to God Shiva in the matter of poison digestion' (p. 19). The true meaning of an alchemical quest is lost for the author, as well as for his public. Amritnāth only warns his audience that any taking of these products, even in small quantities, is very dangerous for health. Hiranāth's advice, which is perhaps the initiatory teaching of an alchemist, is explained simply as a malevolent action.

Throughout the hagiography the motif of Amritnāth's amazing diet recurs: his consumption of dangerous substances as we have seen, and his capacity to ingest enormous quantities of food[17] or to fast entirely, are seen as proofs of his total mastery over physiological functions.

[15] Or mercuric sulfide, cf. White 1996: 6, 66, 194-6: Mercury [...] is the presence in the mineral world of the sexual essence of the Absolute [...] All that remains is for the alchemist to swallow the mercury in question to himself become a second Śiva, an immortal superman (Siddha) (id. 6) ; 'Cinnabar, mercuric sulfide – composed of mercurial semen and sulfurous uterine blood – is a mineral hierophany of the sexual union of Śiva and the Goddess' (id. 194).

[16] According to McGregor's dictionary (1993: 962), a poisonous plant (as *siṅgiyā*) or perhaps arsenic? 'In India, red arsenic is identified with the uterine blood of the Goddess' (White 1996: 195).

[17] This is also a characteritic of Madhva, according to *Sumadhvavijaya*: 'He eats all the food that is brought to him by six Brahmans [...] He eats 4000 bananas and drinks thirty pitchers of milk [...] Acyutaprekṣa [his guru] is astonished that Madhva eats 200 bananas; Madhva explains

When he was travelling, he could walk 52 *kos* (about 160 km) a day, eating only two millet cakes with a handful of herbs. Sometimes he ate only neem leaves. On the contrary, when he settled in Fatehpur, he ate daily five *ser* (about 5 kg) of flour with butter and fifteen litres of milk. Then for three months he took one kg of honey with water, then only lemon juice for two months, then one litre of milk every hour for two months, and finally sixteen litres of cow urine every day for one month. Then he stopped taking any food.

A physician prescribed him pills of *jamāl goṭe.*[18] He took two hundred at once, without any effect (except to turn the physician into a devotee!) Another time he ordered a pit to be prepared with a huge fire. He placed two stones on the embers, sat there and drank 8 *ser* of boiling water.

Amritnāth's control over natural processes, his *siddhis*, supernatural powers, were not only used for demonstrative purposes but also for the wellbeing of others. Several such stories are told and painted on the walls of the monastery.

On a farm where carrots were growing in abundance, the farmer told Amritnāth to eat as much as he wanted. Amritnāth had already finished all the carrots of the third row so that the farmer worried about his harvest. Amritnāth laughed and the carrots grew again immediately. In Bau (Sikar district) there was no rain and the month of Śrāvan (July-August) was already well advanced; the peasants went praying to Amritnāth who told them to go back and plough their fields, and when they returned it was already raining. When walking near Bikaner Amritnāth became thirsty. Seeing a well he wanted to drink but people told him that the water was brackish. He insisted and drank. The water had become excellent and nobody in the village suffered from thirst any more.

Another story linked to the food habits of the Siddha testify also to his capacity to control and modify natural elements.

---

that the divine force in his belly is the same that consumes the world at the time of *pralaya*' (Zydenbos 1994: 172-3).

[18] 'A small cultivated tree, Croton tiglium, and its nut (used as a purgative)' (McGregor 1993: 359).

Amritnāth laid great stress on a good diet and on the properties of milk products, curd, ghee and buttermilk. With this advice he is said to have cured many sick people.

A shopkeeper, having heard of this, one evening brought a dozen of litres of buttermilk. But Amritnāth thought that it was milk and answered that he didn't drink milk at such an hour, and he would take it the next morning when it had curdled. The shopkeeper then told him that it was not milk but buttermilk; however, as the Siddha had said that it was milk and as his words were 'words of truth', the buttermilk was transformed and the next morning a very creamy curd was discovered.

Many examples of healing were reported in which Amritnāth cured people by giving them a drink such as milk or even water or indeed any substance: Raglāl of Churu was cured from tuberculosis by eating curd, a blind man by drinking water and Durgāprasād's wife by chewing a sort of vegetable gum. Sometimes his methods appeared rougher.

A peasant beseeched him to cure his son who was mad. Amritnāth told him to throw the child over the fence, the man was reluctant but his wife did so. The child came back to her, he was cured! In Lakshmangarh a goldsmith whose eye was terribly painful went to see him and asked for his help. Amritnāth laughed and told him to pick up a firebrand and put it on his eye, which the man did without hesitating. Immediately the firebrand became cold, the pain disappeared and the man recovered his eyesight.

Amritnāth was said not to be able to bear the suffering of others and thus took their troubles on himself. At the end of his life a lame man, Pāgalnāth, was brought before him. Amritnāth blessed him and instantly the lame man started walking. But then the Siddha lay down and didn't move again until his death four years later.

His powers of second sight and ubiquity are also mentioned in anecdotes.

In Fatehpur, as his disciple Jyotināth was fetching water during the night, Amritnāth told him to be careful since there was a snake close to the jar. And in Fatehpur, when he was staying at the *dharmaśālā*, Rāmdev Vaiśya went to see him in his room on the upper floor. But when Vaiśya left him and went down the stairs, he saw the same Amritnāth he just had left, climbing up the same stairs.

The hagiography refers very seldom to the spiritual qualities and religious practices of Amritnāth. Only one example occurs, concerning Nārāyaṇ Girī who longed desperately to obtain the vision of the Goddess and wanted to go to Hiṅg Lāj[19] to worship her. Amritnāth told him: 'You may go but if you have a true devotion, you will have her *darśan* right here'. At midnight he called Nārāyaṇ Girī: 'Get up, the Goddess came to give you her *darśan*, bow in front of her!' Nārāyaṇ, thanks to his guru's powers, had the vision of the Goddess with eight arms, seated on her lion in a circle of light.[20]

Even though Amritnāth spent most of his renouncer life roaming throughout Shekhavati alone with only a few disciples, his reputation continued to grow. In a paradox common to many ascetic lifes, the more rigorous and solitary became his practice, the more attractive he was to the people; soon he was followed by a crowd of people looking for his advice, his help or merely his *darśan*. Among these devotees, the hagiogaphy more and more frequently mentions at the end of his life rich and important people whose patronage became essential for the growth of the future Ashram. We find here all the names of the local big families.

[19] A very ancient pilgrimage place now in Pakistan devoted to the goddess Agni Devī and worshipped by the Śaktā as the place where the cranium of Sati Devī fell. Equally visited by the Muslims, the temple of Hiṅg Lāj was before Partition one of the main destinations of the wandering Nāth Yogīs.

[20] A similar situation is found in the biography of Sahajānanda (the founder of the Swaminarayan movement): 'Sahajānanda's yogīc powers apparently included the capacity to transport others in a state of visionary trance; the object of the vision is generally that of the "chosen deity" (*iṣṭadevatā*)' (Schreiner 2001: 159).

Amritnāth often went to Fatehpur and stayed first near a pond on the southern border of the town, then in a cremation ground near Sātī's temple in the north-east. Close to the cremation ground, a rich merchant of Fatehpur, Jagannāth Siṁhāniyā, had a garden and Amrithnāth stayed there several times. He found there a peculiar peace of mind and in 1969 VS, at the age of sixty, he decided to settle there. It is at this place that he took up definitively his lying yogīc position. Jagannāth together with another of the leading merchants of the town, Gorkharām Rāmpratāp Camaṛiyā, wanted to build an ashram. Gorkharām came often to see Amritnāth. As waṣ common among the Marwaris, he used to speculate financially. Once he was on the point of losing 50 *lakhs* in a transaction and went to ask Amritnāth's protection and, thanks to him, he was spared such a loss. To prove his gratitude, he wanted to build a four roomed pavilion but Swamījī was very reluctant. Finally he accepted a small building of two rooms but said that he hated houses, and would never live in it but only accept a straw shelter, that the ashram would be for his disciple Jyotināth to take care of. A place was chosen at the north-eastern limit of Fatehpur, near to the Camaṛiyā estate and when the building and the shelter were finished, Amritnāth was transported there still in his lying posture.

The news that Amritnāth had settled there spread through Shekhavati; the devotees rushed to the place, among them the Thakur of Sikar, Rāvarājā Mādhosiṁha, who wished to grant an entire village to the Siddha, but Amritnāth refused: 'What do I need of a village when I own the entire world? I will accept only the place I need to lie on. Wealth, land properties, what use are they for the roaming *sādhus*?' And he gave the true knowledge to the Thakur in exchange. Mādhosiṁha finally made him accept for his disciples the donation of 25 *bighas* of uncultivated land which are now attached to the Ashram and called 'Nāthji's grove'.

From 1969 VS (1912 CE) till his death the 15th day of the clear half of Āśvin 1973 VS (1916 CE), Amritnāth remained lying on the ground as he had vowed. He was served by his closest disciples Jyotināth, Santoṣnāth, Lālnāth and Kṛṣṇanāth and visited by hundreds of followers. The hagiography states: 'Every day about thirty people physically, psychologically or spiritually sick were healed. In four years forty-five thousand sick people have been cured, hundreds of people have been relieved from poverty, dying ones have been rescued, criminals have been transformed, all were given enlightenment.'

We have seen that Amritnāth had announced his coming death to Durgāprasād who didn't understood and to his great sorrow was absent. The account that he gave in his book was thus based on the accounts of others.

From the fifth day of Āśvin Amritnāth had stopped eating and talking. He forbade everyone to come close. Then on the fifteenth day at three o'clock he called his dearest disciples. Placing his hand on Jyotināth's head and holding Kṛṣṇanāth's hand, he told them: 'I am a roaming ascetic (*ramtā hūn*). Have no fear and follow the path I showed you. I am pleased with you. You will get a divine place close to me'. Then, a sudden crack was heard, Amritnāth closed his eyes, his breath slowed down and then stopped. A flame broke out of his body. There was a sudden peal of thunder, a thunderstorm broke and it started to rain. Thousands of devotees hurried to come, the prescribed rites were performed and in the evening Amritnāth's body was buried under the shelter where he was living. At the *samādhi*'s place a lamp was put, which is still kept burning.

Amritnāth was 64 years, 6 months, and 6 days old.

ANALYSIS: A HAGIOGRAPHY IN A FAMILIAR SPACE

The growth of the Fatehpur Ashram and its network of branch monasteries is rooted in the person of Amritnāth, so his life story takes on a special importance. The details selected in the hagiography and the way it is presented provide a background, showing how the text and hence the representations of the Ashram are included in a local cultural and sociological context.

The author of the hagiography and his audience were familiar with other biographical narratives and in particular with those of the Sant tradition of *nirguṇ bhakti*; this is quite evident when we compare the hagiography with the common pattern as described by D. Lorenzen who states: 'The basic pattern of life stories of these *nirguṇī* saints is quite staightforward and uniform' (1995: 185). He distinguishes the major elements of the typical pattern of such life stories from birth to death and gives a summary table comparing the lives of the seven main saints of the Sant tradition. Amritnāth's life pattern fits this analysis perfectly:

1. The saint has an unusual birth [...]
2. The saint displays his religious vocation, supernatural power, or outright divinity at a young age,
3. He has a life-changing encounter with his first guru,
4. He may be either a celibate ascetic or a married person
5. He has a number of encounters, often during his travels [... or with] petitioners who request the saint's assistance in solving some difficulty or simply wish for his blessing in exchange for him accepting a gift [... or with] the saint's rivals and opponents.
6. How the saint named his successor and/or instructed his followers to carry on the tradition after his death.
7. The saint has an unusual death (Lorenzen 1995: 185-8)

The general pattern of Amritnāth's hagiography is clearly more inspired by the context of the *nirguṇ bhakti* than by the Nāth corpus of heroic ballads. Amritnāth is very far from the great figures such as Gopicand and Bhatṛhari, Ratannāth, Mannāth – his *panth's* eponymous founder – or, to take a more recent example, Mastnāth, who lived in the eighteenth century but whose biography, written in the twentieth century, was steeped in heroic fantasy and the supernatural, in a world inhabited by wonder-worker ascetics and hostile kings. Amritnāth's hagiography has another flavour; even though it insists on miracles and other extraordinary deeds performed by the Siddha, it shows them happening in a familiar environment and well-known social milieu, which are those of the ordinary devotees.[21]

[21] A useful comparison can be made, in the same cultural context, with the biography of Baldev (died 1947 CE) as narrated by his disciple Banāsā (presentation and translation by Monika Horstmann 2003).

The universe that they share is above all Shekhavati. The geographical scenery of the hagiography appeals to the feelings of the audience and allows for a need for local belonging to focus on the person of Amritnāth.

Amritnāth was born in Shekhavati and spent all his life there, travelling farther to Gujarat and Haridwar only for a brief and limited period. His journeys gradually narrowed around Fatehpur till the place became the fixed point of his network. It is worth noting that the places most often mentioned in the hagiography became those where his disciples established monasteries.

Amrithnāth belonged to a farmer family of Jāṭ caste. His concerns, his teaching, his metaphors, his miracles, all show the imprint of a particular natural and human environment: the dryness of the landscape, the deserts and bushes, the brackish waters, form the background of fragile pastoral and agricultural activity. The eating of dairy products and vegetables is seen as an ideal, both a sign of plenty and an element of physical and spiritual well-being.

The social universe of Amritnāth is also made up of these small towns with their varied populations, their administrative bodies and their merchants, these Seṭhs who made the fame and fortune of Shekhavati. They appear in the hagiography as the privileged interlocutors of Amritnāth, those who give him patronage, who want to build him an ashram and also who ask for his protection and powerful help. Contrary to what happens in the widespread Nāth narratives, the kings' or lords' patronage here comes second. Certainly the Thakur of Sikar visited him, bowed before him and offered him grants and wealth, but these were turned down and the meeting with the Thakur happened late in Amritnāth's life: he was then already quite well known and was not in need for patronage.

The hagiography gives much weight to the miracles performed by Amritnāth, especially the healings. It is a fact common to many Saints' lives[22] but it is particularly stressed in the case of

[22] Cf. Granoff (1985: 391): 'In Hindu India hagiographies and miracles would seem indeed to be closely associated. From philosopher to pious

Amritnāth's life as well as for his successors. It is probably a way of insisting on the exceptional character of Amritnāth and to show his nature of *siddh puruṣ* or *divya puruṣ* (perfect being, divine being). However, even if some of his supernatural deeds were done for demonstrative purposes and some of them in anger, they were mainly done for the benefit of his disciples and could be classified under three topics: prediction, healings and material successes. Such stories were not only told extensively about Amritnāth but also about his four successors. Should we link the care Amritnāth took of the health and well-being of his devotees to the modern trend towards welfare and public good which characterizes new religious movements but also has an influence on the Nāth Yogīs?

For his hagiographer, Amritnāth's holiness revealed itself first by his actions. More than his teachings, his behaviour was exemplary. Even though he claimed to despise academic studies, he also claimed to be more learned than the pandits, and they agreed: 'You have the True Knowledge, we have only argumentation [...] as you have studied in the book of the world'. He did not make doctrinal or philosophical speeches but taught everyone 'without considering *jāti-pānti*,[23] *varṇa-āśrama*, high and low, honour and dishonour, desire and envy, wealth' (Śarmā 2052: 33), attesting in practice his disregard for social norms. Sometimes he asserted his generous message energetically, as in the following case which was reported to me: one of his devotees who was a moneylender, a typical activity of the local Marwari

---

devotee, from reformer to Tantric adept, all are seen to have been capable of and to have performed great miracles'. See also Tulpule on Mahipati, the biographer of the Sants of the Marathi bhakti: 'Miracles play a very prominent role in the lives of saints, and saintliness is equated with miracle-making in the eyes of biographers' (1994: 166).

[23] *Pānt(i)* or *paṅkti*, commensal group which accepts to seat together in a line to share food. Sādhus of different sects may refuse this commensality. The term can be considered as a structural equivalent of caste (*jāti*) for the ascetics.

population, had a son who was very sick. Amritnāth agreed to cure him in exchange for a remission of debt for the poorest debtors. The moneylender agreed but did nothing. The child became mute until his father recognized his fault.

The same desire to open to all the path of detachment and thus of happiness led Amritnāth to simplify what he taught on yoga. 'He was sad that the fruitful path of yoga got lost for lack of good practitioners and loss of ancient texts, he wanted thus to teach and simplify its message, to give rules of life and daily discipline within the reach of everyone' (id. 3). He declared: 'A better food, chastity and concentration on breath, this is *sahaj yoga* (natural yoga), this is *samādhi*'.

The obsessive focus on diet obeys the same need for simplification. Throughout the hagiography we find repeated dietary recommendations and maxims which are now reproduced on the walls of the Ashram: 'Milk, yogurt, ghee, *rābṛi*, consume with love. Fast occasionally. Know the state of your body' and 'eat barley, millet, rice, peas, chick peas, sorghum. Cook lentils, beans, soya. This is *amṛit* for sure,' and also 'cereals and fruits are the basic foods. He who eats meat, disease eats him.' This is simple and practical advice that even devotees caught up in the occupations of the world can follow.

We see how greatly Amritnāth's hagiography corresponds to his devotees and also comes from them. As McLeod says about the *janam-sākhī* of Guru Nānak: 'They do not provide history. What they do provide is rather an interpretation of the Guru's life, one which reflects the piety of his devout followers [...] and which draws extensively upon a fund of the marvellous and the miraculous' (1994: 19). The choice and the account of episodes from Amritnāth's life are in line with what the lay devotees, having the difficulties and hopes of an ordinary life, expect from their guru. His sectarian belonging, thus the characteristics of the Nāth Yogīs, their soteriological quest and their yoga are revisited in accordance with other aims.

However, nowadays the disciples stress the fact that the Fatehpur Amritnāth Ashram belongs to the Nāth tradition. Even the lay devotees proclaim and are proud of this belonging. The next chapter will be devoted to examining the construction of this Nāth identity since the foundation of the monastery, the process by which Amritnāth Ashram slowly acquired its importance in and for the *sampradāya*.

CHAPTER 9

Institutionalization of the Fatehpur Ashram's Nāth Belonging

The personal charisma of Amritnāth was not sufficient to ensure the permanency of such a small Ashram as it was at its founder's death. The Ashram's continuation was secured by organizational factors, the first being adherence to a specific tradition capable of supporting and controlling the new institution. The Amritnāth Ashram declared itself part of the Nāth tradition but the involvement was stated more *a posteriori* than *a priori*, since Amritnāth's links to the Nāth seems to have occurred rather later in his life and perhaps even by chance.

However, Amritnāth's decision to settle in Fatehpur was incidentally a way of reviving an old Nāth affiliation since the town's foundation happened under the patronage of a wonder-working Nāth ascetic, Gaṅgānāth.[1] In 1448 a Muslim conqueror, Phatah Khan, the grandson of Kayam Khan, the founder of the Rajput lineage converted to Islam known as the Kāyamkhānīs, decided to build a fort on a small hill where Gaṅgānāth was living. The ascetic, driven away by the nawab's troops, left carrying his *dhūnī*, his holy fire, inside his shawl.[2] Phatah Khan, hearing about the wonder, went to beg the ascetic to stay there and to accept him as his disciple. The nawab followed Gaṅgānāth's teachings, while remaining a Muslim, and at his guru's death

[1] See Rāmgopāl Varmā (1992: 29-32).

[2] A similar story is at the origin of Jodhpur, but the ascetic Ciṛiyānāth driven away by the Rājā Jodha left the place after cursing the king (Mahendra Singh Nagar 2001: 19-26). See Digby (1970) for Sufi examples.

built him a mausoleum (where a Persian inscription is still visible). The ascetic's *samādhi* became the heart of a monastery established by his disciple in the centre of the newly built town of Fatehpur and was patronized by the Kāyamkhānīs till their eviction in 1731. But at the time of Amritnāth's arrival, the monastery was abandoned and would be renovated only years later by a disciple of Amritnāth's second successor. In any case Amritnāth's independent character made him reluctant to settle in old or established institutions.

AMRITNĀTH'S AFFILIATION

Amritnāth's hagiography tells us profusely of his spiritual longing and his exceptional qualities but very little of his particular religious orientation and even less of any sectarian preference. His initiation as a Nāth when he was thirty-six years old was thanks to his encounter with a group of Nāth *sādhus*, among them his future guru. The quest for the guru is a common topos of the ascetic path and thus of spiritual biographies and generally ends with the sudden encounter with an exceptional personality, with the flash of immediate recognition. Sectarian allegiance generally has more to do with personal relationships than with doctrinal choice: one chooses not so much to become a Nāth, a Dasnāmī or a Rāmānandī as chances upon a guru.[3] This is the case for Amritnāth, who was roaming without any definite purpose apart from a vague spiritual quest, and happened to meet Campānāth. He felt immediate trust and faith in him and Campanāth for his part recognized immediately the exceptional radiance of the newcomer. Thus, despite the first negative en-

[3] The same happened in the Śankarien monastery of Sringeri, with the meeting between the Śankarācarya of Sringeri and his future successor, Bharati Tirtha. As told by Glenn Yocum: 'This initial meeting, according to Bharati Tirtha's own report, was crucial : "At the time it struck me that His Holiness was my teacher and my savior. His beaming smile I felt was giving me a message. I thought I got what I wanted [...] I decided then that he was to be my guru"' (1996: 70).

counter with Motināth and his group of Yogīs, Amritnāth was initiated into the Nāth *sampradāya* and received the earrings soon afterwards. However, he seemed little involved in the sect itself. There is no mention in his hagiography of a special link to Gorakhnāth or to Śiva, of him taking part in any Nāth pilgrimage or festival, or of any role in the sect's organization. Amritnāth is above all an individual charismatic figure. But since he has been initiated by Campānāth, he is inscribed in the Nāth tradition as a member of his guru's *panth*, and his disciples will later insist on the legitimacy of this affiliation.

Campānāth, and thus Amritnāth, belonged to the Mannāthī Panth. This *panth* is part of the canonical list of the twelve *panths* and is mentioned by Briggs and Dvivedi, Briggs alluding to its link with Rājā Rasālū and Rajasthan. I personally only met members of this *panth* in Shekhavati and I believe they were not numerous before the recent development of Amritnāth's lineage.

The Mannāthī Panth takes its name from a disciple of Gorakhnāth called Mannāth, a name given to Rājā Rasālū after his initiation. His legend mingles with that of his half-brother Pūraṇ Bhagat/Cauraṅgīnāth.[4] This legend, of Punjabi origin, is well known, under many variants, as far as south India. I summarize it according to Sāgarmal Śarmā's account (2052 vs: 20-2, translated from Hindi):

The king of Syalkot [now in Pakistan] Śaṅkhabhāṭī had married two queens. The younger one had no child but the eldest one had a son, Pūraṇmal, who was very handsome. He went one day to the palace of the younger queen who made advances to him but Pūraṇmal told her that he had vowed celibacy and that he considered her as his mother. She became furious and declared to the king that Pūraṇmal had tried to do her violence. The king, without making any inquiry, had Pūraṇmal's hands and feet cut off and had him thrown into a well. Somewhat later Gorakhnāth was passing by. With the force of his yoga, he knew what had happened, he took Pūraṇmal out of the well and restored his hands

[4] [Cf. Chapter 4, note 21]. For the north-Indian version see Swynnerton (1908), Temple (1885: vol. 1, pp. 2-65), Briggs (1973: 184-5), Gill (1986: 133-52), Digby (2000: 191-7).

and feet. He initiated him as Cauraṅgīnāth and they went roaming together, and one day they passed through Syalkot. Gorakhnāth sent Pūraṇmal (Cauraṅgīnāth) ask for alms in the palace. The king, hearing about the radiant appearance of the begging ascetic, asked for his blessing. Cauraṅgīnāth answered: 'King, you have been very unjust to your son'. The king answered that his son had commited a great offence. Cauraṅgīnāth then said: 'King! Your words are untrue. I am your son Pūraṇmal. I always considered the queen as my mother. Take her in front of me and if milk comes out of her breast and flow into my mouth, you will see that I am right.' This is what happened, the truth was revealed and the king in his wrath wanted to kill the queen. But Cauraṅgīnāth stopped him, saying: 'You are as guilty as she is. You have to forgive her.' The queen apologized saying that every woman wants to have a son and, in her desire to beget a son as handsome as Pūraṇmal, she tried to seduce him. Cauraṅgīnāth told her: 'Mother you shall have a son as handsome as I am but with his own character'. Sometime later the queen gave birth to a very beautiful child who was called Rasālū. He was very energetic. Later on, Gorakhnāth came back and through the power of his yoga entered Rasālū's soul, destroyed his bad inclinations, gave him his blessing and told him that he would become Nāth in spirit. Rājā Rasālū became Gorakhnāth's disciple, renounced his kingship and did tapas, under the name of Mannāth.

While roaming, he went to Shekhavati and established his hermitage in the village of Tain, close to Bisau in Jhunjunu district. The gurus of the Mannāthī *panth* come from Tain: their graves are there.'[5]

Indeed, close to Tain village is a small and peaceful monastery, locally said to be two-hundred-and-fifty years old. The buildings are set around a courtyard and contain the two graves of Campanāth, Amritnāth's guru, and Keśarnāth, who renovated the place around 1950. It was not possible to recreate the succession line of the *mahants* before Keśarnāth. It is said locally that a certain Śivnāth received a large land donation (1,500 *bighas*, or even 5,000?) from a local landowner and built

[5] This shortened version – as it is known in the Ashram – ignores the many extraordinary episodes that render the life of Rasālū so fabulous, notably in Richard Temple's rendition (1885), which however does not mention Tain or Shekhavati.

the monastery, which perhaps was later abandoned. It seems that it was restored and re-established in importance as a result of the Amritnāth Ashram's wish to reinforce its link to the Nāth tradition. The legitimation of the spiritual lineage issuing from Amritnāth requires reference to a prestigious affiliation; this process is necessary when the question is one of perpetuating a new foundation and 'to institutionalize the founder's charisma', a process that is often required in sectarian movements.[6] The 're-discovery' of Mannāth served this purpose.

AMRITNĀTH'S SUCCESSION

Amritnāth was not exactly enthusiastic at the idea of having an *āśram*; founding a monastic establishement was rather a desire of his lay followers and was entrusted to his main disciples, among them Jyotināth. In his last years of life, Amritnāth relied more and more on Jyotināth, putting into his hands all administrative and management tasks. And on his deathbed he declared publicly his confidence in his disciple. Thus progressively to everyone's eyes Jyotināth became considered as Amritnāth's chosen successor. It is he who organized the burial ceremony of his guru and the *bhaṇḍārā*, the ceremonial feast which ends the funerary rituals of the ascetics. According to Durgāprasād's account, Jyotināth was then consecrated (*abhiṣikt*) as head of the monastery (*Amritāśram ke maṭhādhīś*). However, it seems that the succession was not recognized as simply as that since, after spending some years building his guru's *samādhi*, enlarging and organizing the Ashram, it was only ten years after Amritnāths' death that Jyotināth was able to summon the whole of the Nāths of the thirty-two *dhūnis*[7] of the Mannāthī Panth for a commemorative

[6] Let us recall the groundbreaking article by Richard Burghart (1978a: 121-39): 'Every genealogy is a record of a strategy in which the sect has reinterpreted its past in order to compete more effectively for the [...] limited resources which are necessary for its survival in the present' (p. 127).

[7] The solemn meetings of Nāth officials are called *battīs dhūnī*

ceremony. As told by Durgāprasād, 'the Nāths put an end to their ancient rancours, restored their unity and offered to Jyotināth the shawl[8] with the title of *pīr*. At this occasion his disciple Śrī Śubhnāth was declared his would-be successor' (1990: 297).

It is clear that Amritnāth's will was not sufficient to dispense with a much longer official process in order to establish the existence of the new monastery and to recognize Jyotināth as its head. Jyotināth, who was the closest disciple of an unconnected guru, became responsible for setting up an institution on the grave of his guru. Then the collective recognition by the Nāth authorities, who had ended their quarrels,[9] marked the official birth of the Ashram and its chief. The gift of the shawl sealed Jyotināth's investiture and initiated the transmission process.

As a precaution to secure the continuity of the Ashram, Jyotināth made his disciple Śubhnāth, then sixteen years old, his officially designated successor. As we shall see later *mahants* did the same but their position was more solid.

TABLE OF SUCCESSION OF THE *MAHANTS*

	date of birth	*investiture*	*death*
Amritnāth	1852		1916
Jyotināth	1877	1916/1926	1954
Śubhnāth	1911	(1926) 1954	1971
Hanumānnāth	1935	(1963) 1971	1982
Narharināth	1952	1982	

bhaṇḍārā, 'feast of the thirty-two fires'. According to Yogī Vilasnāth (2005: 339), the *pīr-mahant* make together there *pūjā*, fire offering (*havan*), repeating mantras (*jāp*) and ascetic practices (*sādhanā*), share a meal and receive a *vīdāī* (departing gift). It seems that the number thirty-two is purely rhetorical as another name for the ceremony is *108 dhūnī bhaṇḍārā*.

[8] The traditional investiture rite for monastic heads (see Chapter 5).

[9] I have no explanation on the subject of the quarrels: were they rivalries related to the succession and to growing financial interests, as land donations continued to be made?

Jyotināth was born in 1877 in Haryana, in a Jaṭ family like Amritnāth, and like his guru chose to become a renouncer when already an adult. He went in search of a guru and his meeting with Amritnāth brought an immediate response: he was struck by the ascetic's charisma and Amritnāth, seeing his qualities, accepted him as a disciple and continued to give him serious training and teaching for the rest of his life.

For their part the three following *mahants* were brought up in the Ashram from childhood. It happens frequently and in all ascetic traditions that a family will give a child to a monastic institution: either the family has a particular devotion for a specific guru or *āśram*, or it is considered that the birth of the child is the result of a blessing by a wonder-working ascetic, a vow having been made to give the firstborn after a long period of barrenness. Often too the transmission takes place inside the same biological family, for instance from uncle to nephew: the young nephew is commited to the care of the monastery and trained by his uncle in his future duties.[10]

The case of Śubhnāth is similar. He was from the family of Amritnāth, his grandfather being the ascetic's younger brother. Amritnāth having foretold to Śubhnāth's father that an exceptional child would be born to them, the latter considered the child as a gift from the saint and brought him to Amritnāth when he was three. Amritnāth thought it impossible to care for such a young child and left him with his family till he was seven. In 1918 Śubhnāth entered the Ashram and was initiated by Jyotināth. He studied in the Sanskrit College, was recognized as would-be *mahant* as we have seen in 1926, and helped his guru till the latter's death in 1954. He then took the leadership of the Ashram until his death in 1971.

[10] This is the case for instance in the Nimbārki Monastery of Salemabad where, according to Clementin-Ojha (2006: 555) the succession takes place, at least in recent times, among Gauḍa Brahmin families 'through a system of patronage in which the gift of a son to the monastery played a significant part'. The present head entered the monastery when he was eleven years old (id. 552).

The third successor, Hanumānnāth, born in 1935 in a village near Lakhsmangarh, was brought to the Ashram even before the death of Jyotināth, when he was three years old. His father, a close devotee of the Ashram, asked Jyotināth to take care of the child.[11] He was taken in charge by Śubhnāth who trained him to be his successor. To guarantee a transmission devoid of problems or contests, Śubhnāth organized, as Jyotināth had done for him, a huge meeting of Nāth *sādhus* in order to commemorate the ten-year anniversary of Jyotināth's death and to make the *sādhus* recognize the choice of Hanumānnāth, then twenty-seven years old. Śubhnāth died in 1971 and Hanumānnāth succeeded him as had been decided. Like his predecessors he took care of the building of his guru's tomb and the training of his own future successor, Narharināth, the present *mahant,* born in 1952 to a Brahmin family close to Fatehpur. Narharināth's father was the *purohit* of the Ashram and the child used to come with him and to manifest the desire to stay in the Ashram where he was accepted when he was ten. Hanumānnāth took him as a disciple and initiated him during the great Nāth meeting of 1963. Later Hanumānnāth fell seriously ill and – unable to continue his charge – he had Narharināth registered as his successor and entrusted the care of the institution to him. At his death in 1982, the *mahant* ship was bestowed on Narharināth by the *sādhus* community, the civil authorities and the lay devotees.

The recruitment of the next *mahant* will probably follow the same process. Two young boys are living in the Ashram, one has

[11] It seems that the child was born lame. According to the English version of the hagiography, his father 'a religious minded person [...] came to Jyotināth and requested to take Shri Hanuman Nāth under his shelter [...] At some time Shri Amritnāth came in the dream of the mother of Shri Hanuman Nāth. She requested Baba that a legged [*sic*] boy has been presented at the Ashram. But Baba assured her that the boy is not legged but healthy. So by the saying of Baba, the boy became totally cured and the defect of the leg was removed' (*The Biography of Shri 1008 Vilaxan Awadhoot*: 46).

already received the Nāth earrings and started doing the *pūjās*, while the other is still studying.

The transmission procedure is now well established. The selection by the *mahant* of a young disciple, whom he educates and appoints officially as *uttarādhikāri*, 'the next-in-charge', is accepted both by the sectarian authorities and by the lay patrons. The spiritual legitimacy of the process is reinforced by the current belief in a sort of common essence between the four *mahants*. Even though Amritnāth was included in a prestigious Nāth lineage, in an ancient *panth*, he is regarded by his devotees as an independent saint, direct inheritor of Gorakhnāth's grace. He is mentioned as Śrīnāth, an appellation generally used for Gorakhnāth and for Śiva himself. To call Amritnāth Śrīnāth is to identify him with the divine gurus. But besides Amritnāth, all his successors are referred to in the same way and many stories about the different *mahants* tend to lead to a certain confusion: we don't know which *mahant* is meant by the name Śrīnāth. Another idea is the co-presence of all the *mahants*: behind the current *mahant*, all his predecessors and above all Amritnāth are acting. An anecdote quoted in the hagiography expresses the idea in the following way: once a visitor with supernatural powers came to the monastery, a Tantrika they said, who always saw the *mahant* as a double figure. Behind him, acting like his shadow, there was always Amritnāth!

The transmission of authority from a monastic head to his follower can thus be expressed in a subtle way: it is the tranmission of a spiritual essence, of a quality inherent in the function, which renders personal differences meaningless.[12] The symbol of this common essence, and the guarantee of the permanency of the function, is represented by the *gaddī*, the throne, on which sits

[12] We can compare them with the Sikh gurus: as noted by Hawley and Juergensmeyer (1988: 75), all the gurus of the lineage sign their poems with the name Nānak, 'so Nānak, the guru, is not just a person but a principle'.

the head of the monastery. And as we shall see, the *gaddī* is close to and linked to the founder's tomb.

TRANSMISSION AND GROWTH OF THE MANNĀTHĪ PANTH

The Fatehpur Amritashram is the work of Amritnāth and his four successors. No other disciple had any part in it. The monastic structure of the Ashram is, I think, representative of the way monasticism is organized in Hindu sects in the case of the private or *nijī* monasteries: monasteries are anchored in the person of the superior and in his transmission of the ownership and care of the place to one chosen disciple, the others being supposed to leave the monastery to settle elsewhere, founding their own monastery or reactivating an abandoned place. Stress is laid on the individual capacity to follow the path shown by the guru and to reproduce the foundational model he has given. The Amritnāth Ashram thus developed exponentially, with the many disciples of each generation leaving the Ashram to build their own place. It was said that the duty of the disciples was to propagate the *dharma*, to chant the glory of Amritnāth and to spread his teachings as widely as possible, in as many places as possible. The structural atomism was justified by the necessities of proselytism. However, the disciples of Amritnāth and those of his successors did not go very far, they chose to stay within the geographical limits of Amritnāth's wanderings, i.e. in Shekhavati. They were familiar with the territory and with its inhabitants, who were already impressed by Amritnāth's reputation and eagerly supported the heirs to his spiritual lineage. The Amritnāth Ashram is now at the centre of a vast network of more than fifty monasteries which claim their affiliation to the Mannāthī Panth and to Amritnāth's descent. They mark this affiliation materially in the construction pattern, all monasteries following the model laid by Fatehpur, the founder's and his successors' *samādhi* each being crowned by a shikhara roof (thus the number of shikharas is a visible sign of the age of the place, of the number of *mahants* who have succeeded since the foundation), and all the monasteries having at their heart the same painting of Amritnāth seated in half *siddhāsan*. However, even though all the monasteries go back to a common ancestor, they function quite independently. They are not to be considered as branches of the Fatehpur Ashram but as personal monasteries (*nijī maṭhs*) on their own account, with their own system of management, their own festival calendar, and their own network of lay devotees.

Here is a brief survey of the Shekhavati Mannāthī monastic structure.

Above the Amritnāth Ashram are the places related to Amritnāth's guru. We already talked about Tain, as the place of origin of the *panth* since it is supposed to be the burial place of Mannāth, alias Rājā Raśālu. It was renovated around 1950 by a disciple of Jyotināth and is under the care of his successors. At Jhunjhunu monastery we have the first historical testimony of the implantation of Amritnāth's spiritual lineage under the authority of the latter's 'grandfather guru'. The monastery was founded around 1790 thanks to the donation of a local prince, by a charismatic Yogī known as Cañcalnāth.[13] His two main disciples were Kṣamānāth and Gaṇeśnāth. According to the principle of foundation that we have seen, Kṣamānāth left Jhunjunu to found his own place in Bārvās (close to Loharu in Hanumangarh district) where Amritnāth was initiated in 1888, as one of Kṣamānāth's disciple was Campānāth. The *cuṭ* guru of Amrithnāth continued roaming for a long time before settling in 1908 in Bisau, where he died in 1915. The Bisau monastery had been founded by the other disciple of Cañcalnāth, Gaṇeśnāth; it is thus a very important place since it unites the two spiritual lineages coming from Cañcalnāth around the cult of the two *samādhis* of Gaṇeśnāth (d. 1908) and Campānāth (d. 1915). Perhaps the monastery was left without a *mahant* after Campānāth's

[13] On this Yogī and his friendship with the Sufi Qamrūddin Śāh, see Bouillier 2004 (254-6).

death, since we know only of Dharīnāth settling there in 1927. This dear disciple of Jyotināth had been sent there by his guru at a very young age, probably to take care of the deserted Ashram. A booklet published by the Bisau Ashram tells us:

> One night when the young Dharīnāth was lying full of sadness, suffering from loneliness and fever, longing for his guru, he had a vision: he saw a Sant [Campānāth] coming out from the *āśram* meditation cave at the same time as another Sant wearing wooden chappals (Gaṇeśnāth) went out from the *samādhi*. The first one greeted the second one and told him: 'Your disciple is troubled and sad'. The Sant from the *samādhi* then addressed Dharīnāth: 'Brother, I brought you here with much effort to make our *pūjā*. You are not alone, we are with you. Don't be anxious'. The two Sants went back to their respective places and Dharīnāth remembered: 'I was feeling full of happiness and strength, the fever fell immediately. Since this day, I never felt feverish nor disheartened any more.'

Dharīnāth stayed fifty-three years at the head of the monastery and made many improvements. He was also well-known for his taste and skill in writing devotional songs which are now part of the repertoire of the Mannāthi Panth's *āśrams*. He was succeeded by his disciple Bhaktanāth, presently in charge.

GENEALOGY OF THE FOUNDING GURUS

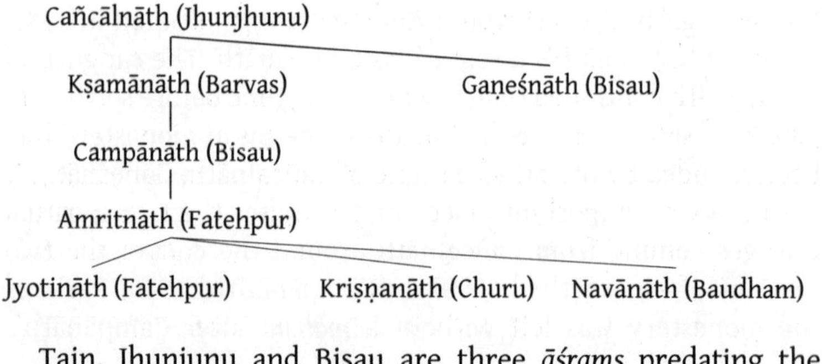

Tain, Jhunjunu and Bisau are three *āśrams* predating the Fatehpur one, which belong to the generation preceding Amritnāth but were later developed thanks to the network of his disciples. Subsequently other *āśrams* were founded by direct disciples of Amritnāth. Among them Jyotināth was the most important, not only as the successor in Fatehpur but also thanks to the many disciples that he initiated himself and who founded establishments all over Shekhavati.

The bigger monasteries nowadays were founded by two of Amritnāth's disciples: Baudham (near Lakshmangarh) by Navānāth, and Churu by Krişņanāth. The Churu *āśram* is quite impressive, with its four high shikharas in white marble, surmounting the four *samādhis* of Krişņanāth, Bhaninath (a disciple of Jyotināth who was the first *mahant*), his successor Dvārkānāth (another disciple of Jyotināth) and Sanjaynāth, the guru of the present *mahant* Devināth. The support of the local Seṭh community was decisive, as well as the gift by the Bikaner *rājā,* Ganga Singh, of 125 *bighās* of land in the north of the small town.

Amritnāth's disciples were responsible for the construction of some of the most important monasteries. In the next generation the expansion becomes exponential and the Mannāthi Nāth network widespread, especially through Jyotināth's disciples. It is possible to list ten disciples who, in their turn, transmitted Amritnāth's message:

JYOTINĀTH

- Śubhnāth, his successor in Fatehpur
- Keśarnāth, the renovator of Tain
- Dhaṛināth, the renovator of Bisau
- Dwārkānāth and Bhānīnāth in Churu
- Bhūrnāth in Palvas (near Sikar)
- Śankarnāth in Than Matui
- Duṅgarnāth in Jasasar (Churu district)
- Makṛināth in Satra (Churu district)
- Pūrṇanāth in Lakshmangarh (in the '*Nāthjī kā maṭh*').

This strategy of expansion was also followed by Śubhnāth, Jyotināth's successor. The Fatehpur *mahant* from 1954 to 1971, he also had many disciples who founded new monasteries, now in full development.

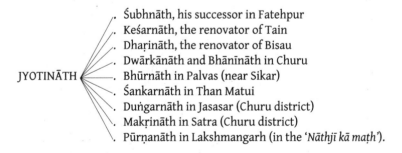

ŚUBHNĀTH
- Hanumānnāth, his successor in Fatehpur
- Śernāth in Rukanser (between Bisau and Tain)
- Bihārināth in Udasar (Churu district)
- Bisambarnāth in Tidiasar
- Kalunāth in Gusainsar (Churu district)
- Ravināth in Jaipur
- Rattināth in Baudham
- Jarnanāth in Taranagar
- Bharpurnāth in Mukundgarh
- Gyannāth in Tain
- Śraddhanāth in Lakshmangarh ('*Nāthjī kā āśram*')

The success and the constant growth of this Shekhavati network contrasts with the derelict state of many former Nāth monasteries that lost princely patronage. The Amritnāth Ashram and its monastic network represents a model of development which relies on three factors: a charismatic founder whose memory is kept alive, skilful institutional management, and a supportive group of rich lay devotees. The fact that this development occurred recently allows better access for the observation of its different steps.

THE THRONE AND THE TOMB

A monastic institution, be it *maṭh* or *āśram*, rests on the person of its superior. This identity between the institution and its head is symbolized by the permanency of the throne, the *gaddī*. Like the royal throne, the *gaddī* of the monastic heads embodies the function; ascending the *gaddī* or 'assuming the *gaddī*' (Mayer 1985: 205) means acceding to the headship. The installation ceremony, as we have seen in relation to Kadri, is performed on the *gaddī*, where the new head receives a special *tilāk* and is wrapped with the ceremonial shawl by the sectarian authorities.

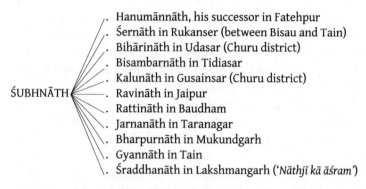

The throne is placed in the centre of the monastery, and is generally of 'the commonest form [i.e.] that of the cotton-stuffed mattress, with bolsters serving as back rest and arms' (Mayer 1985: 207). The *mahant* sits here most often but especially on formal occasions, such as welcoming visitors, giving *darśan* to his devotees, or giving religious speeches. The *gaddī* is considered to be endowed with special sacredness. Adrian Mayer quotes the opinion of some of his respondents for whom 'gaddis were said to have retained the qualities of their more distinguished occupants' (id. 210) and this is evidently the case for the monastic *gaddīs* such as Fatehpur. Morning and evening, at *pūjā* times, the officiant, after having worshipped the *samādhis* of Amritnāth and his three successors, enters the main room and honours the *gaddī*, giving homage with light (*ārti*) and incense (*dhūp*). Another way of considering the sacredness of the *gaddī* is to see it as the seat of the *śaktī*, the power of the *mahant*; the *gaddī* is not personalized as a particular deity[14] but it nevertheless embodies the feminine energy which gives the *mahant* the power to fulfil his office.

The foundation of a monastery raises the question of the installation of a new throne. The founding of many new *āśrams* in Shekhavati shows how this question is answered, how the legitimacy of a throne is conferred on a new line of *mahants*. It is by the close association between the monastic throne and the grave of the founder, between *gaddī* and *samādhi*.

The first act of the prospective successor, the one who would sit on the *gaddī*, is to organize the funeral of his predecessor and guru and to build him a tomb.[15] Closeness is maintained between the dead guru and the chosen disciple: as we have seen in the case of Amritnāth and Jyotināth, the disciple assists his guru in his last moments, he presides over his burial and organizes the funeral feast, three days after the death. Ideally his enthronement is

[14] Compare with the presence of deities in the royal throne, most often the royal Goddesses (Mayer 1985: 207-9), and their worship at *Daśahrā*.

[15] When there are conflicts of inheritance between different disciples, this is a criterion which has juridical value: see for instance the decisions of *pañcāyats*, followed or not by the British lawcourts, in the cases reported by Cohn (1964: 177-8) and Pinch (2004: 591: 'The senior-most chela received the greatest share [of the mahant's personal property] but also the responsibility of performing the death-rites and erecting a fitting samadhi monument').

performed the same day in front of all the ascetics who came for the *bhaṇḍarā*. The *gaddī* does not remain empty.

However, in Fatehpur ten years were needed for the assembly of the Yogīs to recognize Jyotināth's rights and thus to ratify the existence of the ashram. Jyotināth spent this time building up the place: the grave of Amritnāth was dug in exactly the same place where he had spent his last years. Jyotināth subsequently made the pit covered by an altar in white marble and surrounded by four walls, which makes the place a sort of shrine called *samādhi-mandir*. On top of it he had built a high pyramid-shaped roof, a shikhara, also in white marble. This was the centre of the monastery-to-be, and it was preceded by a hall where the *gaddī* was placed for Jyotināth to sit on and for his successors to be enthroned on. The tomb built for Amritnāth was later used as the model for all tombs of the successive *mahants* in Fatehpur and in all the Shekhavati monasteries in Amritnāth's lineage.

Amritnāth's *samādhi-mandir* is a small square room facing north, crowned by the 5-metre-high shikhara roof, and closed by two massive doors in silver.[16] Inside, at the exact place where Amritnāth has been buried in the sitting position, is the *samādhi* which is preceded by a small square platform engraved with the *caraṇ-cinh* (the footprints) which symbolize the holiness of the worshipped saint.[17] The *samādhi* itself is quite peculiar and differs from the ordinary form in *śivaliṅga*. Sitting on a square base it has the form of a pyramid with a rounded top and is covered with an orange silk cloth. The appearence is, in short, that of the Muslim tombs called *kalamdāni*, or pen-box shaped. Of course the ochre colour of the cloth is definitely Hindu, but the general ambiguity of the shape remains and a young Yogī

[16] This is a common form of the classical religious architecture of the area (see Cooper 1994: 46-8 and Sgroi-Dufresnes 2000: 267-94). Let us remark that the inspiration comes from temple architecture and not from the cenotaph (characterized by *chatrīs*, small domes on columns).

[17] See the Dādūpanthī cenotaphs always with these engraved platforms (Mishra 1991: 106, Hastings 2002: 100) or the Sannyāsī tombs on top of which these footprints are carved (Yocum 1990: 260).

told me once that the form of the *samādhi* was Muslim but that they were obliged to build it in this way to please the Muslim sovereigns.[18] I could not get any clear explanation of this peculiarity, reproduced in all the *samādhis* of the Shekhavati Mannāthi Panth. It is perhaps a Rajasthani characteristic of a syncretic culture such as that expressed in the Runicha shrine of Rāmdev who, for his Hindu devotees, is a warrior saint and a Viṣṇu's incarnation; nevertheless, 'Ramdeo *samadhi* [...] shows all the characteristics of a tomb of the Muhammedan style (*mazar, turbat*) – a rectangular structure topped by a cylindrical stone (*kalamdani* a device used to distinguish males from females); this grave, as in Sufi *dargahs*, is covered with a rich ornate textile and erected in a north-south line' (Khan 1995: 305). Amritnāth and his disciples situate themselves in a different tradition from the Nizārī Ismaelism of Rāmdev; nevertheless the wide diffusion of the Islamic-style funerary monument is quite striking.

Amritnāth's *samādhi-mandir* and those of his successors constitute the core of the Fatehpur Ashram. They are worshipped morning and evening by the Nāth *pujārī* who makes the usual offerings of light, incense, and holy water, before kneeling in front of each place and blowing three times into his small *nād* whistle. These *samādhis* are the only cult places inside the monastery, the places where all the devotees gather to honour the yogī saints. Evidently there is no idea of death impurity attached to the places; on the contrary they are considered as places of power where one still encounters the śakti – the energy – of the deceased *mahants* and especially of Amritnāth, who is seen as perpetually alive in *jivit-samādhi* and thus united with Śiva.

It is a common feature of the ascetic monasteries, especially when they are Śaivas,[19] to include the tombs within their build-

[18] We have to remember that the first construction dates from 1916: the Muslim powers had disappeared since a long time (be they Kāyamkhānī Nawābs or Mughals)....

[19] See for instance the remarks of Yocum (1990) concerning the Śaiva Siddhanta monasteries: in the Thiruvavaduthurai Adheenam

ings and to worship daily the deceased *mahants* and even the anonymous ascetics who have died and been buried here. For instance in Fatehpur, just behind the kitchen and close to the *mahants' samādhis,* is a gravesite where a dozen small stone pyramids mark the burial place of ordinary ascetics. The same thing can be seen in Churu, where small tombs are lined up just behind the big *samādhis* in the middle of the ashram courtyard.

The enrootedness of such monasteries on the tomb of the deceased founder, which alone allows for the perpetuation of the institution and its transmission to a chain of sucessors who sit on the *gaddī,* is also manifested in the choice of the anniversary of the founder's death as an annual festival. Every year, for instance in Fatehpur for Śaradpūrṇimā (full moon of Āśvin), there is a great festival where lay devotees and ascetics from the various monasteries of Amritnāth's lineage gather to celebrate his memory with a long worship of the *samādhi*, devotional chanting, and a communal feast. The same thing is done at each monastery, each one on the date of its own founder's death. This is clear evidence of the otherwordly orientation of these ascetic monasteries, of their purpose to ensure liberation. As Gleen Yocum says: 'Mutt in many ways may be like a temple but temples are not located on gravesites and do not have festivals set by death anniversaries [...] for the mutt is also like a grave' (1990: 264)

DHŪNĪ AND *GUPHĀ* (THE FIREPLACE AND THE CAVE)

These soteriological justifications are also expressed in two important places in each monastery, where access is more restricted and which link the monastery and its present residents to the Nāth tradition of austerities and yogic discipline: they are the *dhūnī* or fireplace and the *guphā,* the meditation cave.

Maṭh, the two public temples are the *samādhis* of the founder and his successor, both considered as being in living *samādhi* (*jivansamādhi*). A little outside are the tombs of the ten successors worshippped once a week by the present *mahant.*

The *dhūnī* is the fireplace of the itinerant ascetics, the centre of their campsite when they travel in groups (*jamāt* and *jhuṇḍī*) but it has also an important place in the settled monasteries. The fire is supposed to have been lit by the founding figure (for instance by Paraśurām in Kadri, Ratan in Caughera, Amritnāth in Fatehpur) and never extinguished. Generally the *dhūnī* is kept in a separate room in the monastery and worhipped by the *pujārī* every day before he officiates in front of the *samādhis* and altars (when there are any). The ashes of the *dhūnī,* carefully filtered, are used by the ascetics to mark themselves on the forehead and the body with the *tripuṇḍra*, the three parallels lines of Śiva's followers. The Amritnāth Ashram has the curious tradition of fuelling the fire with camel dung, instead of holy cow dung, but as pragmatic Rajasthani Nāths say, the camel is as precious, thus as sacred as the cow, in such a desert landscape!

Another element tells of the ascetic polarity of the place. A few steps going downwards, which are sometimes hidden in the main sanctuary or sometimes in a corner of the courtyard, remain unnoticed most of the time. A flight of stairs, always steep and dark, leads to an underground chamber. This *guphā* is the secret heart of the monastery, the place where the ascetics are said to come for meditation or yogic practice and where the different steps of Nāth initiations may take place. The Tantric connotation is manifest in Fatehpur since the *guphā* has for its only furniture a tiger skin on which the meditant sits, and a stuffed tiger head in a niche. The contrast between this dark and frightening underground place and the rest of the monastery, modern, vast with large open spaces, is rather striking.

The existence of a *guphā*, a meditation cave, is a characteristic feature of the Nāth monasteries[20] and stories are told about the main famous Nāth sanctuaries where caves are associated with the meditative presence of famous Yogīs, for instance Gorakhnāth in Gorakhmadhi (in Kathiawar), Gorkha (in Nepal),

[20] See Bouillier 2008 ('Grottes et tombes : les affinités des Nāth Yogīs avec le monde souterrain') which I briefly summarize here.

and Gorakhpur (in Uttar Pradesh), and Bharthṛhari in Haridwar and Ujjain.

As a place for meditating and practising *sādhanā*, it suits the advice given in *Haṭha Yoga Pradīpikā* (1.12): 'a yogī should practise Haṭha Yoga in a small room situated in a solitary place, measuring four cubits square (or four *haṣṭha*, four times the forearm), with a small door, without windows or holes or clefts, etc., and outside, there should be a raised platform and a compound'.

Being shut up in a *guphā* (be it a natural cave or a subterranean chamber), being underground, refers to the universal motif of the womb and to the metaphor of the initiatory birth. A Yogī publication makes the association explicit in calling the meditation cave of Haridwar monastery, *bhūgarbha*, earth-womb (Vilāsnāth 2001: 12). It is the place where the Siddha Bhartṛhari practised asceticism; it is a *tapasthalī*. However, the rebirth which occurs in the womb-cave is only made possible by the meditative practices of the yogī who follows his yogic *sādhanā* and reaches the blissful state of enlightenment.[21] The double meaning of the word *samādhi* takes here all its importance, being both on one side the last step in the path of yoga, the final outcome of all practice, the state of absolute concentration leading to blissful release, and on the other side the grave of the ascetic.

The link between the subterranean confinement of the *guphā*, the meditative process ending in ultimate release and the memorial foundation of the *samādhi*, is well illustrated by

[21] A story told in the Nāth monastery of Jhunjunu makes explicit that the underground chamber is a place dedicated to ultimate bliss: in the monastery whose abbot was a locally famous Yogī called Cañcalnāth, a mother brought her leprous son, asking for help. The Yogī, who was meditating, misundertood the mother and thinking it was some gift, he shouted: 'Throw it in the *guphā*'. Six months later, the mother came back asking about her son. Cañcalnāth suddenly understood his mistake, and opened the door of the *guphā*. The boy was seated there, in perfect shape, completely healed, and explained that everyday a sweet and some water appeared and that he was immersed in deep meditation and perfect joy.

the small sanctuary of Kalunāth in Nāthana village (Punjab); this Nāth holy man, living probably at the beginning of the seventeenth century, is said to have remained twelve years in a small *guphā*, ventilated by two narrow channels. When he died there, he was buried exactly under the place where he was meditating (a second cave dug under the first cave). Now in the Nāthana sanctuary are superposed the grave where Kalunāth is buried, the *guphā* where he was practising yoga and reached the state of *samādhi*, and a memorial building, a cenotaph called also *samādhi*, a kind of cement platform with a door and a flight of stairs giving direct access to the subterranean chamber (where the *pādukā* (wooden sandals), the *cimṭā* (fire-tongs) and the meditation staff supposedly owned by Kalunāth are kept). We thus have here three levels on top of each other: the cenotaph-temple (*samādhi mandir*) with a *pujārī* making offerings to a symbolic tomb, the meditation room with the paraphernalia Kalunāth was using, and the grave itself.

The Amritnāth Ashram has no other shrine inside its compound than the *samādhis* and the *dhūnī*. Visiting ascetics, as well as lay devotees, go there at will for the morning and evening *pūjās* or for a private homage during the daytime. This is the ritual centre of the Ashram. However, outside the compound the present *mahant* has had built a Śiva temple, with a marble *śivaliṅga*, small statues, and a surrounding gallery, where the Nāth *pujārī* of the monastery carry out daily worship. The consecration of the building was the occasion for a large gathering of devotees bringing holy water in procession to the site. It was one of the many occasions when the lay devotees are considered as the main targets for the religious performances organized in the ashram. The massive presence of lay householder worshippers and their centrality in the functioning of a Nāth monastery is a modern development that we shall consider next.

CHAPTER 10

Lay Followers, Patronage and *Sevā*: Fatehpur and Gorakhpur

Nijī maṭhs depend on their own network of resources, on land grants given in former times by kings and landlords and nowadays on cash donations made by wealthy lay devotees. A new type of relationship has developed between the Nāth Yogīs and the people around them in which the Yogīs have to compete for support with other religious institutions, sects, or gurus, and are induced to respond to the needs of their lay followers. Material gifts are included in the *sevā*, the 'service' that the followers are expected to provide in exchange for the spiritual advice and protection they obtain. In addition, the wealth accumulated in some monasteries allows for a redistributive process.

In this chapter and the next I will study the way three important modern personal monasteries function in their relation to the lay devotees, what kind of service they provide and what is at stake in this exchange. As we have already seen, the Fatehpur monastery developed in close contact with the surrounding Marwari community; relationships are grounded on an equilibrium between the duties of the devotees and their expectations, and they are spectacularly enacted during great festivals, yearly events of religious performances. The two monasteries of Gorakhpur (Uttar Pradesh) and Asthal Bohar (Haryana) have a much longer history than Fatehpur but both are keen to show themselves to be part of modern India: first their buildings are constantly modified and extended, with older remains being implacably suppressed; second, the wealth they acquire is devoted to the construction of prestigious educational and health institutions and the prestige thus garnered is invested in the political game. However, if Asthal Bohar retains a strong Nāth identity, Gorakhpur tends to present itself as belonging to a more orthodox Hindu surrounding.

FATEHPUR, THE MARWARI NETWORK

As we have seen, since its foundation the Amritashram has been connected with the most important merchant families of Fatehpur: Singhania, Poddar, Devra, Saraogi, Chaudhari, Ganeriwala, and Chamaria. Indeed, all over Shekhavati there are powerful families who would invite the ascetics of the Amritnāth branch to settle nearby, who would offer them the means to build a monastery and who would attend the place in a close relationship with these ascetics and monastic heads they regard as their gurus.

These families belong to the community which is now known as Marwari (from the Marwar region), and constitute the diaspora of the Shekhavat merchants who from the beginning of the nineteenth century sought their fortune beyond the limits of their natal province. However, many of the families encountered in the Amritashram dated their departure from Fatehpur only from the 1920s, saying they had followed advice given by Jyotināth.[1] Today a good number of devotees live in Calcutta (as do many Marwaris), others stay in Assam where they are engaged in the timber business while some six-hundred families have settled in the Raniganj area, a coal district in Jharkhand. However, the network of devotees extands all over India and reflects the economic situation of the Marwaris. Thus apart from

[1] Cf. Hardgrove: 'It was only after the 1920s and 1930s that many Marwari families took up full-time residence in Calcutta and other big cities' (1999: 737). She adds: 'There was no pre-existing "Marwari" community in Western India before the migrations. It is this fact of migration – and this diasporic location outside of Rajasthan – which makes the migrant Rajasthani business community into Marwaris' (id. 732).

some local residents and the people working for the Ashram, the majority of the devotees belong to the urban middle class, be they industrialists or businessmen. Import-export activities oblige them to travel abroad and some of their children study in the US.

This geographical dispersion of the Marwaris goes together with a strong attachment to their original land, which is part of their identity construction and also a factor in their success as a community in their new environment.[2] Every family maintains a link with the ancestral property and the lineage temple which they return to for lifecycle rituals, but the magnificent *havelis* they owned are now sadly decayed, shared by dozen of heirs and neglected by those families used to modern facilities who do not want to live there anymore. The Fatehpur Ashram became a sort of 'family home' for these scattered communities, a place of identity and spiritual resource. Followers do not hesitate to make long trips to reach the Ashram for festivals, such as Śivarātrī, Guru Pūrṇimā or the commemoration of Amritnāth's death, and before any important business trip. These festivities are also the occasion for meetings of the kinship network, for discussing business agreements or marriage prospects. And even on private family matters, the *mahant* is asked for advice and approval.

Attendance at the Ashram is most frequently a result of family transmission. Devotees tell of initial episodes: the encounter of a parent or grand-parent with a *mahant*, the benediction and favour granted, even the occurrence of a miracle. The link to the Ashram then becomes part of the family memory: the life of the guru and his good deeds are told and shared by all the members and the Ashram is the place where this memory is rooted. Young women who marry outside the circle of devotees try to persuade their in-laws to attend the Ashram; many stories are told about their profound frustration and sadness if they do not succeed.

The present *mahant,* like his predecessor, encourages this

[2] Cf. Markovits (2003: 153-4), Hardgrove (1999) on the importance of attachment to native land and solidarity networks.

relationship with the lay community. He is welcoming and travels all over India in order to meet his devotees, even to stay in their houses – a much sought-after honour. He is always accompanied by a small group of close devotees, male and female, who who always travel with him during the pilgrimages he organizes and the Nāth ritual occasions he attends (Kumbh Melā or consecration of the *rājā* in Mangalore). To encourage the devotion and gathering of the Ashram followers, he has founded in four towns (Calcutta, Raniganj, Delhi, Jaipur) what he calls 'branch maṭh': not monasteries but prayer rooms containing Amritnāth's image and intended for the lay devotees.

The link with the Ashram is symbolized by the mantra given by the *mahant* to the lay devotees. The *mahant* hence becomes their guru. The Nāth sect being for celibate ascetics, there is no room for lay householders to be initiated as Nāth. However, it is always possible for a Nāth Yogī to give a mantra, i.e. to solemnly give a formula to be repeated, to someone who wants to improve his behaviour, follow a discipline and have a spiritual goal. This is what happened in Fatehpur where the devotees, while retaining their normal way of life, wanted to remain close to the ascetics, asking them for teaching and advice.

For instance, in Amritnāth's hagiography, we find the case of Śrikānt Śarmā, a professor in Darbhanga, who went to Amritnāth in his quest for the ultimate truth. Following his guru's teaching he came close to his goal, but his family appeared asking him for Rs. 2,500. Distressed, he went to Amritnāth to ask for his help. But the guru answered: 'Anyone who is looking for the felicity of the soul cannot look for the felicity of money!'. He sent him, however, to borrow the sum from another disciple, but Śrikānt then lost the benefit of his *sādhanā*. He came back to Amritnāth, begging forgiveness for his greediness, and recovered his peace of mind (Trivedi 1990: 51-2).

The giving of the mantra is the outcome of a personal relationship between the guru and the disciple. The wording of the formula has less importance than the confidential way it is imparted. The mantra, which is here nothing other than the brief Śiva mantra, *Om Namaḥ Śivāya*, or the mantra to Gorakhnāth, *Om*

Śiva Gorakśa, is known by everyone: its value comes from the circumstances of its enunciation. The guru, here the *mahant* of the Amritashram, speaks the mantra in the ear of the disciple, makes him repeat it and explains to him how and when to repeat it daily. He may end with some personal advice. From now on, the disciple feels strong links with his guru, he evokes him in his mind several times a day, he comes to the Ashram or telephones as often as he can, and ultimately calls his guru mentally to his rescue whenever he is any kind of trouble. But anyone who has received the benediction of the guru has to obey his commands: one young woman even recounted how, in order to repeat her mantra as many times as requested, she was counting with her prayer beads in one hand and doing her household chores with the other hand!

DEVOTEES' DUTIES

The lay disciples at the Ashram are mostly called *sevak* - one who does *sevā*, service to the guru and to the Ashram. This word, common in the bhakti context to refer to devotion towards a qualified deity, *saguṇ*, and the process of worship, is more and more employed in the modern devotional milieux and the new Hindu religious movements to signify obedience to the guru and complete dedication of one's person to his service. *Sevā* is also the giving of 'body, mind, and wealth' (*tan, man, dhan*), a formula well known to the Krishnaïtes.

The wealth of the Ashram's closer devotees is evident, as well as their generosity, judging from the way the Ashram is spending lavishly on festival performances, despite its lack of resources of its own. Besides the ceremonial expenses, devotees also finance multiple constructions for the monastery, as well as generous dispensations of money to chosen villages, to build a well, help poor families, provide fodder to cows during drought, contribute to marriage expenses in a follower's family, etc.

Devotees consider their financial donations as a way of performing their *sevā*. They fulfil their duty, behave rightly, earn merit, avoid bad uses of their wealth: their moral discourse is grounded on an ethic of beneficence which is relatively modern but devoid here of any practical consideration of efficacy. What is important for the *sevak* is to give: what use is made of the gift is not important. The gift can also be considered as a token in the tacit exchange relationship between the guru and the devotees: they expect to be rewarded with guru's protection and blessing. Material gifts *versus* spiritual benefits. Gift giving is also the occasion for worldly competition between devotees to be recognized as the most generous. The *sevā* ideal is somewhat perverted as conspicuous gifts become issue of status and prestige.[3] Positions of honour such as physical closeness to the guru are reserved for the more important donors. It is very difficult for a monastic head to avoid this sort of dependency and compromise: in Fatehpur, the *mahant* reacts sometimes by allowing the humblest of his devotees to perform a prestigious task, but the risk of becoming hostage to his most generous and wealthy disciples is quite strong.

Besides the financial support which can be displayed publicly in piles of banknotes, devotees show their dedication to the guru by staying close to him, accompanying him, anticipating his wishes and worshipping him by bathing his feet. Their *sevā* to the guru expresses also by giving service to others, as in the Ashram where everyone is supposed theoretically to share the domestic duties: cleaning the place, cooking and helping serve food. A devotee must offer his time and labour, especially during festivals when the Ashram is full of people. The close male devotees serve the food themselves, making sure that the humblest and poorest people get a good portion. It is an obvious sign of the *sevā* which subverts social hierarchies, as was Amritnāth's message proclaiming social equality without any

[3] Cf. Maya Warrier's remarks concerning Mata Amritanandamayi Mission and the part played by 'the personal recognition by the Mata' (2003a: 274): 'rewarding seva' is a key element of the functionning of the institution. However as she writes: 'Seva, as practised within MAM, diverges significantly from its ideal of rendering service selflessly, anonymously and without the expectation of reward' (id. 279).

gender or caste discrimination. What is important is purity of heart and selfless devotion: many stories insist on the priceless value of even the smallest gift made sincerely.

Service to the guru includes obedience to his teaching (*updeś*). The strength of Amritnāth's and his sucessors' message is to appear quite simple: it is directed mainly towards lay disciples who live in the world and are not able to follow complex and strenuous ascetic practices. This teaching focus on three axes: way of life, *sahajyoga*, and devotional song.

The way of life, *āhār vyavahār*, concerns food habits. Echoing the pan-Indian belief that 'you are what you eat', written on the Ashram walls as '*Jaisā khāyā anna vaisā huā man*' ('such as the food one eats such is the state of mind'), Amritnāth always advocated a simple diet, of course vegetarian. He thought that it was only possible to purify one's behaviour by starting with eating habits and that this was possible for everyone: lay people even in the modern world can adopt a pure diet based on milk products, cereals and fruits. The purification of the body and thus of the mind by a controlled diet goes with a great care for cleanliness: people as well as places have to be spotless. The Shekhavati *āśrams* are constantly swept and washed and many critical comments have been made on the dirtiness of many other holy places. Cleanliness is identified with purity.[4] Devotees having purified their body are thought to be able to master their passions, to be chaste,[5] fit for practising meditation and even able to reach Liberation. His disciples thank Amritnāth for having summarized in a simple way the *Yogasūtrā* teachings on personal discipline. As Cetannāth Yogī said: 'Our sacred texts gave us the Perfect Knowledge but they are out of reach for the ordinary people. Amritnāth, as Kabīr did, revealed the core of

[4] Cf. Gross: 'One sādhu remarked that "from ācāra ['behaviour'] comes *vicāra*" ['thought']. In other words, from outer cleanliness and ritual purity comes mental and spiritual purity' (1992: 299).

[5] Chastity means here control of the body and of the authorized marital sexual activities. There is no question of advocating sexual abstinence for lay people.

this knowledge and founded an *āśram* to teach it in a simple and direct way. He thus gave happiness to many *sevaks*.'[6]

The spiritual path to reach this supreme state is called by Amritnāth *sahaj yog*.[7] He said (in Trivedi 1990: 122):

By modifying one's dietary habits, one preserves one's semen. By breath control, the fluttering mind is quieted, equanimity is reached and there only remains the vision of the Self; one attains the place of *nirvāṇ*, one feels the eternal bliss of one who is a *jivan-muktā*, liberated in his life; *sahaj yog* is perfected, the place of immortality (*amrit*) is reached.

What makes *sahaj yog* different from what is supposed to be the Nāths' Haṭha Yoga? In Trivedi's biography of Amritnāth the description of his guru's spiritual teaching is not always very clear; he gives a summary of all the different spiritual techniques and attitudes which he puts together as 'the sixteen sorts of yogas',[8] which culminate in the sixteenth, the *sahaj yog*, allowing the vision of the Self (*ātmā darśanārth sahajyog*), this *sahaj yog* which can be translated as 'natural, spontaneous, easy'.

The term *sahaj* applies to the Ultimate Reality as non-dual state as well as to the means to attain this Reality, as in the Tantric Buddhist school – called *Sahajiyā* – which flourished in Bengal between the ninth and twelfth centuries.[9] The term was

[6] Translated from the commemorative booklet published for 2002 Mahotsava (*Amritanjali*, p. 3).

[7] I never saw these two terms – *sahaj yog* – together in traditional texts. The expression only figures in a very modern religious movement which appeared in the 1970s; calling itself '*Sahaja Yoga*', it was founded by Mataji Nirmala Devi Srivastava and refers to the main principles of *Haṭha Yoga*.

[8] The first eight are the *sāmsārik yog*, yogas of this world (including *karmyog, jñānyog*, etc.). Then come four *saguṇ upāsnā*, adoration of divine with attributes (among them curiously is included the *haṭhyog* and more logically *bhaktiyog*). Then three *nirguṇ upāsnā*, adoration of the unqualified divine, and finally the last, *sahaj*.

[9] On Sahajiyā Buddhism see the groundbreaking book of Dasgupta 1976: 3-109; on the Vaiṣṇava Sahajiyā movement, which inspired a great

borrowed by the Nāths then by devotional Vaishnava currents, as well as in the Sant literature: 'Sahaja is a non-dual state of supreme bliss' (according to Kabīr, quoted by Dasgupta 1976: 361), 'Sahaja is vacuity and is pervading the whole universe as the ultimate reality behind all phenomena' (according to Dādū, Dasgupta, id. 363). In the *Haṭha-Yoga-Pradīpikā* (cf. Tara Michaël 1974: 216), *sahaj* is part of the list of words given by Svetarama as equivalents to designate the Supreme State 'where there is no difference nor separation between the individual soul and the supreme Self' (id.), *sahaja* or *sahaj-avashta* being 'the natural state of the atman, the innate state, a state which is always there but not apparent because of the subjection to the material world' (id. 218).

This 'natural state' can also be reached by natural means, it can be obtained in a spontaneous and immediate way, in a *sahaj* way. It is what Kabīr says about meeting God: 'If we come upon God, or God comes upon us, the moment is apt to have a simple, easy feel to it, at once empty and full, what Kabīr calls [...] 'spontaneous' (*sahaj*)' (in Hawley & Juergensmeyer 1988: 42). Hawley adds: 'The Nāth Yogīs of Kabir's day practised a spiritual discipline involving *hatha yoga* that led to an immediate, spontaneous (*sahaj*) experience of truth in which the True Guru (*satguru*) revealed himself in the adept' (1988: 44).

Amritnāth situates himself in this current: *sahaj* is the ultimate accomplishment, the final step (*antim sādhanā*) as described previously (Trivedi 1990: 120-2), but his original contribution is in the technique to attain it. As we have seen, *sahaj yog* rests essentially on control and appropriateness of food habits and breathing. Amritnāth rejects the complex techniques of restraining the breath: 'Stopping breathing is not natural and is painful. Bliss can be obtained by concentration and a natural respiration of fifteen times per minute' (Śarmā 2052 vs: 33); 'Being afraid of the pain caused by restraining the breath many people turned

---

number of poetical compositions in which the *sahaj* metaphysics is pervaded with the motives of love and devotion belonging to Vaiṣṇava bhakti, see also Dasgupta (1976: 113-16) and Dimock (1966).

away from the quest for *samādhi*, which is a pity for society and the country' (id. 34). This is a very peculiar attitude, as generally breath restraining (*kumbhak*) is considered essential in Haṭha Yoga[10] where control of the breath, of the rhythm for breathing in and out, is considered necessary for the purification of the *nāḍīs*, but only techniques of restraining and blocking the breath make possible the awakening and rising up of the *kuṇḍalinī*. The same trend towards simplicity and natural movement can also be seen in the position of Amritnāth regarding the postures (*āsan*). Trivedi's text describes several postures then adds: 'What is the use of numerous other postures when one can attain perfection in *siddhāsan?*'[11]

Alongside a purified diet and simplified yoga, Amritnāth and his successors invite their disciples to practice devotional singing (*bhajan*). In fact, every morning and evening the people present in the monastery meet in the courtyard to sing songs and hymns, reading the words in small booklets published locally. These popular sessions of *kīrtan*[12] have been adopted in the urban annexes of the Amritashram: they unite the community of lay devotees in sharing their emotions. It is again a simple and attractive practice, the most well known songs being daily repeated, as is this 'prayer to the guru' (*prārthana gurūjī*):

Fix your mind on the guru's feet, meditate on the guru's feet.
Guru is Brahmā, guru is Viṣṇu, guru is identical with Śiv.
Guru is Gaṅgā, guru is Yamuna, guru is like a *tirtha*.
Guru is a mother, guru is a father, guru is a god.
On the forehead the beautiful saffron *tilāk*, on the neck the jasmine garland.

[10] To the point that the term *kumbhak* is sometimes employed instead of *prāṇāyām* (Leccia 2003: 27).

[11] The perfect *āsan* or the *āsan* of the Siddhas (*HYP* 1, 35). On new developments of postural Yoga, see Mark Singleton 2010.

[12] 'The terms *kīrtan* and *satsaṅg* ("devotional song/singing" and "good company") are the terms most often used by devotees to refer to a *bhajan* singing session' (Schaller 1995: 108). Regarding the importance of *bhajan* for Nāth householders in Rajasthan, see Gold 2002.

What kind of lamp do you have ? What kind of wick? What kind of ghee?
The body is the lamp, the heart is the wick, the knowledge is the ghee.
Theft, injustice, insult, we turn away from these three.
That the guru gives me the knowledge of the Self, that he comes to me at the last moment]
That I serve the guru from birth to birth, that he makes my boat cross the ocean of life.

Durgāprasād Trivedī has collected and published many songs in his hagiography of Amritnāth and they are attributed to Amritnāth or Śankar. Many others are attributed to Kabīr.[13] The way the songs insist on the absolute without form or name, *alakh nirañjan*, as well as the aniconic nudity of the shrines and monasteries clearly locate Fatehpur in the *nirguṇī*[14] tradition. However, contrary to some theories[15] seeing in the *nirguṇ* bhakti a low caste movement, Amritnāth and his successors belong to a milieu which is neither humble nor anti-establishment.

[13] On the relationship between Kabīr and the Nāth Yogīs, as seen through their literatures, see among others Vaudeville (1974), Offredi (2002), Lorenzen and Thukral (2005), and Daniel Gold explaining how Kabīr appears as 'a knower of esoteric secrets' to the *grihastha* Nāths of Rajasthan (2002).

[14] On the distinction between *nirguṇ* and *saguṇ*, see Schomer and McLeod eds. (1987), Gold (1992), Lorenzen ed. 1995 (Introduction) and 1997 and the cautious statement of Hawley (1995a: 160-80). As was already said by Vaudeville: 'For the Sants already as for earlier Shaiva and for later Vaishnava bhaktas, *nirguṇa* is a somewhat magic word. They would talk of the ultimate object of their own bhakti as *nirguṇa*, but for them, *nirguṇa* should not be interpreted as "that which is deprived of qualities" but rather as "that which is beyond the three *guṇas*" (inherent to material culture, *prakṛti*) and even beyond the traditional distinction between the *nirguṇa* and the *saguṇa* aspects of the Godhead' (1987a: 27-8).

[15] Cf. Lorenzen (1995: 21): 'When we come to the nirguṇī religion, the lower-class and lower-caste identity of most of its followers and many of its leaders and poets is not in doubt. In particular, Brahmins are almost completely absent'.

Narharināth, the present *mahant*, is a Brahmin and his devotees are rich Vaiśyas. But, in accordance with the *nirguṇ* and sectarian ideology, their public discourses deny caste discrimination: the monastery is open to all, male and female devotees, high and low castes, who pray together and share food. All devotees, whatever their status, worship in the same way and submit to the same duties: what is meaningful is to be a *bhakta* and a *sevak*, to serve the guru with devotion. This form of religiosity suits the lay devotees: mild, not actively trangressive, it proposes a quest where wealth is not an obstacle to Liberation and where love for the guru meets love for the native land. Liberation, *mokṣa*, is reinterpreted in a very limited way, in tems of moral and psychological behaviour.[16]

DEVOTEES' EXPECTATIONS AND GURU'S POWERS

Amritnāth's biography as well as the testimony of current devotees attest to the attractiveness of the powers attributed to the guru. Even the more spiritually-minded devotees talk enthusiastically about the many wonders or miracles performed by the Ashram's *mahants*. As is the case with many new or self-proclaimed gurus, the numerous stories told about their superhuman capacities have a huge importance for the growing number of devotees.

This absolute faith in the powers of gurus, sect leaders, sants, is reinforced by the Ashram's Nāth Yogī tradition, where the quest for superhuman powers plays a essential part in their *sādhanā*

[16] I agree with the analysis made by Fuller and Harriss on the attractiveness of the neoguru Dayananda Saraswati for the businessmen of Chennai; in the words of Dayananda: 'my concept of *moksha* is freedom from the sense of limitation and the sense of dependence for your security and happiness ... freedom from the sense of inadequacy'; Fuller adds: '*moksha* has been redefined as a psychological state that is fairly easy to attain, instead of a formidable objective that is achieved only through awesome austerities or superabundant devotion' (2005: 224).

and where their miracles are attributed to their *yogbal*, their 'yogic power'. As we have seen, Amritnāth's hagiography focuses mostly on his miraculous deeds. In a way his successors have inherited his powers when seated on the *gaddī*: of course, they practise their own *sādhanā* but their initiation and installation as *mahants* confer on them 'the charisma of the office', and the different personalities merge into one charismatic and encompassing figure of *mahant,* called here Śrī Nāth: many devotees' stories recall the miraculous intervention of someone they call Śrī Nāth, a merging of the present *mahant*, his predecessors, Amritnāth and even Gorakhnāth and Śiva.

Devotees expect the powers of their guru to be employed in their favour. In this context, gurus are considered less as saints or spiritual models than as deities to appeal to. The worldly successes of the devotees and the wealth of the Ashram are the marks of both the powers and the kindness of the guru.

Life takes on a different meaning when it is constantly under the control of the guru. Luck does not exist. A happy event is due to the guru's grace, and misfortune is merely a test.[17] To a true devotee every incident is meaningful and just.

[17] It is a common belief among any guru's devotee: see Clementin-Ojha (1990) regarding Shobha Ma's disciples, or Warrier on Amritanandamayi's disciples: 'Most devotees come to see the Mata as controlling every aspect of their lives, such as the smallest piece of chance or good/bad fortune comes to have meaning in terms of the Mata's divine working [...] Every incident, every chance [are] happening as proof of her grace and protection. They come to see such mundane incidents as getting train reservations during rush season, or discovering a petrol station close at hand after being stranded with an empty tank in an unfamiliar part of town, as miraculous experiences of the Mata's love' (Warrier 2003b: 235-6). Lawrence Babb says much the same of Sathya Sai Baba: 'Given the up-to-date sophistication of many of his followers, Sathya Sai Baba's emphasis on magic seems anachronistic [but...] there is something fondamentally confident about the "Sai" outlook on the world. For his devotees the world is suffused with his love, a place in which nothing is impossible and in which events always serve a benevolent purpose' (1986: 74-6).

Looking at the followers' testimonies as they are regularly published in small booklets commemorating the Ashram's main festive events, or listening to their narratives, the *mahants*' interventions can be divided in three categories: predictions, miraculous healings and financial successes.[18]

The *mahant* is said to know the future, thus he may suggest directly a course of action or answer his followers' questions, sometimes with a cryptic sentence, the meaning of which may only be discovered many years later by the grateful devotee. His advice can be very precise and respond to urgent situations, such as for instance the conflict of one devotee working in Assam with a terrorist group: 'When I finally decided to go meet the group, Bābājī called me and said: 'Stay where you are and do your work!' After that I worked quietly. Thanks to Mahārāj's compassion, terrorists did not trouble me any more.'

The most frequent stories concern health problems. Miraculous healings are recounted: the many details involving modern medicine are contrasted with the immediacy and simplicity of the miraculous cure, as in the following story:

> I had a pleurisy when I was living at Indore. Many times hospital people made a hole in my back and introduced a pipe to take water out of my lungs. I suffered so much that I wanted to die. It was Kumbh Melā time in Ujjain ! My mother went there to pray to Bābā Śubhnāth to cure me, but he sent her back. After a few days, when doctors had not hope any more to cure me, I was put on the ground, sacred words were said in my ear and Gaṅga water poured in my mouth. I was dying. Then a jeep stopped in the courtyard, Mahārāj Śubhnāth got out to see me and said: 'He wants to eat some yoghurt. Without it he will die'. Mahārāj Śubhnāth poured some yoghurt in my mouth, slowly put me in a seated position and left. Thanks to the Mahārāj's compassion, I am now alive and in good health. (*Amritāñjalī* 2002)

Many stories are also told about avoiding a sudden danger by the intervention or sometimes the mere remembrance of the

[18] See the examples described in my 2008 article: 'Un monastère Nāth dans la Shekhavati: patronage marchand et démonstration de pouvoir'.

guru. Road hazards are a favourite topic: in Bengal a devotee's car is passing a truck, another is coming head on, no space for both!

We all thought that we will have the darśan of Yāmrāj... I started to pray for Mahārāj's help and claimed loudly 'Jay Śrīnāthjī'. And the miracle happened. Our car hit the first truck in front then the second one on the side and fell in a ditch twelve feet deep. The car was in pieces but as for us, we didn't even have a scratch. We came back from the death doors. Thanks to the kindness of Sri Nāthji Mahārāj, we cheated Yāmrāj. (*Amritāñjalī* 2002)

Commercial and financial successes are also credited to the guru. Amritnāth helped his followers even in such matters as we have seen when Gorakhrām Camaṛiyā asked his guru to spare him the loss of 50 lakhs rupees. 'Bābājī made possible a rise in the price of cotton and rescued Gorakhrām thanks to his yogīc power'. Nowadays businessmen still make the trip to Fatehpur or at least call the *mahant* before any important transaction or business trip. As explained by the manager of a successful business based in Kolkata, who gave his export company the Ashram's name:

All our success is due to the blessing of Nāthjī Mahārāj. *Mahant* Narharināth told us that the blessing of Nāthjī Mahārāj was with us, that we start this export business, that we obtain success and thus make Nāthjī's name be heard in all the four directions. His blessing showed itself with a wordly (*bhautik*) appearance because among multiple forms, only this one is visible to the eyes (oral communication).

Hence the Amritashram *mahants* have a close and intimate relationship with their lay devotees and share their concerns even in the most worldly enterprises.[19]

[19] The attitude is quite similar to the description given by Feldhaus of the Mahānubhāva Guṇḍam Rāüḷ and his many actions in favour of his devotees (1984, nos. 25, 26, 173, 305, 306).

FESTIVALS

The occasion of the most intense exchange between *mahant* and lay disciples, between the spiritually powerful guru and generous *sevaks*, are the many festivals organized in the ashram. They celebrate Amritnāth's anniversaries, Śivarātrī, Gurūpūrṇimā; but the most spectacular event was performed in 2002 for the 150th anniversary of the birth of Amritnāth. However, for various reasons it was celebrated at the date of his death (full moon of Āśvin, September/October).[20] The festival then called Amrit Mahotsav extended over the two weeks leading up to the full moon climax and attracted thousands of people. It included elements that are quite unusual in the Nāth Yogī tradition, i.e. a ritual arrangement, borrowed from Vedic and Agamic models, used for a cult to Durgā then to Śiva, and culminating in a *homa*, a fire offering, performed in eleven sacrificial firepits with 108 Brahmins. To these rituals performed in a *yajña śālā* were added a recitation of the *Śiva Purāṇa*, two daily performances of ritual theatre inspired by Vishnuite bhakti (*rāmlīlā* and *rāslīlā*), a triumphal procession around the town, fire-walking and folk dance groups.... Thus we have the paradoxical situation of a profusion of rituals, devotional and festive activities, all of them performed in a monastery, in a place normally devoted to the veneration of ascetics and the personal quest for salvation.[21] But these festivals are intended to please the lay devotees and to present them with a sort of concentrated ecumenical Hinduity,

[20] See a more detailed description in Bouillier 2008: 227-60, and 2012 ('Modern Guru and Old Sampradaya. How a Nāth Yogī Anniversary Festival became a Performance on Hinduism').

[21] A similar situation is described by Babb (1998: 25-6) among the Jains: 'The periodic rites [...] are frequently occasion for the display of great wealth [...] They seem to have little to do with liberation from the world's bondage. And yet here is the paradox. [...] At the center of all the spending, the celebration, the display, the stir, is the figure of the Tīrthankar. He represents everything that the celebration is apparently not, for he is, above all else, an ascetic. [...] Wealth is not worshiped; wealth is used to worship the wealthless'.

encompassing the diversity of cultural forms offered by traditional Hinduism without any sectarian cleavage. Thus the Amritashram devotees can both follow the high individualistic spiritual quest the Ashram teachings provide and an anchorage in traditional modes of religious faith.

GORAKHPUR: A POLITICAL MONASTERY

The huge monastic complex of Gorakhpur in Uttar Pradesh is striving to appear as the main centre of the Nāth *sampradāya.* The impressive marble temple of Gorakhnāth, topped by a roof with three shikharas, is situated in a vast compound enclosing temples to various deities, galleries with statues and paintings, tombs, a reception hall with a library, the living quarters of the *mahants* and resident *sādhus*, a *gośālā* (cowshed), gardens, water tank, etc. Many daily visitors frequent the place, which is a quiet and peaceful spot in the congested and noisy town. However, the institution owes its present success and importance to its last three politically-minded *mahants.*

As one of the *sampradāya*'s philosopher and devotee, Akshaya Kumar Banerjea, wrote:

> Though the monastery with the temple is so very old and of such historical importance, neither the present temple building nor the other structures are old enough. It is quite probable that it had been of the nature of an old hermitage of all-renouncing Yogīs [...] Though its spiritual wealth was shedding lustre upon the minds and hearts of all classes of people for so many centuries its material wealth was perhaps never considerable [...] When the present Mahant succeeded to the *guddee*, he found the institution economically in a poor condition. (1979: 15-16)

However, this was not the opinion of H.R. Nevill who wrote at the beginning of the twentieth century in the *Gazetteer of Gorakhpur* (1909: 239): 'The institution is in a very flourishing condition and is still the resort of numerous pilgrims and worshippers whose offerings bring a considerable income to the Kanphata Jogis in attendance at the temple'. But we have very few elements to document the recurrent assertion of the place's 'undoubted antiquity' (Nevill id.) Its name is interpreted as a reference to Gorakhnāth's seat, as in the following legend:

One day Gorakhnāth when roaming reached Jvālā Devī.[22] The goddess asked him to remain there and to accept some *prasād*. But Gorakhnāth replied that she had only tamasic food and that he could not enjoy anything. The goddess told him that she would light a fire and fill some pots with water for the *khicṛī*[23] food that he would have begged himself. She did as she said and the fire is still burning today but Gorakhnāth never came back. He went to Gorakhpur and settled where the temple is today, the villagers built him a hermitage and his miraculous begging bowl was filled with *khicṛī*. That is the reason why one offers *khicṛī* for the main festival of the temple on Makarsamkrānti (translated from the booklet *Mahayogī Gurū Gorakhnāth*. Gorakhpur mandir. 2010).

Local stories reproduced also by Briggs talk about 'an original shrine converted into a mosque by Alaud-Din [Khilji] (1296-1316). Then a shrine was built in a nearby place by Gorakhnāthis. Aurangzeb (1659-1707) converted this also into a mosque. Afterwards, on the present site, a third shrine was built by Buddhnāth' (1973: 86-7). The many rebuildings continue until the present day: Briggs in the 1930s thought that 'the present buildings were erected about AD 1800', then the shrine was enlarged, a roof raised in 1924. New additions have constantly been made since then.

The *mahants* belong to the Dharamnāth *panth*. The names of some important figures are still remembered, but a precise dated genealogy starts only in 1758 with Bālaknāth (1758-86). He was succeeded by Manasānāth (1786-1811), Santoṣnāth (1811-31), Meharnāth (1831-55), Gopālnāth (1855-80), Balbhadranāth

[22] I.e. the sanctuary dedicated to the Goddess in the place in Uttarkashi called Jwalamukhi.

[23] A mix of rice and lentils, which is traditionnally offered for Makar Saṃkranti, on the first day of the month of Magh, which is also the ceremonial inauguration of the month-long festival in Gorakhpur.

(1880-9), Dilbarnāth (1889-99). Dilbarnāth was succeeded by Sundarnāth, who seems to have been 'weak-minded' (Banerjea 1979: 16) and had entrusted the management of the institution to Gambhīrnāth, 'a great Mahayogī who was universally recognised as a perfectly enlightened saint with superhuman Yogīc powers' (id.), whose *samādhi* is the main one in the recently built memorial complex adjacent to the temple. Sundarnāth was succeeded by Brahmānāth, the chief disciple of Gambhirnāth, till 1934, when Digvijay Nāth was chosen.

Briggs mentions a dispute arising after the death in 1924 of Sundarnāth, who 'died without naming a successor' (1973: 36), and appears to have had no *celā* (disciple), which led to a lawsuit in the civil courts. Briggs adds that 'one Nanhoo Singh who was involved in the suit and who hoped to win the gaddi, was not a Yogī at all. He stated that if he had won his case at law, he had intended to undergo initiation, become a Yogī and have his ears split' (id. 37). Briggs added in a note that Nanhoo Singh won his suit and is now *mahant* of Gorakhpur. In fact Nanhoo Singh is none other than Digvijay Nāth, but the later seems to have been nominated only ten years after Briggs's comment, after Brahmānāth's death.

What is described in Digvijay Nāth's hagiography (published by the temple press, and on the website) is rather different and makes no mention of a court case: Rana Nanhu Singh was a member of the princely family of Mewar, born in 1951 VS (AD 1895) in Kakarva, the fief of the family of the third brother of Rana Pratap Singh. His father, Udai Singh Rāmāvat, had vowed to give one of his sons to a great yogī who was living near Udaipur and whose name was Phulnāth, the disciple of Balbhadranāth and the guru-*bhāī* of Sundarnāth from the Gorakhpur Temple. The child was thus given to Phulnāth who brought him to Gambhīrnāth in Gorakhpur. Brahmānāth was his guru-*bhāī* and chose him as his successor. Digvijay Nāth was thus in charge of the *gaddī* from 1934 to 1969. As stated by Banerjea: 'Being an English-educated person with modern outlook and great organising ability, he has made many improvements of the monastery in external features' (1979: 80). He renovated the buildings, founded trusts (Mahant

Digvijay Nāth Trust, Maharana Pratap Siksha Parishad Trust) and many educational institutions. He took the leadership of the Yogī Mahāsabhā and involved himself actively in the Hindu Mahāsabhā, of which he was nominated president during the Gwalior meeting of vs 2017. Digvijay Nāth was the first to involve himself in politics and to claim to be working for the promotion of Hinduism and for the greatness of the Hindu nation. He was a true *karma yogī* (as claimed on the monastery website), but also an heir of the Ranas of Mewar. At his death in 1969, he was succeeded by his disciple Avedyanāth, who was already a very active member of the Hindu Mahāsabhā, was elected MLA in 1962 in one of the Gorakhpur constituencies and had served in Lok Sabha representing Gorakhpur for four terms. His political agenda within the Hindu right wing reached its climax with the formation in 1984 of the Sri Ram Janmabhumi Yajna Mukti Samiti, the Committe for the Sacrifice for the Liberation of the Birthplace of Ram, whose chairman he was, and which led to the destruction of Ayodhya Babri Masjid in December 1992. Heavily involved in the Vishva Hindu Parishad, in 1994 he nominated as his successor on the *gaddī* of Gorakhpur Maṭh, *uttarādhikarī,* the young Ādityanāth (born in 1972) and entrusted to him the care of the many activities of the *maṭh.* A final homage to the now very old and sick *mahant* was organized in 2012, with the publication of books in his honour and in the presence of many leaders of the Hindu Right. His death in September 2014 and his burial in the *samādhi* part of the monastery was widely reported in the Press, as well as the subsequent consecration of his successor, Ādityanāth.

Ādityanāth inherited the two sides of his guru's activism, in politics and in the *sampradāya.* He has been Member of Parliament (for the Gorakhpur constituency) since 1998, when he was the youngest member in the 12th Lok Sabha, on a BJP ticket. He was re-elected in 1999, 2004, 2009, 2014, but his relations with the BJP are sometimes conflictual.[24] His extremism led him to

[24] See the analysis of Subhash Gatade (www.sacw.net, October 2004) on what he calls division of labour between BJP and the Yogī

the foundation of the Hindu Yuvā Vāhinī, a nationalist youth movement judged responsible for the anti-Muslim riots of 2007.[25] His speeches (like his website) combine *Hindutva evam Bikas,* Hinduity and Development, and he constantly points to the many welfare (including the protection of cows) and educational institutions the *maṭh* is responsible for in the Gorakhpur area. However, alongside his general political agenda and his personal Hindutva propaganda, Ādityanāth also puts forward his belonging to the Nāth. As an influential member of the Yogī Mahāsabhā, he sponsors publications about the *sampradāya* and tries to appear at all the important functions where the press is welcomed. Refering to the age-old dimension of the sect he insists on its link to yoga, seen as a Hindu cultural specificity but sees no contradiction in attacking the Muslims with whom the Nāth Yogīs had a long history of close relationships.[26]

To visit the Gorakhnāth temple gives an insight into its *mahants*' ideas of an encompassing Hinduism under Nāth leadership. First, the place is generally referred to in publications and on websites as 'Gorakhnāth *mandir*', temple, and not *maṭh*, monastery, which clearly testifies to its desire to appeal to the vast group of lay devotees and occasional visitors. These visitors, going first through a compound occupied by small shops and

---

organization. However, for the 2014 elections, Yogī Ādityanāth was still standing on a BJP ticket. About his last campaign (autumn 2014) and the so-called 'love jihad', see Atul Chaurasia, 'The Yogi and his Tricks', *Tehelka* (http://www.tehelka.com/yogi-adityanath-bjp-hindutva-uttar-pradesh-elections-by-poll/#.VBrQY-c9a2x).

[25] Holding Ādityanāth guilty for involvement in communal riots, the state government had withdrawn the security cover provided to him. The HYV has somewhat quietened down after 2007.

[26] See references in Bouillier 2015. Regarding the situation in Gorakhpur, I am thankful to Shashank Chaturvedi, who let me consult parts of his Ph.D. on 'Religion, Culture and Power: A Study of Everyday Politics in Gorakhpur' (2014), where he describes the difficult situation of the Muslim communities in growing regional communalism and the departure from the Nath ideal.

food stalls, have to pass a metal detector to enter the temple area. A flowering alley adorned with fountains leads to the main temple: the Gorakhnāth Temple with its shikhara roof. A large hall ends in the deity's chamber: an altar where a recent statue of Gorakhnāth has replaced the former simple footprints, and where morning and evening the officiating Yogī offers a very choreographic form of *ārtī*. Surrounding Gorakhnāth's chamber, a gallery contains the four huge statues of Śiva, Gaṇesh, Kālī and Kāl Bhairav, in front of which sits a Brahman priest who puts *ṭikās* in exchange for a few coins. The same gallery shows small painted bas-reliefs of the nine Nāths, all seated cross-legged, naked apart from a red *kaupīn*, the earrings, the *selī* and the *nād* well visible. The same didactic and 'artistic' intention prevails in the nearby sculpture gallery, where the great figures of the Nāth tradition are placed side by side with the icons of Hindu deities and rishis, and in the library hall adorned with another set of statues and paintings of deities, yogīs, and yoga postures. This visual accumulation seems to have taken the place of the former emphasis placed on printed materials: bookshelves and previous issues of the temple journal, the *Yogvāṇī*, are now covered in dust. The visitors can also visit the place where the *dhūnī* is maintained and the platform where the *samādhis* of the last *mahants* are erected, but they are more numerous worshipping in the many small temples devoted to the many gods of the Hindu pantheon, including *navagrahas* and Haṭṭhī Mātā (elephant mother) or Baldevi Mātā, worshipped for giving children to women. The biggest temple in front and the closest to Gorakhnāth's *mandir* is devoted to Hanumān and large canvases reproduce invocations to the one who is now considered as the champion of Hinduism. His conspicuous presence here is no surprise.

The residential unit of the ascetics, priests and *mahants* is just outside. Avedyanāth in his last years stayed mostly in his room on the first floor. Now there are the private apartment of Ādityanāth and his offices where he receives his visitors, supplicants and political clientele. Jeeps and armed guards are accompanying his daily local movements.

A visit to Gorakhnāth *mandir* can be part of the daily routine of Gorakhpur people, even if it is for its quietness and the coolness of its water-tank and pedal-boats! A visit to the temple is also part of marriage ceremonies and a guesthouse and meeting hall can be provided. But of course the place is mostly crowded during the month-long festival which starts on Makar Saṃkranti.

Like the Fatehpur *mahotsav,* the Gorakhpur festival and temple offers multiple occasions to satisfy the religious aspirations of the lay devotees as well as a didactic and encompassing demonstration of the diversity of cultural Hinduism. Paradoxically, Nāth ascetics who may appear as the center of such festivals, are much less numerous. Nāth enrootedness is more apparent in the third of the three personal monasteries we are studying here, in Asthal Bohar, which offers an original synthesis of the different elements that contribute to the success of modern Nāth *sampradāya.*

CHAPTER 11

Asthal Bohar, a New Synthesis

A huge brand-new plaster figure of an impressive bearded ascetic welcomes visitors to the monastery of Asthal Bohar, near the town of Rohtak in Haryana. The enormous compound includes both religious buildings in Indo-Mughal style and modern civil buildings devoted to education and healthcare. These two styles of construction reflect very well the double trend of the *maṭh*: on the one hand a place anchored in Nāth traditions, a *nijī maṭh* with a charismatic founder, on the other the most up-to-date alliance of the charitable and the political, which its recent *mahants* have successfully promoted.

This double orientation finds an institutional expression, since Asthal Bohar has the peculiarity of being the seat of two transmission lines: the monastery contains two thrones, a big one and a small one (*baṛī gaddī* and *choṭī gaddī*), or as is sometimes said, referring to the ascetic fireplaces, a big and a small fire (*baṛī dhūnī* and *choṭī dhūnī*). This division allows the combination in the same place of both the ultramundane dimension of ascetic quest and the worldly dimension of an institution involved in the socio-political life of its time. However, in Asthal Bohar, the small *dhūnī* of the *tapasvī*, the ascetic Yogīs, is placed under the authority of the big *dhūnī* of the monastic heads-cum-administrators.

FOUNDATION LEGENDS

Cauraṅgīnāth

The present monastery was founded at the end of the eighteenth century CE, but the Yogīs consider it to be a refoundation, the place having been occupied by Caurаṅgīnāth (the disciple of Gorakhnāth we met previously in Kadri and Fatehpur) and his disciples, to practise the *sādhanā* peculiar to his *panth* (the Pāgal Panth), a meditation in reversed yogic position (head on the ground, feet towards the sky). No testimony remains of this prestigious past, but the site was probably occupied in ancient times, judging from some half broken statues which have been found there. Whatever happened in the past, the reference to a prestigious ancestor whose presence is 'rediscovered' gives prestige and legitimacy to institutions which would like to appear as old as the sect itself, Caurаṅgīnāth having been initiated directly by Gorakhnāth. Nevertheless, the history of the monastery as we know it today starts in the seventeenth century with Mastnāth. It is his image which stands at the entrance of the compound; this is the place where he left his traces that the pilgrims now visit.

Mastnāth

Mastnāth's hagiography, written at the end of the nineteenth century and published for the first time in 1968, has been constantly republished ever since. The most recent edition under the patronage of the present *mahant*, Cāndnāth, includes a presentation of the monastery and the lifestory of the six *mahants* who succeeded Mastnāth. As in Fatehpur, the printed text plays a prominent role in securing the canonical image of the founding saint, and as in Fatehpur also, it has been illustrated on numerous canvases collected in a kind of memorial gallery. To these pictures of episodes in Mastnāth's life have been added marble statues and biographical stone slabs of the six successive *mahants*. Asthal Bohar monastery and its *mahant* being involved in the Yogī Mahāsabhā, Māstnāth's hagiography and fame benefit from its network and are widely spread.

The hagiography, as written by Śaṅkarnāth, is rather peculiar, as David White has underlined (2001: 139-61). Local geography as well as modern history (as Mastnāth is depicted as having agency in the fall of Shah Alam II) combine with episodes borrowed from multiple legendary lives of other famous Nāths. The narrative offers a kind of palimpsest of the many deeds for which Nāth Yogīs were widely known and which are attributed by the hagiographer to Mastnāth!

I will limit myself here to the episodes which are in direct relation to Asthal Bohar. The story starts with the appearance of Māstnāth:

In the province of what is now Haryana and in Rohtak district, in a village named Kansareṭī, a man whose name was Sabalā became exceedingly rich thanks to his business. He was a Vaiśya. The merchant Sabalā was rich but had no children. One day he met Gorakhnāth and worshipped him; Gorakhnāth was pleased and promised to grant him a boon. Later on, when Sabalā and his wife were going through a forest, they found a one-year-old child and they understood that the saint had blessed them. This was in 1764 VS [1707 CE].

The text specifies that these merchants (*byāpārī*) were known under the name of Raibārī, as transportation was done by camel.[1] It is interesting to see here an attempt to enhance the status of this community of nomadic camel breeders to the level of the Vaiśya *varṇa* and therefore to justify the strong link which persists nowadays between them and Asthal Bohar: Raibārīs have made numerous donations to the *maṭh*, they have a specific *dharmaśālā* built for them, and they participate in large numbers in the yearly festival.

As is a common topos in hagiographies, Mastnāth's childhood was marked with wonders, since he is no other than Gorakhnāth's incarnation. He was only twelve years old when a Yogī called Narmāī appeared in his village and accepted him as a disciple. He initiated him as Mastāī, in his *panth* Āī.

[1] On this community, also known as Raikā, see Sandrine Prevot (2007) and Vinay Kumar Srivastava, who remarks on the closeness between the Raikās' way of life and religiosity and the renunciatory values, and refers to their frequent visits to Nāth centres (1997, on Asthal Bohar see pp. 91 and 105).

Mastnāth and the Āī Panth

We already know the particular place of this *panth*, the only one to have a female figure at its origin, Vimlā Devī, who is also its tutelary deity. Vimlā Devī lived in Assam, a stronghold of Śaktism and one of the various places where Nāth mythology situated the kingdom of women. As we have seen (Chapter 2), she had two sons, Bhuśkaināth and Khaḍkaināth, who went roaming in western India while she remained in Assam. They were the founders of the Āī Panth to which Narmāī belonged.

The Āī Panth, whose name signifies Mother (Āī equivalent of *māī*, mother), well-known for having a strong link to Śakti, is supposed to delegate members for any function requiring power. Asthal Bohar's links with the Āī Panth perhaps explains its present importance. However, the local legendary corpus and iconography are astonishingly poor regarding Vimlā Devī.

After his first initiation, Mastāī started wandering and went to the old Caurangināth monastery in Asthal Bohar, where a few ascetics from the Pagal Panth were still staying. Disregarding the sectarian rules of hospitality, those ascetics sent Mastāī to collect grass for the monastery's horses. Mastāī came back with a giant bundle on his head: seeing his prowess the ascetics apologized, but Mastāī cursed them and vowed to destroy the monastery.

He went on his way and reached the village of Pehvā where a huge feast was to be held for the Nāth community. The *darśanī*, the initiated Nāths wearing the earrings, wanted their superiority be recognized over a simple *aughaṛ* like Mastāī who, moreover, asked for the absurd gift of twelve cows and twelve shawls. The Yogīs of the twelve *panths* were very angry. Then Mastāī showed himself as *virāṭ*, as the supreme being in whom the whole of creation is manifested; he opened his mouth and revealed to the amazed Yogīs the whole world it contained.[2] All

[2] An episode directly based on Kṛṣṇa's childhood in the *Bhāgavata Purāṇa*.

Yogīs paid him homage and gave him the title of Swamināth. He was afterwards called Mastnāth and seems to have received the earrings spontaneously: his hagiography does not mention any guru nor any earpiercing ceremony, even though he is now always depicted with the earrings. It is probably impossible at the present time to represent a great Yogī without the full insignia of his status.

Mastnāth is also always portrayed naked, wearing only a *langoṭi* (loincloth); this nakedness, which today marks the *tapasvī* itinerant ascetics, is at the origin of biographical anecdotes, such as this one about the encounter between Mastnāth and Pāī Devī.

> Mastnāth and his group of disciples went one day close to the village of Bohar, in the vicinity of the ancient monastery of Cauraṅgī where Mastnāth had established his *dhūnī*. There, among the women gathered around the well, Pāī Devī, the young wife of a Jaṭ peasant, mocked his nakedness. Mastnāth replied her: 'You also will be naked!' And since he was only saying 'words of truth', his prediction had to come true. Soon the young woman felt in her soul the radiance of renunciation; she stood naked before the domestic fire-place and covered her body with ashes. Her husband decided to kill the ascetic and hit him three times but in vain. The village members consulted with each other and decided to commit the young women to the care of Mastnāth. She was intitiated as Pāī Devī, practised a severe asceticism in remaining always standing and spent her life as a disciple of Mastnāth.

Nowadays the only trace of her existence in the *maṭh* is a painting showing her standing, chastely covered by her long hair and animal skins. It was said that a memorial will be built for her close to Mastnāth's grave, but this does not seem to have been done yet. However, the presence of Pāī Devī, as a close disciple of Mastnāth, reminds us of the specificity of the Āī Panth (the initiatory name of Pāī is of course the sign of her belonging to this *panth*), its origin in the feminine figure of Vimlā Devī, and thus its *śakti*-oriented particularism.

Mastnāth and the two Brothers who Became his Disciples

Another wandering of Mastnāth took him to the village of Kharak. There, two Rajput children, Raṇpat and Mandhātā, went running to him and wanted to follow him. Mastnāth recognized them as old disciples from a former life[3] and agreed. The parents implored their children not to go, described to them the harsh life of wandering ascetics, and resisted until they finally had enough of seeing their children distribute all their money to the poor and feeding them with the milk from their cows. They accepted the situation and the two brothers went with Mastnāth to Asthal Bohar where they were initiated.

A well-known episode of their wandering life with their guru tells how they were collecting firewood for the *dhūnī*. They took a large beam that the people of Khiṛavālī village intended to use to build a hall. People protested and tried to take it back, but Mastnāth cursed them and said they would not be able to build any building till they were visited by an ascetic on the back of a white elephant.

The two young disciples started their ascetic life by making the vow to stay standing near a fire without moving for twelve years (or for thirty-six years in some versions of the legend).

A rather transgressive story was told to me, which for obvious reasons is not mentioned in the printed versions of the hagiography:

Once, while they were meditating, they nevertheless perceived the excitement of the Holi festival which surrounded them and they became nostalgic for their house and for the alcohol that the Rajputs were drinking in this occasion. Bābā Mastnāth felt their longing thanks to his yogic powers and had a bottle of alcohol sent to them. They opened their eyes, saw the bottle and were full of remorse. They told

[3] We may see a reference to the twin sons of Vimlā Devī, Bhuśkaināth and Khaḍkaināth, but no connection is made in the hagiography nor by the *maṭh* people.

Mastnāth that they had relinquished all desire but Mastnāth did not believe them. Since then, the tradition has been to offer alcohol at their *dhūnī*.

A discussion arose among the listeners of this story, some saying that their longing for alcohol was because they were from low caste, that they were even longing for meat ! No offering of alcohol is to be seen today, but what is clear is that Ranpaṭ and Mandhātā belong to a more extreme tradition, a violent asceticism which brings them closer to Bhairav.

THE FIRE OF THE ASCETICS: THE *CHOṬĪ DHŪNĪ*

The *choṭī dhūnī* of the Asthal Bohar monastery is said to be situated at exactly the spot where Raṇpat and Mandhātā performed their ascetic exercies. It is placed under the patronage of Bhairavnāth: on a small platform covered with tridents and *śivaliṅgas* stands a small statue of the god – Bhairav with the Nāth earrings – under the cover of an acacia tree (*khair*) which was supposed to shelter the meditation of the two brothers. In front was their *dhūnī*, where a statue of Śiva has been recently installed.

Further down lies the *samādhi* of the brothers, at the place where the earth is said to have split open to receive them, as she does in the case of true ascetics who take a living *samādhi*. Thus Raṇpat and Mandhātā are considered by the people to be still and forever alive, a belief expressed in the custom of putting two waterpipes on their grave every evening after *pūjā*, the reason being that, shortly after their burial, people heard the gurgle of hookah water coming out from under the soil.

The former *dhūnī* has recently been displaced and set in an open hall with a shikhara roof. But it is still considered as the *dhūnī* of Raṇpat and Mandhātā, constantly burning, and constitutes what is called in the monastery the small *dhūnī* or the small throne, the *choṭī gaddī*. However, this throne is double: the two bothers are represented by two *mahants* who take their place on two *āsan*, two seats made of thin mattresses placed on either side of the central fireplace and constituting the throne.

These two *mahants* are said to be *tapasvī bābās*, devoted to asceticism, and must remain naked, i.e. with only a loincloth, as were Raṇpat and Mandhātā. This nudity places them in the category of the ascetic Yogīs, the wandering Yogīs of the *jamāt*, even though their function obliges them to be sedentary. Their main duty is to keep up the *dhūnī* and to make *pūjā* in the different places sanctified by the practices of the two brothers. They also have to prepare the *roṭ*, the bread cooked in the *dhūnī's* ashes, which has to be offered on special occasions such as the anniversary of the death of former *mahants*. They may also prepare amulets with the same ashes for suffering visitors and whisper some protective formulas to them.

The *choṭī gaddī* testifies to the wild side of Mastnāth's heritage. Like Amritnāth in Fatehpur, Mastnāth is a roaming Yogī, a wonder-worker ascetic, naked and unconventional, in sum a '*jungli*' *sādhu*. It is to this tradition that the *choṭī gaddī* is connected and this explains the commentaries made by Briggs: 'Followers of Mastnāth are not very respectable [...] There are two divisions of [them]: (1) the Baṛī Dargah who avoid flesh and liquor and (2) the Chhoṭī Dargah, who indulge in both. The latter group was founded by a Cāmār [a leather worker, untouchable]' (1973: 68). We find here again a possible allusion to the low status of Raṇpat and Mandhātā and to their unbrahmanic eating habits.

The *dhūnī* was previously surrounded by a wall and separated from the rest of the monastery, and the *samādhi* was in an open space, but in 2001 some construction work was carried out. The *samādhi* was recarved and nested in a sumptuous mausoleum of white marble, which cost Rs. 1.5 crore (15 million) according to the commemorative plaque which gives the name of the donor, Mahant Cāndnāth.

The restoration of the *samādhi*, the removal of the *dhūnī* into a roofed hall, and the destruction of the enclosure, testify to the present *mahant's* will to reunite, under his authority, the two halves – the two aspects – of Mastnāth's tradition: the *baṛī gaddī* and the *choṭī gaddī*, the big and small thrones.

The display of the *baṛī gaddī* constrasts with the former simplicity of the small *gaddī*, which was close to the tradition of the wandering ascetic Yogīs. As Mastnāth was said to have declared: 'After the *faqīrs* come the *amīrs*', 'after the begging ascetics, the rich lords'! Anyone who visits the monastery and looks for the history of the six *mahants* who succeeded Mastnāth will be struck by its opulence.

THE *BAṚĪ GADDĪ* (THE 'BIG THRONE')

This is the official throne of the person who bears the title of *mahant* of the Asthal Bohar Maṭh, thus the seat of the monastery's public activities.

The various different buildings surround the tomb of Mastnāth. The tomb, a white marble slab covered with a black wool cloth, sits in a dark room containing a sort of cave (*guphā*) with a statue of Gorakhnāth. This *guphā* probably communicates with the former sanctuary, an old unrestored building, which contains the *dhūnī* of the *baṛī gaddī*. This ancient part of the monastery is now surrounded by the modern rooms of the *mahant*, the new throne room where thousands of visitors queue up on festival days to pay him homage, a large meeting hall, a memorial room with paintings and statues, storehouses, kitchen, etc. This huge compound consists of buildings of various styles and periods. It contains also a vast garden containing the four Indo-Mughal mausoleums of the four *mahants* who preceded Cāndnāth, the present *mahant*. And new constructions are still in progress.

Mahants *and Kings*

The first successors of Mastnāth wanted to settle and develop their institution and thus sought patronage.

Totānāth, the first successor, was initiated by Mastnāth and started acting for the monastery while his guru was still alive. Born in Rajasthan, he had privileged relationships with local *rājās*, especially the Bikaner *rājā*.

The link with Bikaner had been established previously with a miracle performed by Mastnāth. The *rājā* had organized a great feast for his kingdom's Brahmins and Mastnāth, who was camping in the vicinity, sent one of his disciples to throw a camel bone into the pot where the rice was cooking. The Brahmins of course protested and went complaining to the *rājā*. Mastnāth replied that he only wanted to give some *dakṣinā*, and that they empty the pot before judging! The Brahmins then discovered a golden bone. The *rājā*, Sūrat Singh, acknowledged the greatness of Mastnāth, so when a terrible drought fell on his kingdom, he was happy to welcome Mastnāth's disciple, Totānāth, who was on his way to visit the royal courts of Jodhpur and Udaipur. Totānāth assured him of his protection and made the rain come down in torrents. Surāt Singh, most grateful, donated him a piece of land of 5,250 *bighās* at Gangani Tehri (the northern limit of the Bikaner kingdom, near present-day Haryana). This was the starting point of the wealth of the monastery. These land grants were confirmed by the successive Bikaner *rājās* and the place is still in the possession of the monastery which constructed several buildings there.

The beginnings of Asthal Bohar Maṭh exemplify the traditional patronage relationships between kings and Nāth Yogīs, which we have also seen for instance in Dang Caughera; Yogīs used their exceptional powers in favour of the kings, who showed their gratitude by granting land and privileges, and by various marks of respect: they went to meet the ascetics, they bowed in front of them, they gave them symbolic goods such as special cloth, horses and elephants, paraphernalia such as umbrellas, etc. It is said, for instance, that the unusual headdress, a conical brocade cap, worn during ceremonies by the Ashtal Bohar *mahants* after Totānāth, was a gift from the Bikaner *rājā*. This reciprocal relationship of dependence between spiritual and temporal powers continued until modern times, even though it took different forms.

Alongside the patronage of Rajasthani kings and landlords, Ashtal Bohar developed strong links with the surrounding villages (even though the relationship was sometimes conflictual). The villagers of Bohar had given 750 *bighās* to help build the monastery, according to the *Ashtal Bohar Maṭh ka Itihās* (Mahant Cāndnāth Yogī 133). The text alludes to a *dān-patr* (donation act), unfortunately without dating it, which mentions the donation to the *maṭh* of the village of Bohar and two others as *dohlī* (land given for a religious purpose, not taxable nor transferable). The text adds: 'Today still, the peasants of these village make a gift to the *maṭh* in proportion with the amount of land they have' (id. 186), a euphemistic way of describing the land taxes! However, the agrarian reform would allow the monastery to keep only three acres, the remaining land being allotted to the cultivators.

The close relationships with the surrounding villages also explain the decision of Mastnāth to 'relinquish his body' in the village of Bidharan, its inhabitants having begged their guru to visit them one last time. Mastnāth gave out his last breath on the ninth day of the clear half of Phālgun 1864 VS (1807 CE) and Totānāth organized the solemn transfer of his body to Ashtal Bohar for the funeral rites.

Totānāth ordered the building of his guru's *samādhi*, thus ensuring the enrootedness of the monastic institution.

He died in 1894 VS (1837 CE) and was succeeded by Meghnāth (1894-1992 VS) who increased the network of disciples, especially among the Raibaris. Then came Meharnāth till 1935 VS (1878 CE). His memorial slab mentions that he corrected bad behaviour and that 'during his time horses and elephants were introduced into the *maṭh* and hence that the *sādhus* were able to travel far away to collect donations in order to give charity'. After him Cetnāth stayed on the *gaddī* from 1935 to 1963 VS (1906 CE): beginning a tradition that was to develop considerably under his successors, he founded a Sanskrit college in Asthal Bohar itself. His successor Pūrṇanāth (1906-39 CE) was probably skilful in politics: he cultivated his relationships with the Udaipur *mahārājā* and received from the British the prestigious title of Kaiser-i-Hind for his assistance during the 1914-18 War, a fact which did not stop the monastery's ascetics from enrolling in the nationalist movement (judging from the number of Asthal Bohar Nāths who made what they called the '*jel-yātrā*', the journey to jail!). Most importantly, he got involved in the organization and reforms of the *sampradāya* and was at the origin of the foundation of the Yogī Mahāsabhā. At the end of his life, Pūrṇanāth asked his disciple Śreyonāth to join him and settled him on the *gaddī*, himself leaving Asthal Bohar for a Himalayan pilgrimage then a death by immersion, *jal samādhi*, in the Ganga in Haridwar.

The New Mahants*: Social Service and Politics*

Śreyonāth represents a new type of monastic head. He was born in a Jaṭ peasant family from the Delhi area, and pursued Sanskrit then Ayurvedic studies in Ahmedabad. Called by his guru in 1937, he was enthroned as *mahant* in February 1939 during the monastery festival, and, according to his biography spent Rs. 1 lakh on this occasion. Soon after Independence, Śreyonāth embarked on a vast programme of development and construction which, after more than fifty years, still characterizes the ambition of Asthal Bohar.

In 1952, he inaugurated the first building of the future huge medical complex in the compound of the monastery, an ophthalmic clinic; then a general ayurvedic and allopathic hospital and in 1958 an ayurvedic college. This college, which according to the foundation plaque cost Rs. 6,74,000, was inaugurated by the then Chief Minister of Punjab (the Rohtak district was still attached to Punjab), Pratap Singh Kairon, who declared: 'Mahant Śreyonāth is the only monastic head in the whole Punjab area to put all his maṭh's resources at the service of the needs of the people, be they in education or in health.' Patronage changes with the times: political leaders and state ministers take the place of former kings and, by giving protection and backing of the civil power to the monastery, they display themselves as the beneficiaries of the support of well-known spiritual leaders.

A further step would be taken by Śreyonāth: claiming his 'will to place himself in the service of the people', he entered the political arena and, with Caudhari Sricand, an ex-member of the Congress party, he founded a party called Navīn Haryāṇa Janatā Dal and was elected in the 1967 state elections. Nominated Haryana state health minister, he tried to improve the water supply, and in a different context, fought for recognition of Hindi as the official language.

His successor was to follow his line of conduct. Cāndnāth was nominated *uttarādhikarī* (successor) in May 1984 and was enthroned in January 1985, two days after his guru's death. Born in 1956 into a peasant family, he was initiated in 1978 and put in charge of the administration of the monastery's properties in Hanumangarh district. After his accession to Asthal Bohar *gaddī*, he initiated many changes and projects in order to make Asthal Bohar the leading institution of a modernized Nāth *sampradāya*. As we have seen, he transformed the *maṭh* buildings, ordered the building of a new *samādhi* for Raṇpat and Mandhātā and a new *dhūnī*, as well as changing the mural paintings, having effigies sculpted of former *mahants* and commissioning a huge statue of Mastnāth at the entrance of the compound. Most of all, he added a considerable number of new medical and teaching institutions around the *maṭh*,[4] in addition to schools in Rohtak, and an ophthalmic clinic in Hanumangarh. Something like twelve new institutions were created between 1995 and 1999: the success is impressive and the reputation of the educational and medical institutions quite good.

A conflict with Haryana state in 2000 stopped Cāndnāth from founding new establishements. However, he turned his energy to Chhattisgarh and founded there in 2003 the 'Baba Mastnāth University of Raipur' which has been authorized by the Chhattisgarh Governement to conduct classes and grant degrees and diplomas.

This leads us to Cāndnāth's complex and conflicting relations with politics. Following the example of his guru Śreyonāth, he stood as candidate for the legislative elections in Narnaul constituency under the Congress banner but was defeated. He was afterwards approached by the BJP for Alwar constituency (2004 Lokh Sabha elections) and he was still the BJP candidate

[4] A pharmaceutical research and teaching centre, a dental college and clinic, a physiotherapy centre, a science college, a research institute, a Sanskrit college, an Institute in educational sciences, an engineering college with three sections (see the list on the website: http://babamastnāthuniversity.com/services.html)

for the 2014 elections (gaining the support of Baba Ramdev, the Yoga guru). Candnāth seems thus to be politically involved with the BJP, an affiliation which agrees with the political trend of the Gorakhpur monastery's leaders, and which perhaps expresses a general shift in the attitudes of the Nāth Yogīs. Though Cāndnāth's political involvement perhaps has other motives, since he was involved in a scandal. He was accused of organizing the murder of a certain Azadnāth in 1999; his defence, or counter-attack, was that the case had been fabricated by his political opponent, who was allied to the BJP, to discredit him (he was then a Congress candidate). His opponent Om Prakash Chautala became Chief Minister in 2000 and was the one who opposed the educational expansion of the monastery.[5] The case is still pending, but in the meantime Cāndnāth changed his political affiliation.

The entrance of Asthal Bohar *maṭh* and of its *mahant* into the public arena is, according to Cāndnāth, part of a strategy aiming at promoting the Nāth *sampradāya* and to place it at the service of society (*samāj sevak*). According to his biographer: 'Bābā Cāndnāth has no taste for politics [...] If he stands as a candidate in Rajasthan, it is to bring to attention the Nāth *sampradāya* in the land of Bhartṛhari' (2005: 238). Indeed Cāndnāth is very active on behalf of the Nāth *sampradāya*; he is the vice-president

[5] Curiously, Om Prakash Chautala, the chief minisiter and leader of the Indian National Lok Dal, was then involved in a scam regarding the illegal recruitment of junior teachers in Haryana in 1999-2000. According to a Jaṭ website, 'Mahant Chand Nāth Yogī disclosed that in 1999 the Math has proposed setting up a Medical College at Asthal Bohar and submitted its plans to the government and the Medical Council of India. However, just when the council nominees were visiting the institute the state government had initiated criminal proceedings against him and Dr Markandey Ahuja' (21 October 2003). Another contributor concludes: 'It should be a matter of deep concern to all people in Haryana when political parties shape the future of education in the state according to their own wishes and agendas... Asthal Bohar Math is doing a great service to the state by establishing fine education in rural Haryana' (www.jatland.com/forums/archive).

of the Yogī Mahāsabha for which he supports publications and meetings and he attends the most important events of the sect, since he presided over the enthronement of the Kadri *rājā* in 2004.

The Asthal Bohar monastery thus attests to a new development in the sect, with massive investment in welfare and educational institutions. This new care for the public good goes with some sense of publicity, as testified by a large signboard presenting the activities of the 'Shri Baba Masthnāth Group of Institutions'; having at its top photos of Mastnāth's statue and of Cāndnāth, it translates Mastnāth's name with the following acrostic: 'Massive Accredited Sacred Technical Novel Achiever Talented Helper'.

THE ANNUAL FESTIVALS

As was the case in Fatehpur, the *utsav* or anniversary festivals are the occasion for a sort of performance expressing the different components of the monastery's identity. In Asthal Bohar the double polarity of the *choṭī* and *baṛī gaddīs*, of the *tapasvī* and settled *mahants*, is clearly visible.

The festival happens, as is traditional, on the anniversary of the founder's death, here the ninth day of the clear half of Phālgun. It lasts three days and comes to its climax when the *mahant* of the *baṛī gaddī*, seated on his throne, wearing a brocade coat and conical headdress, protected by an umbrella, thus having all the symbols of sovereignty, receives the homage of his devotees, and first among them, of the dignitaries of Haryana state and of Rohtak town. Afterwards the *mahant* ceremoniously makes his way towards Mastnāth's tomb to pay homage, which in turn legitimizes him as successor.

During the course of these three days a considerable crowd attends the *maṭh*, visiting both the *choṭī* and the *baṛī gaddīs*. Among them can be seen the colourful dress and the musical band of the nomadic Raibaris.

Most noteworthy is the presence of the group of itinerant Yogīs of the *jamāt*, led by the two *mahants*. They camp in an open space close to the *choṭī gaddī* and spend these days of obliged sedentariness in quiet idleness and cannabis smoking, under the curious gaze of the visitors. Besides the *jamāt mahants*, the camp is under the authority of a third leader, called *pañcāyatī dhūnī mahant*, who depends on the sectarian collective institutions. Usually the *mahant* of the nearby monastery of Pinjore,[6] he takes this responsibility for three days, becoming, as he told me 'a *nāgā sādhu*', i.e. a *ramtā tapasvī*, an itinerant ascetic. However, as in the case of the *mahants* of the *choṭī dhūnī*, the designation defines a status more than a practice.

The status of *pañcāyatī dhūnī* given to the central fireplace of the *jamāt* is very important. It shows how institutions are intertwined, how the collective institutions interfere with the working of private monasteries. Asthal Bohar is effectively a private, *nijī*, monastery, even though the *mahant* Śreyonāth virtuously declared: 'Asthal Bohar is not a *nijī maṭh* in the sense that it is not the personal property of the *mahant*. The *mahant* is only the protector of the *maṭh* properties.' Evidently we can consider that, given the importance of Asthal Bohar, the *jamāt* has only a nominal power of control and sanction over the *maṭh*. We note also that the *pañcāyatī dhūnī mahant* comes from a monastery which has been founded by a disciple of Mastnāth, which is thus a sort of subsidiary of Asthal Bohar. Thus what is clearly at stake is more a question of association than of control or regulation; however, this presence of the *jamāt* and of the *mahants* means that the collective dimension of the sect has its place even inside the private institution of the Mastnāth's disciples.

[6] The role given to the Pinjore *mahant* is explained by the link between the two monasteries, Pinjore having been founded by Mastnāth's disciple Topnāth. One day, Topnāth, sent by his guru to Pinjore, found himself in the path of the *mahārājā* of Patiala. Ordered to move his *dhūnī*, he just blew in his *cilām*. From the *cilām* emerged a bullet, which damaged the *rājā's* palace. Faced with the wrath of the king, Topnāth blew two more bullets which completely destroyed the palace. The *rājā* had then no other choice than to bow in front of the ascetic and to give him land to found a monastery.

In parallel, with the joint presence of the two *gaddīs*, Asthal Bohar offers a synthesis between the two poles of the sect: the wild ascetic and itinerant life and the regulated, settled and institutionalized monastic life. And Asthal Bohar, like Gorakhpur, adds to these two dimensions the modern valorization of social service and political involvement.

PART IV

YOGĪS BY CASTE

So far our concern has been the ascetic Yogīs of the Nāth Yogī *sampradāya*. We have dealt with their recruitment, their organization, their behaviour according to the type of institution they belong to. However, we began this study by saying that the generic appellation of yogī referred and still refers to a much wider category of people than the Nāth *sampradāya*. We can now look inside this wider category and try to describe, define and characterize the vast number of people who claim a Yogī identity, who see themselves as related to Gorakhnāth, even using Yogī or the vernacular form Jogī as a caste name, but are married and householders (*grihastha*). Incomparably more numerous than the ascetic Nāth Yogīs, they can be encountered all over India and Nepal. Who are they, do they have common characteristics, what are their relations with the Nāth *sampradāya*, and do we have some clues about their history?

CHAPTER 12

The *Grihastha* or Householder Yogīs

CELIBACY AND THE NĀTH *SAMPRADĀYA*

We have seen that, to be fully initiated into the sect, the would-be Yogī has to pronounce a vow of *brahmacārya*, usually taken at the same time as the ear-splitting ceremony. This vow of *brahmacārya*, or celibacy, is symbolized by the giving of a particular loincloth (*langoṭ* or *kopīn*), accompanied by the appropriate mantra.[1] From what I have seen in the present time, the Nāth Yogīs, be they itinerant or living in monastery, are supposed to be celibate and the present statutes of the *sampradāya* are very strict on this point. The 1995 statutes specify that they concern the *Avadhūt* Yogīs, those 'who have renounced wordly aspirations and are not *grihastha*' and they enjoin 'the removal of any Sādhu or Mahant who disobeys the rules of the Nāth Sampradāya and becomes a householder (*grihastha*) or tries to become a householder (*grihastha banane kā prayatna kar rahe hai*)' (article 11). The secretary of the Mahāsabhā commented in relation to the rule: 'Those who cannot keep celibacy, they have no control and constitute a major problem. They are not Yogīs. Married Yogīs represent a corrupt tradition' (personal communication). A folk etymology echoed by Dvivedi (1981: 21) relates *grihastha* to *girast*, and to *girnā*, to fall, to be disgraced.

However, whatever the present enforcement of the celibacy rule which goes together with a puritanical trend, we are left with many questions unanswered: where do the huge number of Yogīs by caste come from? Why are some traditions more

[1] See its text in Vilāsnāth 2005: 486-7.

flexible and even some *mahants* married? How is the Tantric dimension accounted for?

First, let us observe that the breaking of celibacy rule can be taken rather lightly. For instance, in the Ḍholībuvā tradition in Gwalior, which I will return to later, the lifestories of the *mahants* mentions: 'In the flow of the Nāth *panth*, a shift occurred and Udbodh was the first *mahant* to be in the *āśrama* [life stage] of *grihastha*. Because of that, the signs of Nāth belonging are worn inwardly'. The ear-splitting too was done inwardly.'[2] The same shift happened in the transmission line of a temple in Orissa; according to local reports, the king made the land donation in the name of Siddhayogī Paraśurāmnāth. Later on 'Paraśurāmnāth became *grihastha* (*bād main grihastha ho gaye*) and his lineage (*vaṁṣ*) is still settled in the district' (*Yogvaṇī* 1990: 25, p. 232). And even though the Yogīs now acknowledge the injunction to remain celibate, I remember how casually someone explained to me in the Dang monastery: 'Sure, the Yogīs have to remain celibate ! Their lovers, they must keep them outside the *maṭh*!'

AMBIGUOUS CATEGORIES

Looking at the various British ninenteenth and early twentieth century reports, gazetteers, and censuses listing castes and religious groups, we are faced with a complex situation. The encompassing denomination under which the community appears is Jogī and it is subdivided into different categories, sometimes listed under a different entry.

Let us take, for instance, the report given by Crooke (1975: 59-63, 153-9), which contains well-documented information. Under the

[2] Cf. the anonymous booklet recording the tradition of the *maṭh* published on the occasion of the anniversary festival in 1975: *Śrī 1008 rājyogī Śrīsadgurū Mahipatināth Mahārāj kā 151vān samādhi mahotsav* (no pagination). With many thanks to Françoise 'Nalini' Delvoye who generously shared with me her familiarity with this Gwalior tradition.

entry 'Jogi', he specifies: 'The last Census [1891] divides the Jogis into two main classes of Aughar and Gorakhpanthi... Besides the respectable members of the sect who are contemplative ascetics, there are others who do not bear such a reputable character' (id. 59). And he gives the figures in the census according to the different districts, for instance:

Dehra Dun: Aughar 86; Gorakhpanthi 90; Others 927; Muhammadans 0; Total 1,103

Agra: Aughar 32; Gorakhpanthi 48; Others 2,165; Muhammadans 758; Total 3,003.

We can see the remarkable discrepancy between those that could be considered now as Nāth Yogīs (Aughar and Gorakhpanthi, who are, according to Crooke, celibate) and the vast number of 'Others' whose occupations he details (for instance the Bhartari Jogis, itinerant singers and beggars, and the Nandiya Jogis, begging with a deformed ox). The mention of the Muhammadan Jogis reminds us of the possibility of former absence of a clear-cut division between Muslims and Hindus (Bouillier 2015). Let us add that in many districts, no Gorakhpanthi are recorded, but only 'Others'. However, this is not the only entry for the community, since under the label 'Kanphata' Crooke gives the following account: 'A class of Jogis, known also as Gorakhnāthi from the name of their founder or Darshani, because they wear a special earring'. From the census that he quotes, it is clear that these Kānphaṭā or Gorakhnāthi Jogis are the same as the Gorakhpanthis.

The categories change from one census to another. In the 1901 census, the subdivision is between Jogīs and Nāth, the Nāths, corresponding probably to the Gorakhnāthis of the previous decade, being absent in many districts while the Jogīs remain numerous.

Thus we have in the censuses as in the present situation a small percentage of Gorakhnāthis, Gorakhpanthis, Kānphaṭās or Nāths, whatever the name given in these texts to the ascetic celibate yogīs belonging to the *sampradāya*; and a vast mass of

Jogīs qualified with various local epithets, who are married and householders, who may retain tenuous links with the *sampradāya* and who are considered as forming a caste, a *jātī*.

We have already seen the Bhartari Jogis mentioned by Crooke. 'They wear a beard and a long sort of coat dyed with ochre [...] an arm wallet (*jholi*) dyed in ochre and a turban of the same colour. [...] They play on the fiddle and sing songs in honour of Bhartrihari [...] These people are hereditary beggars, and keep house and families. The boys are initiated into the order at the time when the ceremonial shaving (*mundan*) is carried out' (1975: 60).[3] In the same category Crooke places the Nandiya Jogis who 'wear the same dress, but do not carry a fiddle. They lead about with a deformed ox, an animal with five legs, or some other malformation. He is decorated with ochre coloured rags and cowry shells. They call him Nandi or the vehicle of Mahadeva, and receive gifts of grain from pious Hindus' (id.).

Syed Siraj ul Hassan in *The Gazetteer of the Bombay Presidency*[4] gives a very detailed description of two groups of Jogis found in Maharashtra (1989: 279-85):

> The Davre Jogis or Bharadi – derive their name from the *dabara*, a small drum shaped like an hour glass, on which they play when begging or singing religious hymns in honour of Bhairava. [...] These are mostly children, dedicated by their parents to the god Bhairava in fulfilment of a vow. The ceremony of initiation is performed generally at the temple of Bhairava, at Sonari, when the novice, male or female, is eight years of age. A pious Bharadi is called in and the neophyte, squatting before him, has his ear-lobes bored with a knife and *mudras* or brass rings,

[3] Crooke distinguishes between the Bhartari as Hindus and the Bhaddari, 'very often Musalmans' (1975: 60). However, according to Catherine Servan-Schreiber who studied the Bhartrihari Jogīs of U.P. they are Muslims, 'they obey to the five commands of the Islamic law and follow the calendar of the Muslim festivals' (1999: 29) even though they sing the songs of the Nāth tradition during their wanderings from Muslim shrines to Hindu temples.

[4] Syed Siraj ul Hassan, *The Castes and Tribes of H.E.H. the Nizam's Dominions*, 1989, New Delhi, Asian Educational Service (1st edn. 1920).

inserted in them. The *guru* gives to the convert a *shinghi* or hornpipe, and a *dabara* or small drum, and enjoins him not to eat with low-caste people, to collect alms by singing hymns in honour of Bhairava, and to perform the *bharad* dance [...]The Davre Jogis bury their dead in a sitting posture, with the face turned towards the east [...] On the third day after death, offerings of flowers, *bel* leaves and *vibhuti* are again made at the grave and a feast, known as *bhundara* is given to caste brethren. No regular *ṣradha* is performed, nor is mourning observed by the members of the caste. (279-81)

The Raval Jogis are said to be very numerous.

The ceremony of initiation slightly differs from that of the Davre Jogis [...]Their ears are not necessarily bored, but, when they are perforated, *mudras* or earrings made of conch shell, are inserted in them [...] In matters of religion, the Ravals differ very little from the Davre Jogis [...] Reverence is paid to Gorakhnath, the founder of the sect, Machindranath, and also to the 'Trident' and *linga* of Siva [...] The members of the caste eat all flesh, except beef and pork, and indulge in strong drink. Their characteristic occupation is the collecting of alms in the name of Bhairava. Many of them have now taken to cultivation and trading and a few have adopted the profession of tailors. (Siraj ul Hassan 1989: 281-5)

The official recognition of the Jogīs as being a caste appellation is made evident in the modern political context, with various Yogīs' associations fighting to be considered as OBC, Other Backward Classes, and thus beneficiaries of the advantages linked to this status.[5] Lists given by the National Commission for Backward Classes give for each state the official entries in the

[5] See Gold (1999b: 83) on the ambivalent attitude of some associations' organizers who 'on the one hand, seeking to make [their] community seem more respectable, [...] advocate closer conformity to standard Hindu householder norms [... and] on the other hand, seek official recognition of the group as a "backward class" of "religious mendicants" [...] Urban Rajasthani Nāths I spoke with were not so enthusiastic about this latter idea. Still proud of their former princely association [...] most did not feel that the economic advantages of being a "backward caste" would be worth its social stigma'.

OBC category: in each Indian state we find the category variously labelled Jogī, Yogī, Nāth, Nāthjogī, and/or Jogināth, recognized as OBC generally since 1993.

National and regional associations of caste Jogīs such as Akhil Bharatiya Nāth Samaj Mahasangh or Rajasthān Nāth Samāj for instance may have websites and/or publish journals and booklets publicizing their community and announcing the main events it organizes. The Jaipur-based Śrī Nāth Press publishes books reminding the Yogīs about the rituals they have to follow as members of the '*jāti sampradāya*', blurring the distinction between caste and sect.

GRIHASTHA YOGĪS AND NĀTH *SAMPRADĀYA*

I will now present a few cases illustrating the multiple ways the Yogīs by caste relate themselves to the Nāth *sampradāya* and their various statuses and particularities.

Dang Caughera

The first case will take us back to the Nepalese Dang Valley and the monastery of Caughera. Just outside the *maṭh*, at the front gate, a simple cuboid sanctuary contains a *śivaliṅga* on a *yoni*. It is considered as the 'exterior temple' (*bahira mandir*) of Ratannāth, also called 'small Ratannāth' (*sānu* Ratannāth); in front of it another simple shrine is dedicated to Kāl Bhairav and contains the *dhūnī*, and there is also a stone representing Bhagavatī. This ritual complex is now the property of a lineage of Yogīs by caste, i.e. by birth or *janmā* Yogīs, as they are called in Nepali. The history of the lineage and of the Ratannāth's outside temple are intrinsically linked to the main Caughera monastery; thus in this example we will see how the conditions of the *grihastha* and ascetic Yogīs could be intertwined.

The foundation story tells of a Dang *rājā* who vowed never to eat before having saluted his god Ratannāth. But, as we have seen, the god is supposed to leave his temple every year during the month-long journey to Devi Patan. Afraid of the prospect of a month-long fast, the king decided to build a temple to Ratannāth for his own usage. The present location of this temple suggests that it was included in the royal palace compound, and inscriptions mention that the priest of this sanctuary had the title of *rājgūru*, king's guru. Together with the title and the temple, the king instituted a *guṭhi*, which means that he allotted some lands to the functioning of the cult and the support of his officiant.

These land revenues have been the sources of many conflicts among the successors of the *rājgūru*. Even after the suppression of the independent kingdom of Dang (in 1786 CE), many petitions were made to the Nepalese state, denouncing usurpations or false documents. Today's *Grihastha* Yogīs legitimize their rights as being the descendants of a wonder worker yogī whose name was Gopināth and who benefited from a royal edict in 1827 CE. Gopināth and his immediate successor were said to be celibate; however, already in 1853 CE a letter from the then Prime Minister Jang Bahadur Rana examines a petition made by the Nāth sectarian authorities, saying: 'Since the beginning, Ratannāth's service was performed only by the pardeśī Jogīs [i.e foreigner, the celibate Indian Yogīs], but now the *gharbāri* [i.e. householder] Jogīs do the service. This is a disorder and Ratannāth's dignity is not respected'.[6] To which the *Grihastha* Jogīs replied with economic arguments: 'We are deprived of our residence. We have always lived on this land and we paid our taxes like everyone else. We must have our residence'. The Minister decided: '*Pīr, bhaṇḍāri*, the *pardeśī* Jogīs of the *dhūnī*, you stay at the service of the temple; the *gharbāri* Jogīs, you don't stay but continue, in living in your houses and paying the taxes, to farm the land like you did before'. The present lineage of *pujārīs* would be descended from the third successor of Gopināth, who was the first to marry. In 1881 CE a conflict broke out between two

[6] Narharināth, *IPS*: 498, 500. See details on the various documents in Bouillier 1997: 157-62.

candidates, Bhaktināth and Kalyanāth, who asked for an edict to be made in his name as had been done for his grandfather (Nep. *baje*).[7] This was apparently not done and Bhaktināth kept the office and fathered two sons, who are at the origin of the two lineages presently in-charge of the cult.

In the 2000s, the 35 initial *bighas* were divided between the three sons of the first lineage and the two of the second one. But each family was also able to buy land for its own use or to find other occupation; not wishing to be mere officiants they were paying another *Grihastha* Yogī to take care of the *pūjā*, which is now rather simplified.[8] However, the families of these *Grihastha* Yogīs remain very close to Ratannāth's main monastery: they live in the hamlet surrounding the *maṭh*, which they visit daily, they are members of the committee which assists the superior in his management, and they have their say in every important decision concerning the *maṭh*.

Like all Hindu Nepalese lineages they have a tutelary deity, a *kuldevatā*, whose festival is performed, as is mostly the case in Nepal, during the full moon of the month of *Mangsir* (November-December). And their *kuldevatā* is none other than Kāl Bhairav, the deity worshipped in the *maṭh* and also in the outside temple. The transformation of the wild anomic Bhairav into a deity protecting a lineage of sedentarized palace officiants is symbolic of the change from sect to caste.

[7] As is often the case, the use of kinship terms for spiritual filiation makes it difficult to know when the transmission by spiritual descent gives way to biological filiation: thus we cannot be sure of Kalyannāth's condition.

[8] An agreement signed between the State department for religious affairs (*Guṭhi Samsthan*) and the officiants in 1953 CE show that the rituals were precisely defined and important, including notably the offering of a *roṭ* bread every Tuesday to Ratannāth and a daily meal of rice and lentils (*khicaṛi*) to Bhairav, fire offerings and big celebrations including animal sacrifices for Dasaĩ (*Daśahrā*) [Kathmandu, National Archives, K316/31].

Mangalore

Another example of a close relationship between a Nāth Yogī ascetic monastery and a community of *Grihastha* Jogis can be seen in Mangalore around the Kadri Maṭh. But in this case there is no question of the sort of ritual competition we have seen in Caughera. The *Grihastha* Jogis of Mangalore are a strong and numerous community which plays an important role in Mangalore city since one former mayor came from their ranks, and they tend to consider the Kadri Maṭh as their caste temple. They have founded different committees in charge of the promotion of the *maṭh* and are also very busy every twelve years in organizing the festival which accompanies the enthronement of the new superior. As we have seen, the new *rājā* is foreign to the place, thus the leaders of the committees and the elders of the *grihastha* community may help him to manage the institution and may also complain if they feel excluded by the personal network of the *rājā*. This was for instance the case when a former *rājā* relied on his own Marwari connections instead of on their network.

The origin of this community is not documented. We do not know if they developed around and from the monastery; however, in any case, the monastic Nāth system which is centred on a few individuals, does not allow for the growth of a wide community (even though some heads were known to have had children!). Whatever their initial situation, the *Grihastha* Jogīs now consider the Kadri *rājā* as their guru and they receive from him the first initiation to which they are entitled; with the mantra which confirms their belonging to the Yogīs' community, they receive the small whistle or *nād* which they blow before their daily *pūjā* in their house shrine and in front of their guru. Most often now the initiatory mantra is collectively given by the *rājā* during a general ceremony in the monastery. This *Grihastha* caste was described in 1909 by Thurston and Rangachari, under the name of 'Jogi Purusha' (1909: II, 499-500). They specify:

Their special deity is Bhairav but some regard Gorakshanāth as their god... All Jogi Purusha who have become the disciples of a guru of their cult ought to have a brass, copper or silver pipe called singanātha tied on a thread round the neck... The dead are buried in a sitting posture. *Bojja* or final death ceremony is on the 12th day. The ceremony consists in offering food to the crows, making presents to Brāhmans, and undergoing purificatory rites for the removal of death pollution.

Pushkar

The coexistence of two distinct communities, one of the celibate ascetic Nāth Yogīs and one of the householder caste Jogīs, but sharing an identical reference to the tradition of Gorakhnāth, finds an institutional expression in the sacred pilgrimage town of Pushkar. I have already mentioned the *pañcāyatī maṭh* named 'Śrī Gorakṣa Mandir Bārah Panth Dalīcā' with its *pātradevatā* worship and the obligation for new Nāth initiates to register with the sect genealogist. On another side of the lake stands the Śrī Mahāyogī Gorakhnāth Mandir which is dependent on the Pushkar Sarva Grihastanāth Mahāsabhā: it is the temple of the *grihastha* Yogīs' caste, close to the other temples which belong to and represent the main Rajasthani castes, as is the tradition in Pushkar. This Gorakhnāth *mandir* has been recently expanded and embellished thanks to the donations of the devotees. It is under the care of *Grihastha* Yogīs who wear the *nād-selī* but not the earrings; interestingly they claim to belong to the same *sampradāya* as those they call *avadhūt* and to have the right to wear the earrings: if they don't take this initiation, it is because of the many constraints and obligations it would be impossible for a householder to observe. However, even though *Grihastha* Jogīs may worship in the *Avadhūt* Nāth monastery, its Yogīs never go to the *grihastha mandir*.

In all these three cases, the two groups of the Nāth ascetics and the householder Jogīs acknowledge their coexistence and their relatedness even though they recognize the distinctiveness of their statuses and the superiority of the celibate ascetics.

There are other cases where the distinction between the two

categories appears less evident, where the *grihasthas* benefit from rights and duties which seem similar to those of the ascetic and monastic Yogīs.

This may be because they kept their married condition hidden. That was the case in one Udaipur Maṭh, well known for the special ceremonial role played by its *mahant* for the *Daśahrā* festival. However, at the same time as the festival and the renewal of the maharaja's power thanks to the ascetic performance of the *mahant* were abandoned, as the lands of the *maṭh* were sold for construction, the tradition of the *mahant*'s celibacy was changed to one of marriage, disguised as a *gūru-śiṣya* relationship.

Gwalior: Ḍholībuva Tradition

In contrast, the Gwalior Nāth monastery known as Ḍholībuva Maṭh is very openly a monastery of householder Yogīs. The spiritual lineage was first settled in Paithan where Udbodhnāth was the first to marry. After him the transmission was made from guru to the *putra aur śiṣya*, the 'son and disciple': from Udbodh to Kesarīnāth, then Śivadinnāth, then Narharināth.[9] Narharināth was the guru but not the father of Mahipatināth, who was the first to settle in Gwalior after being summoned by the Maharaja Daulat Rao (r. 1794-1827). The tomb of Mahipatināth is the centre around which the monastery was built by his sucessor and nephew Kaśināth, originally from Poone, who started the family transmission in the Purandare lineage; the anniversary of Mahipatināth's death (on the 13th day of the clear half of Pauṣ 1823 CE) is the main festival of the *maṭh*. Mahipati's lineage was famous for its musical tradition and especially for the playing of a big drum, a *ḍhol*, hence the name of Ḍholibuva ('*Buwa* is a Maharashtrian honorific', Gold 2011: 53); Mahipati himself was a performer and a composer and his successors played an important musical role in most Gwalior celebrations;[10] the present *mahant*,

[9] According to the *Śrī 1008 rājyogī Śrīsadgurū Mahipatināth Mahārāj kā 151vān samādhi mahotsav*.

[10] See Daniel Gold 2011: 53: 'Members of the extended Dholi Buwa

Śrī Kānt Nāth, despite his old age, is well known for his singing of the *Hari Kathā* on festive occasions. The compound of the *maṭh* includes the family habitations of the members of the Ḍholibuva lineage but its centre is the *samādhi* temple of Mahipatināth, surrounded by all the *samādhis* of his successors. We find here the archetypal features of the personal monasteries, built around the memory, and the *samādhi*, of the founder and continuing to be the graveyard of his successors. Another anchorage into the Nāth ascetic tradition can be seen in the importance given by the Ḍholibuva Maharaj to his begging tours; he insists on going regularly around Gwalior streets to beg (*bhik magne)*[11] in order to finance the feasts offered in the *maṭh*. However, nothing in his dress alludes to Nāth affiliation; as I said before, the Ḍholibuva Maharaj's tradition claims to wear the Nāth symbols inwardly: not Nāth earrings but long gold earrings worn in the earlobe; no ochre dress but a silk robe and necklaces, and a high brocade headdress, the whole looking more like a princely outfit than an ascetic one. Is this an indication of the close connection between the Ḍholibuva lineage and the Gwalior Scindya dynasty? Mahipatināth was considered as the *rājgūru* of Daulat Rao and their successors continue to exchange ceremonial visits at each festive occasion, the Gwalior *rājā* visiting for instance the *maṭh* on the back of an elephant during the *utsav*.

---

lineage are known in town primarily as religious performers, presenting a Maharashtrian-style story and song programme that features a signature introductory drumbeat. In addition to presentations at their own math, other temples, and private religious events, they also perform frequently at public fora', and most remarkably at Sufi celebrations such as Shah Mansur Samaroh, Tansen Samaroh and Raja Bhakshar Urs (Gold 2005).

[11] He also uses the term '*phir*' (*phirnā*, to turn, to walk to and fro, to wander) as was the case in Nepal for the tours (Nep. *phiri lāune*) the Yogīs were making around villages to ward off evil spirits, singing mantras and blowing horns (Bouillier 1986: 156-7).

Gorkha

There is no monastery in the Nepalese town of Gorkha, the former capital of the Shah kings, but there is a lineage of *Grihastha* Jogīs who played a principal role in the worship of Gorakhnāth as the protective deity of the kingdom.[12] Their householder status was no hindrance to their function as *pujārīs* of Gorakhnāth and Bhairav, and they officiated in an underground chamber under the royal palace, which was said to be the place where Gorakhnāth meditated during his Himalayan sojourn. They claim to have been obliged to marry by the Gorkha kings who wanted to be sure of the succession process. They settled during the seventeenth century and benefited from royal land donations in exchange for worship, which is now done alternately by the four families of descendants of the first settlers. They live in small hamlets called '*Jogī gāūn*', Jogīs' village, and their families practise farming. However, in contrast with their lives as royal officiants and with the common practice of the *Grihastha* Jogīs, they are fully initiated and thus wear the Nāth earrings. Their Nāth belonging is also manifest in the complex rituals they organize for initiations and funerals and which are adapted from the *śaṅkhaḍhāl* (see passim).

Rajasthan

The many studies made by Ann and Daniel Gold of the Rajasthani householder Nāths give us a deep insight into the complex position of the Nāth caste. Nowadays mainly settled as farmers in rural Rajasthan, these *Grihastha* Yogīs have retained many links with the Nāth tradition. Inheritors of the reputation for power of their ancestors, some settled in villages to protect them from hail and locusts thanks to their magical skills and were given land by local landlords. Often priests of local shrines to Bhairav, they transmitted their rights to their children, together with

[12] See Bouillier 1986, 'La caste sectaire des Kanphata Jogi dans le royaume de Gorkha'.

the knowledge of many epics and songs which portray the main heroes and themes of the Nāth lore (Grodzins Gold 1992). Some *grihasthas* choose to combine the settled life of the householder with periods of itinerance during which they travel to pilgrimage places or sing religious hymns for song-fests (Daniel Gold 1999b: 78). They combine alternative identities as roaming ascetics and settled householders, both related to their Nāth belonging.

As studied by Gold (2002) these Rajasthani *Grihastha* Nāths are enthusiastic singers of a repertoire of hymns which belong to what Gold calls the *nirguṇ bhajan* tradition, inherited from the Sants: 'There were songs dedicated to warnings and to guru devotion, as well as to esoteric secrets in a familiar Sant jargon [...] Despite the familiar topics and some familiar names, the Nāths not only sometimes gave the songs [...] interpretations diverging radically from those I would have anticipated, but also sang them in a very different way' (2002: 145). Songs are replete with sexually explicit metaphors which refer to 'the great secrets of the Nāths' (id.: 152), the householder Nāths being their exclusive repository.

This *bhajan* tradition is, according to Gold, related to an esoteric funeral cult, called in Rajasthan *dasnāmī pūjā*. The villager Nāths are in Rajasthan the officiants of this cult which is prescribed for the initiates who, besides the Nāths themselves, may belong to various low and middle castes. The cult is performed at the death of the initiated member[13]. 'Whenever a member of the cult dies someone else had to take their place and the cult tends to perpetuate itself in families, and all the Nāths we knew were seriously involved in it' (Gold 2002: 150). The cult is done in secrecy, during the night, devoted to the goddess Hing Laj and includes the singing of many hymns with *nirguṇ* themes

[13] Such a cult among the Meghwals has been described in detail by Mahendra Bhanāwat under the title '*mṛtak-samskār śankhāḍhāl*' (1986: 121-7, with many thanks to Dominique-Sila Khan for providing me with chapters of the book where it appears, *Ajubā Rajāsthān*). It seems that a similar cult exists in Malwa among the low caste and tribal people belonging to the Māī Panth sect (see Samata 1997).

(cf. Gold and Gold 1984: 120-3, Gold 2002: 120-3) but which could also be understood in a Tantric context.

Dasnāmī Pūjā, Updeśī

The performance of this Rajasthani ritual appears quite similar to the one I attended to among the *Grihastha* Yogīs of central Nepal. It was done in the middle of the night in a remote place, behind closed doors and was in two parts, the first one being the initiation of new members and the second a funeral ceremony for recently departed members (see Chapter 2). But in contrast to the Rajasthani case, the ceremony was limited to the Nāths and the initiation was given to all members of the *grihastha* community, male and female, and was regarded as the way to be incorporated into the caste. The ritual was called *updeśī* and in close connection with the dual status of the *grihasthas* was considered as an initiation both into the caste (*jātī*) and into the sect (*sampradāya*), entitling the members to the specific funerals which secure them access to liberation.

However, as we have seen, the ritual called *updeśī* was considered among the *avadhūt*, the celibate Yogīs, as a final initiatory step, performed only for advanced Yogīs. Their reluctance even to talk about it contrasted with the lack of restriction of the *grihasthas* who gave *updeśī* to young children.[14] Thus, even though it was impossible for me to attend an *updeśī* among the ascetic Nāths which, as in Nepal among the *grihasthas,* is related and coupled with funerals, the few descriptions I obtained from informants and read about in the works of Yogī Vilaśnāth (2004 and 2005) correspond closely to the ritual I was permitted to attend in Nepal.

[14] And even to me, without my asking for! It can be a problem since, as in the Rajashtani ritual, 'once people had witnessed the ritual, it had to be done for them at their death; if not, trouble could ensue for everyone involved. The ritual's secrecy here is seen to stem from a practical occult danger' (Gold 2002: 150-1).

Thus, both the Nepalese and Rajasthani ritual performances of the *Grihastha* Yogīs share a common background with the Nāth initiatory tradition. But the circumstances of the performance of the *dasnāmī pūjā* and the *updeśī* give them different consequences. The *dasnāmī* cult seems to gather around *Grihastha* Nāth performers a circle of initiates who consider themselves as belonging to a special *panth*. This *panth* appears to be related to a still more secret, esoteric and transgressive current, the Bisnāmī Panth, which the low caste initiates met by Dominique-Sila Khan (1994) also call Kuṇḍā Panth ('path of the vessel'): the *bisnāmī* form has overtly sexual rituals, including ritual intercourse between random partners and consumption of shared sexual fluids.[15] Beyond the aura of scandal, we could see the *panth* and hence the *Grihastha* Yogīs as the holders of 'a great secret', as Daniel Gold puts it (2002), which they express in the double-entendre of their *nirguṇ* songs and which would relate them to a Tantric interpretation of the Sant tradition.

GRIHASTHAS AND TANTRISME

As was explained to Daniel Gold: 'In the Nāth community there is another way. It's Shiva's way: the union of Shiva and Shakti takes place in it. This is the *bisnāmī panth*. The great way of the Nāths is this one' (2002: 152). 'If the great secret of the Nāths are to be found in sexual practice' (id.), evidently the *grihasthas* are in a better position than the *avadhūts* to succeed in their quest. Beyond this self justification by some *grihasthas*, what can we know about the former position and the evolution of the Nāth *sampradāya* in the case of householders?

The long history of Tantric Śivaism as explained by Alexis Sanderson (1988) is marked by the succession and juxtaposition of the two currents of the Atimārga and the Mantramārga:

[15] See also a description of this *panth* and of the sexual aspect of ritual intercourse in Mahendra Bhanāwat (1986: 32-7, chapter entitled '*Kuṇḍā evam undriyā panth*').

These are termed the Outer Path (Atimārga) and the Path of Mantras (Mantramārga). The first is accessible only to ascetics, while the second is open both to ascetics and to married home-dwellers (*gṛhastha*). There is also a difference of goals. The Atimārga is entered for salvation alone, while the Mantramāga promises both this and, for those that so wish, the attainment of supernatural powers (*siddhis*) and the experience of supernal pleasures in the worlds of their choice (*bhoga*). (1988: 664)

Whatever the multiplicity of schools emerging in the Mantramāga, 'there is complete solidarity in a basic faith that it is enough to be a Śaiva in a purely ritual sense, that the least gnostic of their common audience will attain liberation simply by being processed by the rituals of the community' (id. 691).

Following the same line of argument, Mallinson questions the origin of the Nāth *sampradāya* and proposes a joint emergence of the two currents of ascetic and *Grihastha* Nāths. Giving some reports of the mentions of famous Nāths as married (including possibly Gorakhnāth), he even says that

The *Nāth* ascetics' existence as a pan-Indian *sampradāya* has given them more prominence in *Nāth* historiography than their disparate lay counterparts. In interactions between the two, the ascetics are known to emphasize their superiority in spiritual matters, not to mention their subordinating householder Nāths by claiming that the latter are the descendants of fallen ascetics. It is quite possible that the householder Nāths are in fact heirs of the oldest *Nāth* traditions (2011a: 426).

The sexual 'secret' of the *Grihastha* Yogīs would make them the inheritors of former sexual-yogīc practices that were later internalized in the Haṭha yoga of Gorakhnāth. That the propounder of this sexual-yogic trend would be Matsyendranāth is not unrelated: Matsyendranāth who, according to his most famous legend, went into the women's kingdom, got married to the queen, and begot two sons, before being brought back to his yogī condition by Gorakhnāth (see Chapter 1), is taken by the *Grihastha* Yogīs as their hero, or as an excuse for their married condition.

However, as told by Yogī Vilaśnāth (pers. comm.): 'The *gri-*

hasthas use Matsyendranāth's story as a justification for their lapse. They forget that Matsyendranāth took the body of a king after leaving his true Self in a cave. He did that in order to demonstrate the dangers of attachment. How to stand in water but not to drink water!'

OBSERVATIONS

One way to contrast householders and ascetics is to oppose *janmā* (Nep.) and *karma* Yogīs, the Yogīs by birth and by act (by ritual). Another opposition mentioned by Gold (1999: 73) is between *bindu paramparā* and *nād paramparā*, succession through seed (*bindu*) and through sound (*nād*): the transmission from father to son, and the transmission from guru to disciple through the giving of an initiatory mantra. However, this double qualification is ambiguous. *Bindu* is the seed, the semen, and refers naturally to the biological succession of householders, but *bindu* also has yogic connotations. *Bindu* as semen is what the sexual-yogic practices seek to retain or to make ascend;

> [*Bindu* is also] a point of concentration in the body ... sometimes paired with *nād* as a localized point at which yogīs in meditation hear the eternal sound power of the universe. In this sense *bindu* indicates an experience of selfhood concentrated so densely that it implodes into the eternal substrate beyond the finite self. *Bindu* and *nād* are thus polar opposites that eventually converge. Used primarily to present a contrast, the terms also point to an ultimate continuity. (Gold 1999: 74)

Whatever the past history, and whatever the scornful disdain of present-day ascetic Nāths, it is possible to consider the *Grihastha* Yogīs as double winners. Gaining initiation by birthright, they are sure to obtain ultimate liberation without submitting to the strenuous requirements the celibate ascetic Nāth Yogīs have to endure. They can enjoy both ways: to live in the world and to get liberation, or, as a *grihastha* guru from the group of the Kālbeliyās said to Gold: 'With us you can split your ears and still live as householders' (2002: 158). To be born liberated,[16] even though this liberation has to be ensured and confirmed by initiatory and funeral specific rituals, is quite a privilege.

[16] To paraphrase the title of the book I devoted to *Grihastha* Sannyāsīs in Nepal: 'Naître renonçant. Une caste de Sannyasi villageois au Nepal central' ('To be Born a Renouncer: A Caste of Sannyasi Villagers in Central Nepal').

CHAPTER 13

Conclusion

At the end of this journey into the world of the Nāth Yogīs, we have followed different paths, encountered many different situations, discovered various ways of being a yogī. However, we also discovered, beyond this diversity, common features and connections which tell of a shared belonging.

I have shown the importance of the monastic organization, a fact which is, in my view, a principal component of Indian sectarian asceticism. Monastic structures give institutional continuity and preserve sectarian movements from splits. Among the Nāth Yogīs, we have seen monasteries functioning at two levels:

Collective monasteries are, in a way, the memory of the institution and the place where all Yogīs can find their roots; these monasteries belong to everyone and everyone may have his place there. The rotation of offices prevents personal appropriation and exclusiveness; the collective monasteries are rooted in the foundational myths of the sect, follow the examples proposed by the great Siddhas with their behaviour inspired by yogic Tantrism, and perform esoteric rituals reserved for initiates.

This continuity appears in the succession of events leading to the enthronement of the head of Kadri monastery. It starts with the assembly of the Yogīs of the twelve *panths* and the election of the one who bears the special title of *rājā* during the Nasik Kumbh Melā, thus once every twelve years; it is followed by the long procession which, over six months, leads southward ascetics and sect leaders carrying ceremoniously the *pātradevatā*, a divinized symbol of their condition as Gorakhnāth's disciples;

finally the ceremonial installation of the *rājā* is performed, combining vedic rites of royal consecration and sectarian investiture. These rituals maintain the permanency and the cohesiveness of the sect around values and symbols in which the sect itself is represented.

The monastery of Caughera has its roots in the legendary world of the Siddha Ratannāth, whose enigmatic figure gives us a glimpse of the special relationships the Nāths had with Islam. Caughera is also representative of the system of close association and mutual legitimation occurring between Nāth monasteries and royal powers; interplay between spiritual and worldly benefices found expression in the traditional tenurial system exemplified in Caughera legal documents.

Kadri, Caughera, and Pushkar are among the few monasteries which belong to the Nāth *sampradāya* as a global and pan-Indian institution. Their heads are elected among the community for a limited period, they have no local roots, they serve the institution and have no right to leave the district of the *maṭh* during their mandate.

The personal or private monasteries function on a different basis. They are open to innovation and transformative change, but their stability depends on uncertain factors such as the charisma of the founder and his successors, the patronage of fortunate well-wishers, and the inclusion in local networks. Thus these monasteries are most often rooted in a specific territory from which their *mahants* come and where they travel regularly. In such a context, to build up sacrality thanks to the founder's hagiography is most essential: the narrative of his exceptional life helps to gather a community around his worship and to legitimize the related institution. Such a monastery has to be constantly maintained, being both fragile because of its dependency on an external support, and adaptable to a changing context because of its institutional autonomy. It can then free itself from tradition, introduce some new practices and reject others, and adapt itself to transformation of socio-political conditions or to a change of patronage.

I do not believe the monasteries are the outcome of a long process of 'taming the ascetics', as Carrithers[1] defines it, followed by Van der Veer (1987: 683) who describes: 'a long process of sedentarisation [which] has resulted in the taming of the wild, free-moving ascetic'. In my view, in the Nāth sect, as in many other sects, monastic structures are intrinsic to the nature and even to the emergence of the sect, and many epigraphic testimonies prove their antiquity. Wandering and the monastic life are in a relation of complementarity and between these two modes of Nāth behaviour there is no clearcut or permanent barrier: ascetics easily change their way of life and do not remain permanently sedentary. What is involved is rather a different relation to space, a shift between mobility and steadinesss. The constant moving of the *jamāt*'s itinerant ascetics contrasts with the sedentarity of the monasteries and moreover with the prohibition for certain *mahants* of *pañcāyatī maṭhs* against leaving their seats. Wandering is not devoid of rules, the journey may obey institutional logic (for example, the calendar of monastic festivals). The two worlds are not opposed; we have seen that the mobile group of ascetics can constitute an 'itinerant monastery' (Burghart 1996: 115), with its portable altar and hierarchical structure, and that traditionally this itinerant monastery has authority over the centres it visits. The settled institutions, the *pañcāyatī maṭhs,* are thus subjected to the control of the roaming renouncers. And it was necessary for the Caughera *pīr* and the Kadri *rājā* prior to their enthronement, to adopt the way of life of the itinerant *tapasvī* ascetics, with the self-control and the endurance of physical pain that it supposes. Monasteries, in my view, do not represent sedentarization but come within different possibilities which remain always open and whose values are hierarchized, the *jamāt* adding monastic stability to prestige of itinerant movement.

[1] Carrithers (1979: 294-310). For Carrithers, this process – in a Buddhist Sri Lankan context – is the result of the dependence of the monks on lay donors, for Van der Veer – in a Ramanandi context – of 'devotional worship of images in a localised temple cult' (1987: 693).

One finds much evidence of the fragility of monasteries and of the decrease in importance of the Nāth Yogīs. One can look, for instance, at the former domain of Ayas Dev Nāth, the exceptional guru of the Jodhpur Maharaja Man Singh; his monastery, the Mahāmandir, has now been transformed into a school and the affluent and powerful Nāth community of the early nineteenth century has lost all importance. It is also possible to visit the monastery linked to the temple of the goddess Annapūrṇa ('fertile', 'full of grain') near Jaipur, whose *mahant* was the guru of the Maharaja; the *roṭ* cooked in the *maṭh* for Śivarātrī and kept in the palace kitchen used to bring Annapūrṇa's blessing and abundance to the palace and the king. A succession conflict, the Maharaja's lack of interest, land reform, have left the present *mahant* lonely and impoverished: and as a final misfortune and reversal in the order of things, 'now Annapūrṇa is hungry'.

Decrease in princely patronage and land reforms had a negative economic impact on the Nāth monasteries. Many of them, often sufficiently large to accommodate big gatherings of ascetics and devotees during festivals but otherwise rather deserted, did not survive the decrease in resources nor the loss of their ceremonial functions for royal courts.

Elsewhere the patronage of merchants replaced that of kings. Evidently businessmen, like princes, wish success in their enterprises and for that they look to the special powers of wonder working ascetics. But their activities, less violent – apparently – require more peaceful religious forms: merchant communities more often adopt Jainism or devotional Vishnuism than Tantric Shaivism. However, even some of these merchant groups, in Shekhavati and elsewhere in India, have chosen Nāth gurus, who have been able to come up to their expectations, both in suggesting a personal discipline inspired by Nāth principles and in proposing a collective devotional atmosphere, allowing lay devotees to share in a common, territorially grounded memory.

Monasteries in this context appear less sectarian, they open their doors to everyone and give their devotees the opportunity to combine the modernist trend with a personal spiritual quest and self affirmation, which characterizes many of the new urban middle class, while resorting to the familially inherited tradition of a well-established sect. Fatehpur Ashram is symptomatic of this new openness, which embraces 'vedism' such as has been reinvented in these fashionable broadcast celebrations, as well as emotional bhakti, the strict bodily discipline of Haṭha Yoga, and most importantly, the personal relationship with a guru.

Lay disciples responded eagerly to this opening in their direction. Nāth monasteries, which had a limited audience when they were frequented only by ascetics, became places of assembly. Mukundgarh in Shekhavati is a good exemple of this change from ascetic *maṭh* to public temple: the Yogī Chetnāth has supervised the construction of a huge new temple to Śiva, his own future monastery being just a little square room nearby.

Together with the opening to lay devotees comes media coverage: all the media were present for Fatehpur Mahotsav and Kadri *rājābhiṣek*: the *jhuṇḍī*'s arrival took place in front of the television cameras and daily Press reported the succession of ritual events. At a deeper level, the new standards of modernity can be seen in the development, which is new for the Nāths, of welfare activities. This is the case in Gorakhpur and Asthal Bohar, where the many educational and health institutions make the Nāths participant in the socio-political game. This involvement in the public space inevitably leads the Nāth leaders to enter the political arena, out of concern for efficiency or as a consequence of their leading position: being by tradition the counsellors of princes, they now aspire after ministership or elected positions. The monastery of Gorakhpur was the first to take this path, followed by Asthal Bohar. Until now the Hindutva extremist position of Gorakhpur *mahants* has remained limited, perhaps under the influence of a clientele of devotees who prefer successful business to communalist violence.

However, the adaptation to modern religiosity, to a kind of sweet devotion which appears for instance in the long sessions of devotional singing, practised everywhere even by the itinerant ascetics of the *jamāt*, goes together with a certain denial of Tantric and unorthodox ritual forms (such as *śaṅkhaḍhāl* and cannabis smoking). This belongs of course to the general trend in India towards puritanism, only more so for the sects which have a well known Tantric reputation and want to acquire an image of respectability. Will the Tantric side become the exclusive privilege of the *Grihastha* Yogīs, among whom certain communities have kept to specific secret practices?

The position of the Mahāsabhā is quite interesting, as the association has to play two contradictory roles: to promote the Nāth Yogī sect and also to discipline it. It tries to take control of the existing institutions and to include them in a bureaucratic organizational structure, according to the rules of functioning of modern institutions (with assemblies, committees, elections, presidents and vice-presidents, and statutes). The Mahāsabhā wants to know the identities of all the ascetics, to list them, to register them and to be able to check on their behaviour and expel them if necessary. It also wants to publicize the philosophy, history and particularity of the Nāth tradition, and it sponsors the publication of books, which incidentally reveal practices elsewhere disapproved of. The Mahāsabhā has both to testify to the originality of the Nāth contribution to Hindu tradition and to ensure its conformity with the prevailing ideology; a symbol of this attitude appears in the rules of the Mahāsabhā which forbid the smoking of cannabis and encourage the practice of Haṭha Yoga.

The Nāth Yogīs' *sampradāya* remains important in the Indian religious landscape; it is even experiencing new development and prosperity, thanks to the innovative capacities of its monasteries, especially the *nijī maṭhs*, but it runs the risk of having its specificity diluted with a vague religiosity, a 'neo-guruism' obeying diverse influences. There the collective monasteries play their part as guardians of tradition. The difference is striking between the *jhuṇḍī mahant* refusing any single change in the performance of the Kadri *rājā's* consecration and the Asthal Bohar *mahant* displacing and modifying age-old sanctuaries in order to give them a magnificent appearance and promote the monastery: on one side, there is fidelity to details transmitted in the sect's tradition and identical repetition of memorial marks, on the other transformation dictated by changing circumstances.

Considering the importance taken by the Mahāsabhā in recent years, its influence will determine the future evolution of the Nāth sect. Will the Mahāsabhā be able to preserve the sect's identity, to accompany its development while protecting what makes it what it is?

Bibliography

Agrawal, Purushottam. 2011. 'The Naths in Hindi Literature', in D.N. Lorenzen and A. Muñoz (eds). *Yogi Heroes and Poets: Histories and Legends of the Nāths*. New York: SUNY Press: 3-18.

Alter, Joseph. 2004. *Yoga in Modern India: The Body between Science and Philosophy*. Princeton N.J.: Princeton University Press.

Amatya, Saphalya, s. d., Guthi records and accounts offices. Series nos. 1, 2, 3, 4. Kathmandu: National History Guide Committee.

Anandanath Jogi. 2003. *Nathapanthakshetra Jogimatha*. Mangalore.

Assayag, Jackie. 1992. *La Colère de la déesse décapitée. Traditions, cultes et pouvoir dans le sud de l'Inde*. Paris: CNRS Éditions.

Atkinson, E.T. 1974. *Religion in the Himalayas*, Delhi: Cosmo (rpt).

_______. 1980. *Kumaun Hills*, Delhi: Cosmo (rpt).

Babb, Lawrence A. 1986. 'The Puzzle of Religious Modernity', in James R. Roach (ed.), *India 2000: The Next Fifteen Years*, Maryland: The Riverdale Company: 55-79.

_______. 1998. *Absent Lord: Ascetics and Kings in a Jain Ritual Culture*. Berkeley: University of California Press.

_______. 2002. 'Paraśurām's Sacrifice: A Myth and Its Local Travels', in V. Joshi (ed.), *Culture, Community and Change*. Jaipur: Rawat: 133-53.

_______. 2004. *Alchemies of Violence: Myths of Identity and the Life of Trade in Western India*. Delhi: Sage.

Banerjea, Akshaya Kumar. 1979. *The Nath-Yogi Sampradaya and the Gorakhnath Temple*. Gorakhpur: Gorakhnath Temple.

_______. 1983. *Philosophy of Gorakhnath, with Gorakhsha-Vacana-Sangraha*. Delhi: Motilal Banarsidass.

Barthwal, Pitambar Datt. 1942. *Gorakh bānī*. Allahabad: Hindi Sahitya-sammelan.

_______. 1978. *Traditions of Indian Mysticism based upon Nirguna School of Hindi Poetry*. New Delhi: Heritage Publishers.

Bedi, Rajesh and Ramesh Bedi, 1991. *Sadhus: The Holy Men of India*. New Delhi: Brijbasi Printers.

Behl, Aditya and Simon Weightman. 2000. *Introduction to Manjhan's Madhumālatī*. Oxford: Oxford University Press.

Bhanāwat, Mahendra. 1986. *Ajubā Rajasthan*. Udaipur: M. Bhanāvāt.

Bhat, P. Gururaja. 1975. *Studies in Tuluva History and Culture*. Manipal: Manipal Power Press.

______. 2000. *The Manjunatha Temple, Kadri, Mangalore* (Kannada and English). Mangalore.

Bhatt, G.P., ed. 2004. *The Forceful Yoga. Being the Translation of Haṭhayoga-Pradīpikā, Gheraṇda-Saṁhitā and Śiva-Saṁhitā*. Delhi: Motilal Banarsidass.

Bhattacharya, France. 1996. 'La secte des Nāth et le Manasā Maṅgal', in Catherine Champion (ed.), *Traditions Orales dans le Monde Indien*. Paris: Editions de l'EHESS (*Puruṣārtha* 18).

______. 2001. 'La construction de la figure de l'homme-dieu selon les deux principales hagiographies bengali de Śrī Kṛṣṇa Caitanya', in Françoise Mallison (ed.), *Constructions hagiographiques dans le monde indien. Entre mythe et histoire*. Paris: Librairie Honoré Champion: 183-204.

______, 2003-4. 'Un texte du Bengale médiéval: le yoga du Kalandar (Yoga-Kalandar). Yoga et soufisme, le confluent de deux fleuves', *BEFEO* 90-1: 69-99.

Biardeau, Madeleine. 1976. 'Etudes de Mythologie Hindoue IV. Bhakti et Avatāra', *BEFEO*, LXIII: 111-263.

______. 1981. 'Paraṣurāma', in Yves Bonnefoy (ed.), *Dictionnaire des Mythologies, II*, Paris: Flammarion, pp. 239-41.

Biardeau, Madeleine et Charles Malamoud. 1976. *Le Sacrifice dans l'Inde Ancienne*. Paris: Presses Universitaires de France.

Bijayanāth Yogī. 2043 vs. *Siddha ratnanāth caritāmṛt*. Dang: Caughera.

Bilimale, Purushottama. 1996. 'Siddaveesa: An Interpretation', in U.P. Upadhyaya (ed.), 1996, *Coastal Karnataka*, Udupi: Rashtrakavi Govind Pai Samshodhana Kendra, pp. 281-91.

Birch, Jason, 2011. 'The Meaning of *Haṭha* in Early Haṭhayoga', *Journal of the American and Oriental Society*, 131. 4: 527-54.

Bouillier, Véronique. 1979. *Naître renonçant. Une caste de Sannyasi villageois au Népal central*. Nanterre: Laboratoire d'ethnologie.

______. 1986. 'La caste sectaire des Kanphata Jogi dans le royaume du Népal: l'exemple de Gorkha'. *Bulletin de l'Ecole française d'Extrême-Orient*, vol. 75: 125-67.

______. 1989. 'Des prêtres du pouvoir: les Yogi et la fonction royale', *in* Véronique Bouillier et Gérard Toffin (eds.), *Prêtrise, pouvoirs et autorité en Himalaya*, Paris: Editions de l'EHESS (*Puruṣārtha* 12): 193-214.

______. 1992a. 'Mahādev Himalayen', in Véronique Bouillier et Gérard Toffin (eds.), *Classer les dieux? Des panthéons en Asie du Sud.* Paris: Ed. de l'EHESS, (*Puruṣārtha* 15), 1992: 173-87.

______. 1992b. 'The King and His Yogi: Prithvi Narayan Shah, Bhagavantanath and the Unification of Nepal in the 18th Century', in J.P. Neelsen (ed.), *Gender, Caste and Power in South Asia: Social Status and Mobility in Transitional Society*, Delhi: Manohar: 3-21.

______. 1993. 'Une caste de Yogi Newar, les Kusle-Kapali', *Bulletin de l'Ecole Française d'Extrême-Orient*, 80 (1): 75-106.

______. 1997. *Ascètes et Rois. Un monastère de Kanphata Yogis au Népal.* Paris: CNRS Editions (Ethnologie).

______. 1999. 'The Royal Gift to the Ascetics: The Case of the Caughera Monastery', *Studies in Nepalese History and Anthropology*, 3, 2: 213-38.

______. 2003. 'The Violence of the Non-Violent, or Ascetics in Combat', in Denis Vidal, Gilles Tarabout and Eric Meyer (eds.), *Violence/ Non-Violence: Some Hindu Perspectives.* Delhi: Manohar: 27-64.

______. 2004. 'Samādhi et dargâh: hindouisme et islam dans la Shekhavati', in V. Bouillier and C. Servan-Schreiber (eds.), *De l'Arabie à l'Himalaya. Chemins croisés. En hommage à Marc Gaborieau.* Paris: Maisonneuve et Larose: 251-72.

______. 2008a. *Itinérance et vie monastique. Les ascètes Nâth Yogîs en Inde contemporaine.* Paris: Editions de la FMSH.

______. 2008b. 'Un monastère Nath dans la Shekhavati: patronage marchand et démonstration de pouvoirs', in C. Clementin-Ojha and P. Lachaier (eds.), *Divines Richesses.* Paris: Editions de l'EFEO, 2008: 113-31.

______. 2008c. 'Grottes et tombes: les affinités des Nath Yogis avec le monde souterrain', *Rivista di Studi Sudasiatici*, III: 33-48.

______. 2009. 'Y a-t-il des monastères dans l'Hindouisme? Quelques exemples shivaïtes', in *La Vie monastique dans le miroir de la parenté*, A. Herrou et G. Krauskopff (eds.), Paris: l'Harmattan, 2009: 25-35.

______. 2011. 'Kānphaṭās', in *Brill's Encyclopedia of Hinduism*, vol. III. *Society, Religious Specialists, Religious Traditions, and Philosophy.* Knut A. Jacobsen (ed.), Leiden: Brill, 347-54.

———. 2012. 'Modern Guru and old Sampradaya: How a Nath Yogi Anniversary Festival became a Performance on Hinduism', in John Zavos et al. (eds.), *Public Hinduisms*, New Delhi: Sage, 2012: 373-91.

———. 2013. 'Religion Compass: A Survey of Current Researches on India's Nath Yogis', *Religion Compass* 7/5 (2013): 157–68 (online 10.1111/rec3.12041).

———. 2015. 'Nāth Yogīs' Encounters with Islam', *South Asia Multidisciplinary Academic Journal* [online], Free-Standing Articles, Online since 13 May 2015. URL: http://samaj.revues.org/3878

Bouillier, Véronique and Dominique-Sila Khan. 2009. 'Hajji Ratan or Baba Ratan's Multiple Identities', *Journal of Indian Philosophy*, 37: 559-95.

Bouy, Christian. 1994. *Les Nātha-Yogin et les Upaniṣads*. Paris: Collège de France.

Briggs, George Weston. 1973. *Gorakhnath and the Kanphata Yogis*. Delhi: Motilal Banarsidass (1st edn. 1938).

Bronkhorst, Jan. 1998. *The Two Sources of Indian Asceticism*. Delhi: Motilal Banarsidass.

de Bruijn, T. (2012). *Ruby in the Dust: Poetry and History in Padmāvat by the South Asian Sufi Poet Muhammad Jāyasī*. Leiden: Leiden University Press.

Brunner-Lachaux, Hélène. 1963, 1968, 1977, *Somaśambhupaddhati*, vols. I, II and III, Publ. IFI 25, Pondichery: Institut Français d'Indologie.

———. 1985. *Mṛgendrāgama. Section des Rites et Section du Comportement.* Pondichéry: Institut Français d'Indologie.

Bühler, Georg and Bhagvanlal Indrajit. 1880. 'Inscriptions from Nepal', *The Indian Antiquary*, vol. IX, 163-94.

Bühnemann, Gudrun. 2007. *Eighty-four Āsanas in Yoga: A Survey of Traditions*. New Delhi: D.K. Printworld.

Burchett, Patton, 2011, 'My Miracle Trumps Your Magic: Encounters with Yogīs in Sufi and Bhakti Hagiographical Literature', in Knut Jacobsen ed., *Yoga Powers*. Leiden: Brill, 2011.

Burghart, Richard. 1978a. 'The founding of the Ramanandi Sect', *Ethnohistory*, 25, 2: 121-39.

———. 1978b. 'The History of Janakpurdham: A Study of Asceticism and Hindu Polity', Ph.D. thesis, University of London (SOAS).

———, 1987, 'Gifts to the Gods: Power, Property and Ceremonial in Nepal', in D. Cannadine and S. Price (eds), *Rituals of Royalty: Power and Ceremonial in Traditional Societies*, Cambridge: Cambridge University Press: 237-70.

______. 1996. *The Conditions of Listening: Essays on Religion, History and Politics in South Asia,* ed. C.J. Fuller and J. Spencer. Delhi: Oxford University Press.

Callewaert, W. and B. Op de Beeck. 1991. *Nirgun Bhakti Sagar: Devotional Hindi Literature*, 2 vols. Delhi: Manohar.

Callewaert, Winand M. and Rupert Snell (eds.). 1994. *According to Tradition: Hagiographical Writing in India*. Wiesbaden: Harrassowitz Verlag.

Cāndnāth, Yogī Mahant, s.d. *Asthal Bohar Maṭh kā Saṅkṣipt Itihās*. Rohtak: Asthal Bohar.

Carrithers, Michael. 1979. 'The Modern Ascetics of Lanka and the Pattern of Change in Buddhism', *Man*, 14, 2: 294-310.

Chalier Visuvalingam, Elisabeth, 1989, 'Bhairava's Royal Brahmanicide: The Problem of the Mahābrāhmaṇa', in A. Hiltebeitel (ed.), *Criminal Gods and Demon Devotees*, New York: SUNY Press: 157-230.

Champion, Catherine. 1989. 'A Contre Courant (Ulṭā sādhanā). Tradition orale du Nord-Est de l'Inde: l'exemple des récits chantés bhojpuri', in R.K. Barz and Monika Thiel-Horstmann (eds.), *Living Texts from India*. Wiesbaden: Otto Harrassowitz: 63-85.

Chattopadhyaya, D.P. 1970, *Taranath's History of Buddhism in India*, Simla: Institute for Advanced Studies.

Chaturvedi, S., D.N. Gellner and S.K. Pandey. 2016. 'Politics in Gorakhpur since the 1920s: The Making of a Safe "Hindu" Constituency', unpublished ms.

Chaturvedi, Shashank. 2014, 'Religion, Culture and Power: A Study of Everyday Politics in Gorakhpur'. Ph.D. thesis, University of Delhi, Mss.

Clementin-Ojha, Catherine. 1990. 'Image animée, image vivante. L'image du culte hindou', in André Padoux (ed.), *L'image divine: Culte et méditation dans l'hindouisme.* Paris: Editions du CNRS: 115-32.

______. 2006. 'Replacing the Abbot: Rituals of Monastic Ordination and Investiture in Modern Hinduism', *Asiatische Studien/Etudes Asiatiques* LX-3: 535-73.

Cohn, Bernard. S. 1964. 'The Role of Gosains in the Economy of Eighteenth and Nineteenth-Century Upper India', *Indian Economic and Social History Review*, 4: 175-82.

Colas, Gérard. 2009. 'Images and Territory of Gods: From Precepts to Epigraphs', in Daniela Berti and Gilles Tarabout (eds.), *Territory, Soil and Society in South Asia*. Delhi: Manohar: 99-139.

Cooper, Ian. 1994. *The Painted Towns of Shekhawati*. Ahmedabad: Mapin Publishing.

Crooke, W., 1975, *The Tribes and Castes of the North Western Provinces*. Delhi: Cosmo (1st edn. 1896).

Dalmia, Vasudha, Angelika Malinar and Martin Christof (eds.). 2001. *Charisma and Canon: Essays on the Religious History of the Indian Subcontinent*. Delhi: Oxford University Press.

Dasgupta, Shashibhusan 1976, *Obscure Religious Cults*. Calcutta: Firma KLM (1st edn. 1946).

Dejenne, Nicolas, 2007. 'Du Rāma Jāmadagnya épique au Paraśurāma contemporain. Représentations d'un héros en Inde.' PhD dissertation, Université Sorbonne Nouvelle.

Despande, M.N. 1986. *The Caves of Panhale-Kaji (Ancient Pranaluka)*. Delhi: Archeological Survey of India.

Digby, Simon. 1970. 'Encounters with Jogis in Indian Sufi Hagiography', Mss. (London, SOAS).

———. 2000. *Wonder-Tales of South Asia*. Jersey: Orient Monographs.

Dimock, Edward C. 1966. *The Place of the Hidden Moon: Erotic Mysticism in the Vaiṣṇava-sahajiyā Cult of Bengal*. Chicago: University of Chicago Press.

Diwan, Paras. 2002. *Dr. Paras Diwan on Hindu Law*. Delhi: Orient Publishing Company.

Djurdjevic, Gordan, 2008. *Masters of Magic Powers: The Nath Yogis in the Light of Esoteric Notions*. Saarbrücken: VDM Verlag Dr. Muller.

Dowman, Keith. 1985. *Masters of Mahāmudrā: Songs and Histories of the Eighty-Four Buddhist Siddhas*. Albany: State University of New York Press.

Dumont, Louis, 1960, 'World Renunciation in Indian Religions', *Contributions to Indian Sociology*, no. IV: 33-62

———. 1966. *Homo hierarchicus. Essai sur le système des castes*. Paris: Editions Gallimard.

Dvivedi, Hajārīprasād. 1981. *Nāth Sampradāy*. Ilāhābād: Lokbhāratī Prakāśan.

Eaton, R.M. 1978, *The Sufis of Bijapur, 1300-1700*, Princeton: Princeton University Press.

Ernst, Carl W. 1996. 'Sufism and Yoga according to Muhammad Ghawt', *Sufi* 29 (Spring 1996): 9-13.

______. 2003. 'The Islamization of Yoga in the *Amrtakunda* Translations', *Journal of the Royal Asiatic Society*, Series 3, 13, 2: 1-23.

______. 2005. 'Situating Sufism and Yoga', *Journal of the Royal Asiatic Society*, Series 3, 15, 1: 15-43.

Farquhar, J.N. 1967. *Modern Religious Movements in India*. Delhi: Munshiram Manoharlal.

Feldhaus, Anne. 1984. *The Deeds of God in Ṛddhipur*, New York: Oxford University Press.

Flatt, Emma. 2011. 'The Authorship and Significance of the *Nujūm al-'ulūm*: A Sixteenth Century Astrological Encyclopedia from Bijapur'. *Journal of the American Oriental Society*, 131.2: 223-44.

Frederic, Louis. 1987. *Dictionnaire de la civilisation indienne*. Paris: Laffont (Bouquins).

Freeman, John Rich. 2006. 'Shifting Forms of the Wandering Yogi', in David Schulman and Deborah Thiagarajan (eds.), *Masked Ritual and Performance in South India*. Ann Arbor: University of Michigan Press.

Fuller, Christopher J. 1984. *Servants of the Goddess: The Priest of a South Indian Temple*. Cambridge: Cambridge University Press.

______. 1985. 'Initiation and Consecration: Priestly Rituals in a South Indian Temple', in Richard Burghart and Audrey Cantlie (eds.), *Indian Religion*. London: Curzon Press.

Fuller, Christopher J. and John Harriss. 2005. 'Globalizing Hinduism: A "Traditional" Guru and Modern Businessmen in Chennai', in Jackie Assayag and Christopher J. Fuller, *Globalizing India: Perspectives from Below*. London: Anthem Press: 211-36.

Gaborieau, Marc. 1974. 'Les récits chantés de l'Himalaya et le contexte ethnographique', in Christoph von Fürer-Haimendorf (ed.), *Contributions to the Anthropology of Nepal.* Warminster: Aris & Phillips: 114-28.

Ganesan, T. and Christèle Barois. 2003. 'A propos des manuscrits de l'Institut Français de Pondichéry', *Bulletin des Etudes Indiennes*, 21, 1: 255-64.

Gatade, Subash. 2004. 'Hindutvaisation of a Gorakhnath *Mutt*: The Yogi and the Fanatic', www.sacw.net , 7 October.

Ghosh, Amitav. 1992. *In an Antique Land.* London: Granta Books.

Ghurye, G.S. 1953. *Indian Sadhus*. Bombay: The Popular Book Depot.

Gill, Harjeet Singh. 1986. 'The Human Condition in Puran Bhagat: An Essay in Existential Anthropology of a Punjab Legend', in Veena Das (ed.), *The Word and the World.* Delhi: Sage: 133-52.

Gnanambal, K. 1973. *Religious Institutions and Caste Panchayats in South India.* Calcutta: Anthropological Survey of India.

Gold, Daniel. 1987. *The Lord as Guru: Hindi Sants in North Indian Tradition.* Oxford: Oxford University Press.

———. 1992. 'What the Merchant-Guru Sold: Social and Literary Types in Hindi Devotional Verse', *Journal of the American Oriental Society* 112, 1: 22-35.

———. 1995. 'The Instability of the King: Magical Insanity and the Yogi's Power in the Politics of Jodhpur, 1803-1843', in David N. Lorenzen (ed.), *Bhakti Religion in North India: Community Identity and Political Action.* Albany: SUNY Press: 120-32.

———. 1999a. 'Yogis' Earrings, Householder's Birth: Split Ears and Religious Identity among Householder Naths in Rajasthan', in N.K. Singhi and Rajendra Joshi (eds.), *Religion, Ritual and Royalty.* Jaipur: Rawat: 35-53.

———. 1999b. 'Nath Yogis as established Alternatives: Householders and Ascetics Today', *Journal of Asian and African Studies*, XXXIV, 1: 68-88.

———. 1999c. 'The Yogī who Pissed from the Mountain', in Alan W. Entwistle et al. (eds.), *Studies in Early Modern Indo-Aryan Languages, Literatures and Culture.* Delhi: Manohar: 145-56.

———. 2002. 'Kabīr's Secrets for Householders: Truths and Rumours among Rajasthani Nāths', in Monika Horstmann (ed.), *Images of Kabir.* Delhi: Manohar.

———, 2005. 'The Sufi Shrines of Gwalior City: Communal Sensibilities and the Accessible Exotic Under Hindu Rule'. *The Journal of Asian Studies* 64, no. 1: 127-50.

———, 2011, 'Different Drums in Gwalior: Maharashtrian Nath Heritages in a North Indian City', in D.N. Lorenzen and A. Muñoz (eds.). *Yogi Heroes and Poets: Histories and Legends of the Nāths.* New York: SUNY Press, 51-62.

Gold, Daniel and Ann Grodzins Gold. 1984. 'The Fate of the Householder Nath', *History of Religion*, 24, 2: 113-32.

Goodall, Dominic and Marion Rastelli (eds.). forthcoming. *Tāntrikābhidanākośa* IV. Wien: Verlag Osterreichischen Akademie Wissenschaften.

Goswamy, B.N. and J.S. Grewal. 1967. *The Mughals and the Jogis of Jakhbar: Some Madad-i-Ma'ash and Other Documents.* Simla: Indian Institute for Advanced Studies.

Goudriaan, Teun (ed.), 1992, *Ritual and Speculation in Early Tantrism: Studies in Honor of André Padoux*, New York: SUNY Press.

Gowda, K. Chinnappa. 1996. 'Jalaata: A Form of Bhuta Worship', in U.P. Upadhyaya (ed.), *Coastal Karnataka.* Udupi: Rashtrakavi Govind Pai Samshodhana Kendra: 265-79.

______. 2003. 'Bhuta Worship', in B.Surendra Rao and K. Chinnappa Gowda (eds.), *The Retrieved Acre*. Mangalore University: 55-65.

Granoff, Phyllis. 1985. 'Scholars and Wonder-Workers', *Journal of the American Oriental Society*, July, 105, 3: 389-403.

Grierson, George A. 1885. 'Two Versions of the Song of Gopi Chand', *Journal of the Asiatic Society of Bengal*, I: 35-55.

Grodzins Gold, Ann. 1989. 'The Once and Future Yogi: Sentiments and Signs in the Tale of a Renouncer-King', *The Journal of Asian Studies*, 48, 4: 770-86.

______. 1992. *A Carnival of Parting.* Berkeley: University of California Press.

Gross, Robert Lewis. 1992. *The Sadhus of India*. Jaipur: Rawat.

Gupta, B., 1979. *Magical Beliefs and Superstitions*, Delhi: Sundeep Prakashan.

Gupta, Sanjukta, D.J. Hoens and T. Goudriaan. 1979. *Hindu Tantrism*, Leiden, Köln: E.J. Brill.

Hardgrove, Anne. 1999. 'Sati Worship and Marwari Public Indentity in India', *The Journal of Asian Studies*, 58, 3: 723-52.

Hassan, Syed Siraj ul. 1989: *The Castes and Tribes of H.E.H. the Nizam's Dominions*. Delhi: Asian Educational Service (1st edn. 1920).

Hausner, Sondra L. (2007). *Wandering with Sadhus: Ascetics in the Hindu Himalayas*, Bloomington: Indiana University Press.

Hastings, James M. 2002. 'Poets, Warriors and Brothers: The Shifting Identities of Rajput Dadupanthis, *c.* 1660-1860 CE', in Varsha Joshi (ed.), *Culture, Community and Change*. Jaipur: Rawat: 85-103.

Hawley, John Stratton. 1995a. 'The Nirguṅ/Saguṅ Distinction in Early Manuscripts Anthologies of Hindu Devotion', in David N. Lorenzen (ed.), *Bhakti Religion in North India: Community Identity and Political Action.* Albany: SUNY Press: 160-80.

Hawley, John Stratton and Mark Juergensmeyer. 1988. *Songs of the Saints of India.* New York: Oxford University Press.

Heesterman, Jan C. 1957. *The Ancient Indian Royal Consecration*, The Hague: Mouton & Co.

______. 1981. 'Householder and Wanderer', *Contributions to Indian Sociology*, vol. 15, nos. 1–2, pp. 251-71.

______. 1998. 'The Conundrum of the King's Authority', in J.F. Richards (ed.), *Kingship and Authority in South Asia.* Delhi: Oxford University Press (1st edn. 1978): 13-40.

Höfer, Andras. 1979. *The Caste Hierarchy and the State in Nepal: A Study of the Muluki Ain of 1854*, Innsbruck: Universitätsverlag.

Horovitz, J. 1914. 'Baba Ratan, the Saint of Bhatinda', *Journal of the Panjab Historical Society*, II, 2, pp. 97-117.

Horstmann, Monika. 2001. 'Charisma, Transfer of Charisma and Canon in North Indian Bhakti', in Vasudha Dalmia, Angelika Malinar and Martin Christof (eds.), *Charisma and Canon: Essays on the Religious History of the Indian Subcontinent.* Delhi: Oxford University Press: 171-82.

______ (ed.). 2002. *Images of Kabir*. Delhi: Manohar.

______. 2003. *Banāsā: A Spiritual Autobiography*. Wiesbaden: Harrassowitz Verlag.

______. 2005. 'The Two Sides of the Coin: Santism and Yoga in Rajasthan' (unpublished mss.).

Inden, Ronald. 1998. 'Ritual, Authority, and Cyclic Time in Hindu Kingship', in J.F. Richards (ed.), *Kingship and Authority in South Asia.* Delhi: Oxford University Press (1st edn. 1978): 41-91.

Ishaq, M., 1955, *India's Contribution to the Study of Hadith Literature*, Dacca: The University of Dacca.

Jaini, Padmanabh S. 1980. 'The Disappearance of Buddhism and the Survival of Jainism: A Study in Contrast', in A.K. Narain (ed.), *Studies in History of Buddhism*, Delhi: B.R. Publishing Corporation: 81-91.

Jarrett, H.S. (ed.). 1978. *The A'īn-i-Akbarī* by Abū'l-Fazl 'Allāmī, Delhi. Munshiram Manoharlal.

Kane, Pandurang Vaman. 1930-62. *History of Dharmaśāstra*. Poona: Bhandarkar Oriental Research Institute, 5 vols.

Kasturi, Malavika. 2009. '"Asceticising"' Monastic Families: Ascetic Genealogies, Property Feuds and Anglo-Hindu Law in Late Colonial India', *Modern Asian Studies*, 43, 5: 1039-83.

______. 2015. *Sadhus, Sampradaya, and Hindu Nationalism: The Dasnamis and the Shri Bharat Dharma Mahamandala in the Early Twentieth Century*. Delhi: NMML Occasional Paper, History and Society, New Series, 79.

Khan, Dominique-Sila. 1995. 'Ramdeo Pir and the Kamadiya Panth', in N.K. Singhi and R. Joshi (eds.), *Folk, Faith & Feudalism*. Jaipur: Rawat: 295-327

———. 1997b. *Conversions and Shifting Identities: Ramdev Pir and the Ismailis in Rajasthan.* Delhi: Manohar and CSH.

Kiss, Csaba. 2011. 'The *Matsyendrasaṃhitā*: A Yoginī-centered Thirteenth-century Text from the South Indian Śāmbhava Cult', in D.N. Lorenzen and A. Muñoz (eds.), *Yogi Heroes and Poets: Histories and Legends of the Nāths.* New York: SUNY Press: 143-62.

Kolff, D. 1990. *Naukar, Rajput and Sepoy: The Ethnohistory of the Military Labour Market in Hindustan, 1450-1850*, Cambridge: Cambridge University Press.

Kramrisch, Stella. 1981. *The Presence of Śiva*, Princeton: Princeton University Press.

Krauskopff, G. 1989. *Maîtres et Possédés. Les rites et l'ordre social chez les Tharu (Népal)*, Paris, Editions du CNRS.

Krauskopff, Gisèle. 1996. 'Rencontre des déesses et des dieux du lieu: le Dasai et les changements de pouvoir à Phalabang (Salyan)', in Gisèle Krauskopff and M. Lecomte-Tilouine (eds.). *Célébrer le pouvoir. Dasai, une fête royale au Népal.* Paris: CNRS Editions, Editions de la MSH: 167-208.

Lapoint, Elwin C. 1978. 'The Epic of Gugā: A North Indian Oral Tradition', in Sylvia Vatuk (ed.), *American Studies in the Anthropology of India*, Delhi: Manohar: 281-308.

Leccia, Marie-Christine. 2003. 'Etude de prānāyāma à travers quelques textes traditionnels indiens', in 'La voie du souffle', *Revue Française de Yoga* 28: 19-32.

Lecomte-Tilouine, Marie. 1996. 'Les dieux-sabres. Etude du Dasai dans une capitale sans roi (Isma)', in Gisèle Krauskopff and Marie Lecomte-Tilouine (eds.), *Célébrer le pouvoir. Dasai, une fête royale au Népal.* Paris: CNRS Editions, Editions de la MSH: 243-80.

Levi, S. 1986. *Le Nepal. Etude historique d'un royaume hindou*, Paris: PUF (1st edn. 1905).

Levy, Robert I. 1990. *Mesocosm: Hinduism and the Organization of a Traditional Newar City in Nepal.* Berkeley: University of California Press.

Lienhard, Sylvain. 1978. 'Problèmes du syncrétisme religieux au Népal', *BEFEO*, LXV, 1, pp. 329-70.

Linrothe, Rob. 2006. 'Siddha Stories in Stone: Nath Narratives at Shri Sailam', *Orientations*, March: 99-105.

———(ed.). 2006. *Holy Madness: Portraits of Tantric Siddhas.* New York: Rubin Museum of Art, Chicago: Serinda Publications.

Locke, John K. 1980. *Karunamaya.* Kathmandu: Sahayogi Prakashan.

Lorenzen, David N. 1972. *The Kāpālikas and Kālāmukhas: Two Lost Śaivite Sects.* Berkeley: University of California Press.

______ (ed.). 1995. *Bhakti Religion in North India.* New York: SUNY Press.

______ 1995. 'The Lives of *Nirguṅī* Saints', in D. Lorenzen (ed.), *Bhakti Religion in North India.* New York: SUNY Press: 181-211.

______. 1997. *Praises to a Formless God: Nirguṅī Texts from North India.* Delhi: Sri Satguru Publications.

______. 2011. 'Religious Identity in Gorakhnath and Kabir: Hindus, Muslims, Yogis and Sants', in David N. Lorenzen and Adrian Munoz (eds.), *Yogi Heroes and Poets: History and Legends of the Nāths.* New York: SUNY Press: 19-50.

Lorenzen, D.N. and A. Muñoz (eds). 2011. *Yogi Heroes and Poets: Histories and Legends of the Nāths.* New York: SUNY Press.

Lorenzen, David N. and Uma Thukral. 2005. 'Los Dialogos Religiosos entre Kabir y Gorakh', *Estudios de Asia y Africa*, 126, XL, 1: 161-77.

Maclean, Kama. 2008. *Pilgrimage and Power. The Kumbh Mela in Allahabad, 1765-1954.* Oxford: Oxford University Press.

Madhava, K.G. Vasanta 1985. *Religion in Coastal Karnataka 1500-1763.* Delhi: Inter-India Publications.

Malamoud, Charles. 1989. *Cuire le Monde. Rite et pensée dans l'Inde ancienne.* Paris: Editions La Découverte.

______. 2003. 'Remarks on Dissuasion in Ancient India', in Denis Vidal, Gilles Tarabout and Eric Meyer (eds.), *Violence/Non-Violence: Some Hindu Perspectives.*Delhi: Manohar: 209-18.

______. 2005. *La Danse des Pierres. Etudes sur la scène sacrificielle dans l'Inde ancienne.* Paris: Editions du Seuil.

Malinar, A. 2011. 'Sampradāya', in K.A. Jacobsen (ed.). *Brill Encyclopedia of Hinduism*, vol. 3, Leiden: Brill: 156–64.

Mallik, Kalyani. 1954. *Siddha-siddhanta-paddhati and other works of the Natha Yogis.* Poona: Poona Oriental Book House.

Mallinson, James. 2011a. 'Nāth Saṃpradāya', in K.A. Jacobsen (ed.). *Brill Encyclopedia of Hinduism* , vol. 3. Leiden: Brill: 407-28.

______. 2011b. 'Haṭha Yoga', in K.A. Jacobsen (ed.). *Brill Encyclopedia of Hinduism*, vol. 3. Leiden: Brill: 770-81.

______. 2012. 'The Original Gorakṣaśataka', in D.G. White (ed.), *Yoga in Practice.* Princeton: Princeton University Press: 257–72.

______ (forthcoming). *Haṭhayoga's Philosophy: A Fortuitous Union of Non-Dualities.*

Mallinson, James and Mark Singleton. 2017. *Roots of Yoga.* London: Penguin Classics.

Mallison, Françoise. 2001. *Constructions hagiographiques dans le monde indien. Entre mythe et histoire*. Paris: Honoré Champion éditeur.

Mallman, Marie-Thérèse de. 1948. *Introduction à l'Etude d'Avalokiteçavara*. Paris: Annales du Musée Guimet, vol. 57.

Markovits, Claude. 2003. 'Merchant Circulation in South Asia (Eighteenth to Twentieth Centuries): The Rise of Pan-Indian Merchant Netwoks', in Claude Markovits, Jacques Pouchepadass and Sanjay Subrahmanyam (eds.), *Society and Circulation*. Delhi: Permanent Black: 131-62.

Matringe, Denis. 1988. *Hir Varis Shah, poème panjabi du XVIIIe siècle*, Pondichery: Institut Français d'Indologie.

———. 1992. 'Krishnaite and Nath Elements in the Poetry of the Eighteenth-century Panjabi Sufi Bulhe Śāh', in R.S. McGregor (ed.), *Devotional Literature in South Asia*, Cambridge: Cambridge University Press: 190-206.

Mayer, Adrian. 1985. 'The King's Two Thrones', *Man*, 20: 205-21.

McGregor, R.S. 1993. *The Oxford Hindi-English Dictionary*. Delhi: Oxford University Press.

McLeod, W.H. 1986. *Guru Nanak and the Sikh Religion*. Delhi: Oxford University Press.

———. 1994. 'The Hagiography of the Sikhs', in Winand C. Callewaert and Rupert Snell (eds.), *According to Tradition: Hagiographical Writing in India*. Wiesbaden: Harrassowitz Verlag: 15-42.

Michaël, Tara. 1974. *Hatha-Yoga-Pradīpikā*, Paris: Fayard.

———. 1992. *Le Yoga de l'Eveil dans la tradition hindoue*, Paris: Fayard (L'Espace Intérieur).

———, 2007, *La centurie de Gorakṣa suivi du Guide des principes des Siddha. Introduction, traduction et notes*. Paris: Editions Almora.

Mishra, Ratan Lal. 1991. *The Mortuary Monuments in Ancient and Medieval India*. Delhi: B.R. Publishing.

Monier-Williams, Sir Monier. 1988. *A Sanskrit-English Dictionary*. Delhi: Motilal Banarsidass (1st edn. 1889).

Mukherjea, Bijan Kumar. 2003. *The Hindu Law of Religious and Charitable Trusts* (Tagore Law Lectures 1951). Calcutta: Eastern Law House (5th edn. by A.C. Sen 1983).

Mumford, S.R. 1989. *Himalayan Dialogue: Tibetan Lamas and Gurung Shamans in Nepal*, Madison: The University of Wisconsin Press.

Muñoz, A. 2010. *La piel de tigre y la serpiente. La identidad de los nāth-yoguis a través de sus leyendas*. Mexico, El Colegio de México.

______. 2011. 'Matsyendra's "Golden Legend": Yogi Tales and Nath Ideology', in D.N. Lorenzen and A. Muñoz (eds.), *Yogi Heroes and Poets: Histories and Legends of the Nāths*. New York: SUNY Press: 109-28

Nagar, Mahendra Singh. 2001. *Marwar ki sanskritik virasat*. Jodhpur, Maharaja Mansingh Pustak Prakash

Nagaraju, S. s.d. 'A Rare Saivo-Buddhist Work with Vaishnavite Interpolations', *Kannada Studies*, 3, 1: 67-75.

Narharināth Yogi. 2013 vs, *Siddharatnanāth*, Dang: Caughera.

______, 2021 vs, *Gorkhā Vaṁśāvali*. Gorakṣa Granthmālā 87, Kasi.

______, 2022 vs, *Itihās Prakāśmā Sandhipatrasaṁgraha*. Varanasi: Kalpana Press.

______, 2025 vs. *Nava Nātha Caurāsī Siddha*, Varanasi: Rashtriya Press.

Nayar, K.E. and J.S. Sandhu, 2007. *The Socially Involved Renunciate: Guru Nānak's Discourse to the Nāth Yogis*. Albany: SUNY Press.

Nevill, H.R. 1921. *Bahraich: A Gazetteer* being vol. 45 of the *District Gazetteers of the United Provinces of Agra and Oudh*. Lucknow: Govt. Press.

______. 1921. *Gonda: A Gazetteer*, Allahabad: Govt. Press.

______. 1921. *Gorakhpur: A Gazetteer*, Allahabad: Govt. Press.

Offredi, Mariola. 1999. 'Some Concepts of Gorakh Yoga through the Analysis of Three Nāthpanthī Manuscripts', in Alan W. Entwistle et al. (eds.), *Studies in Early Modern Indo-Aryan Languages, Literatures and Culture*, Delhi: Manohar: 267-86.

______. 2002. 'Kabir and the Nāthpanth', in Monika Horstmann (ed.), *Images of Kabir*. Delhi: Manohar.

Olivelle, Patrick. 1993, *The Āśrama System: The History and Hermeneutics of a Religious Institution*, New York: Oxford University Press.

______. 2003. 'The Renouncer Tradition', in Gavin Flood (ed.), *The Blackwell Companion to Hinduism*. Blackwell: 271-87.

Padoux, André. 1980. 'Contributions à l'étude du mantrasastra. II: nyasa -l'imposition rituelle des mantra', *Bulletin de l'Ecole Française d'Extrême-Orient*, LXVII: 59-102.

______. 1987. 'Contributions à l'étude du mantrasastra, III: le japa', *Bulletin de l'Ecole Française d'Extrême-Orient*, LXXVI: 117-64.

______. (ed.). 1990. *L'Image Divine. Culte et Méditation dans l'Hindouisme*, Paris: Editions du CNRS.

Parihar, Subhash. 2001. 'The Dargāh of Bābā Hājī Ratan at Bhatinda'. *Islamic Studies*, 40(1): 105-32.

Parry, Jonathan. 1985. 'Aghori Ascetics of Benares', in Richard Burghart and Audrey Cantlie (eds.), *Indian Religion*, London: Curzon Press: 51-78.

Pinch, Vijay. 2004. '*Gosain Tawaif*: Slaves, Sex, and Ascetics in Rasdhan, c. 1800-1857', *Modern Asian Studies*, 38, 3: 559-97.

Pinch, William R. 2005. 'Soldiers, Monks and Militant Sadhus', in David Ludden (ed.), *Making India Hindu: Religion, Community and the Politics of Democracy in India*. Delhi: Oxford University Press: 140-61 (1st edn. 1996).

______. 2006. *Warrior Ascetics and Indian Empires*, Cambridge: Cambridge University Press.

Pauwels, Heidi. 2012. 'Whose Satire? Gorakhnāth Confronts Krishna in Kanhāvat', in M. Horstmann and H.R.M. Pauwels (eds.), *Indian Satire in the Period of the First Modernity*. Wiesbaden: Harrassowitz Verlag: 35-64.

Pran Puri. *The European Magazine*, 1810, vol. 57.

Prévot, Sandrine. 2007. *Les nomades d'aujourd'hui. Ethnologie des éleveurs Raika de l'Inde*. Paris: Aux lieux d'être.

Ramesh, K.V. 1970. *A History of South Kanara (from the Earliest Times to the Fall of Vijayanagar)*. Dharwar: Karnataka University.

Rao, Velcheru Narayana, David Schulman and Sanjay Subrahmaniam. 1992. *Symbols of Substance: Court an State in Nayaka-period Tamilnadu*. Delhi: Oxford University Press.

______. 2001. *Textures of Time: Writing History in South India, 1600-1800*. Delhi: Permanent Black.

Rao, Vasudeva. 2002. *Living Traditions in Contemporary Contexts: The Madhva Matha of Udupi*. Delhi: Orient Longman.

Regmi, Mahesh Chandra. 1976. *Landownership in Nepal*, Berkeley: University of California Press.

Rose, Horace Arthur, Denzil Ibbetson and Edward Douglas Maclagan. 1919. *A Glossary of the Tribes and Castes of the Punjab and North-West Frontier Province*. Lahore, Government Printing.

Rousseleau, Raphaël. 2008. *Les créatures de Yama. Ethnohistoire d'une tribu de l'Inde (Orissa)*, Bologne: CLUEB.

Saletore, B.A. 1936. *Ancient Karnāṭaka*, vol. I: *History of Tuḷuva*. Poona: Oriental Book Agency.

______. 1937. 'The Kānaphāṭa Jogis in Southern History', *Poona Orientalist*, 1, 4: 16-22.

Samata, D.K. 1997. *Sacred Complex of Ujjain*. Delhi: D.K. Printworld.

Sanderson, Alexis. 1988. 'Śaivism and the Tantric Tradition', in Friedhelm Hardy (ed.), *The World's Religions/Religions of Asia*, London: Routledge: 660-704.

———, 2006, *Meaning in Tantric Ritual*, Delhi: Tantra Foundation.

Śarmā, Sāgarmal. 2052 vs. *Śekhāvāṭī ke Sant*: Ciṛāvā: Śekhāvāṭīśodh, Pratiṣṭhān.

Sawyer, Dana W. 1998. 'The Monastic Structure of Banarsi Dandi Sadhus', in Bradley R. Hertel and Cynthia Ann Humes (eds.), *Living in Banaras: Hindu Religion in Cultural Context*. Delhi: Manohar: 159-80.

Schaller, Joseph. 1995. 'Sanskritization, Caste Uplift, and Social Dissidence in the Sant Ravidās Panth', in David N. Lorenzen (ed.), *Bhakti Religion in North India : Community Identity and Political Action*. Albany: SUNY Press: 94-119.

Schomer, Karine. 1987. 'The Dohā and Sant Teachings', in Karine Schomer and W.H. McLeod (eds.). *The Sants: Studies in a Devotional Tradition of India*. Delhi: Motilal Banarsidass: 69-72.

Schomer, Karine and W.H. McLeod (eds.). 1987. *The Sants: Studies in a Devotional Tradition of India*. Delhi: Motilal Banarsidass.

Schopen, Gregory, 2006. 'The Buddhist "Monastery" and the Indian Garden: Aesthetics, Assimilations, and the Siting of Monastic Establishments', *Journal of the American Oriental Society*, 126: 487-505.

Schreiner, Peter. 2001. 'Institutionalization of Charisma: The Case of Shajānanda', in V. Dalmia, A. Malinar and M. Christof (eds.), *Charisma and Canon: Essays on the Religious History of the Indian Subcontinent*. Delhi: Oxford University Press: 155-70.

Servan-Schreiber, Catherine. 1999. *Chanteurs Itinérants en Inde du Nord*. Paris: L'Harmattan.

Sgroi-Dufresnes, Maria. 2000. 'Images, archétypes, symboles au Shekhavati: Problèmes et perspectives de conservation du patrimoine', in Annie Montaut (ed.), *Le Rajasthan. Ses dieux, ses heros, son peuple*. Paris: Publications Langues' 0: 267-94.

Sharma, Mahesh, 2009. *Western Himalayan Temple Records: State, Pilgrimage, Ritual and Legality in Chamba*. Leiden: Brill.

Sharma, Padmaja. 1972. *Maharaja Man Singh of Jodhpur and his Times (1803-1843)*. Agra: Shiva Lal Agarwala & Co.

Singh, Mohan. 1937. *Gorakhnath and Mediaeval Hindu Mysticism*. Lahore: Oriental College.

Singleton, Mark. 2010. *Yoga Body: The Origins of Modern Posture Practice*. Oxford, New York: Oxford University Press.

Sinha, Surajit and Baidyanath Saraswati. 1978. *Ascetics of Kashi*. Varanasi: N.K. Bose Memorial Foundation.

Sircar, Dinesh Chandra. 1973. *The Śākta Pīṭhas*, Delhi: Motilal Banarsidass.

Snell, Rupert. 1994. 'Introduction: Themes in Indian Hagiography', in Winand M. Callewaert and Rupert Snell (eds.), *According to Tradition: Hagiographical Writing in India*. Wiesbaden: Harrassowitz Verlag: 1-13.

Srivastava, Vinay Kumar. 1997. *Religious Renunciation of a Pastoral People*. Delhi: Oxford University Press.

Stietencron, Heinrich von. 2001. 'Charisma and Canon: The Dynamics of Legitimization and Innovation in Indian Religions', in V. Dalmia, A. Malinar and M. Christof (eds.), *Charisma and Canon: Essays on the Religious History of the Indian Subcontinent*. Delhi: Oxford University Press: 14-38.

Swynnerton, Charles. 1908. *Romantic Tales from the Panjāb with Indian Nights' Entertainment*. London: Archibald Constable and Co.

Tambiah, S.J. 1981. 'The Renouncer: His Individuality and His Community', *Contributions To Indian Sociology*, vol. 15, nos. 1-2: 299-320.

Tarabout, Gilles. 1986. *Sacrifier et donner à voir en pays malabar*. Paris: EFEO.

______. 1990. 'Sacrifice et renoncement dans les mythes de fondation de temples au Kerala', in Marcel Detienne (ed.), *Tracés de Fondation*. Louvain-Paris: Peeters: 211-32.

Temple, Richard C. 1885. *The Legends of the Panjab*. London: Trübner & Co., 2 vols.

Thapar, Romila, 1981. 'Householders and Renouncers in the Brahmanical and Buddhist Traditions', *Contributions to Indian Sociology*, vol. 15, nos. 1-2: 273-98.

Thurston, Edgar and K. Rangachari. 1909. *Castes and Tribes of Southern India*. Madras: Government Press, 7 vols.

Tod, James. 1983. *Annals and Antiquities of Rajasthan*. Delhi: Oriental Book Reprint Corporation (1st edn. 1829 and 1832).

Toffin, Gérard. 1993. *Le Palais et le Temple. La fonction royale dans la vallée du Népal*. Paris: CNRS Editions.

Trivedī, Durgāprasād Śarmā 'Śankar'. 1990. Śrī *Vilakṣan Avadhūt*. Fatehpur: Śrī Amritnāthaśram (1st edn. 1942).

Tulpule, S.G. 1994. 'Hagiography in Medieval Marathi Literature', in Winand C. Callewaert and Rupert Snell (eds.), *According to*

Tradition: Hagiographical Writing in India, Wiesbaden: Harrassowitz Verlag: 159-68.

Tuluvite, A. 1966. *A Miniature India*. Mangalore: Sarasvati Printing Works.

Unbescheid, Gunther. 1980. *Kanphata: Untersuchungen zu Kult, Mythologie und Geschichte Sivaitischer Tantriker in Nepal*. Wiesbaden: Franz Steiner Verlag.

Upadhyaya, U.P. (ed.), 1996, *Coastal Karnataka*, Udupi: Rashtrakavi Govind Pai Samshodhana Kendra.

Valle, Pietro Della. 1892. *The Travels of Pietro Della Valle in India*, ed. Edward Grey. London: The Hakluyt Society [from the old English translation of 1664 by G. Havers].

Van der Veer, Peter. 1987. 'Taming the Ascetics: Devotionalism in a Hindu Monastic Order', *Man* (NS), 22: 680-95.

———. 1988. *Gods on Earth*. London: The Athlone Press.

Varenne, Jean (ed.). 1971. *Upanishads du Yoga*, Paris: Gallimard Unesco.

Varmā, Rāmgopāl. 1992. *Nagar Phatahpūr Nagarān Nāgar, 1457-1950*. Phatehpur: Śrī Saravatī Pustakālya.

Vaudeville, Charlotte. 1974. *Kabir*. Oxford: Clarendon Press.

———. 1987a. '*Sant Mat*: Santism as the Universal Path to Sanctity', in K. Schomer and W.H. McLeod (eds.), *The Sants*. Delhi: Motilal Banarsidass: 21-40.

———. 1987b. 'The Shaiva-Vaishnava Synthesis in Maharashtrian Santism', in K. Schomer and W.H. McLeod (eds.), *The Sants*. Delhi: Motilal Banarsidass: 215-28.

Veerathapa, K. (ed.). 1986. *Studies in Karnataka History and Culture*. Bangalore: Karnataka History Congress.

Veluthat, Kesavan. 1978. *Brahman Settlements in Kerala: Historical Studies*. Calicut University: Sandhya Publications.

Venkatachari, K.K.A. 1996. 'Transmission and Transformation of Rituals', in Raymond Brady Williams (ed.), *A Sacred Thread: Modern Transmission of Hindu Traditions in India and Abroad*. New York: Columbia University Press: 177-190.

Verardi, Giovanni. 1996. 'Religions, Rituals, and the Heaviness of Indian History', *Annali*, 56: 215-53.

Vergati, A. 1985. 'Le roi faiseur de pluie. Une nouvelle version de la légende d' Avalokitesvara Rouge au Népal', *BEFEO*, LXXIV: 287-303.

Vilāsnāth Yogī 2001. *Prācīn Bhartrhari Guphā Mahātmya*. Haridwar: Ākhil Bhāratvarṣiya Avadhut Bheṣ Bārah Panth Yogī Mahāsabhā.

______, 2004. *Śrī Nāth Siddhon Kī Śankhaḍhāl.* Haridwar: Ākhil Bhāratvarṣiya Avadhut Bheṣ Bārah Panth Yogī Mahāsabhā.

______, 2005. *Śrī Nāth Rahasya.* Haridwar: Ākhil Bhāratvarṣiya Avadhūt Bheṣ Bārah Panth Yogī Mahāsabhā.

Warrier, Maya. 2003a. 'The Seva Ethic and the Spirit of Institution Building in the Mata Amritananda Mission', in Antony Copley (ed.), *Hinduism in Public and Private.* Delhi: Oxford University Press: 254-89.

______. 2003b. 'Process of Secularization in Contemporary India: Guru Faith in the Mata Amritanandamayi Mission', *Modern Asian Studies* 37, 1: 213-53.

Weber, Max. 1964. *The Theory of Social and Economic Organization [Wirthschaft and Gesellschaft, Teil I]*, ed. Talcott Parsons. New York: Free Press.

White, David Gordon. 1996. *The Alchemical Body: Siddha Tradition in Medieval India.* Chicago: The University of Chicago Press.

______. 2001. 'The Exemplary Life of Mastnāth: The Encapsulation of Seven Hundred Years of Nāth Siddha Hagiography', in Françoise Mallison (ed.), *Constructions hagiographiques dans le monde indien. Entre mythe et histoire.* Paris: Librairie Honoré Champion: 139-61.

______. 2002. 'Le monde dans le corps du Siddha. Microcosmologie dans les traditions médiévales indiennes', in Véronique Bouillier et Gilles Tarabout (eds.), *Images du Corps dans le Monde Hindou.* Paris: CNRS Editions: 189-212.

______. 2009. *Sinister Yogis.* Chicago, IL: Chicago University Press.

______. 2011. 'On the Magnitude of the Yogic Body', in D.N. Lorenzen and A. Muñoz (eds). *Yogi Heroes and Poets: Histories and Legends of the Nāths.* New York: SUNY Press: 79-90.

Wright, Daniel. 1983. 'Nepal: History of the Country and People'. Delhi: Cosmo Publications (1st edn. 1877).

Yocum, Glenn E. 1990. 'A Non-Brāhman Tamil Śaiva Mutt: A Field Study of the Thiruvavaduthurai Adheenam', in Austin B. Creel and Vasudha Narayanan, *Monastic Life in the Christian and Hindu Tradition: A Comparative Study.* Lewinston: The Edwin Mellen Press: 245-79.

______. 1996. 'The Coronation of a Guru: Charisma, Politics and Philosophy in Contemporary India', in Raymond Brady Williams (ed.), *A Sacred Thread: Modern Transmission of Hindu Traditions in India and Abroad.* New York: Columbia University Press: 68-91.

Zimmermann, F. 1987. *The Jungle and the Aroma of Meats: An Ecological Theme in Hindu Medicine*. Berkeley: University of California Press.

Zydenbos, Robert J. 1994. 'Some Examples from Mādhva Hagiography', in Winand C. Callewaert and Rupert Snell (eds.), *According to Tradition: Hagiographical Writing in India*. Wiesbaden: Harrassowitz Verlag: 169-90.

Index